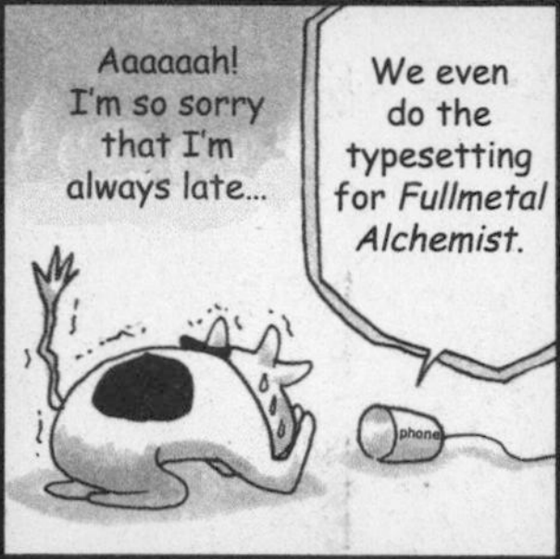
We even do the typesetting for *Fullmetal Alchemist.*
Aaaaaah! I'm so sorry that I'm always late...
phone

I recently found out that the typesetter is a relative of mine.

—*Hiromu Arakawa, 2009*



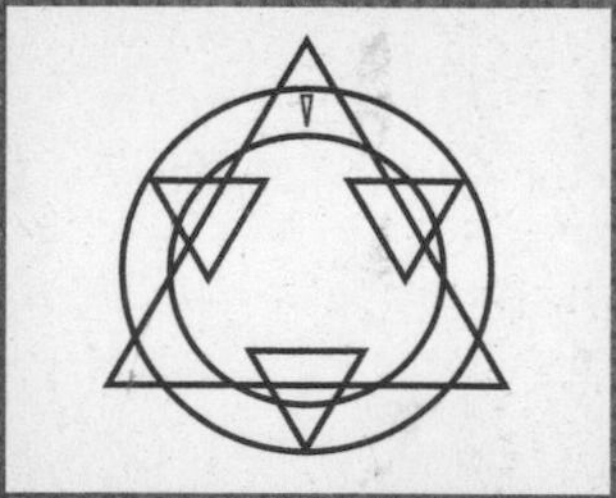

Born in Hokkaido (northern Japan), Hiromu Arakawa first attracted national attention in 1999 with her award-winning manga *Stray Dog*. Her series *Fullmetal Alchemist* debuted in 2001 in Square Enix's monthly manga anthology *Shonen Gangan*.

# FULLMETAL ALCHEMIST
## VOL. 24

VIZ Media Edition

**Story and Art by Hiromu Arakawa**

**Translation**/Akira Watanabe
**English Adaptation**/Jake Forbes
**Touch-up Art & Lettering**/Wayne Truman
**Design**/Julie Behn
**Editor**/Alexis Kirsch

Hagane no RenkinJutsushi vol. 24 © 2009 Hiromu Arakawa/SQUARE ENIX. First published in Japan in 2009 by SQUARE ENIX CO., LTD. English translation rights arranged with SQUARE ENIX CO., LTD. and VIZ Media, LLC.

Printed in the U.S.A.

Published by VIZ Media, LLC
P.O. Box 77010
San Francisco, CA 94107

10 9 8 7 6 5 4 3 2 1
First printing, January 2011

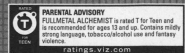

# 鋼の錬金術師

FULLMETAL ALCHEMIST

24

荒川弘

HIROMU ARAKAWA

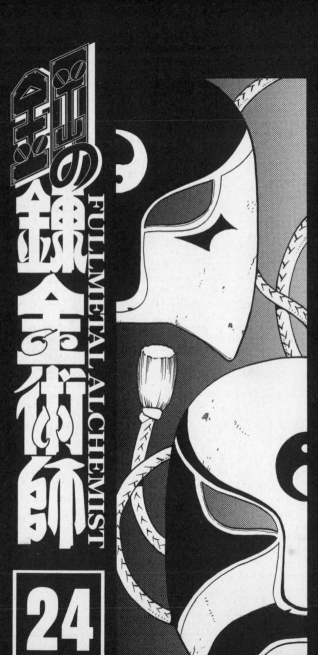

■ アルフォンス・エルリック

Alphonse Elric

■ エドワード・エルリック

Edward Elric

■ アレックス・ルイ・アームストロング

Alex Louis Armstrong

■ ロイ・マスタング

Roy Mustang

# OUTLINE
## FULLMETAL ALCHEMIST

Using a forbidden alchemical ritual, the Elric brothers attempted to bring their dead mother back to life. But the ritual went wrong, consuming Edward Elric's leg and Alphonse Elric's entire body. At the cost of his arm, Edward was able to graft his brother's soul into a suit of armor. Equipped with mechanical "auto-mail" to replace his missing limbs, Edward becomes a state alchemist in hopes of finding a way to restore their bodies. Their search embroils them in a deadly conspiracy that threatens to take the innocence, if not the lives, of everyone involved.

As the "Day of Reckoning" approaches, Central City has become a warzone! On one side, the Homunculi and the military leaders who have sold out their country for power; on the other, a rag-tag alliance of rebel soldiers loyal to Major General Armstrong of Briggs and Roy Mustang, Ishbalan refugees and, of course, the Elric family. Even the Elrics' former teacher, Izumi Curtis, has joined the fight! But deep beneath Central City lies the leader of the Homunculi, the Dwarf in the Flask, aka "Father." The original Homunculus is about to get a long overdue reunion…

# 鋼の錬金術師
FULLMETAL ALCHEMIST

## CHARACTERS
FULLMETAL ALCHEMIST

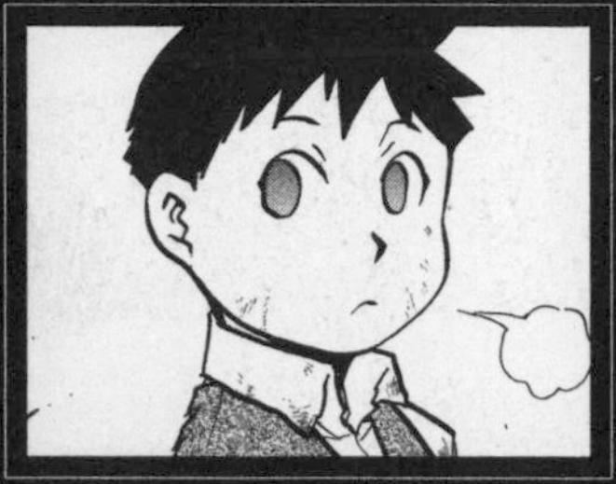

セリム・ブラッドレイ(プライド)
Selim Bradley (Pride)

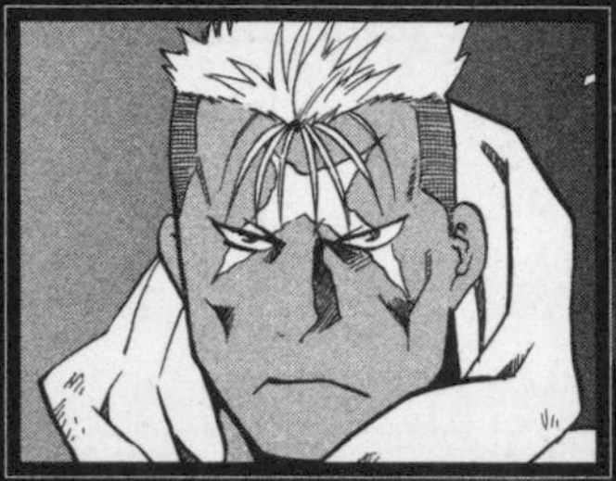

スカー
Scar

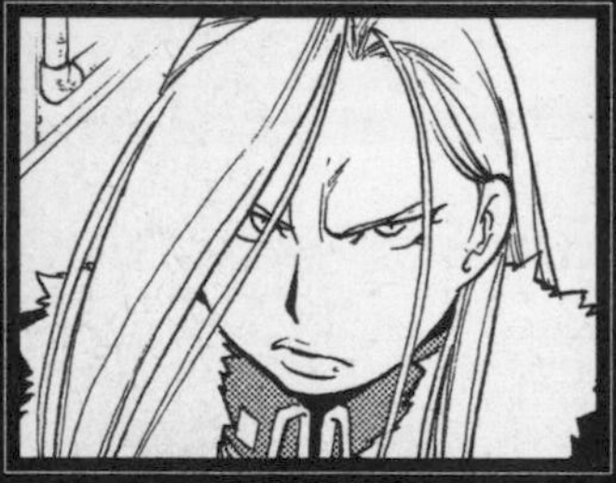

オリヴィエ・ミラ・アームストロング
Olivier Mira Armstrong

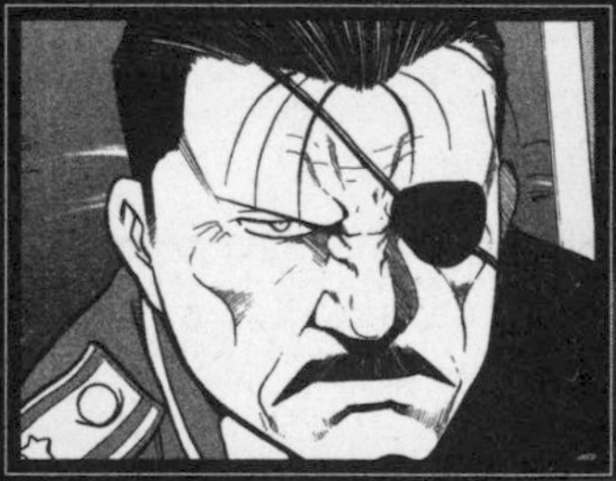

キング・ブラッドレイ
King Bradley

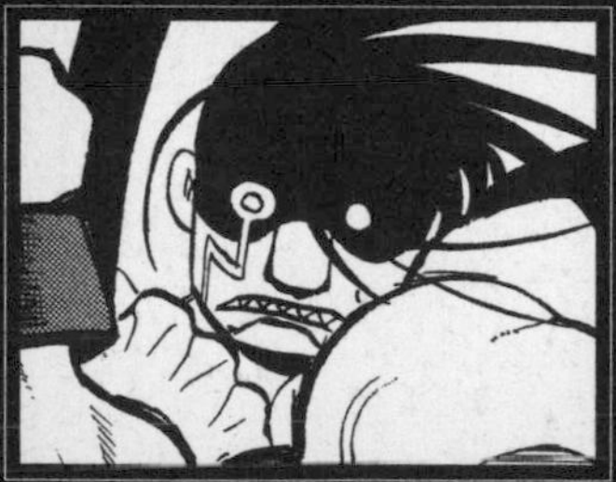

スロウス
Sloth

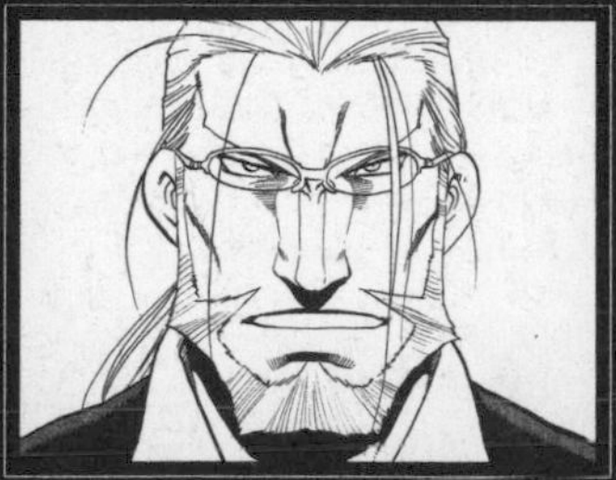

ヴァン・ホーエンハイム
Van Hohenheim

# CONTENTS

# Chapter 96
# Two Strong Women

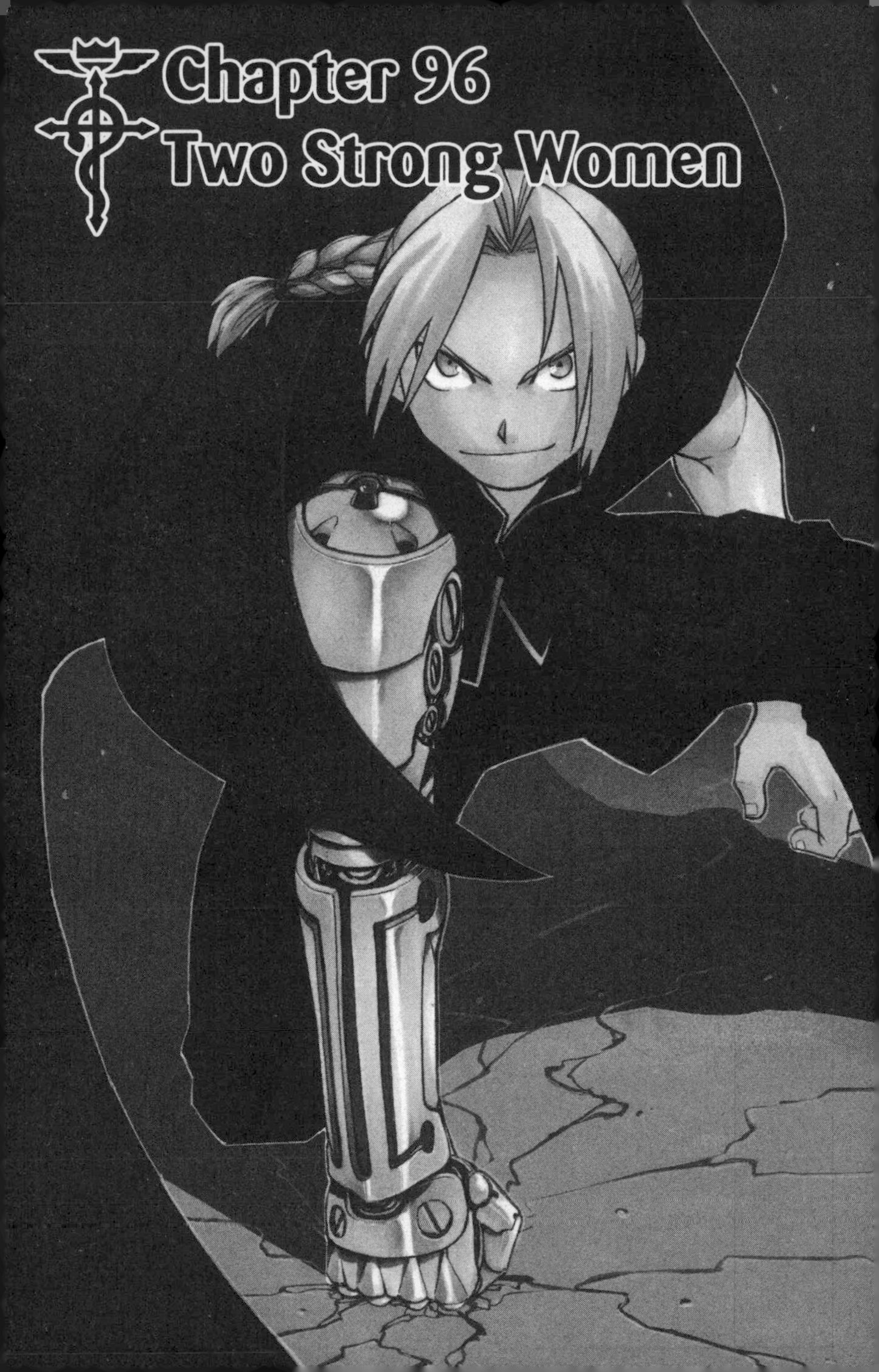

FULLMETAL
ALCHEMIST

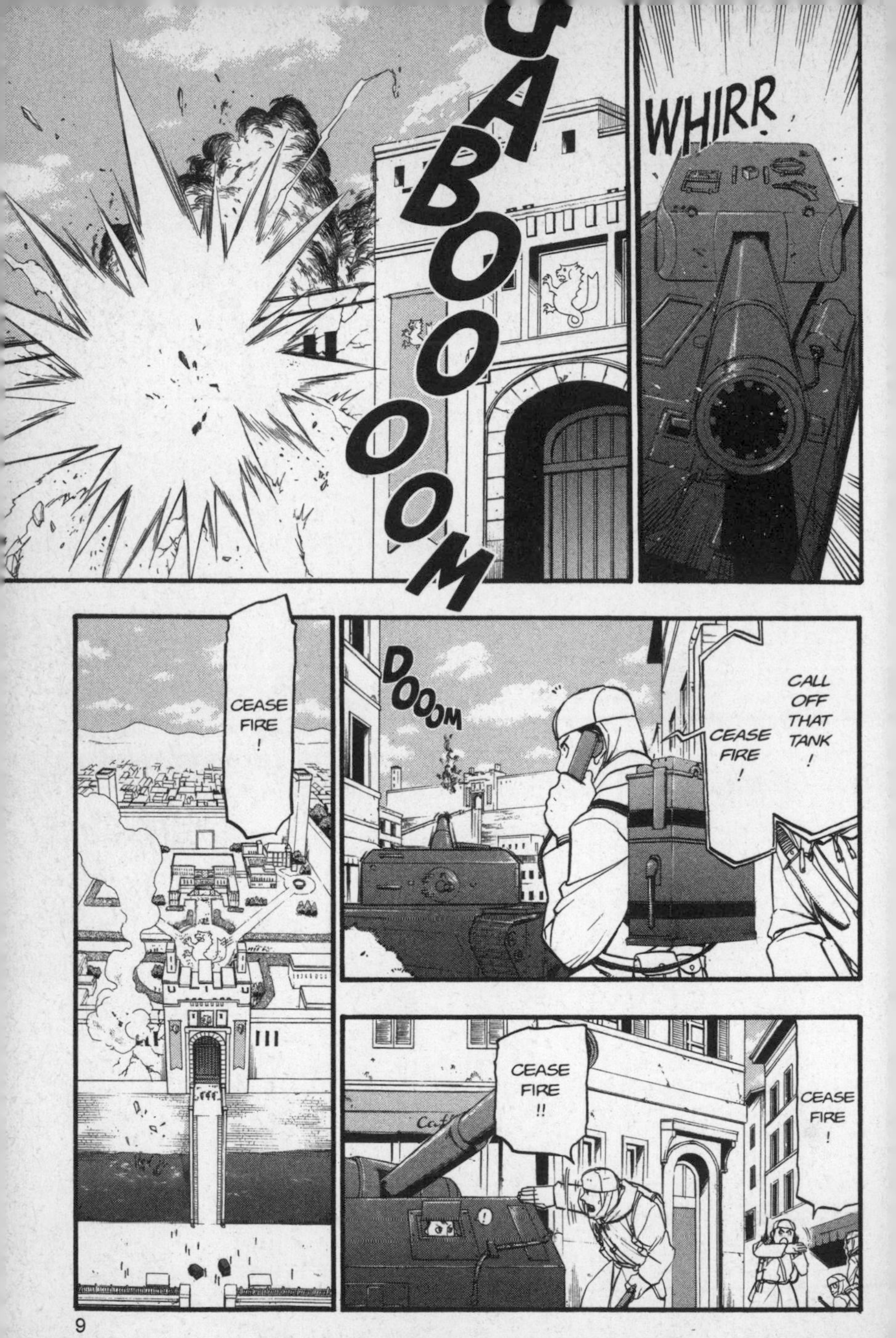
WHIRR
KABOOOOM
CALL OFF THAT TANK!
CEASE FIRE!
DOOOM
CEASE FIRE!
CEASE FIRE!!
!
CEASE FIRE!

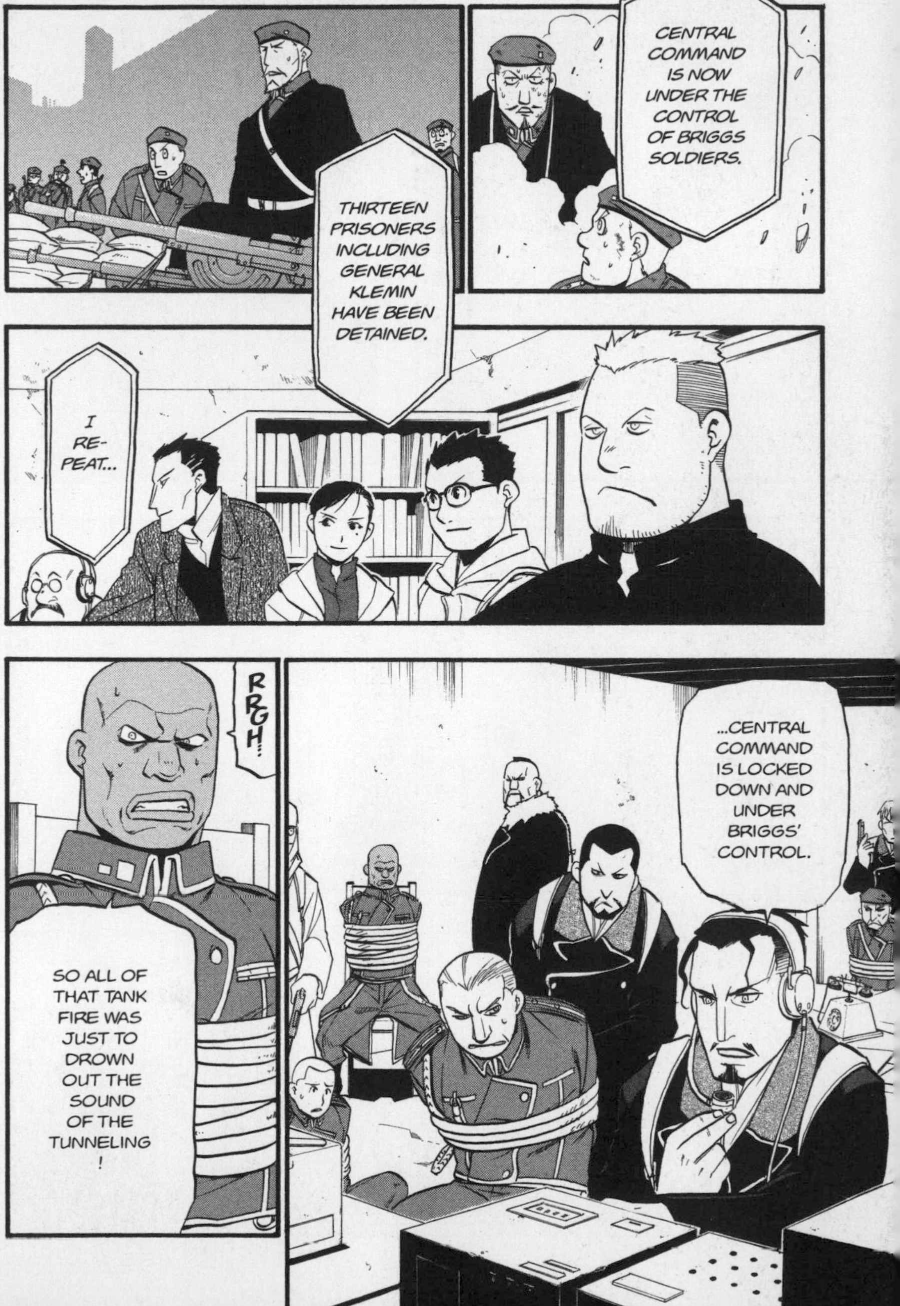
CENTRAL COMMAND IS NOW UNDER THE CONTROL OF BRIGGS SOLDIERS.
THIRTEEN PRISONERS INCLUDING GENERAL KLEMIN HAVE BEEN DETAINED.
I RE-PEAT...
...CENTRAL COMMAND IS LOCKED DOWN AND UNDER BRIGGS' CONTROL.
RRGH!!
SO ALL OF THAT TANK FIRE WAS JUST TO DROWN OUT THE SOUND OF THE TUNNELING!

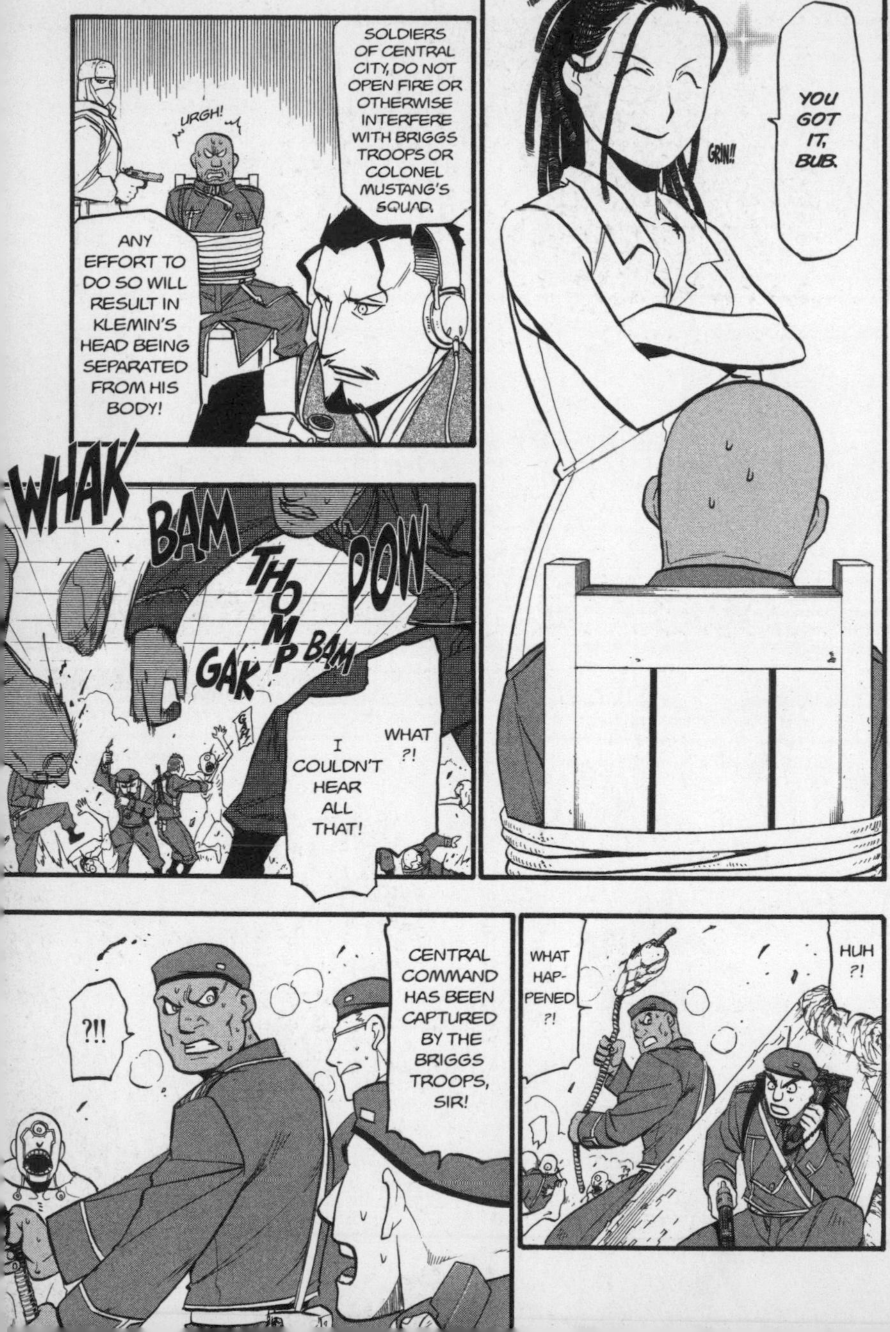
GRIN!!
YOU GOT IT, BUB.
SOLDIERS OF CENTRAL CITY, DO NOT OPEN FIRE OR OTHERWISE INTERFERE WITH BRIGGS TROOPS OR COLONEL MUSTANG'S SQUAD.
URGH!
ANY EFFORT TO DO SO WILL RESULT IN KLEMIN'S HEAD BEING SEPARATED FROM HIS BODY!
WHAK
BAM
THOMP
POW
BAM
GAK
WHAT ?!
I COULDN'T HEAR ALL THAT!
HUH ?!
WHAT HAP-PENED ?!
CENTRAL COMMAND HAS BEEN CAPTURED BY THE BRIGGS TROOPS, SIR!
?!!

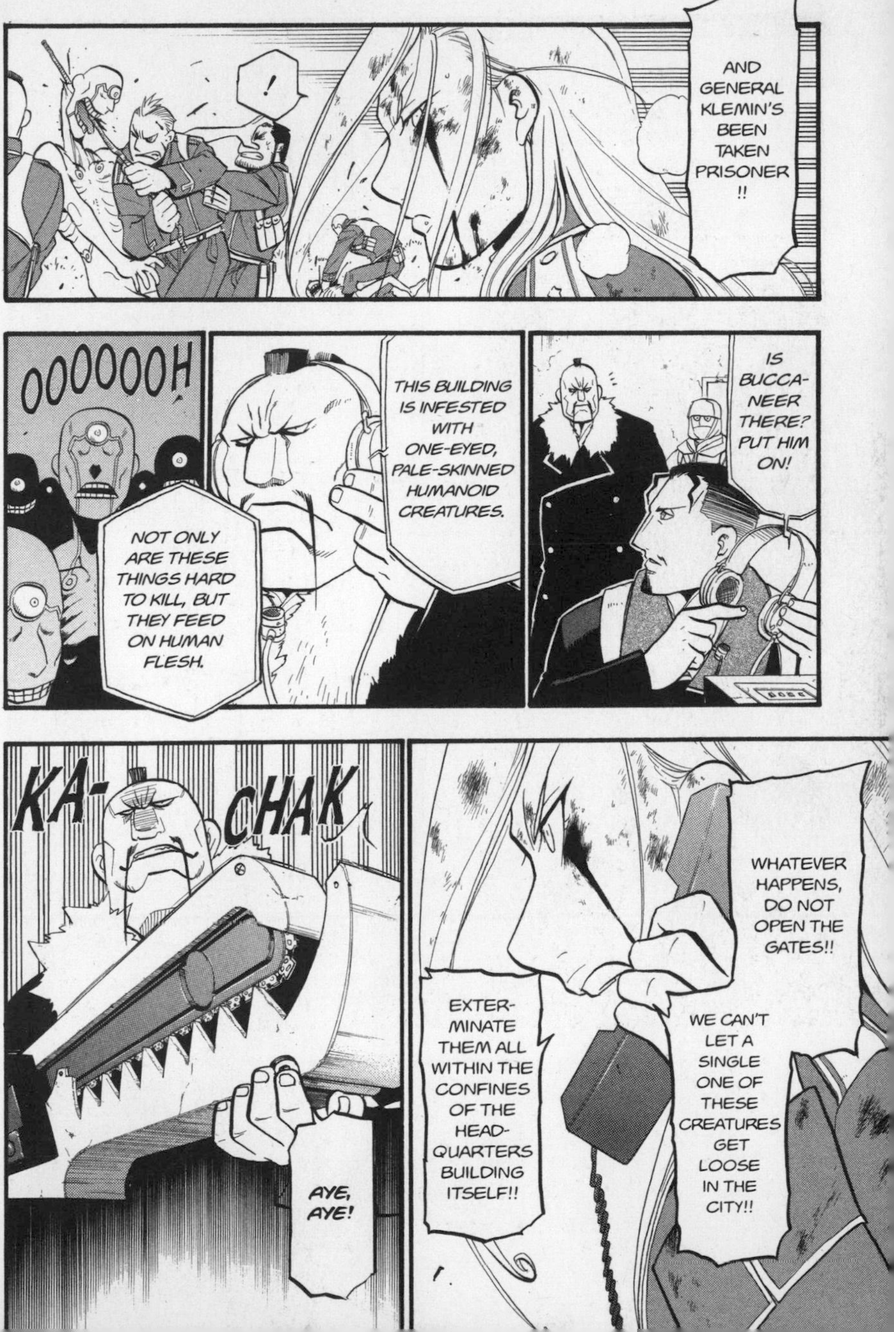
AND GENERAL KLEMIN'S BEEN TAKEN PRISONER!!
!
IS BUCCANEER THERE? PUT HIM ON!
THIS BUILDING IS INFESTED WITH ONE-EYED, PALE-SKINNED HUMANOID CREATURES.
NOT ONLY ARE THESE THINGS HARD TO KILL, BUT THEY FEED ON HUMAN FLESH.
OOOOOOH
WHATEVER HAPPENS, DO NOT OPEN THE GATES!!
WE CAN'T LET A SINGLE ONE OF THESE CREATURES GET LOOSE IN THE CITY!!
EXTERMINATE THEM ALL WITHIN THE CONFINES OF THE HEADQUARTERS BUILDING ITSELF!!
KA-CHAK
AYE, AYE!

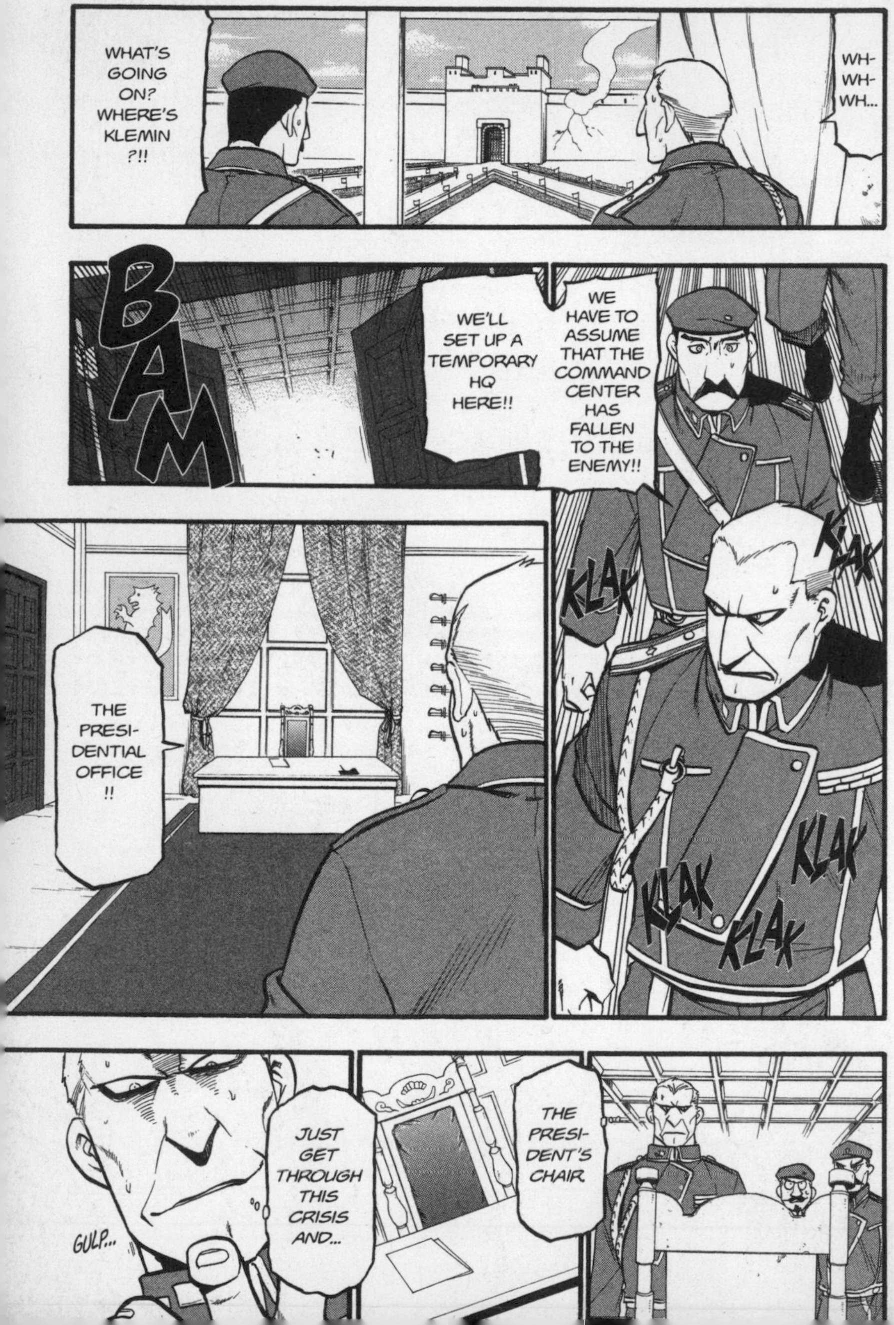
WH- WH- WH...
WHAT'S GOING ON? WHERE'S KLEMIN?!!
WE HAVE TO ASSUME THAT THE COMMAND CENTER HAS FALLEN TO THE ENEMY!!
KLAK KLAK
KLAK KLAK KLAK
BAM
WE'LL SET UP A TEMPORARY HQ HERE!!
THE PRESIDENTIAL OFFICE!!
THE PRESIDENT'S CHAIR.
JUST GET THROUGH THIS CRISIS AND...
GULP...

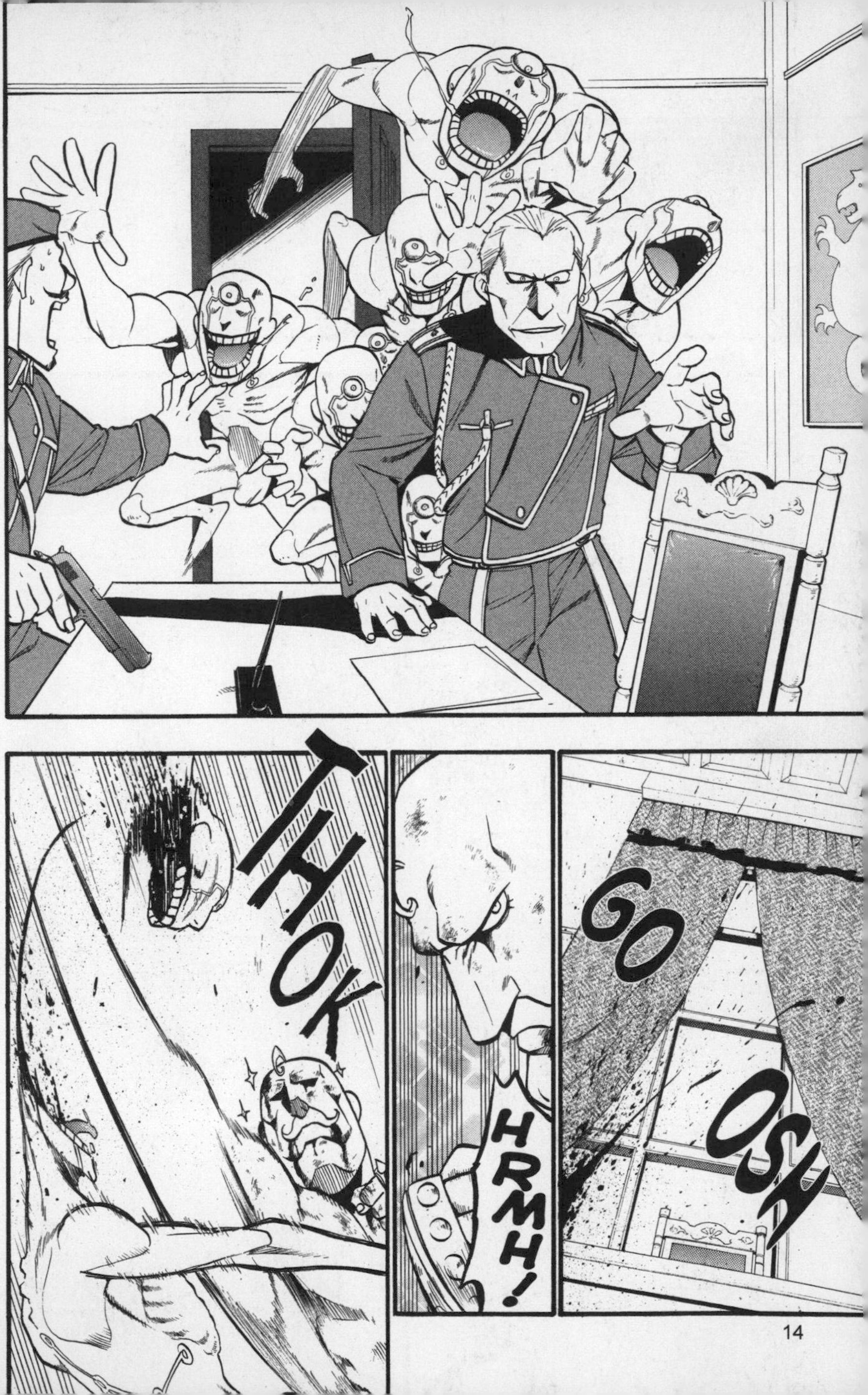
GO
OSH
HRMH!
THOK

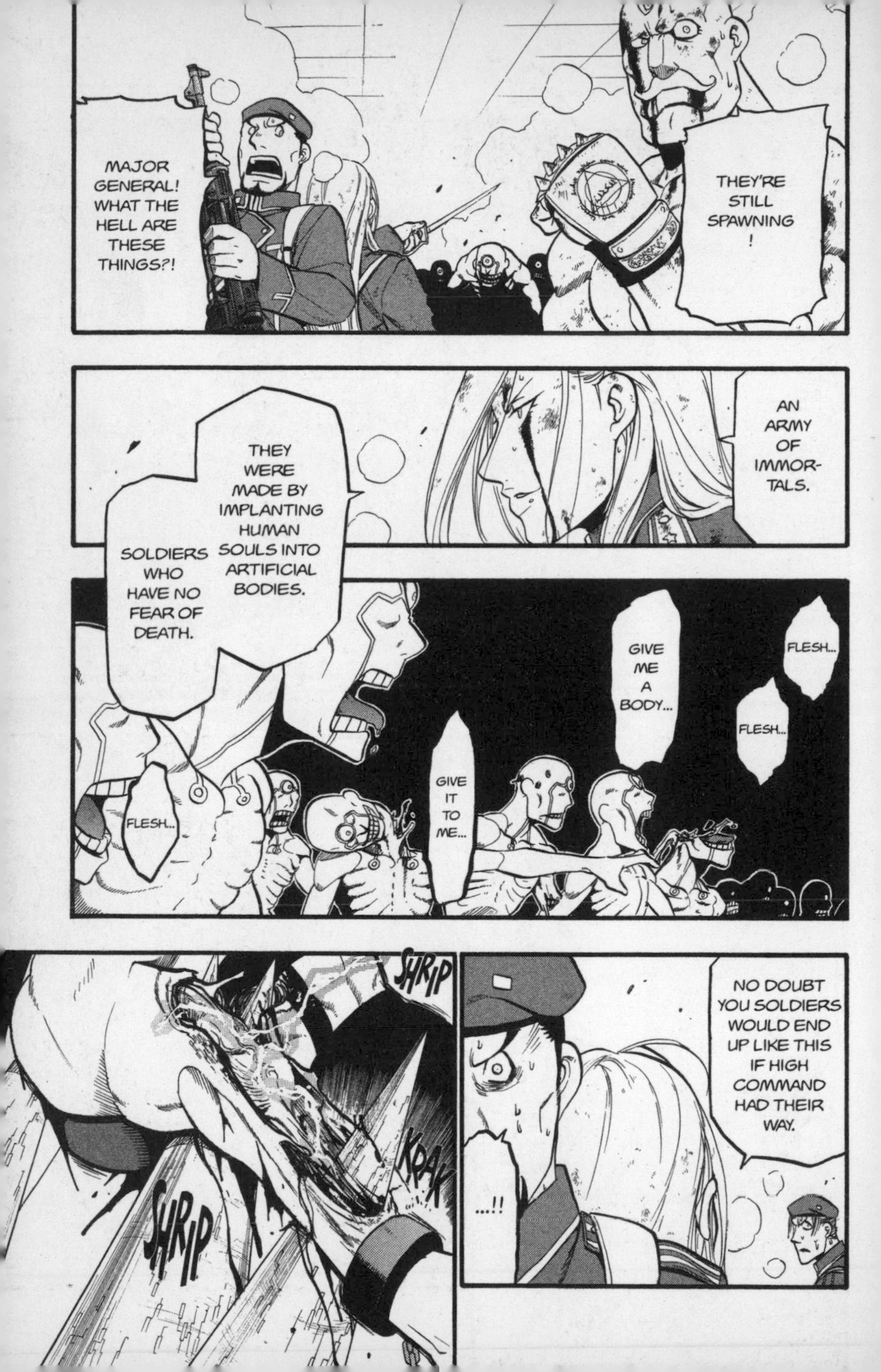
THEY'RE STILL SPAWNING!
MAJOR GENERAL! WHAT THE HELL ARE THESE THINGS?!
AN ARMY OF IMMORTALS.
THEY WERE MADE BY IMPLANTING HUMAN SOULS INTO ARTIFICIAL BODIES.
SOLDIERS WHO HAVE NO FEAR OF DEATH.
FLESH...
FLESH...
GIVE ME A BODY...
GIVE IT TO ME...
FLESH...
NO DOUBT YOU SOLDIERS WOULD END UP LIKE THIS IF HIGH COMMAND HAD THEIR WAY.
...!!
SHRIP
KRAK
SHRIP

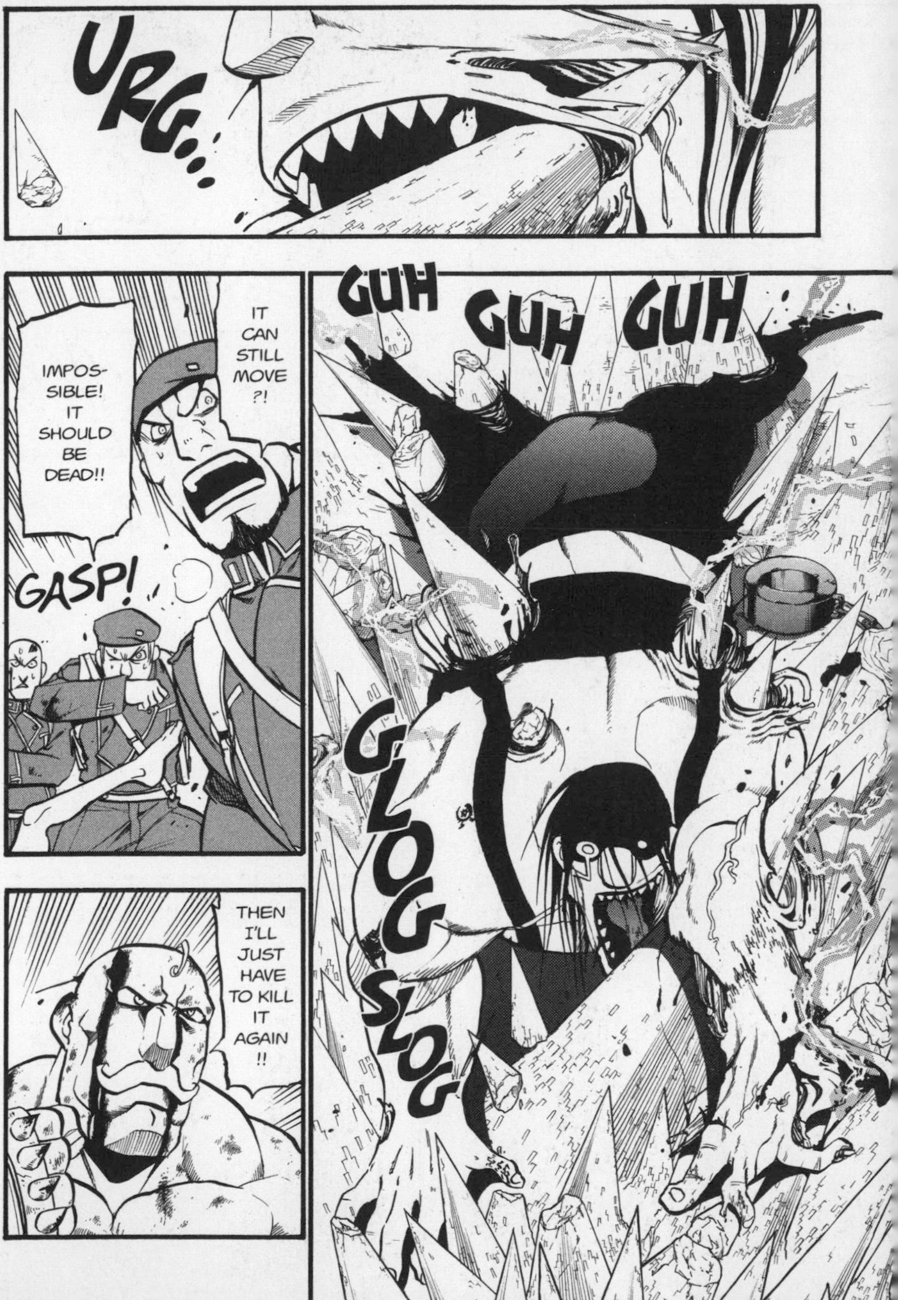
URG...
GUH GUH GUH
GLOG SLOG
IT CAN STILL MOVE?!
IMPOSSIBLE! IT SHOULD BE DEAD!!
GASP!
THEN I'LL JUST HAVE TO KILL IT AGAIN!!

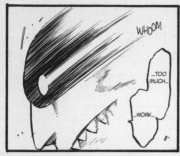

WHOOM

...TOO MUCH...

...WORK...

DY-ING IS...

SLOG

NNGH...

THWOMP!

GRRRRRR...

...WAIT...

ITS AIM IS AS POOR AS EVER!

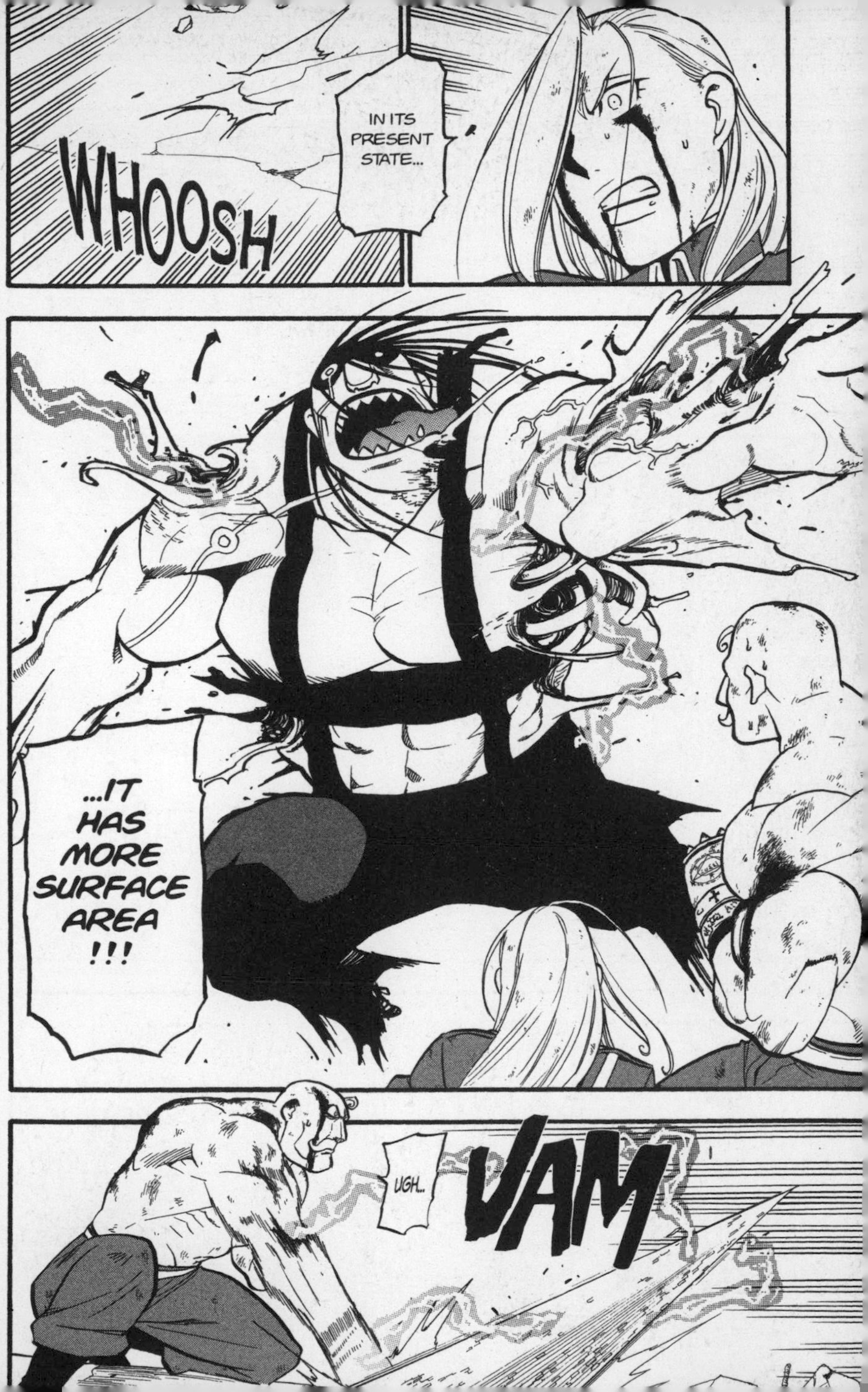
IN ITS PRESENT STATE...
WHOOSH
...IT HAS MORE SURFACE AREA!!!
VAM
UGH...

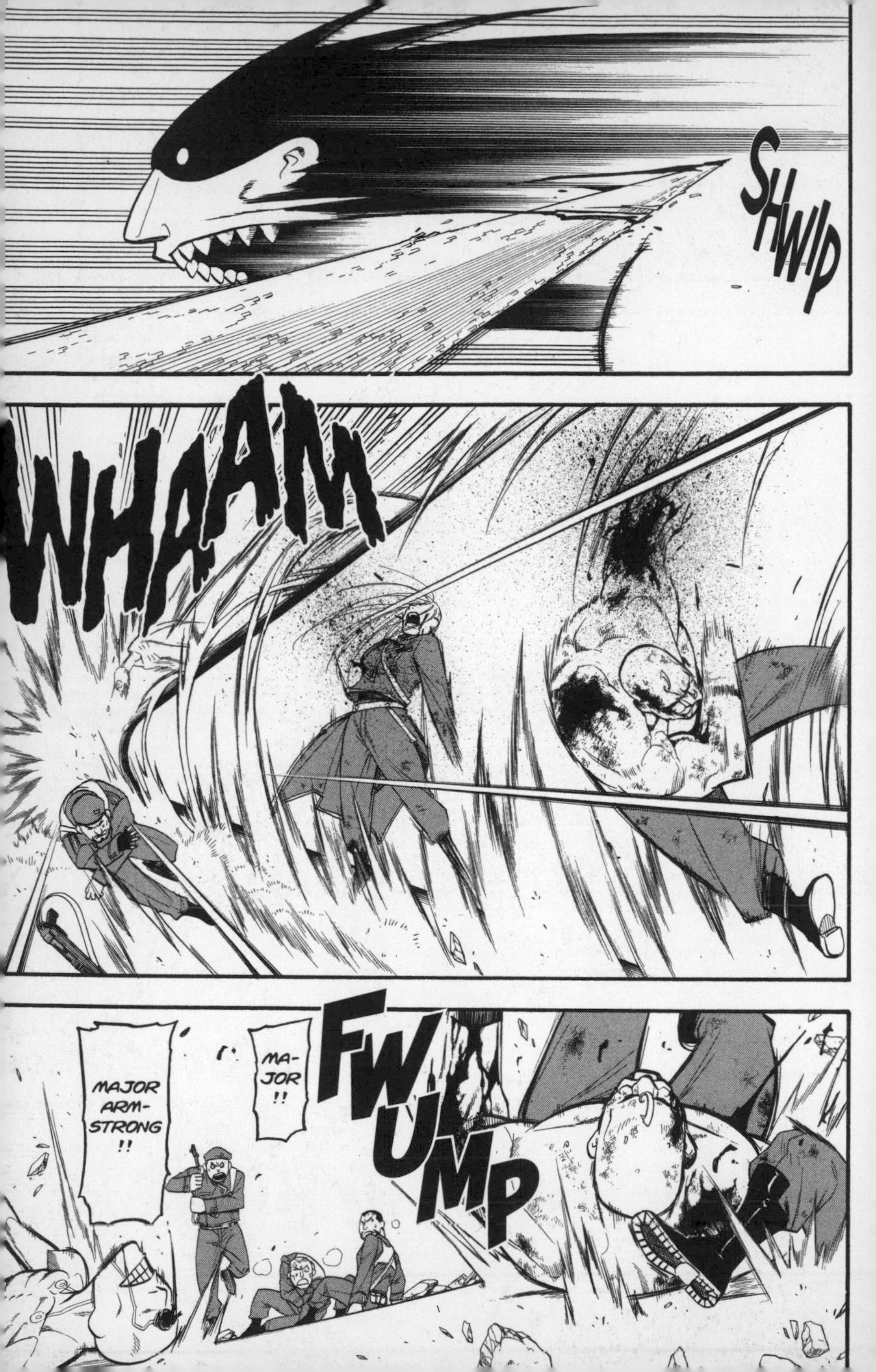
SHWIP
WHAAM
FWUMP
MA-JOR!!
MAJOR ARM-STRONG!!

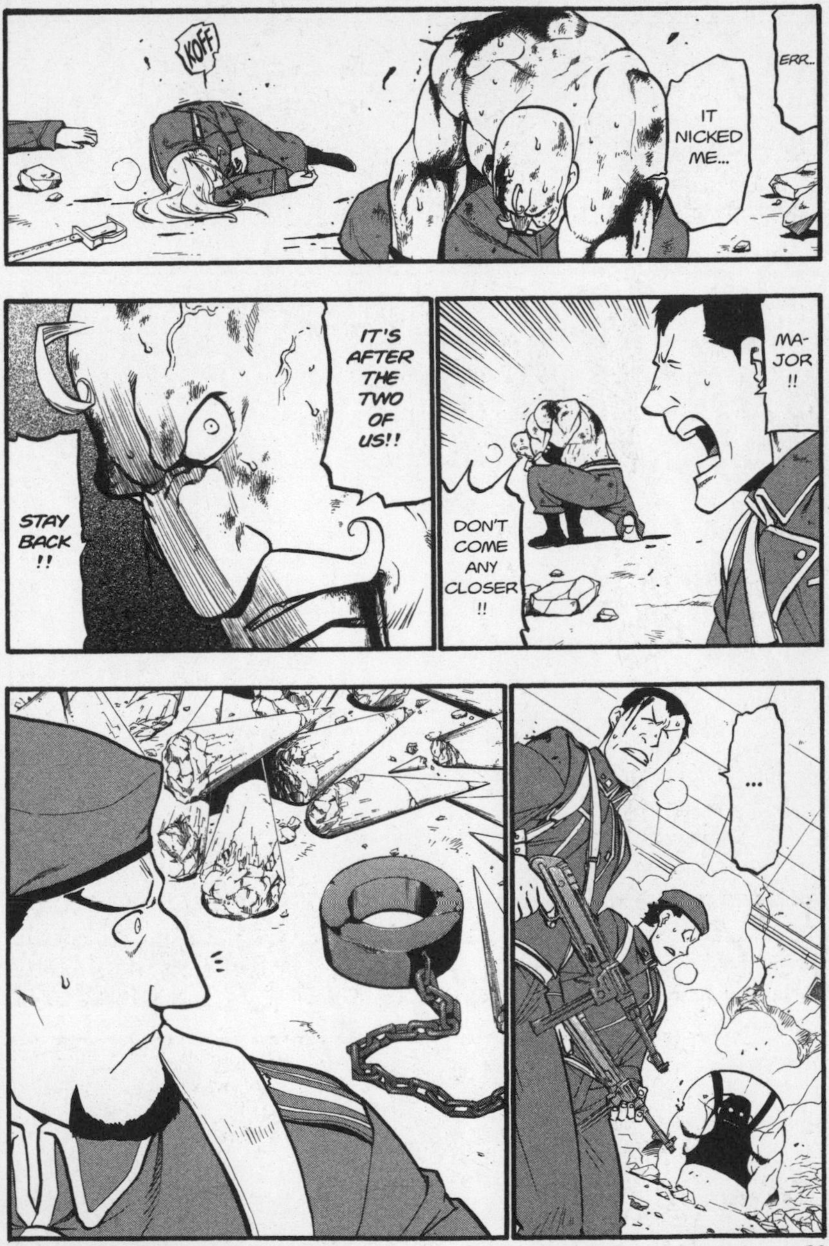
ERR...
IT NICKED ME...
KOFF
MA-JOR!!
DON'T COME ANY CLOSER!!
IT'S AFTER THE TWO OF US!!
STAY BACK!!
...

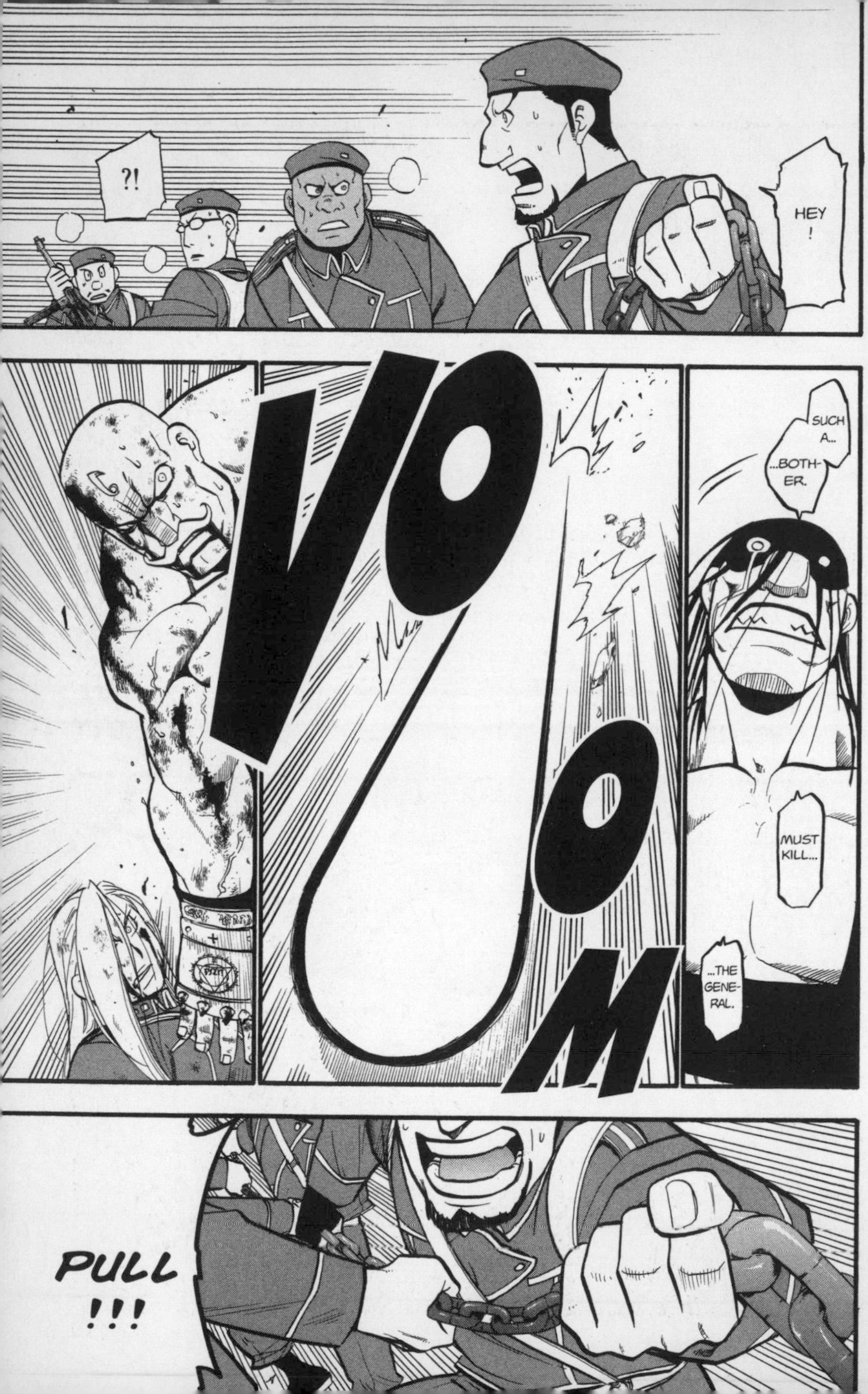
HEY!
?!
SUCH A... ...BOTHER.
MUST KILL...
...THE GENERAL.
VOOOM
PULL!!!

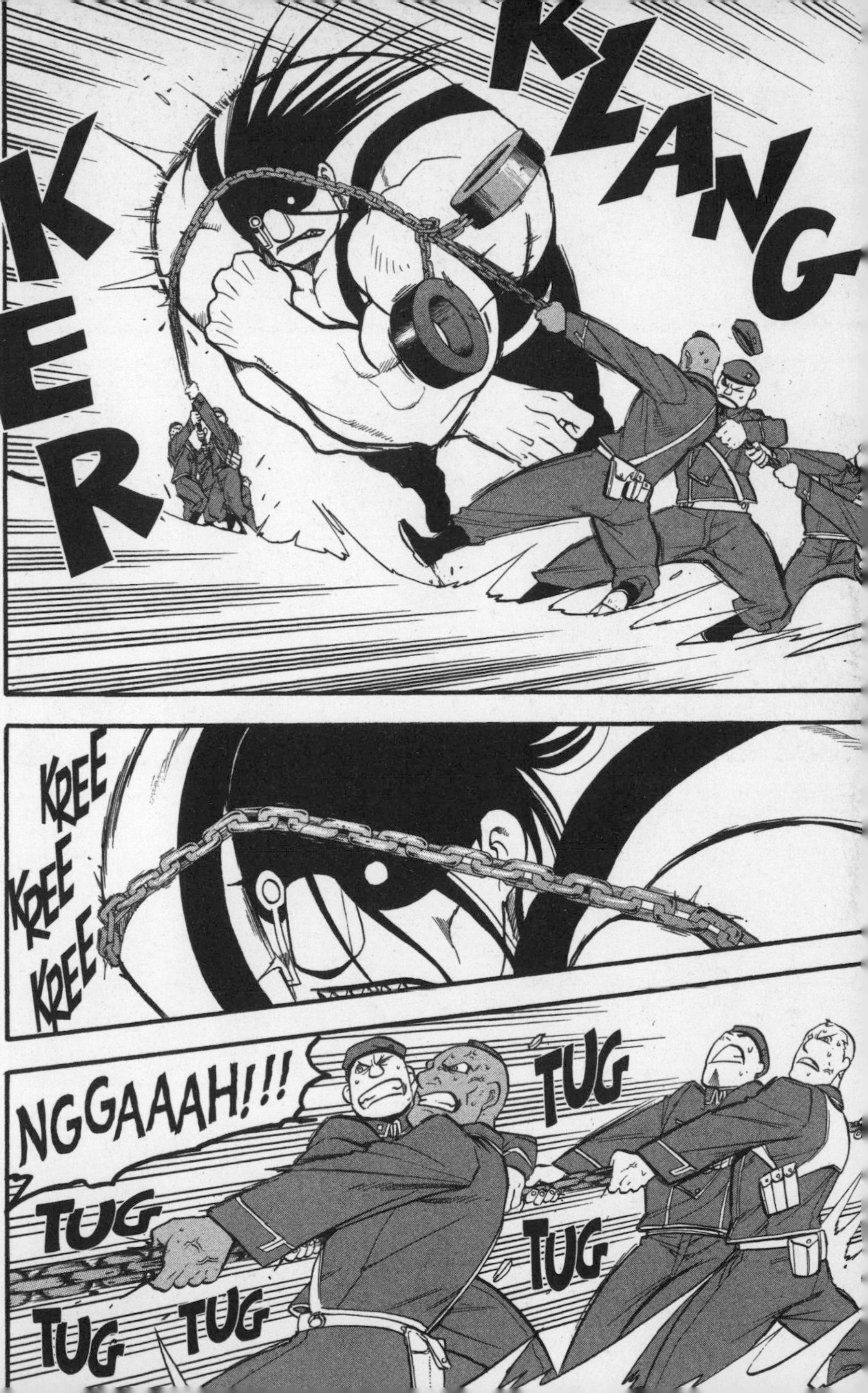
KLANG
KER
KREE
KREE
KREE
TUG
NGGAAAH!!!
TUG
TUG
TUG
TUG

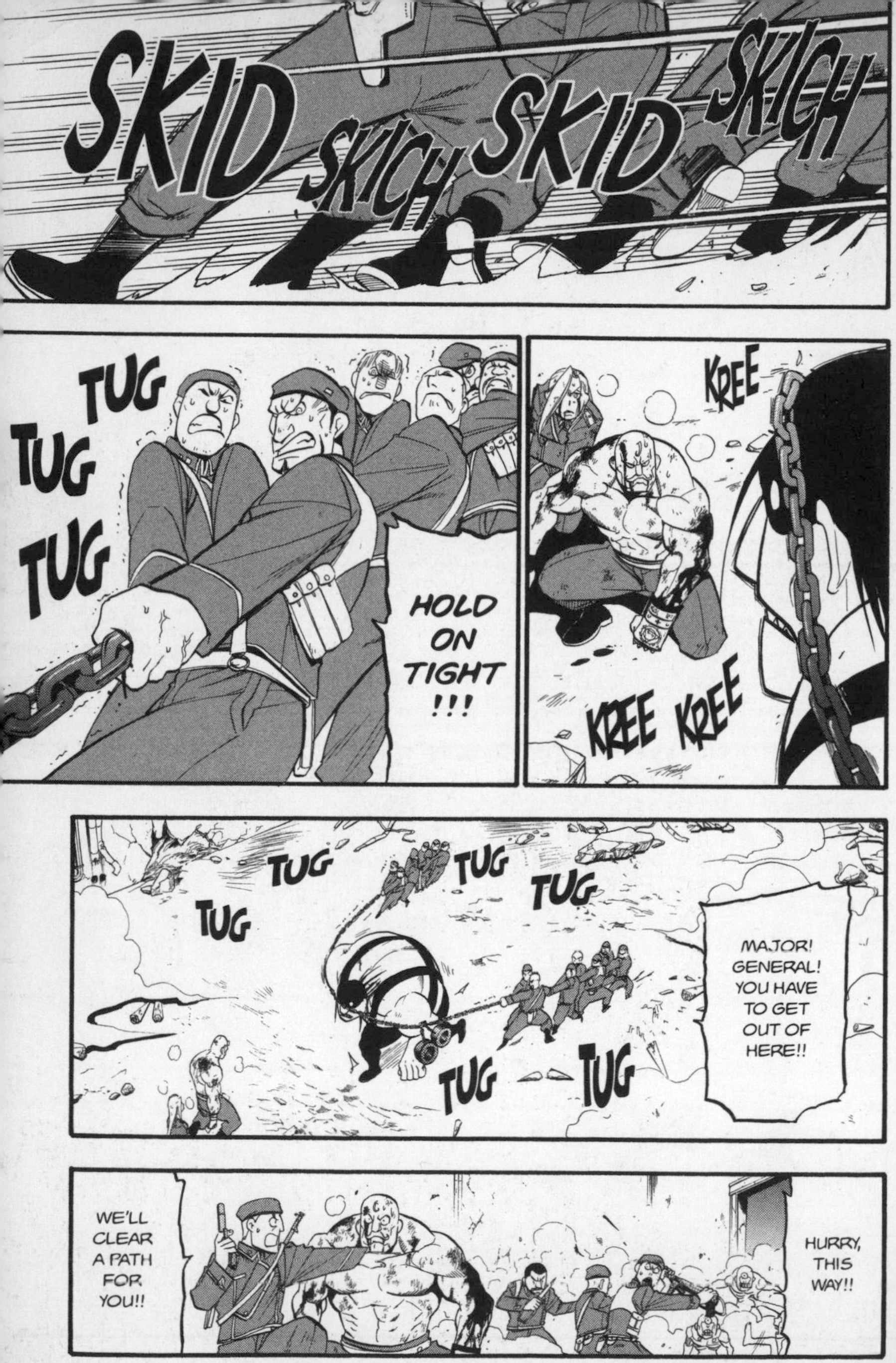
SKICH
SKID
SKICH
SKID
KREE
KREE KREE
HOLD ON TIGHT!!!
TUG
TUG
TUG
MAJOR! GENERAL! YOU HAVE TO GET OUT OF HERE!!
TUG
TUG
TUG
TUG
TUG
TUG
HURRY, THIS WAY!!
WE'LL CLEAR A PATH FOR YOU!!

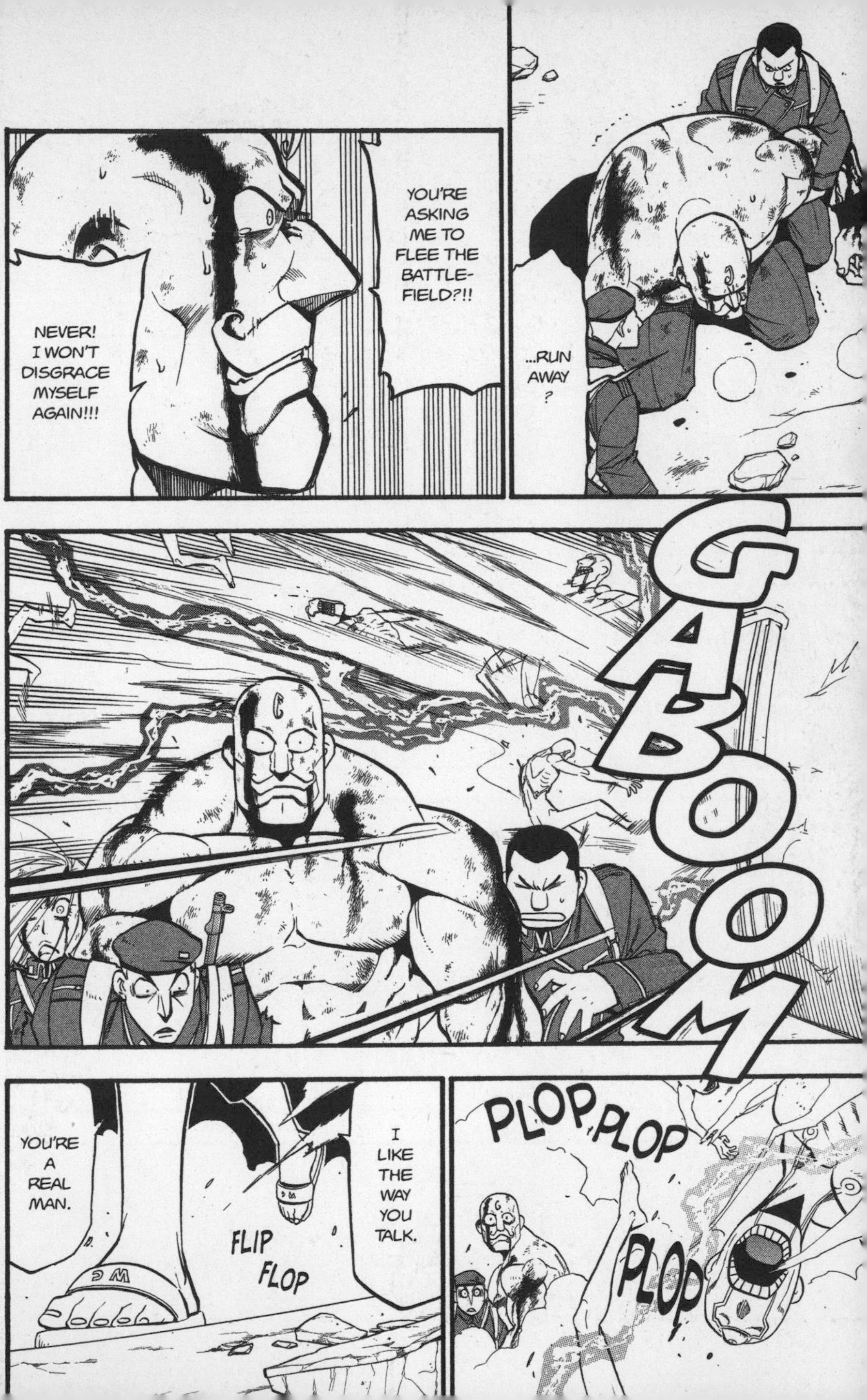
...RUN AWAY ?
YOU'RE ASKING ME TO FLEE THE BATTLE-FIELD?!!
NEVER! I WON'T DISGRACE MYSELF AGAIN!!!
GABOOOM
PLOP, PLOP
PLOP
I LIKE THE WAY YOU TALK.
YOU'RE A REAL MAN.
FLIP FLOP

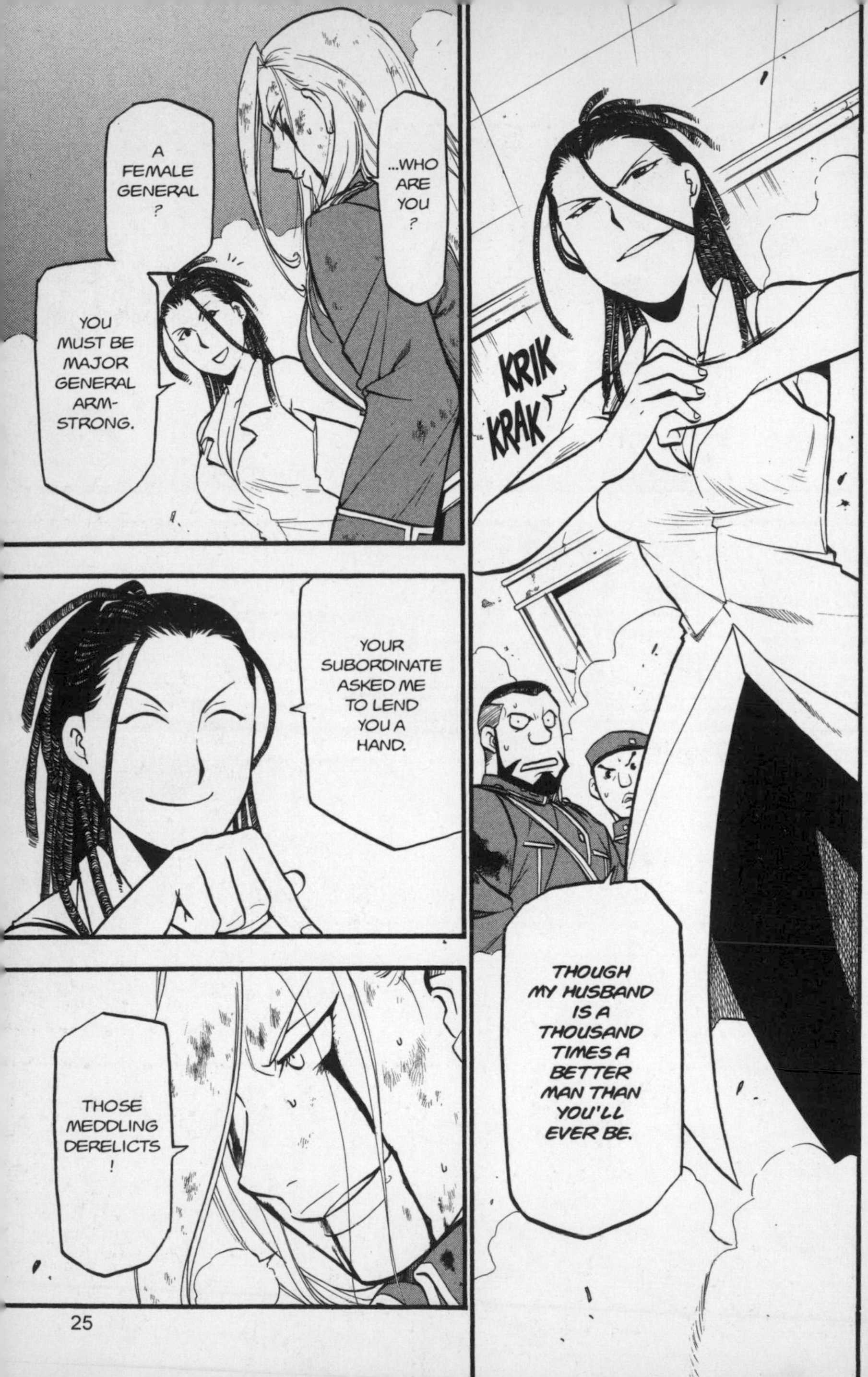
KRIK KRAK
THOUGH MY HUSBAND IS A THOUSAND TIMES A BETTER MAN THAN YOU'LL EVER BE.
...WHO ARE YOU?
A FEMALE GENERAL?
YOU MUST BE MAJOR GENERAL ARM-STRONG.
YOUR SUBORDINATE ASKED ME TO LEND YOU A HAND.
THOSE MEDDLING DERELICTS!

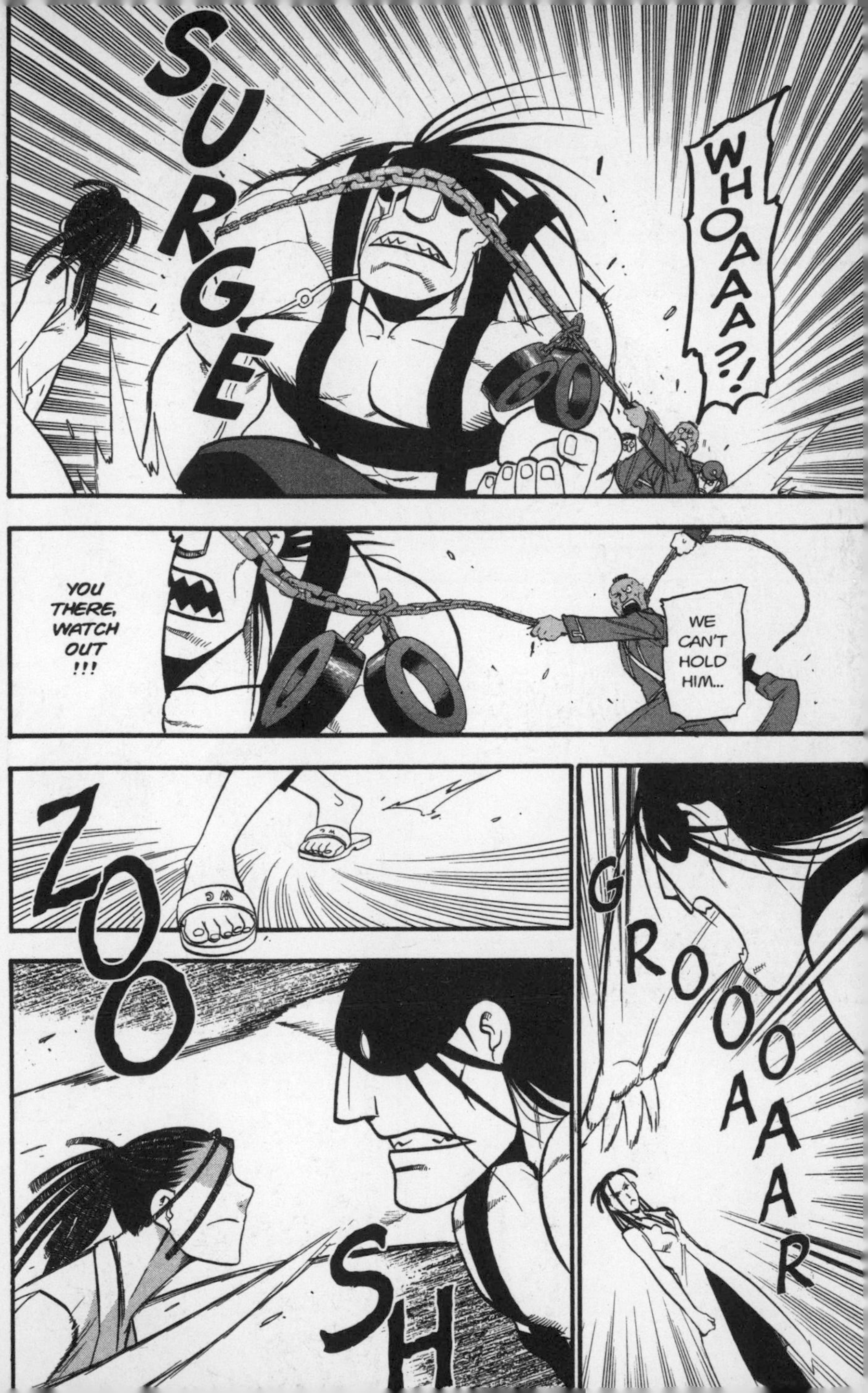
WHOAAA?!!
SURGE
WE CAN'T HOLD HIM...
YOU THERE, WATCH OUT!!!
GROOOAAAR
ZOOO
SH

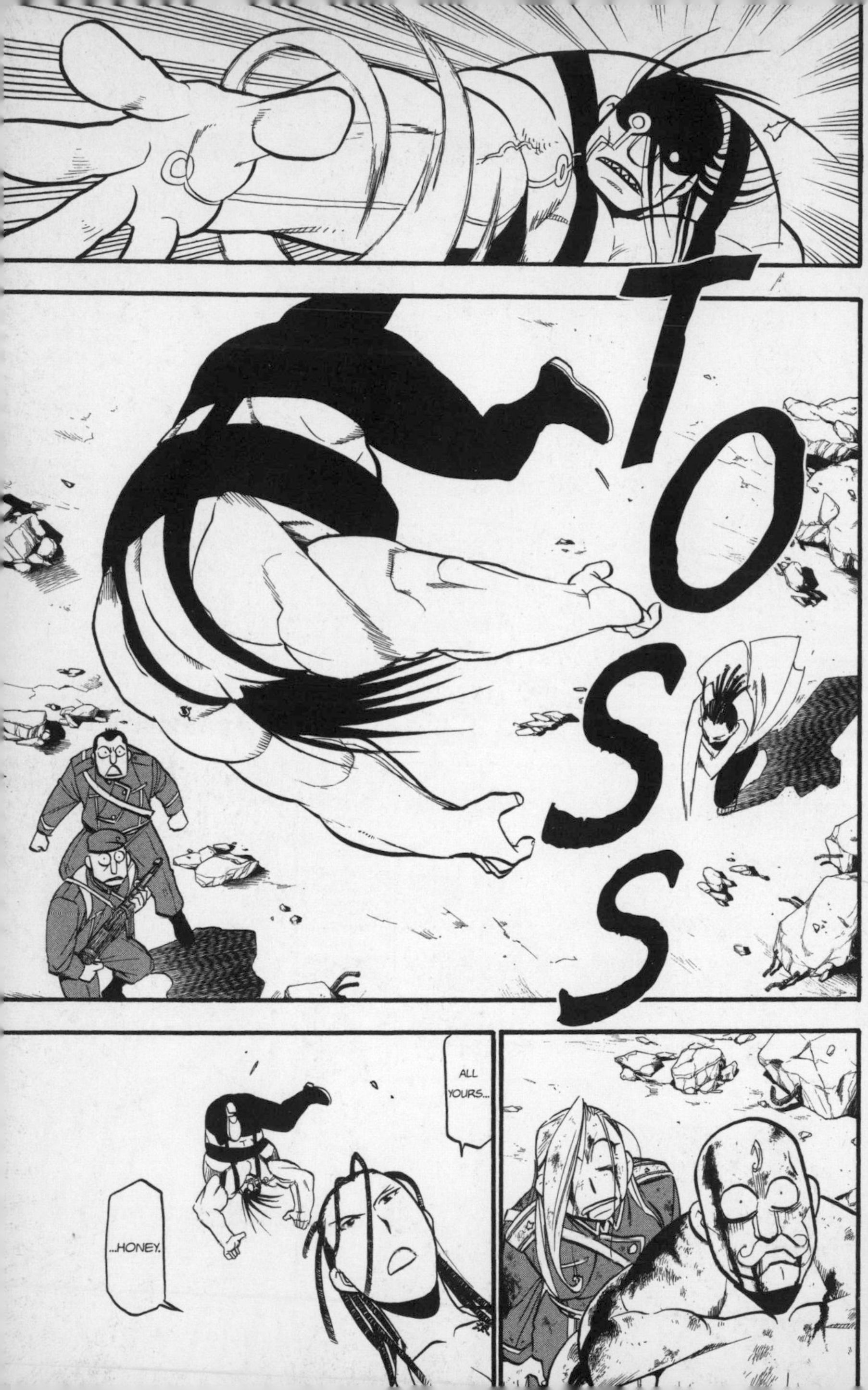
TOSS
ALL YOURS...
...HONEY.

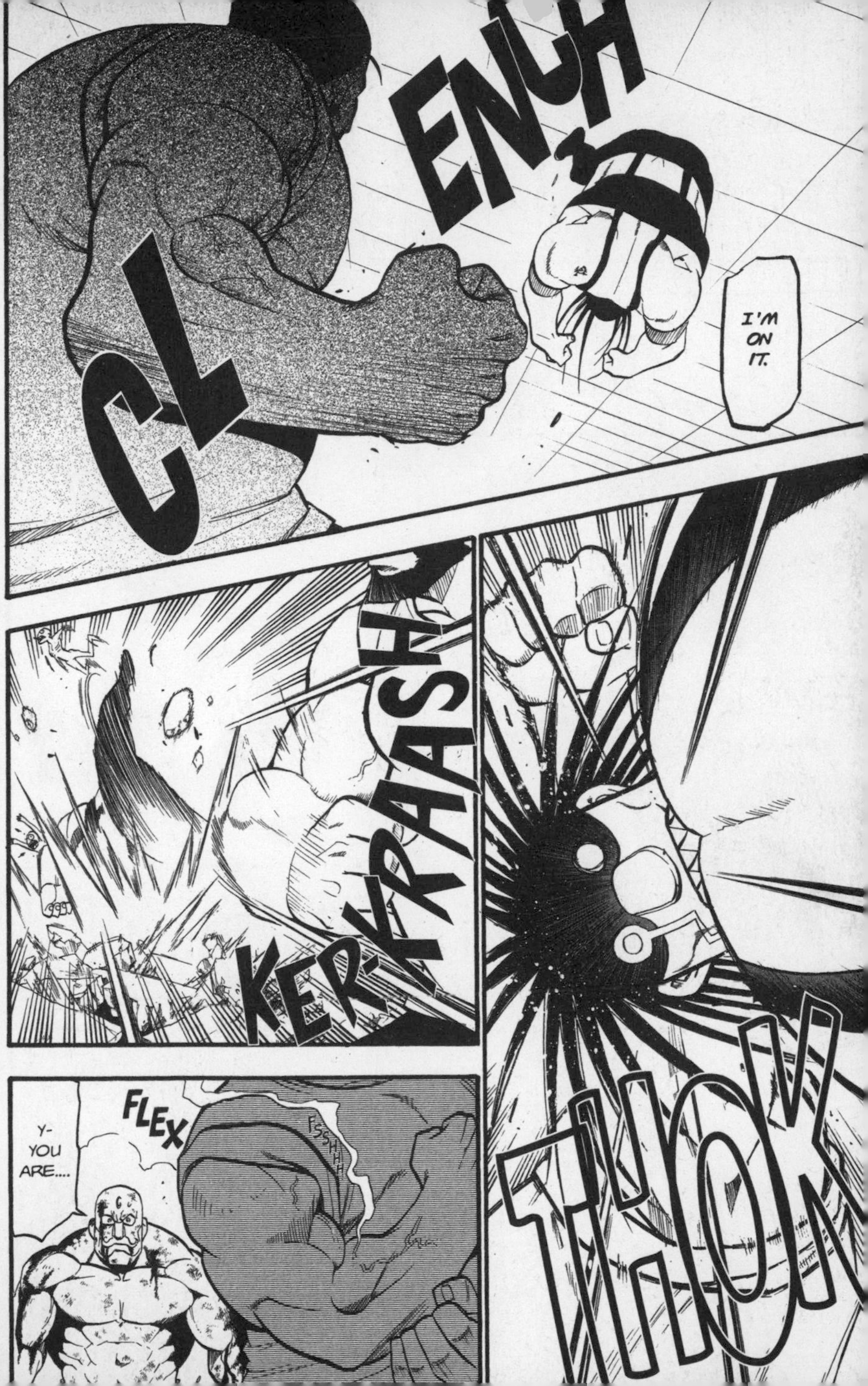
I'M ON IT.
CLENCH
THOK
KER-KRAASH
FLEX
FSSSHHH
Y-YOU ARE....

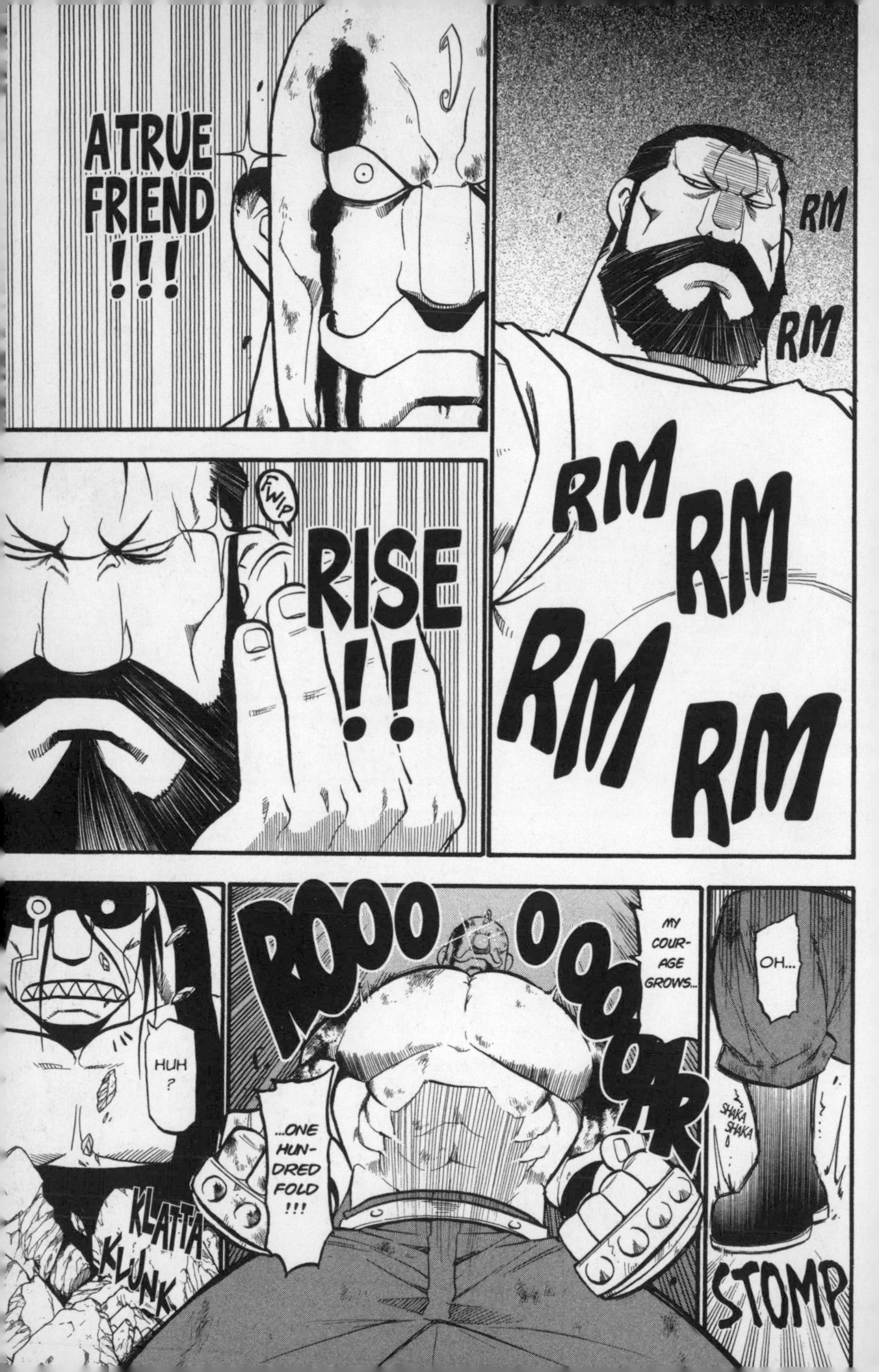
RM
RM
RM
RM
RM
RM
A TRUE FRIEND!!!
FWIP
RISE!!
OH...
SHAKA SHAKA
STOMP
ROOOOOOOAR
MY COURAGE GROWS...
...ONE HUNDRED FOLD!!!
HUH?
KLATTA KLUNK

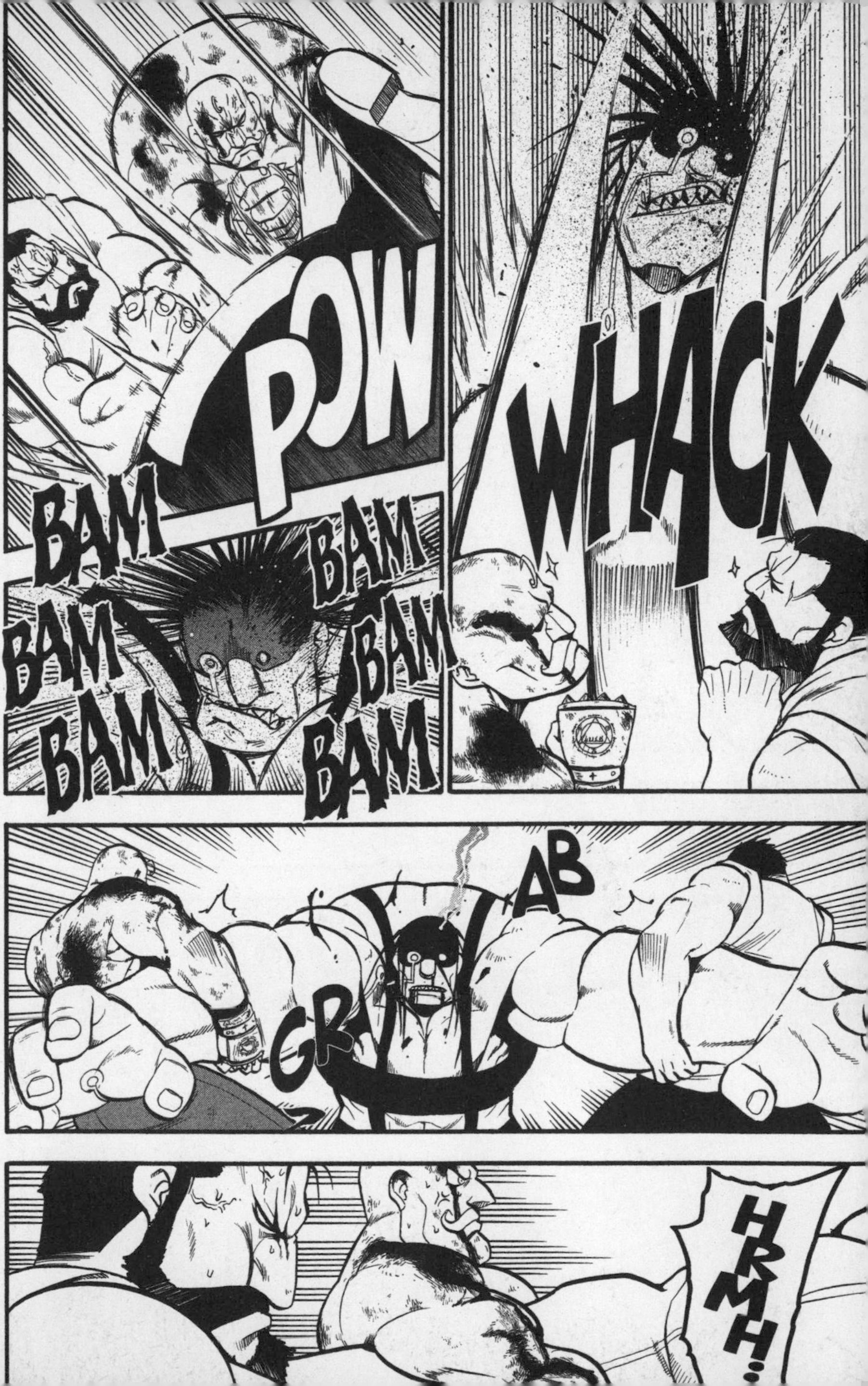
WHACK
POW
BAM BAM BAM
BAM BAM BAM
GR AB
HRMH!

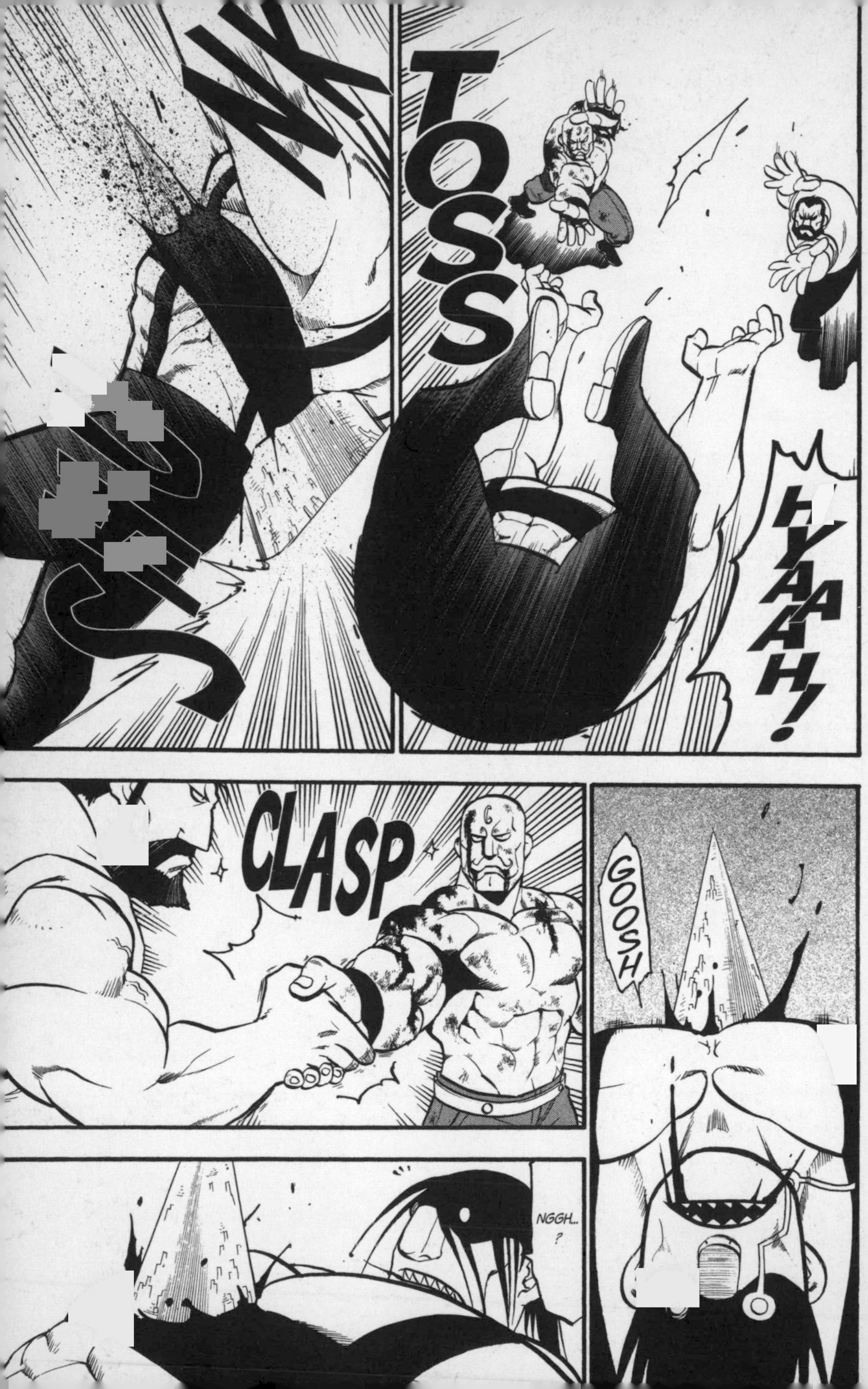
HYAAAH!
TOSS
GOOOSH
CLASP
NGGH... ?

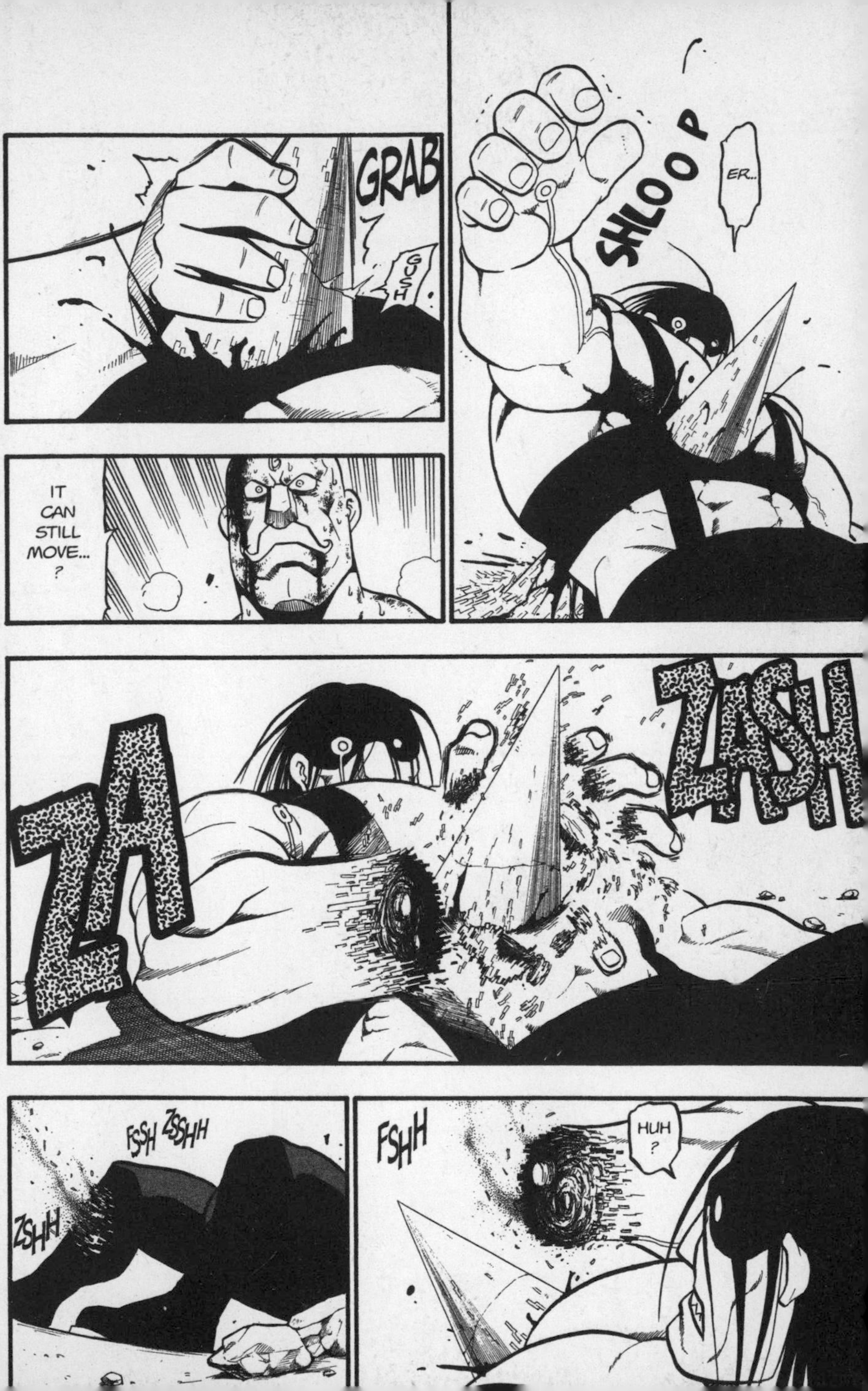
SHLOOP
ER...
GRAB
GUSH
IT CAN STILL MOVE...?
ZASH
ZA
FSHH
HUH?
FSSH ZSSHH
ZSHH

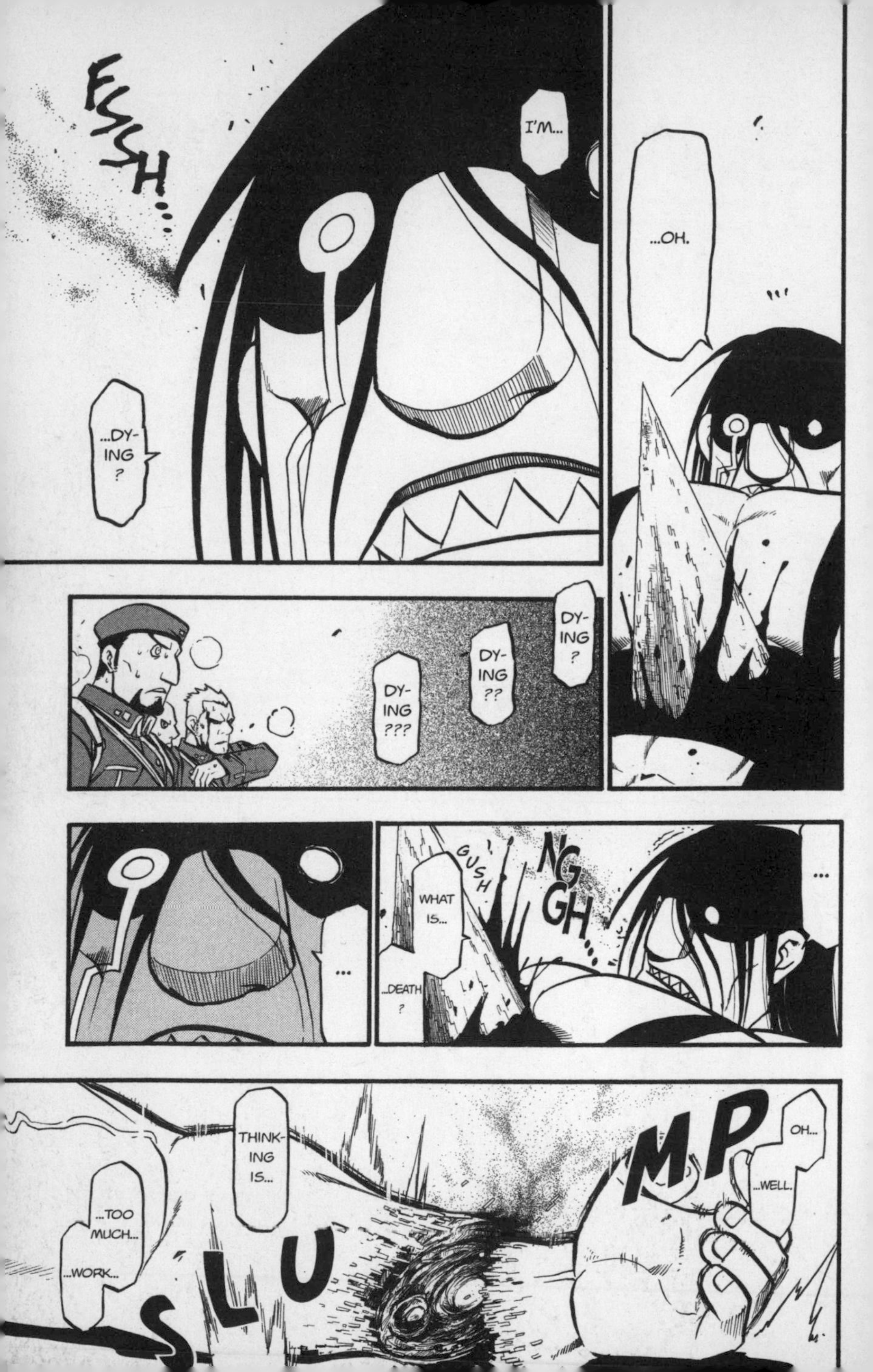
...OH.
I'M...
FSSH...
...DY-ING?
DY-ING?
DY-ING??
DY-ING???
...
NG GH...
GUSH
WHAT IS...
...DEATH?
...
OH...
...WELL.
MP
THINK-ING IS...
...TOO MUCH...
...WORK...
SLU

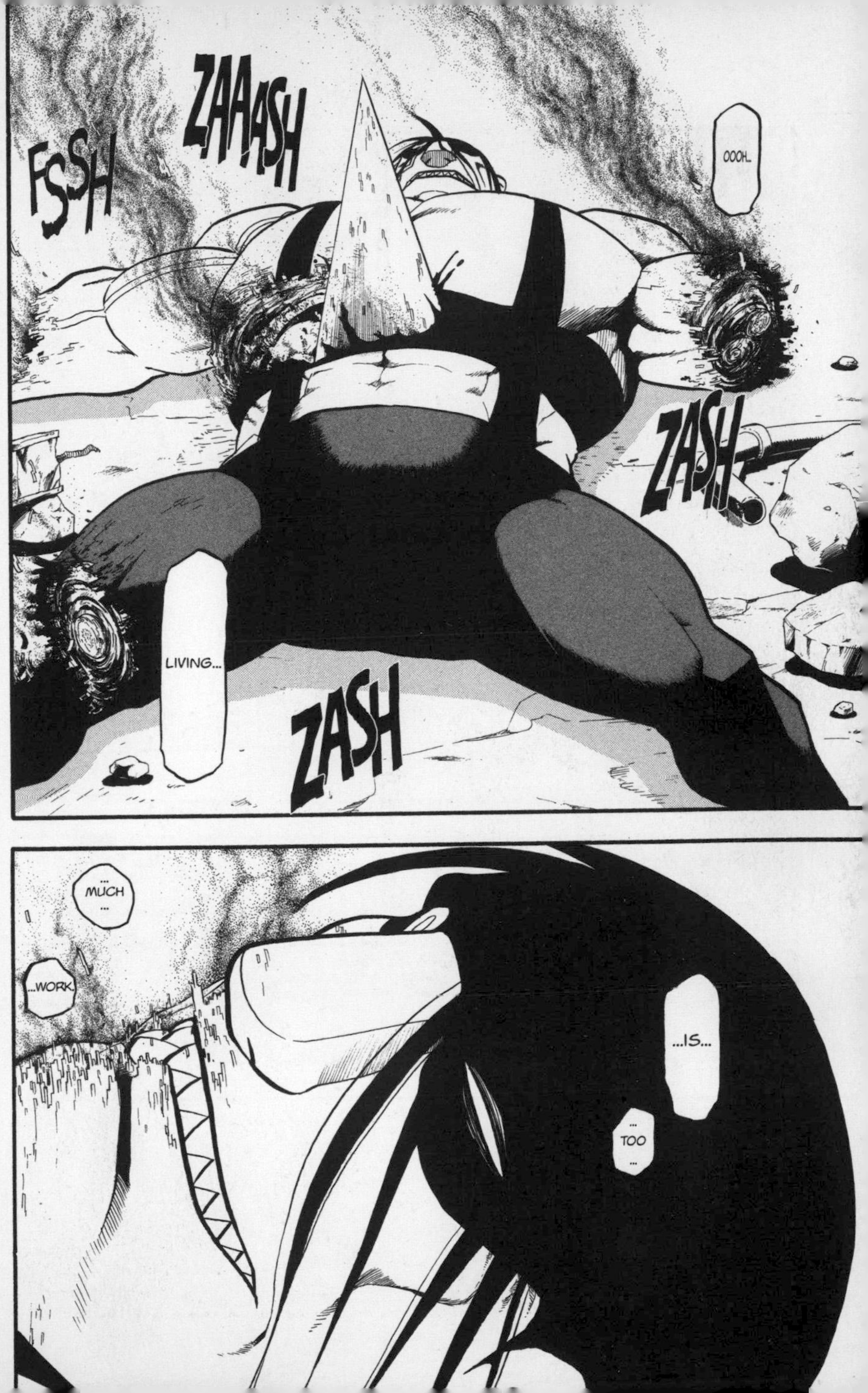
OOOH...
ZAAASH
FSSH
ZASH
LIVING...
ZASH
...IS...
... TOO ...
... MUCH ...
...WORK.

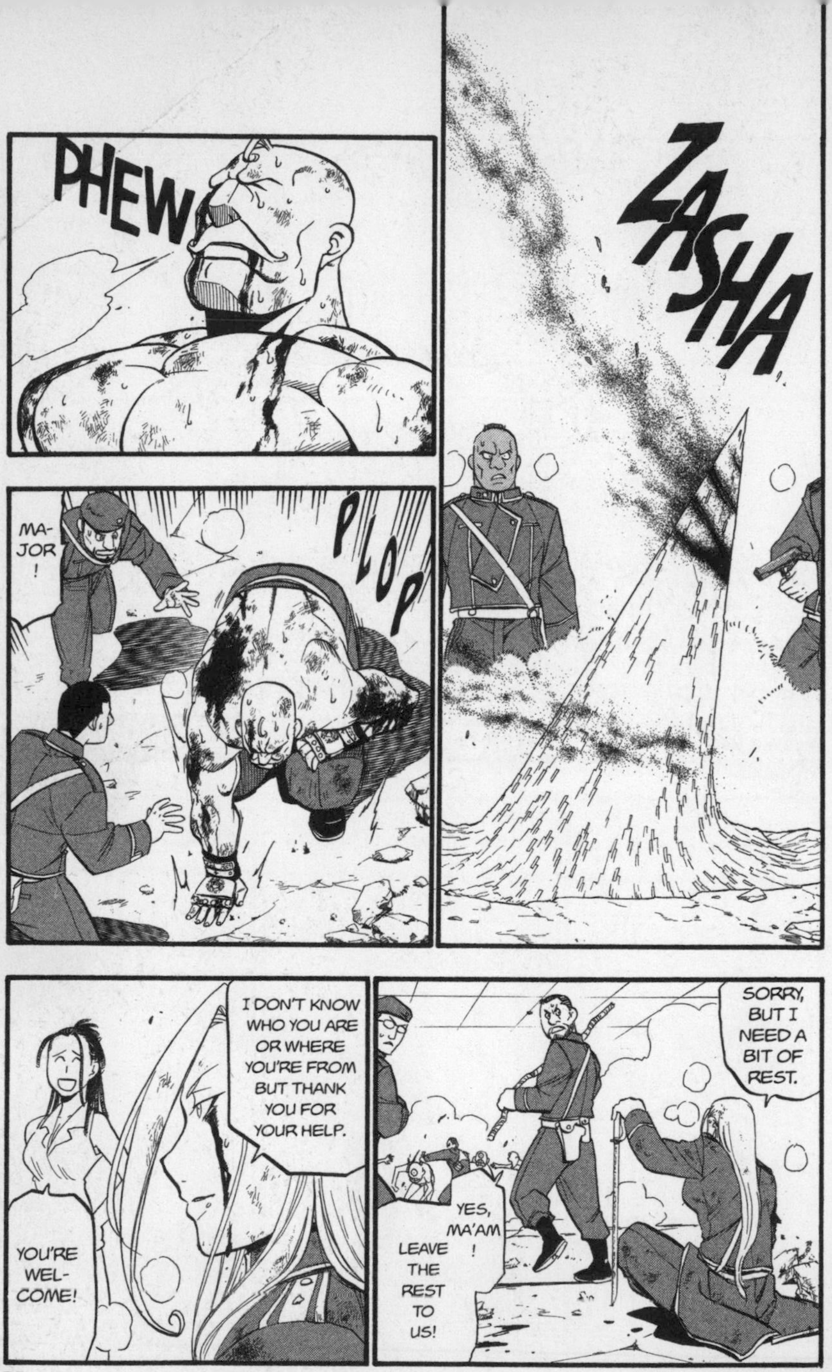
ZASHA
PHEW
MA-JOR!
PLOP
SORRY, BUT I NEED A BIT OF REST.
YES, MA'AM!
LEAVE THE REST TO US!
I DON'T KNOW WHO YOU ARE OR WHERE YOU'RE FROM BUT THANK YOU FOR YOUR HELP.
YOU'RE WEL-COME!

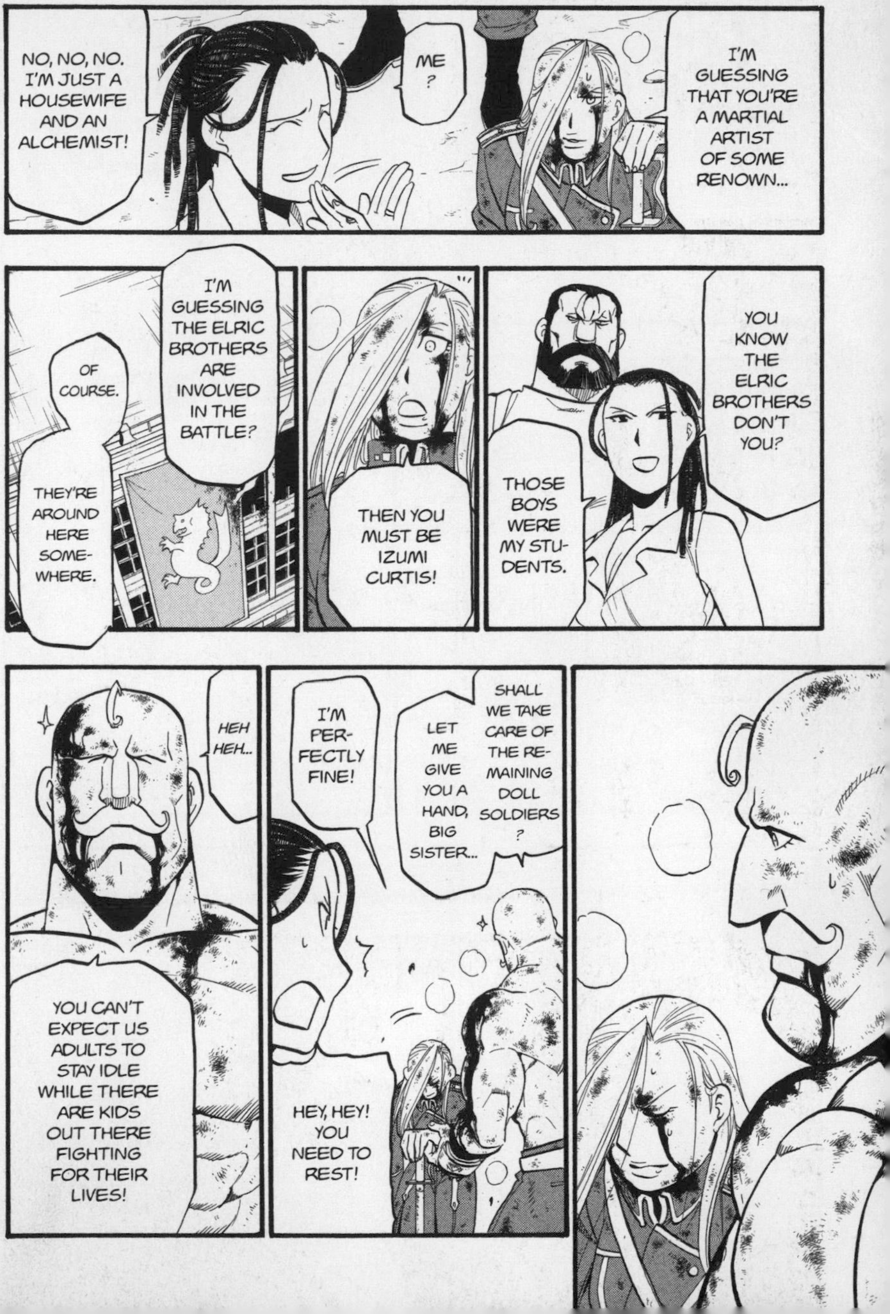
I'M GUESSING THAT YOU'RE A MARTIAL ARTIST OF SOME RENOWN...
ME?
NO, NO, NO. I'M JUST A HOUSEWIFE AND AN ALCHEMIST!
YOU KNOW THE ELRIC BROTHERS DON'T YOU?
THOSE BOYS WERE MY STUDENTS.
THEN YOU MUST BE IZUMI CURTIS!
I'M GUESSING THE ELRIC BROTHERS ARE INVOLVED IN THE BATTLE?
OF COURSE.
THEY'RE AROUND HERE SOMEWHERE.
SHALL WE TAKE CARE OF THE REMAINING DOLL SOLDIERS?
LET ME GIVE YOU A HAND, BIG SISTER...
I'M PERFECTLY FINE!
HEY, HEY! YOU NEED TO REST!
HEH HEH...
YOU CAN'T EXPECT US ADULTS TO STAY IDLE WHILE THERE ARE KIDS OUT THERE FIGHTING FOR THEIR LIVES!

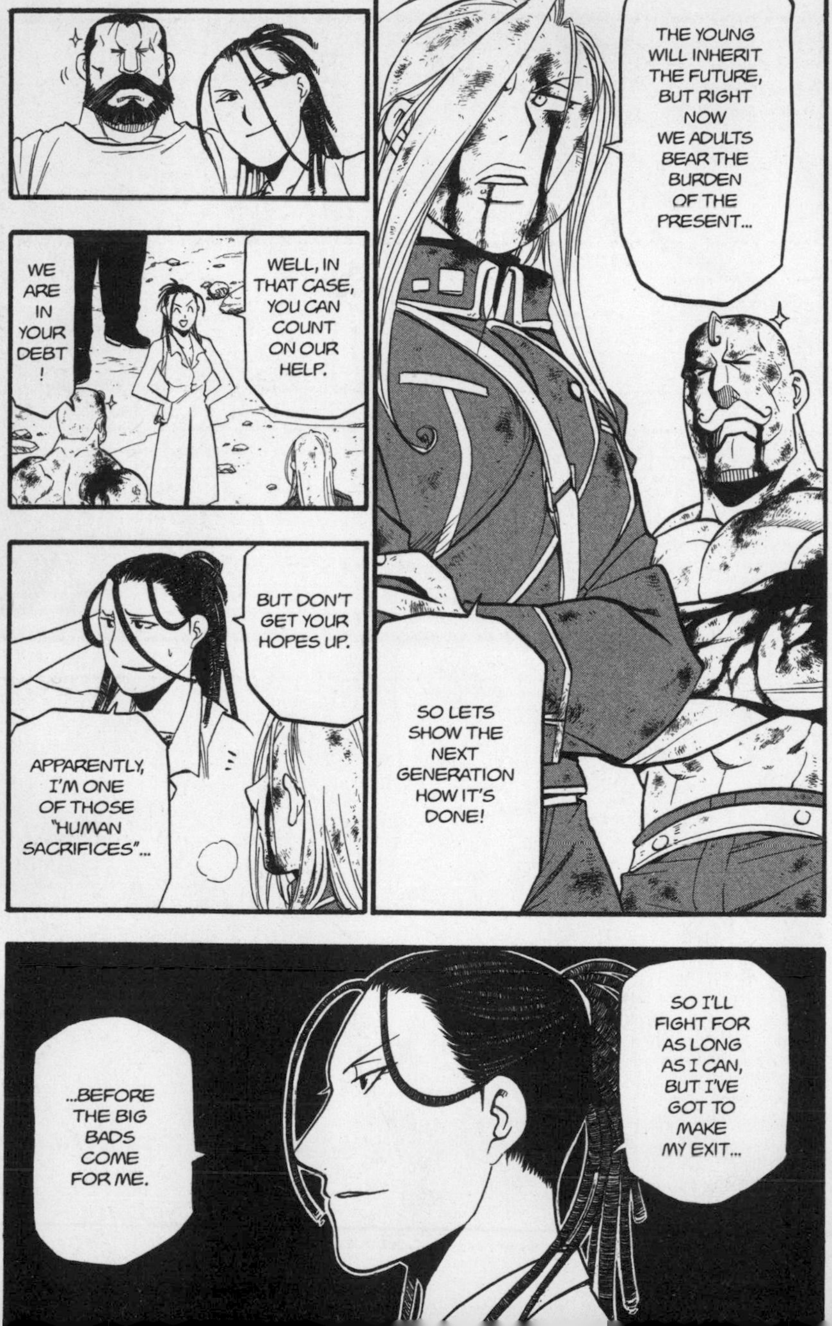
THE YOUNG WILL INHERIT THE FUTURE, BUT RIGHT NOW WE ADULTS BEAR THE BURDEN OF THE PRESENT...
SO LETS SHOW THE NEXT GENERATION HOW IT'S DONE!
WELL, IN THAT CASE, YOU CAN COUNT ON OUR HELP.
WE ARE IN YOUR DEBT!
BUT DON'T GET YOUR HOPES UP.
APPARENTLY, I'M ONE OF THOSE "HUMAN SACRIFICES"...
SO I'LL FIGHT FOR AS LONG AS I CAN, BUT I'VE GOT TO MAKE MY EXIT...
...BEFORE THE BIG BADS COME FOR ME.

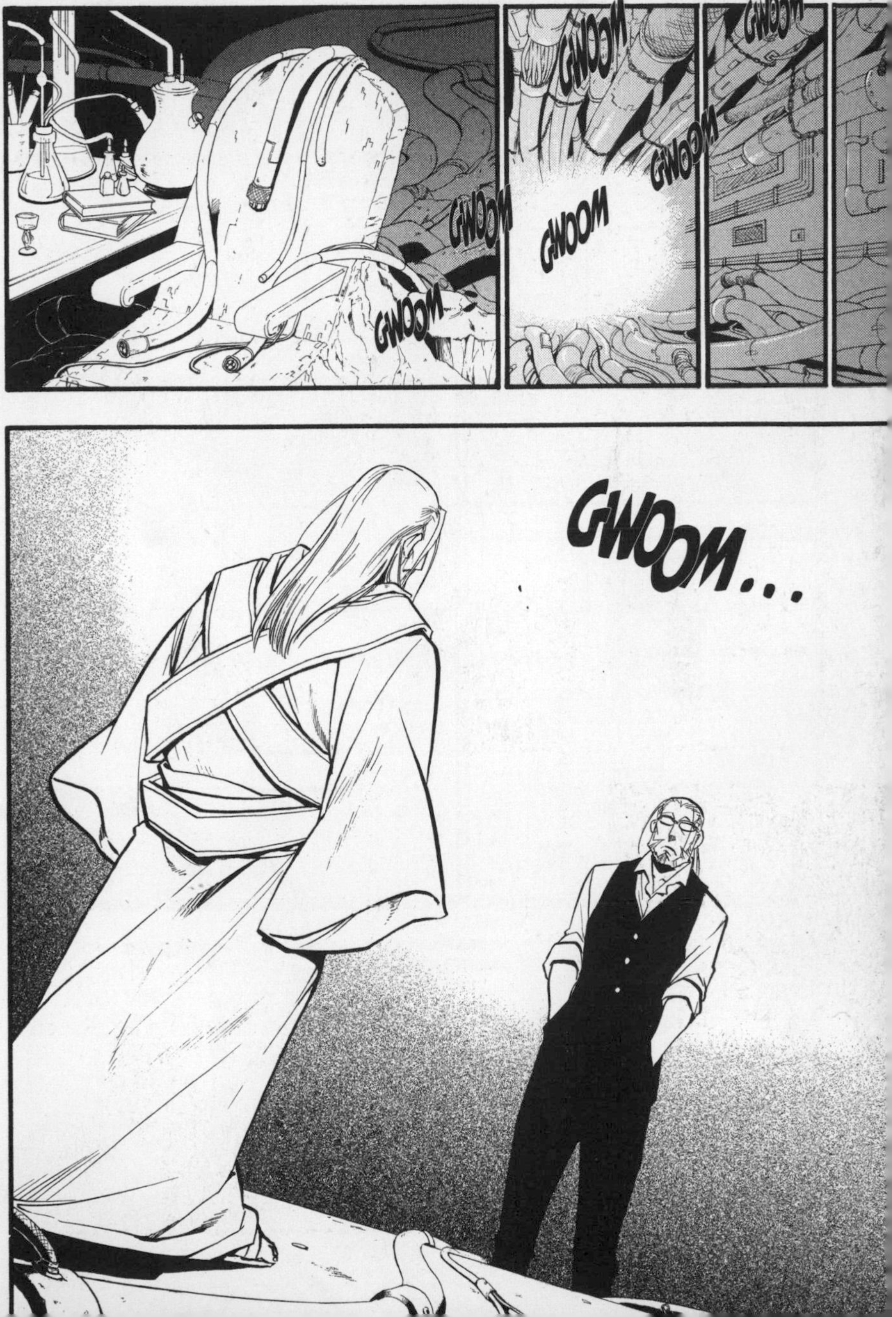
GWOOM
GWOOM
GWOOM
GWOOM
GWOOM
GWOOM
GWOOM...

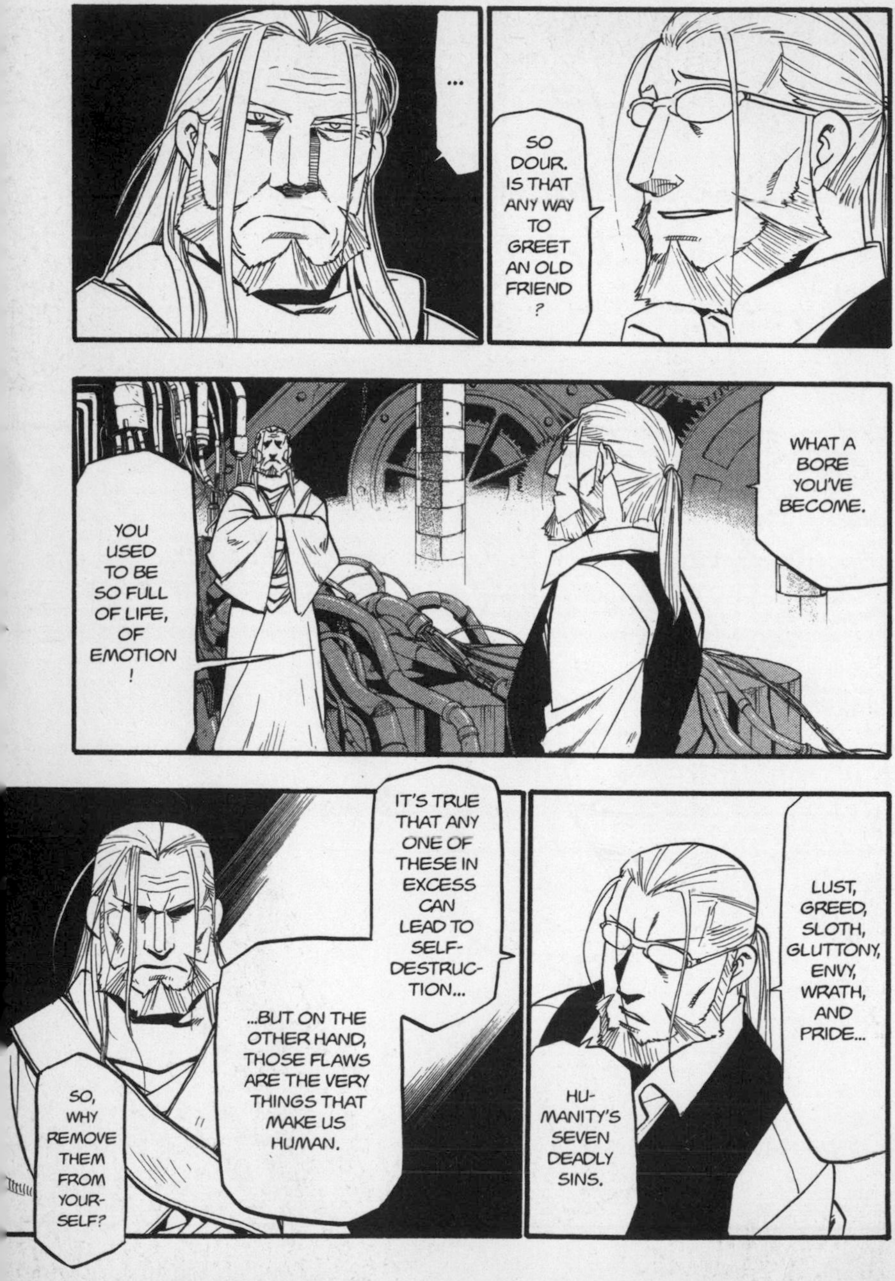
SO DOUR. IS THAT ANY WAY TO GREET AN OLD FRIEND?
...
WHAT A BORE YOU'VE BECOME.
YOU USED TO BE SO FULL OF LIFE, OF EMOTION!
LUST, GREED, SLOTH, GLUTTONY, ENVY, WRATH, AND PRIDE...
HUMANITY'S SEVEN DEADLY SINS.
IT'S TRUE THAT ANY ONE OF THESE IN EXCESS CAN LEAD TO SELF-DESTRUCTION...
...BUT ON THE OTHER HAND, THOSE FLAWS ARE THE VERY THINGS THAT MAKE US HUMAN.
SO, WHY REMOVE THEM FROM YOURSELF?

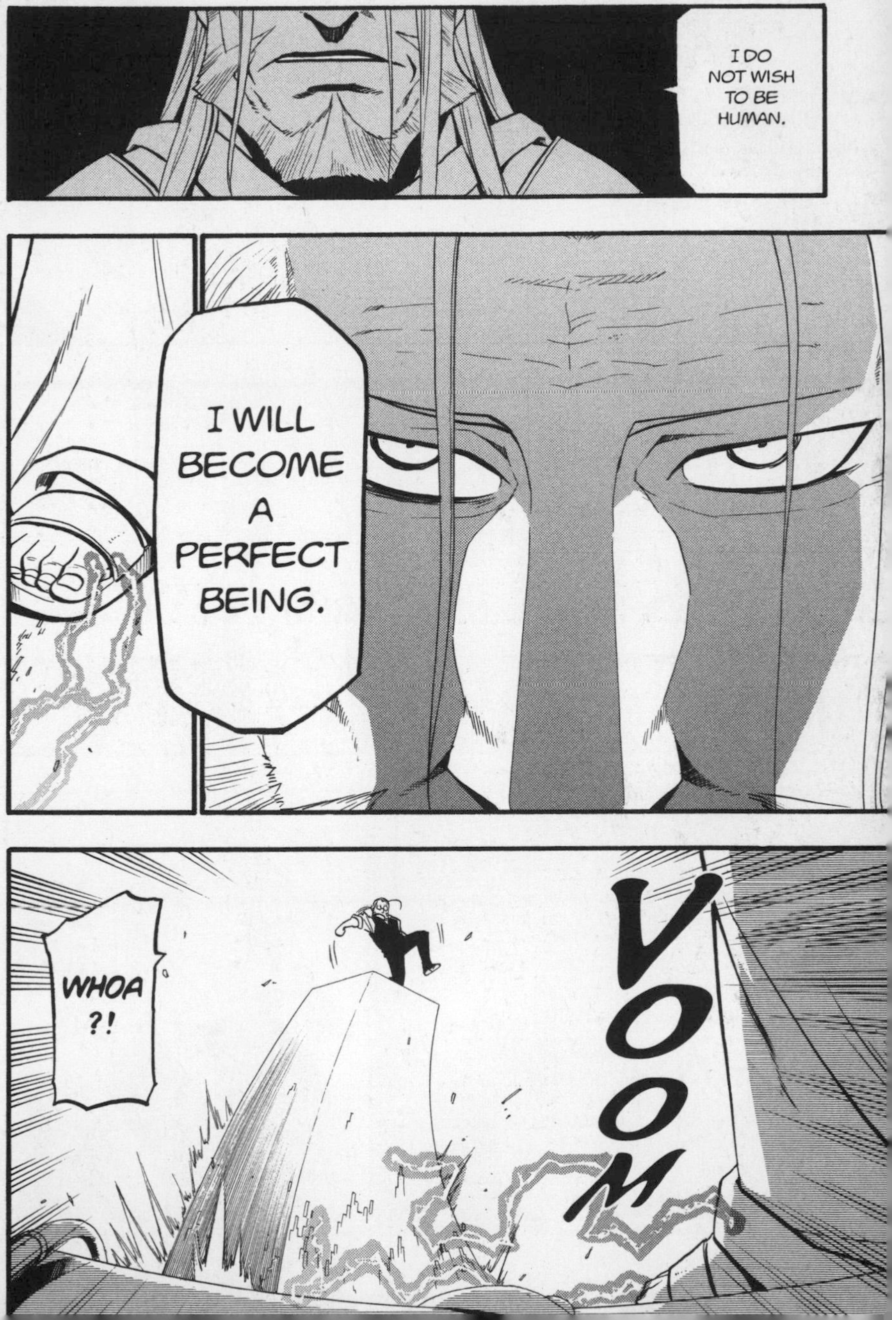
I DO NOT WISH TO BE HUMAN.
I WILL BECOME A PERFECT BEING.
VOOM
WHOA ?!

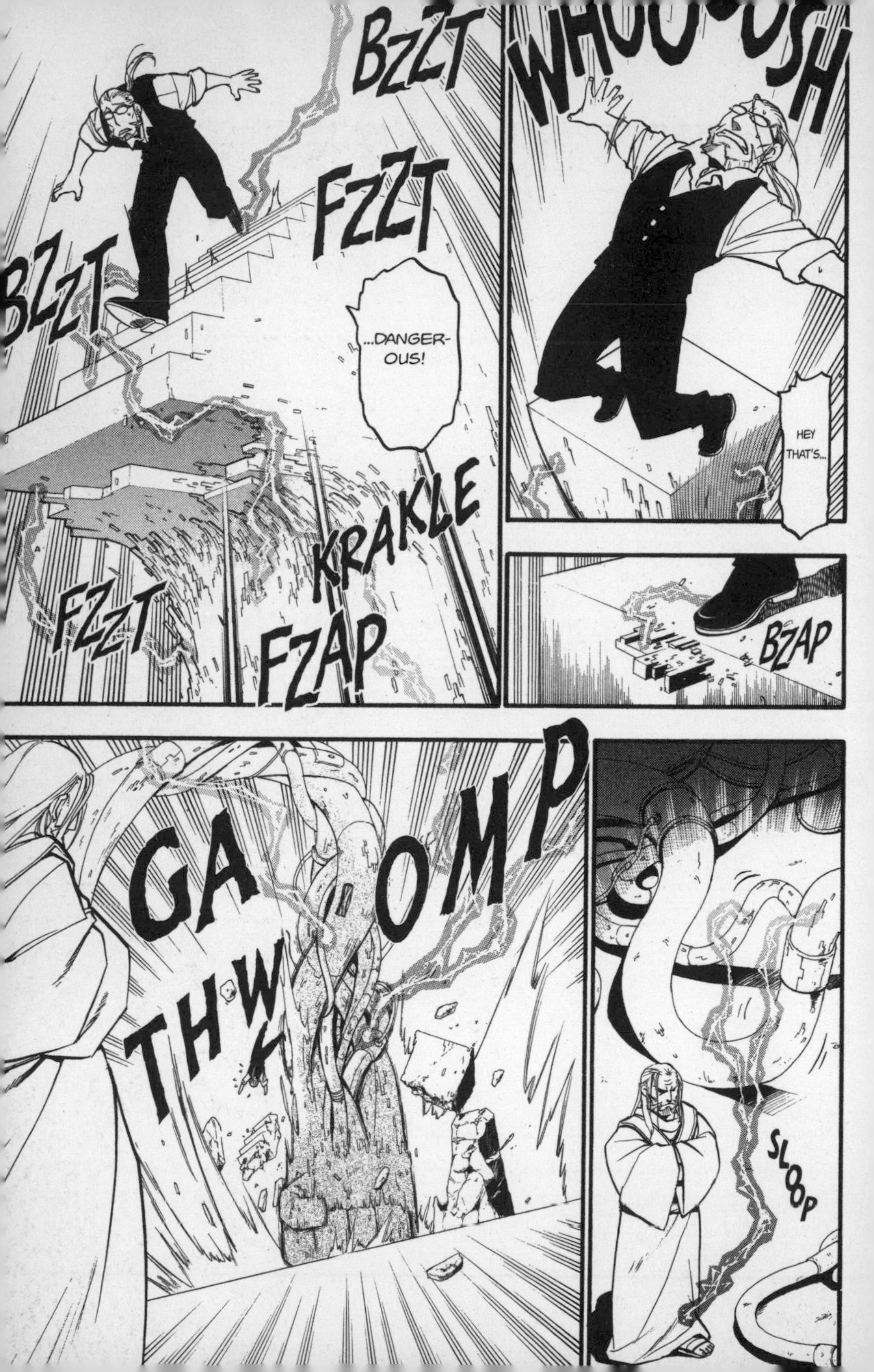

WHOO-OSH
HEY THAT'S...
BZAP
BZZT
FZZT
BZZT
...DANGER-OUS!
KRAKLE
FZZT
FZAP
SLOOP
GA THWOMP

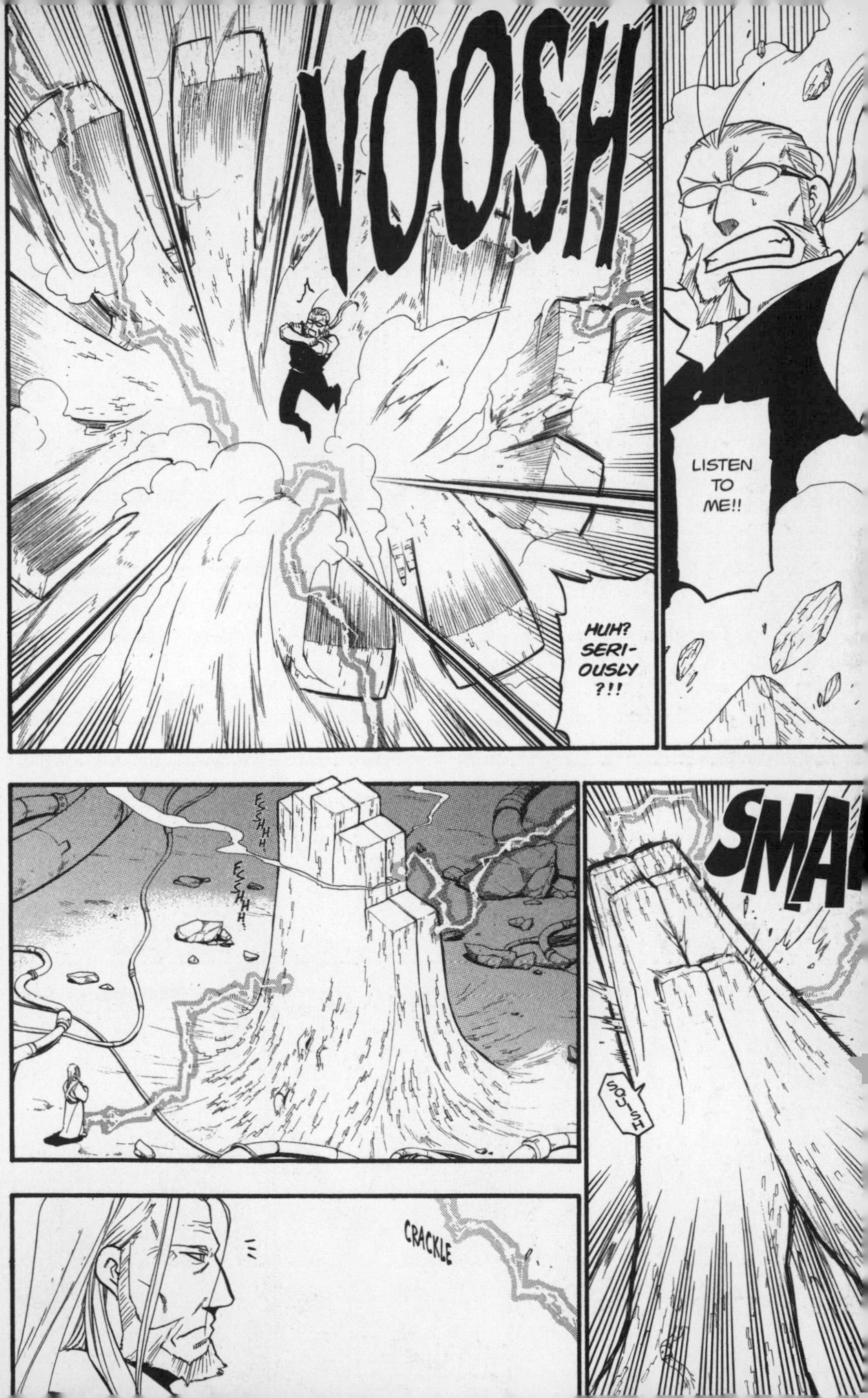
LISTEN TO ME!!
VOOSH
HUH? SERIOUSLY?!!
SMA
SQUISH
FSSHHH..
FSSHHH..
CRACKLE

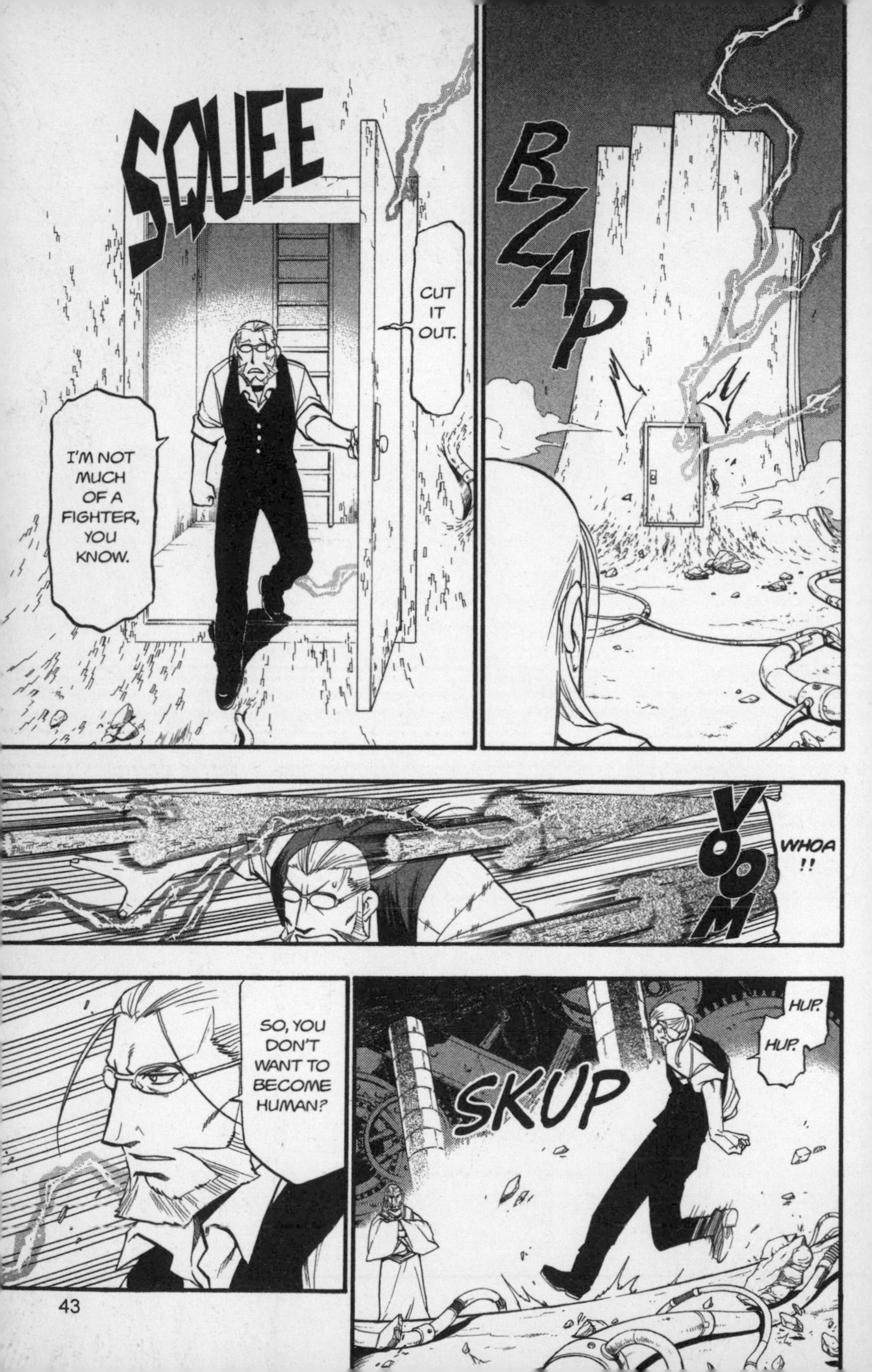
BZZAP
SQUEE
CUT IT OUT.
I'M NOT MUCH OF A FIGHTER, YOU KNOW.
WHOA!!
VOOM
HUP.
HUP.
SKUP
SO, YOU DON'T WANT TO BECOME HUMAN?

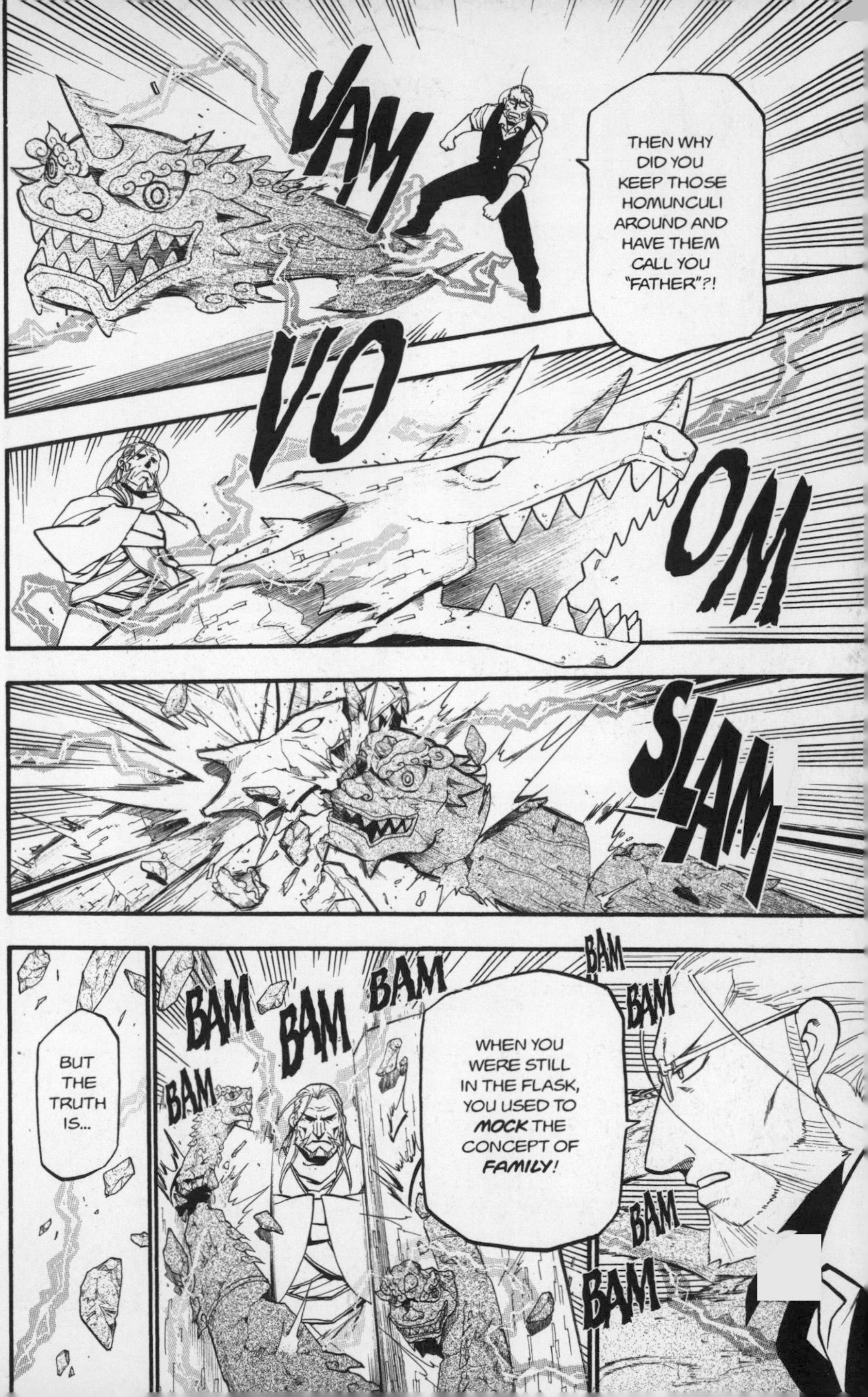
THEN WHY DID YOU KEEP THOSE HOMUNCULI AROUND AND HAVE THEM CALL YOU "FATHER"?!
VAM
VOOM
SLAM
BAM
BAM
WHEN YOU WERE STILL IN THE FLASK, YOU USED TO *MOCK* THE CONCEPT OF *FAMILY*!
BAM
BAM
BAM
BAM
BAM
BAM
BUT THE TRUTH IS...

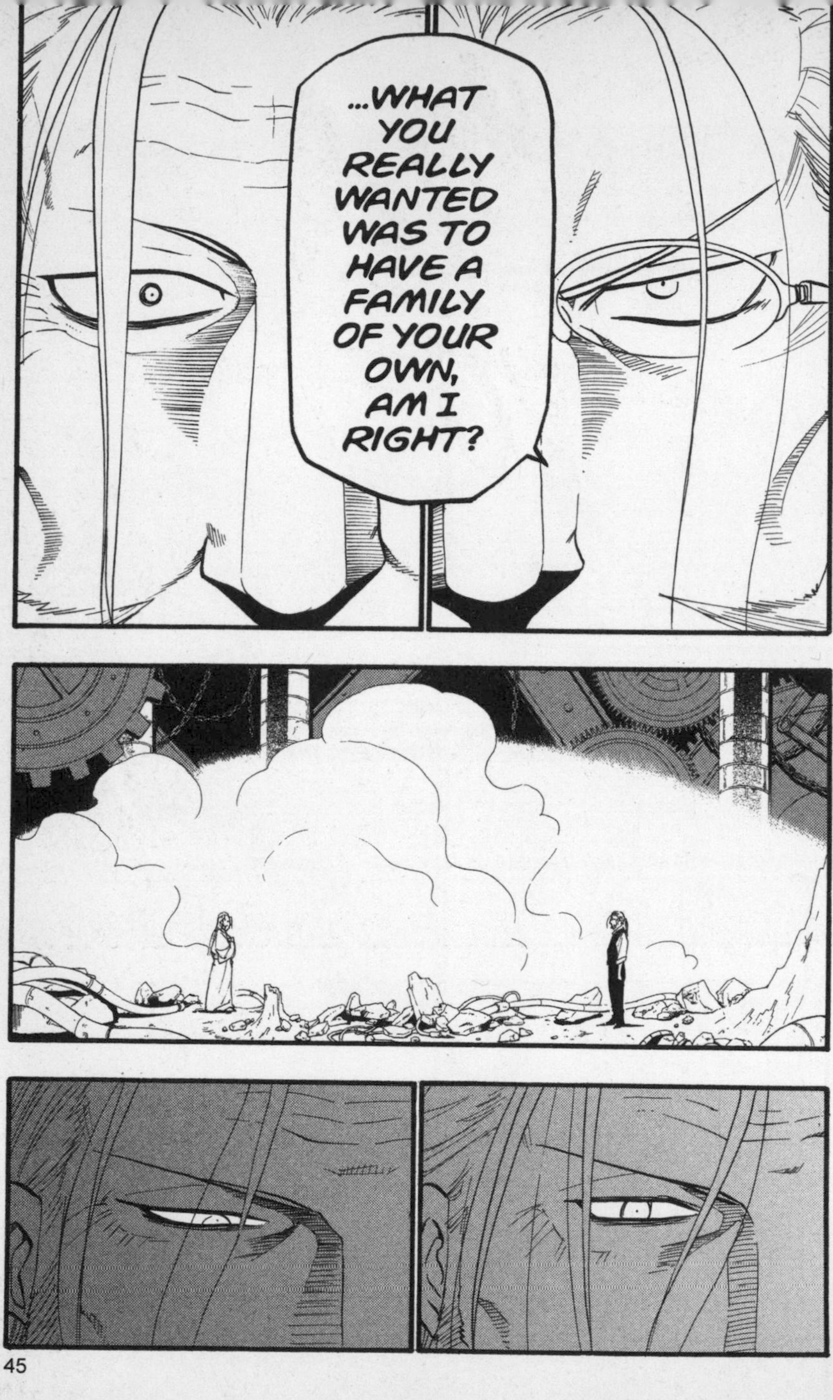
...WHAT YOU REALLY WANTED WAS TO HAVE A FAMILY OF YOUR OWN, AM I RIGHT?

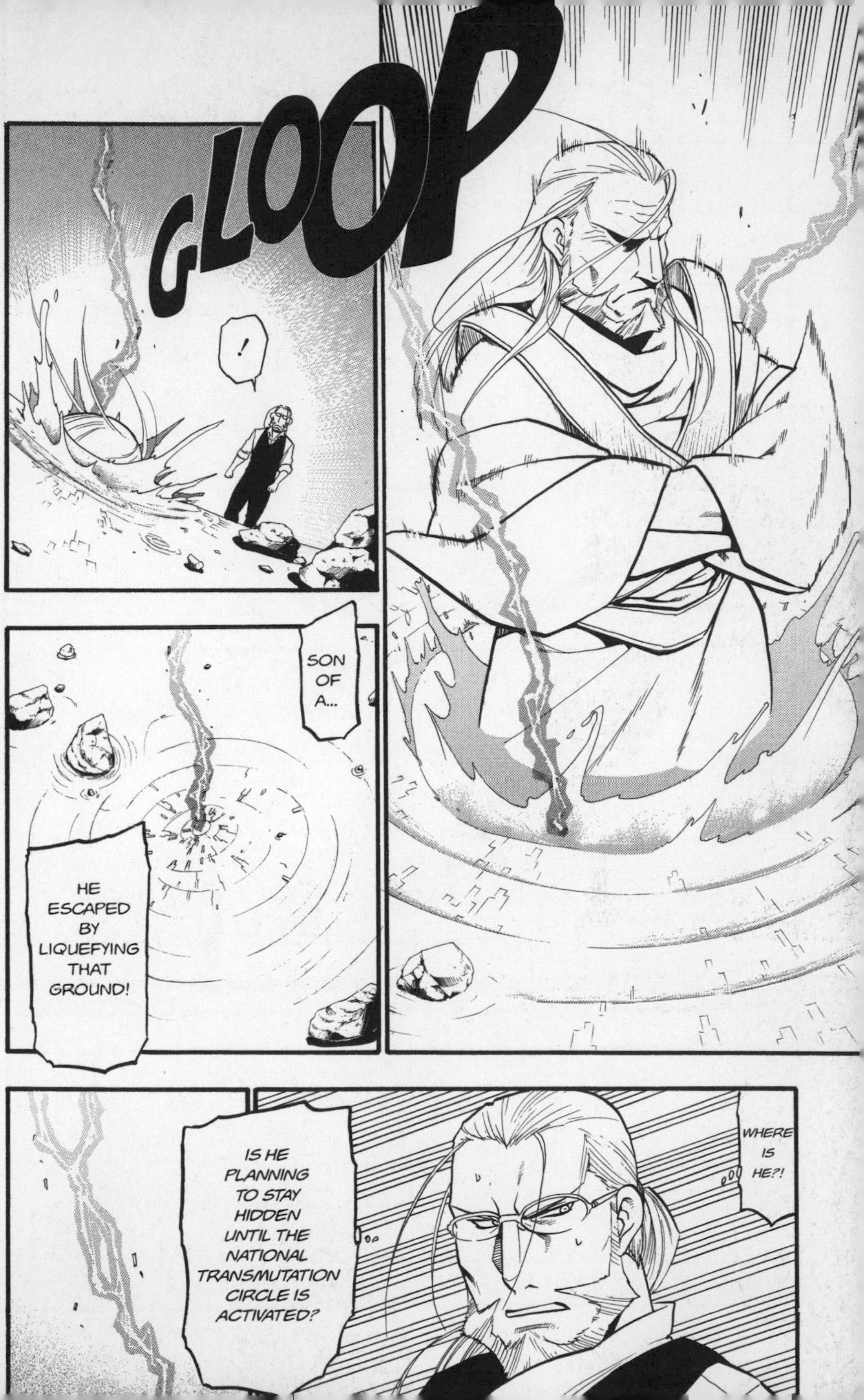
GLOOP
!
SON OF A...
HE ESCAPED BY LIQUEFYING THAT GROUND!
WHERE IS HE?!
IS HE PLANNING TO STAY HIDDEN UNTIL THE NATIONAL TRANSMUTATION CIRCLE IS ACTIVATED?

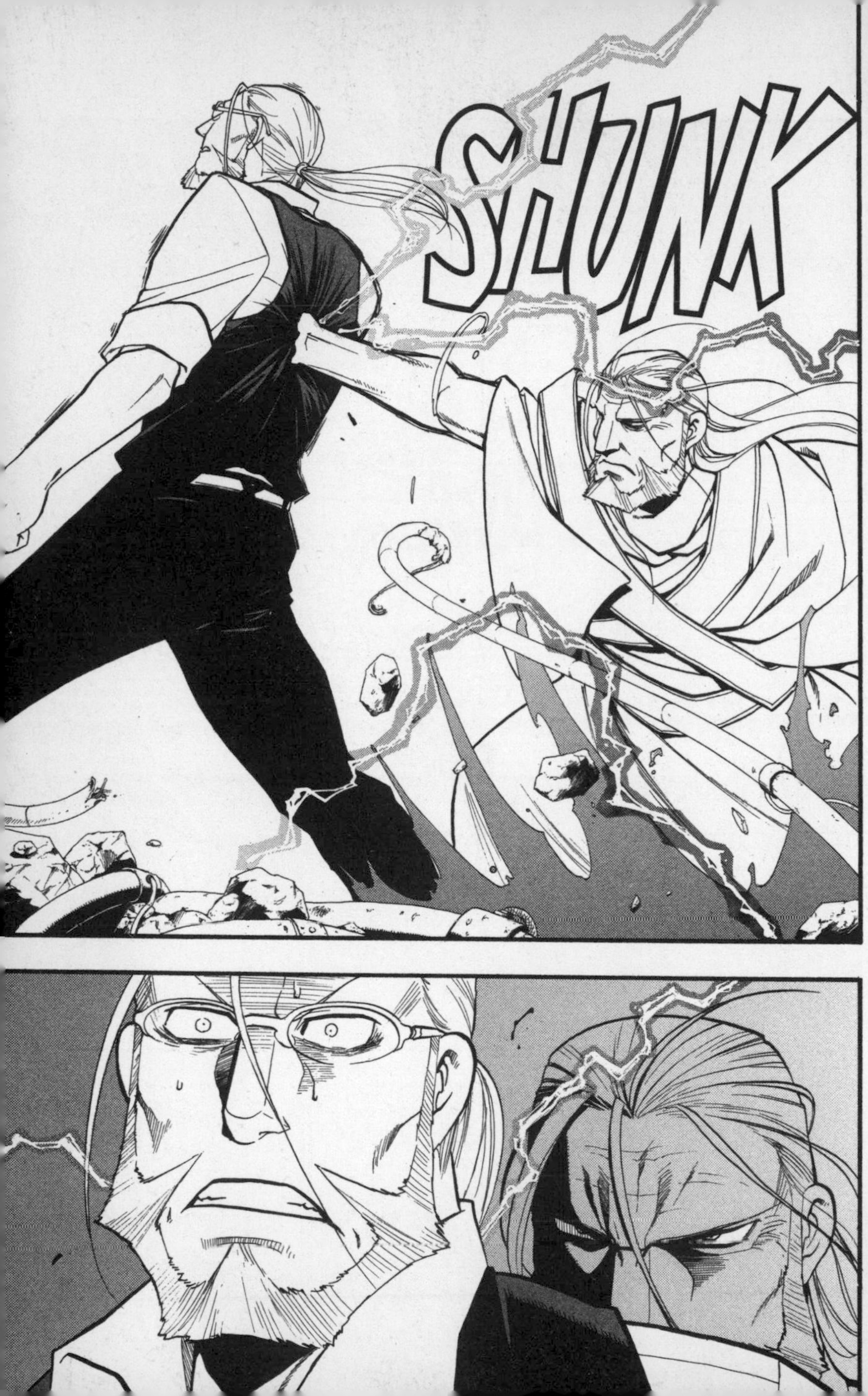
SHUNK

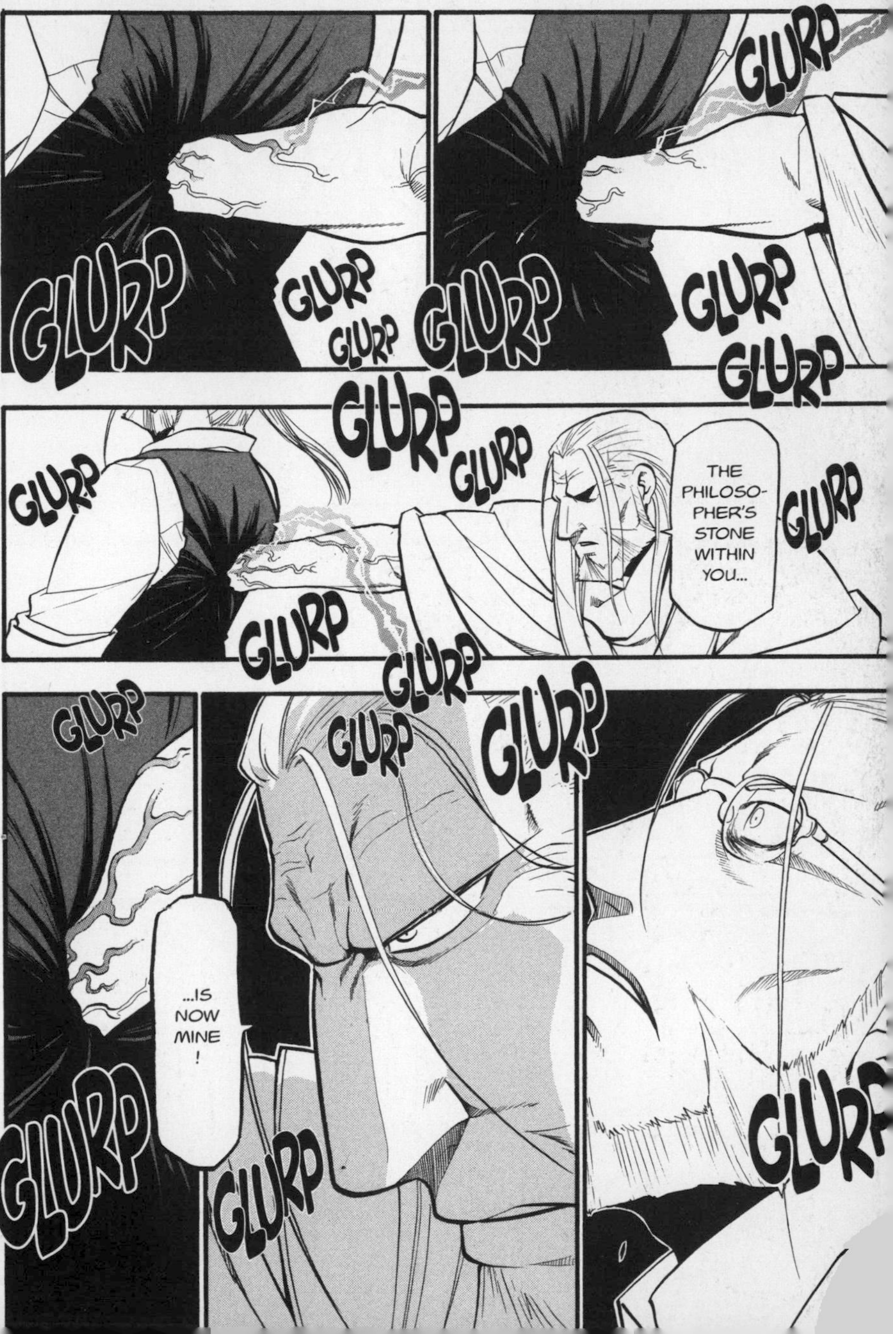
GLURP
GLURP
GLURP
GLURP
GLURP
GLURP
GLURP
GLURP
GLURP
THE PHILOSOPHER'S STONE WITHIN YOU...
GLURP
GLURP
GLURP
GLURP
GLURP
GLURP
...IS NOW MINE!
GLURP
GLURP
GLURP

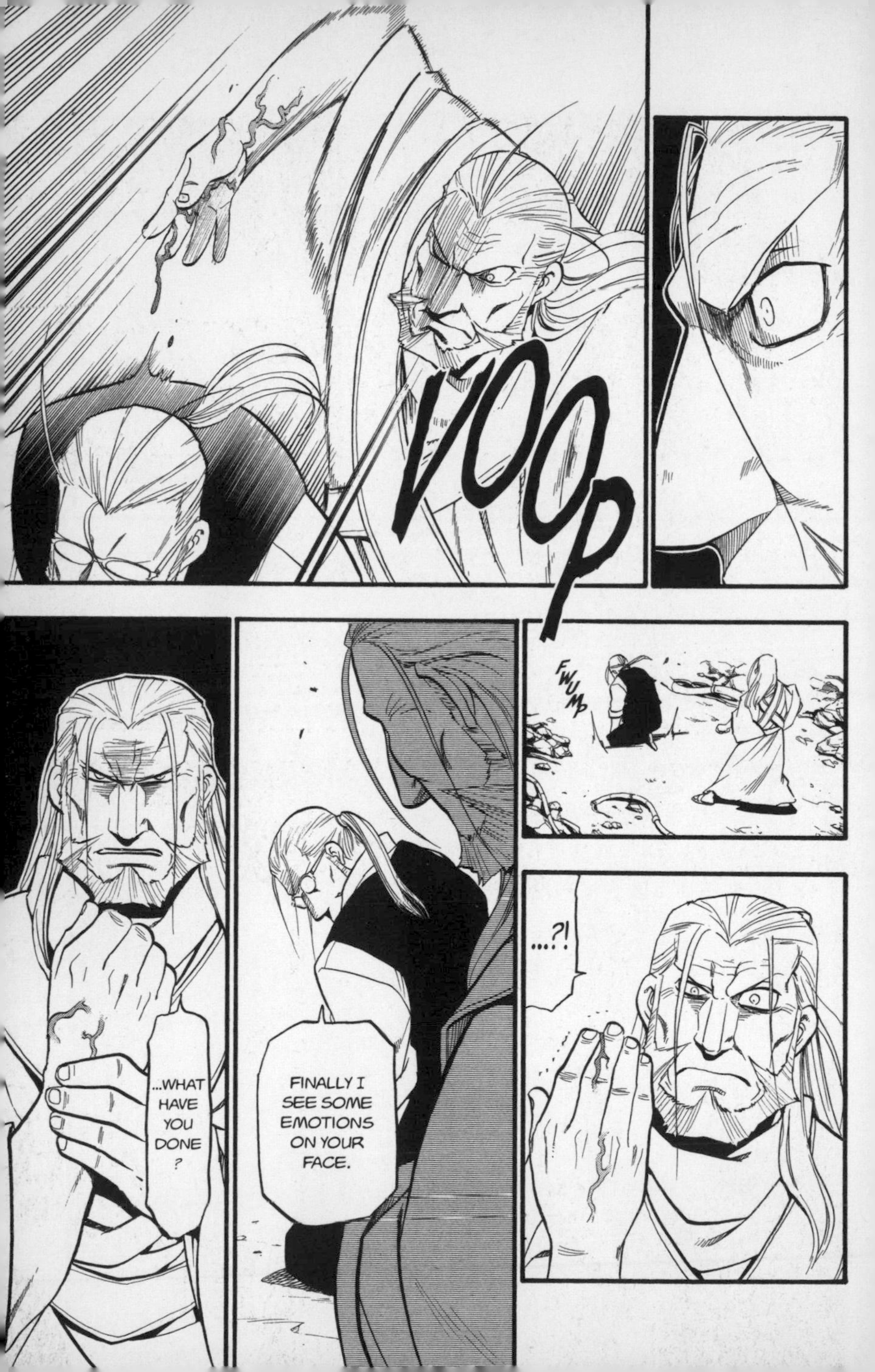
VOOP
FWUMP
...?!
FINALLY I SEE SOME EMOTIONS ON YOUR FACE.
...WHAT HAVE YOU DONE?

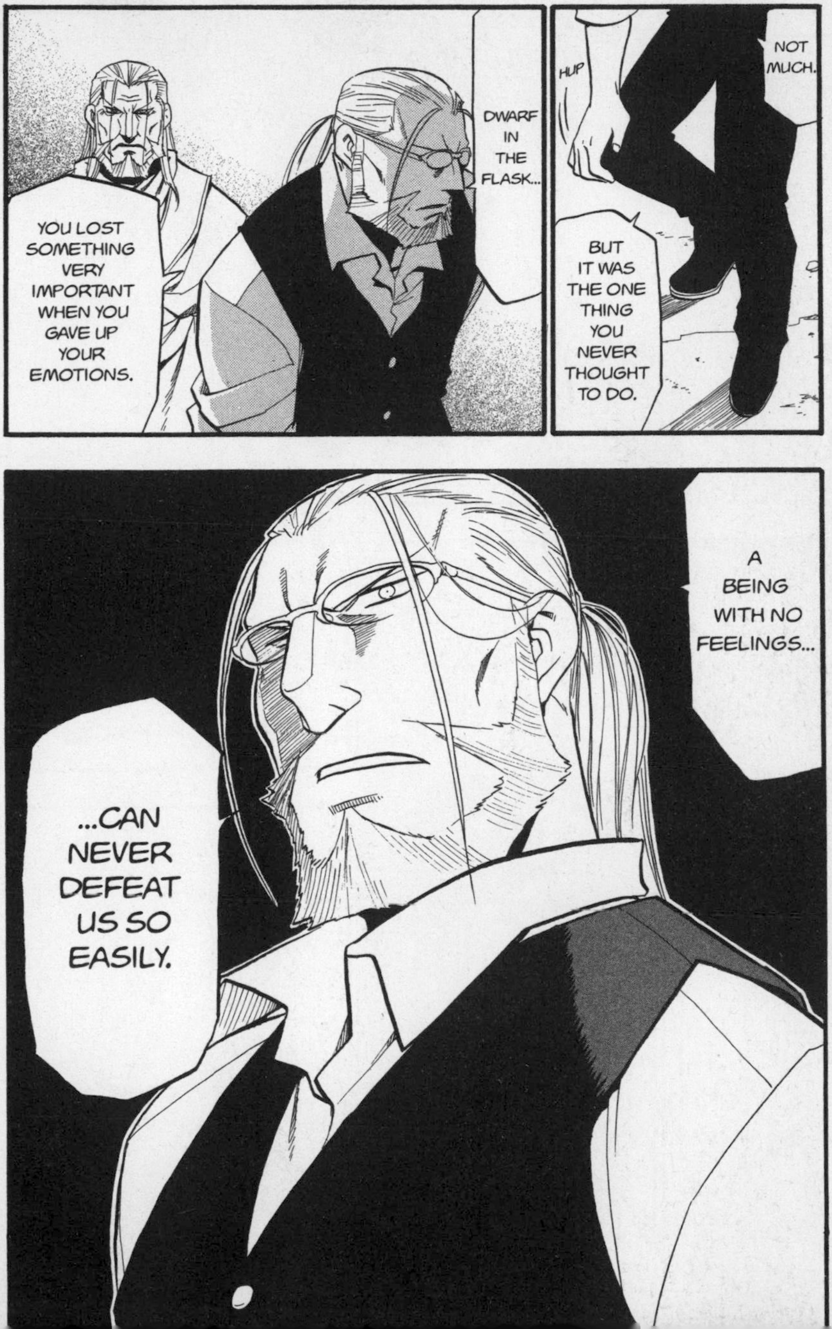
NOT MUCH.
HUP
BUT IT WAS THE ONE THING YOU NEVER THOUGHT TO DO.
DWARF IN THE FLASK...
YOU LOST SOMETHING VERY IMPORTANT WHEN YOU GAVE UP YOUR EMOTIONS.
A BEING WITH NO FEELINGS...
...CAN NEVER DEFEAT US SO EASILY.

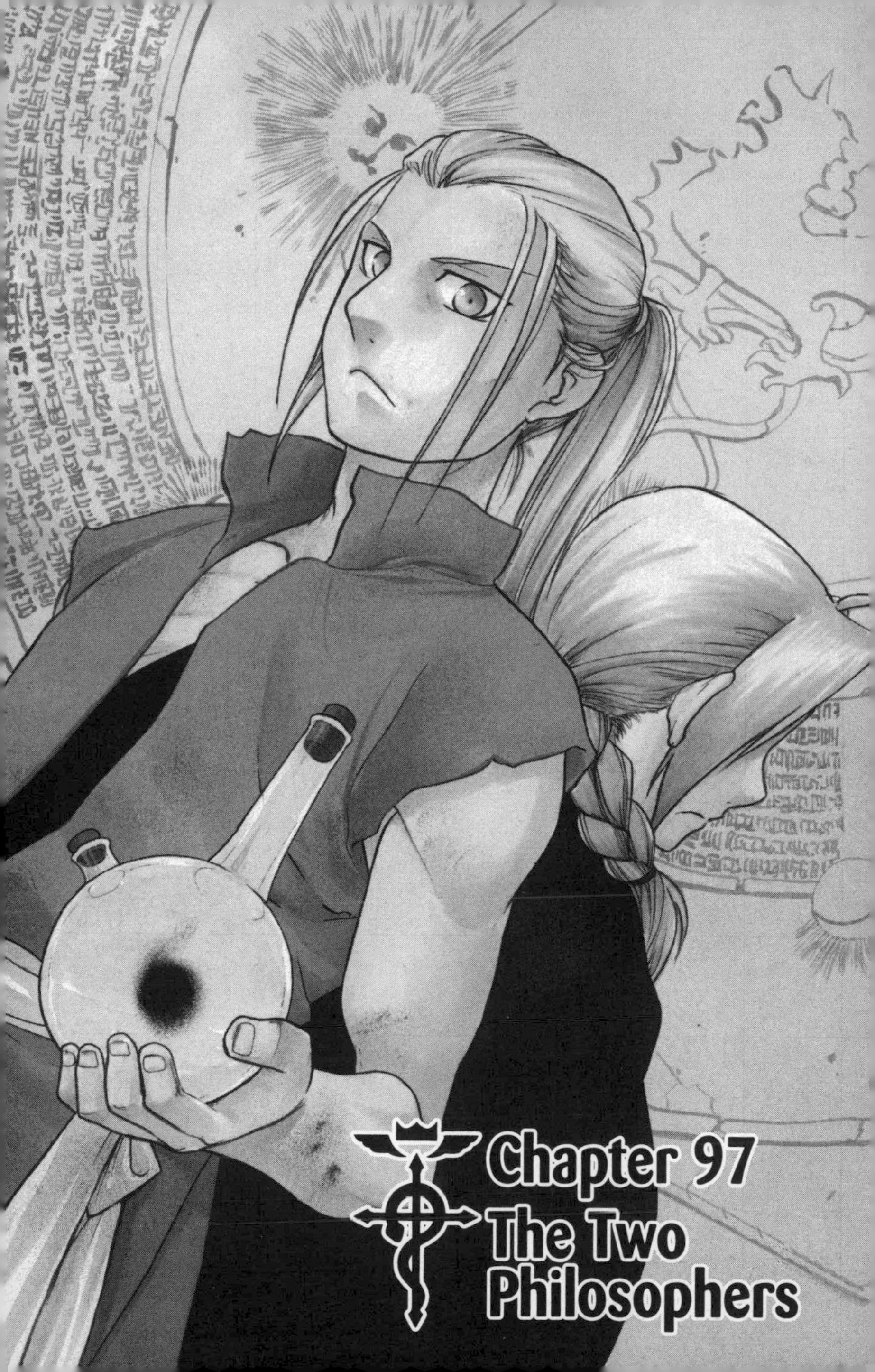
Chapter 97
The Two Philosophers

FULLMETAL
ALCHEMIST

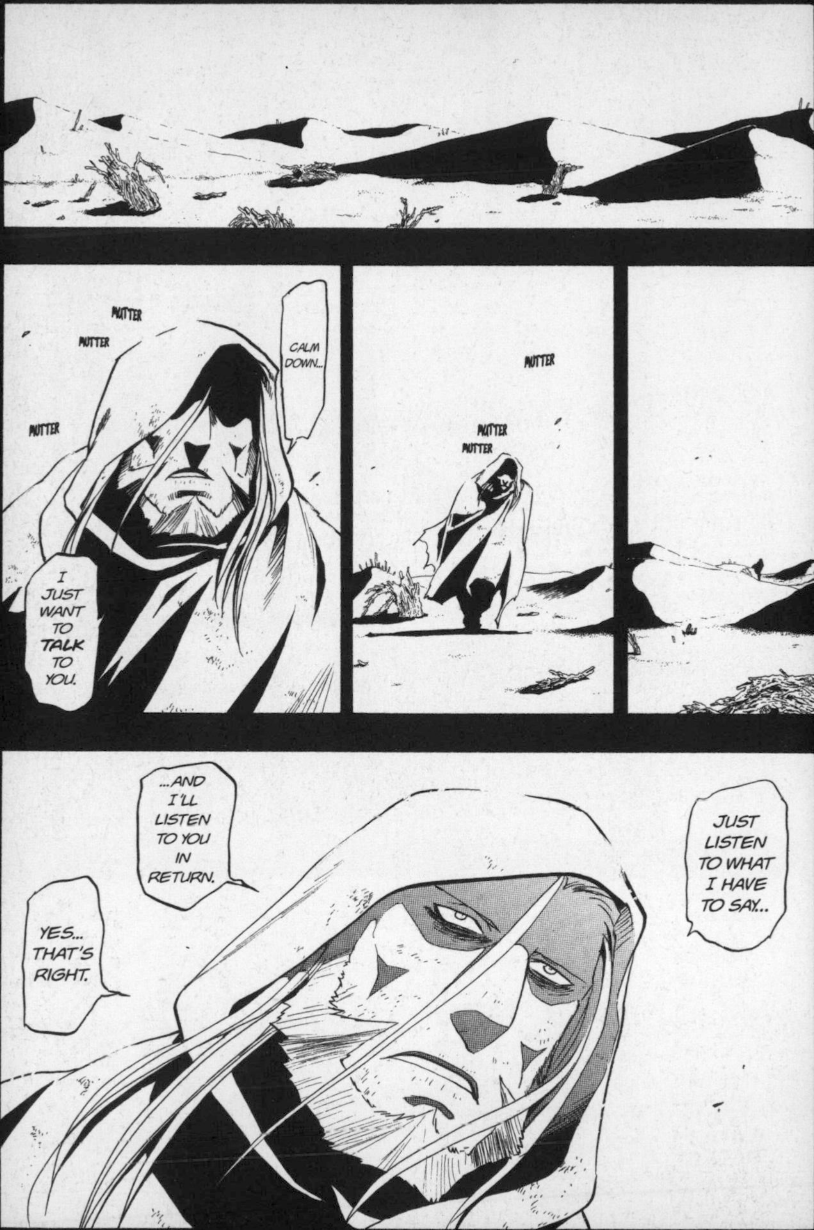
MUTTER
MUTTER
MUTTER
MUTTER
MUTTER
CALM DOWN...
I JUST WANT TO TALK TO YOU.
MUTTER
JUST LISTEN TO WHAT I HAVE TO SAY...
...AND I'LL LISTEN TO YOU IN RETURN.
YES... THAT'S RIGHT.

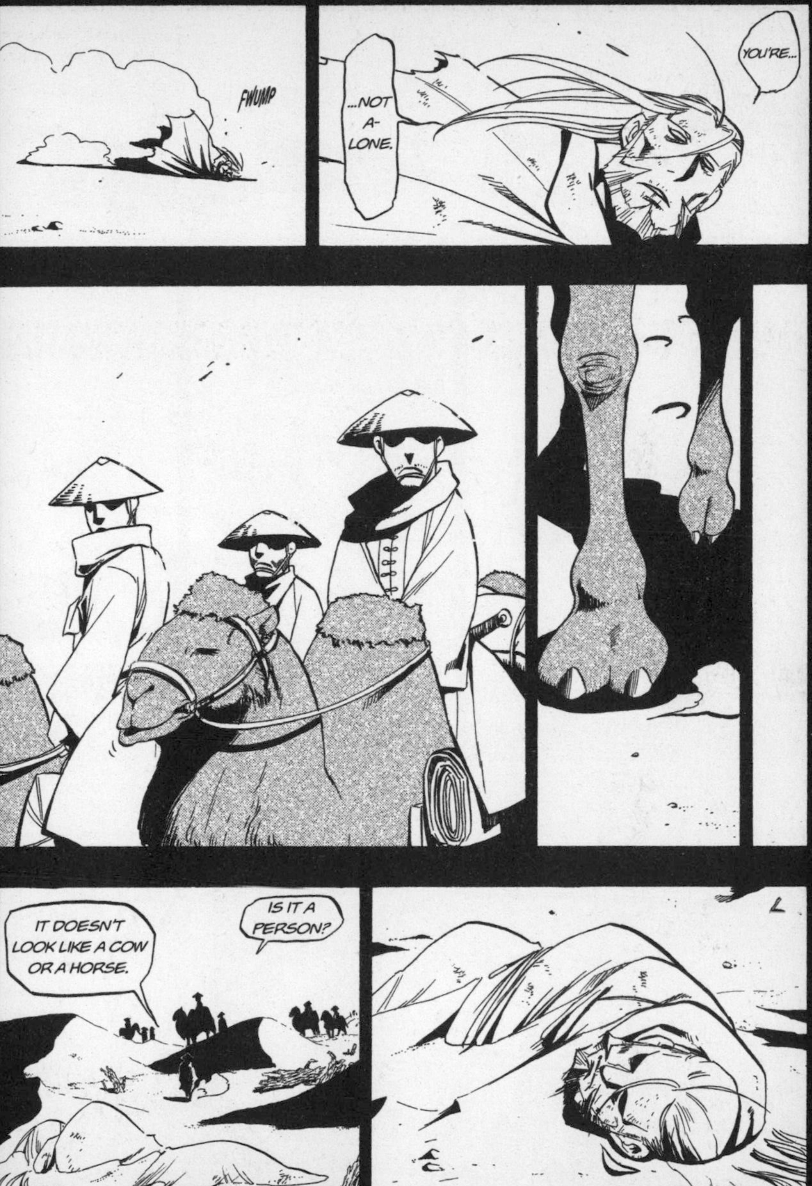
YOU'RE...
...NOT A-LONE.
FWUMP
IS IT A PERSON?
IT DOESN'T LOOK LIKE A COW OR A HORSE.

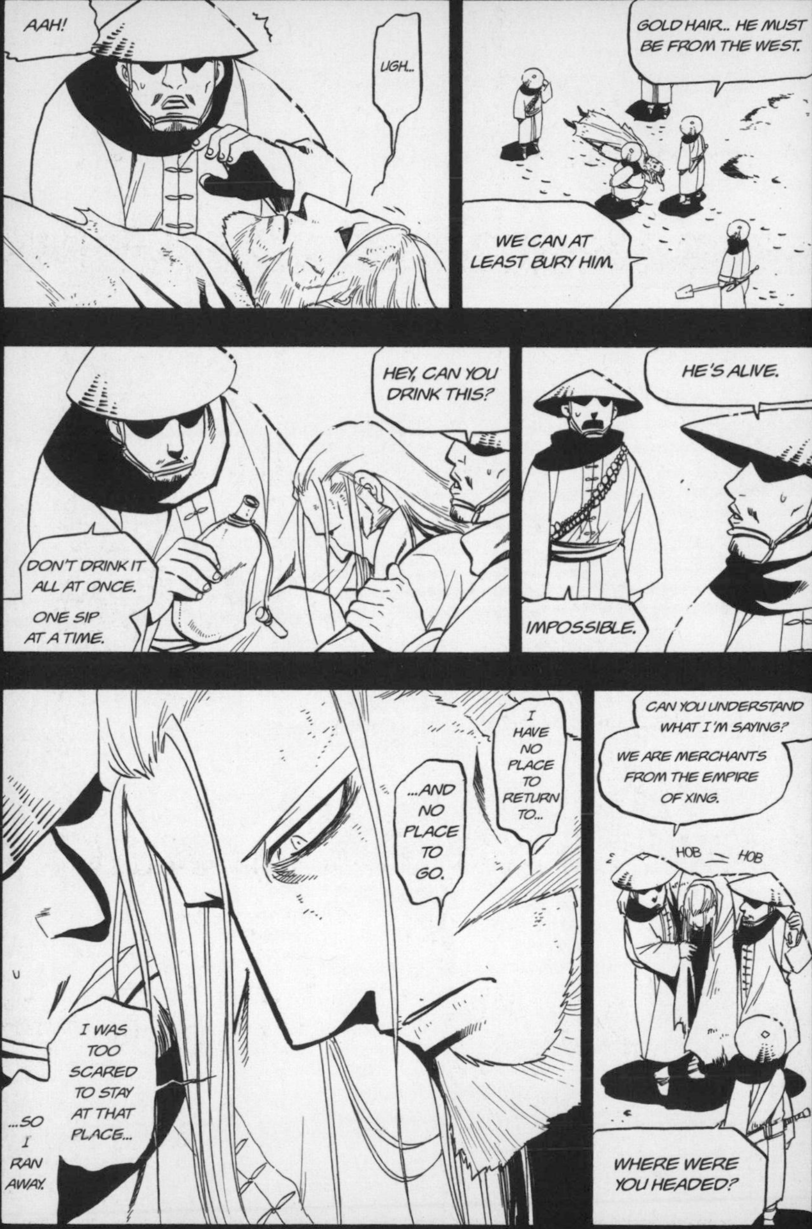
GOLD HAIR... HE MUST BE FROM THE WEST.
WE CAN AT LEAST BURY HIM.
UGH...
AAH!
HE'S ALIVE.
IMPOSSIBLE.
HEY, CAN YOU DRINK THIS?
DON'T DRINK IT ALL AT ONCE.
ONE SIP AT A TIME.
CAN YOU UNDERSTAND WHAT I'M SAYING?
WE ARE MERCHANTS FROM THE EMPIRE OF XING.
HOB HOB
WHERE WERE YOU HEADED?
I HAVE NO PLACE TO RETURN TO...
...AND NO PLACE TO GO.
I WAS TOO SCARED TO STAY AT THAT PLACE...
...SO I RAN AWAY.

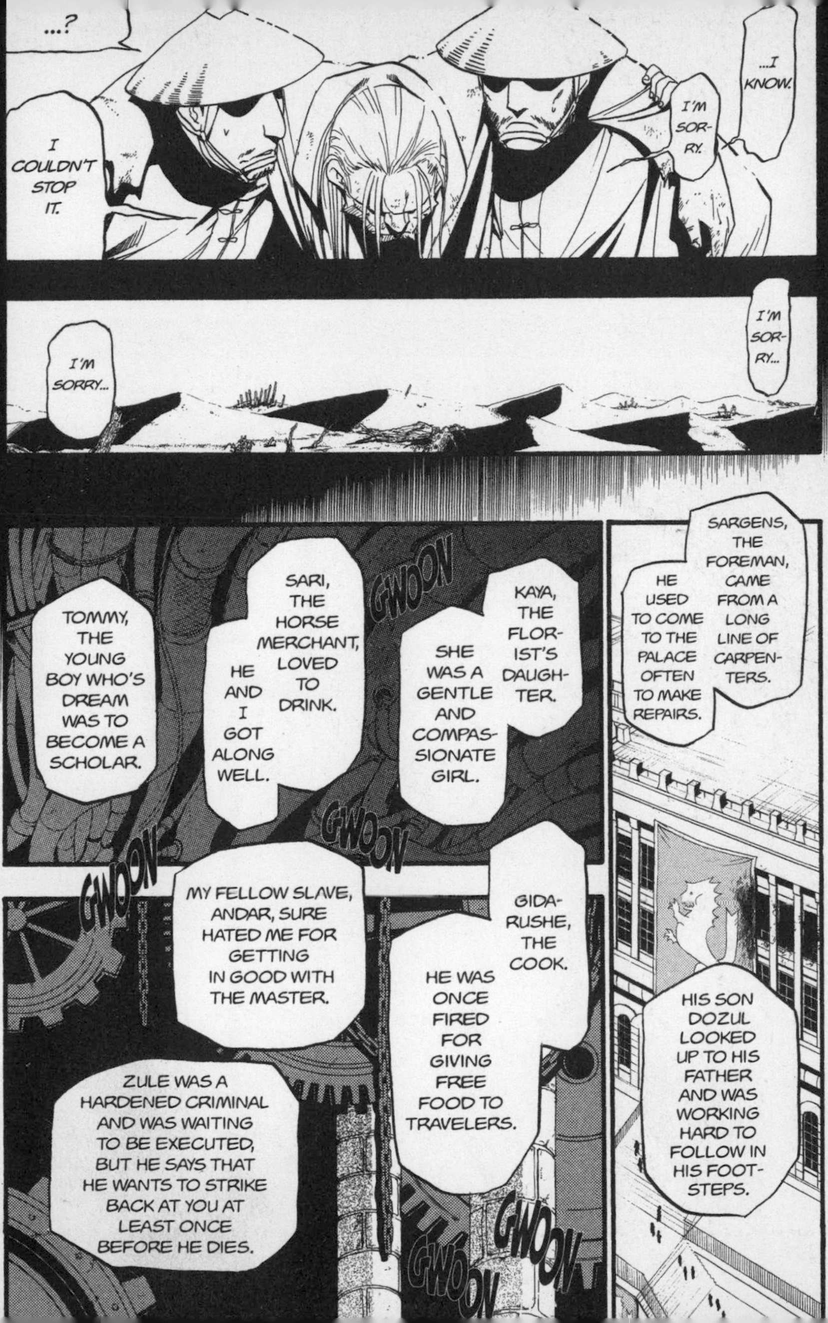
...I KNOW.
I'M SORRY.
...?
I COULDN'T STOP IT.
I'M SORRY...
I'M SORRY...
SARGENS, THE FOREMAN, CAME FROM A LONG LINE OF CARPENTERS.
HE USED TO COME TO THE PALACE OFTEN TO MAKE REPAIRS.
HIS SON DOZUL LOOKED UP TO HIS FATHER AND WAS WORKING HARD TO FOLLOW IN HIS FOOTSTEPS.
KAYA, THE FLORIST'S DAUGHTER.
SHE WAS A GENTLE AND COMPASSIONATE GIRL.
GWOON
SARI, THE HORSE MERCHANT, LOVED TO DRINK.
HE AND I GOT ALONG WELL.
TOMMY, THE YOUNG BOY WHO'S DREAM WAS TO BECOME A SCHOLAR.
GWOON
GIDARUSHE, THE COOK.
HE WAS ONCE FIRED FOR GIVING FREE FOOD TO TRAVELERS.
MY FELLOW SLAVE, ANDAR, SURE HATED ME FOR GETTING IN GOOD WITH THE MASTER.
GWOON
ZULE WAS A HARDENED CRIMINAL AND WAS WAITING TO BE EXECUTED, BUT HE SAYS THAT HE WANTS TO STRIKE BACK AT YOU AT LEAST ONCE BEFORE HE DIES.
GWOON
GWOON

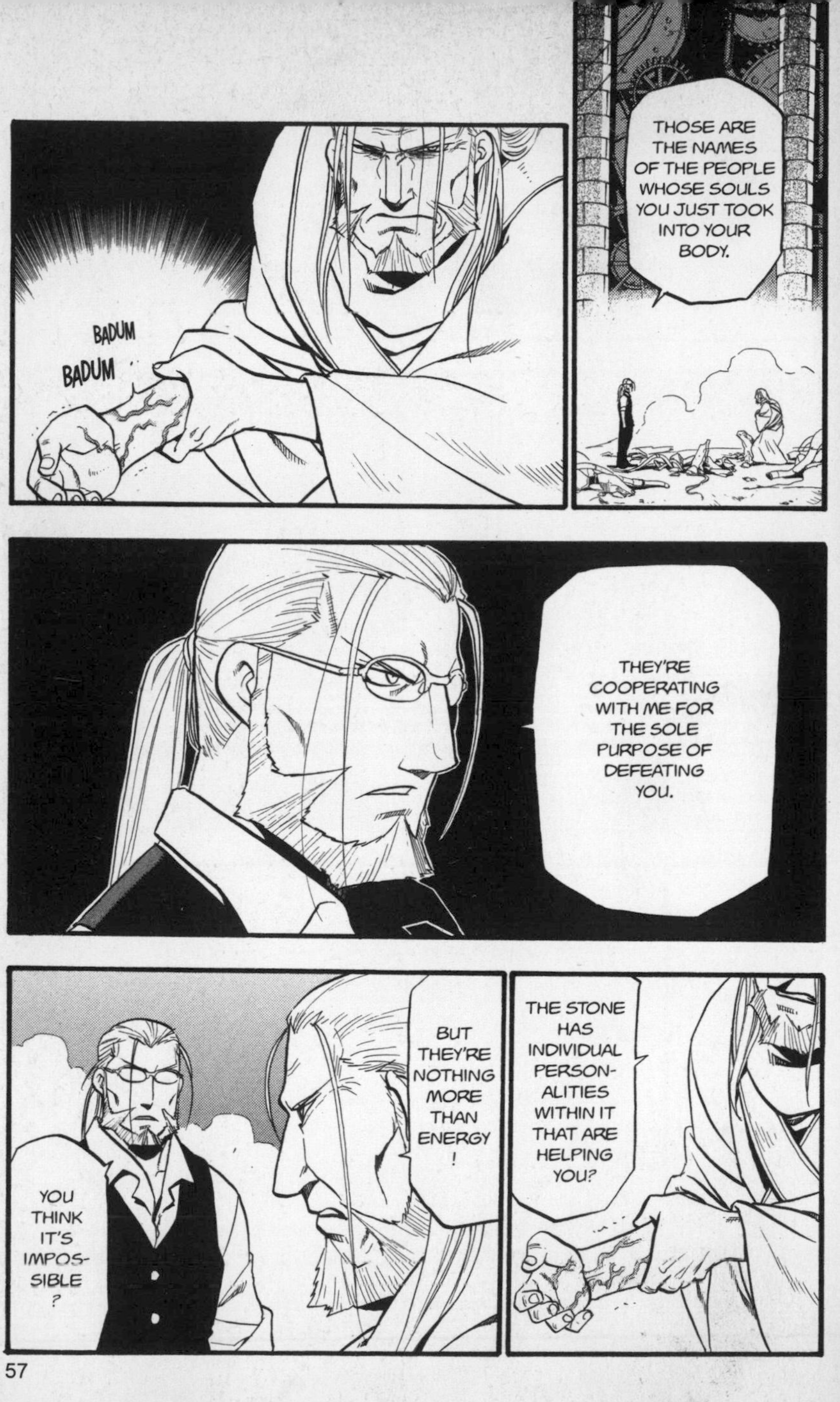
THOSE ARE THE NAMES OF THE PEOPLE WHOSE SOULS YOU JUST TOOK INTO YOUR BODY.
BADUM
BADUM
THEY'RE COOPERATING WITH ME FOR THE SOLE PURPOSE OF DEFEATING YOU.
THE STONE HAS INDIVIDUAL PERSON-ALITIES WITHIN IT THAT ARE HELPING YOU?
BUT THEY'RE NOTHING MORE THAN ENERGY!
YOU THINK IT'S IMPOS-SIBLE?

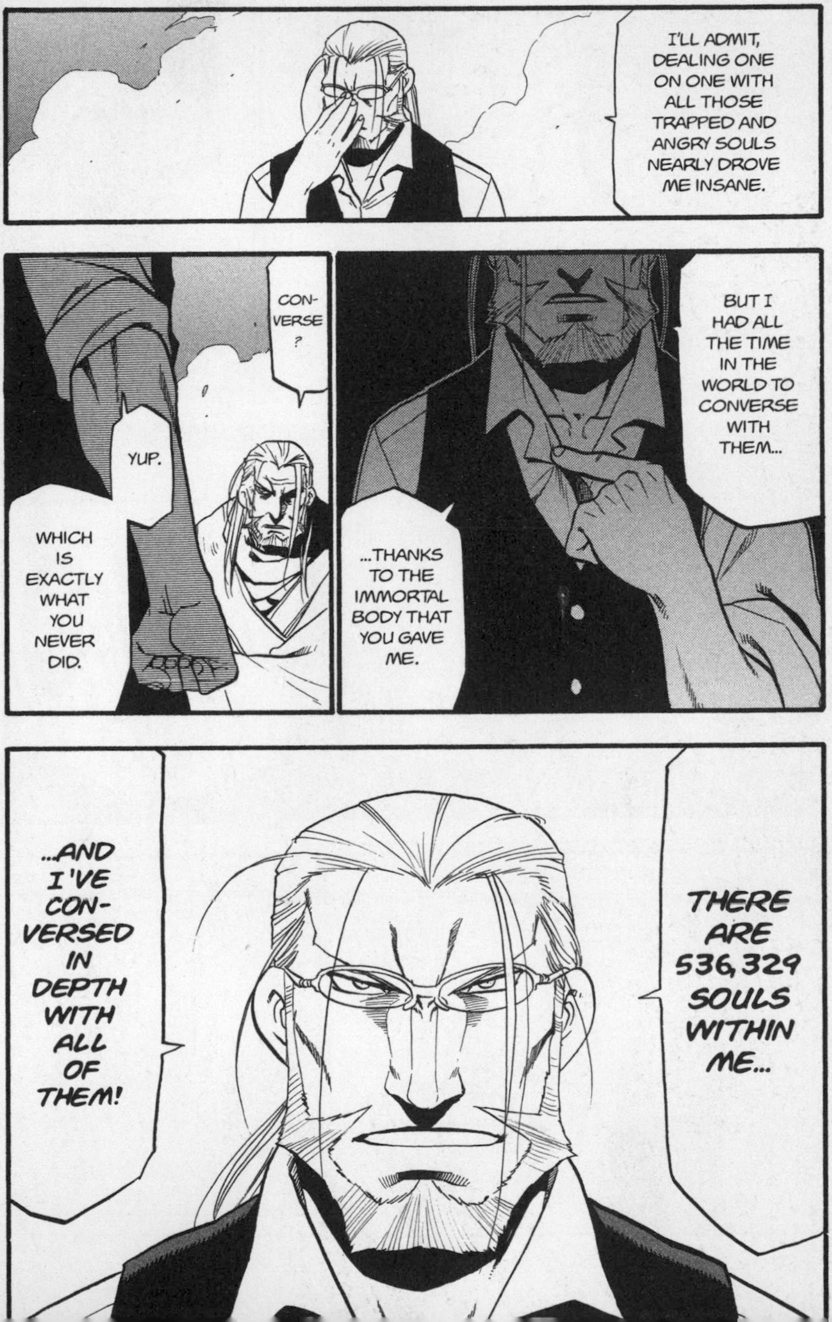
I'LL ADMIT, DEALING ONE ON ONE WITH ALL THOSE TRAPPED AND ANGRY SOULS NEARLY DROVE ME INSANE.
BUT I HAD ALL THE TIME IN THE WORLD TO CONVERSE WITH THEM...
...THANKS TO THE IMMORTAL BODY THAT YOU GAVE ME.
CON-VERSE?
YUP.
WHICH IS EXACTLY WHAT YOU NEVER DID.
THERE ARE 536,329 SOULS WITHIN ME...
...AND I'VE CON-VERSED IN DEPTH WITH ALL OF THEM!

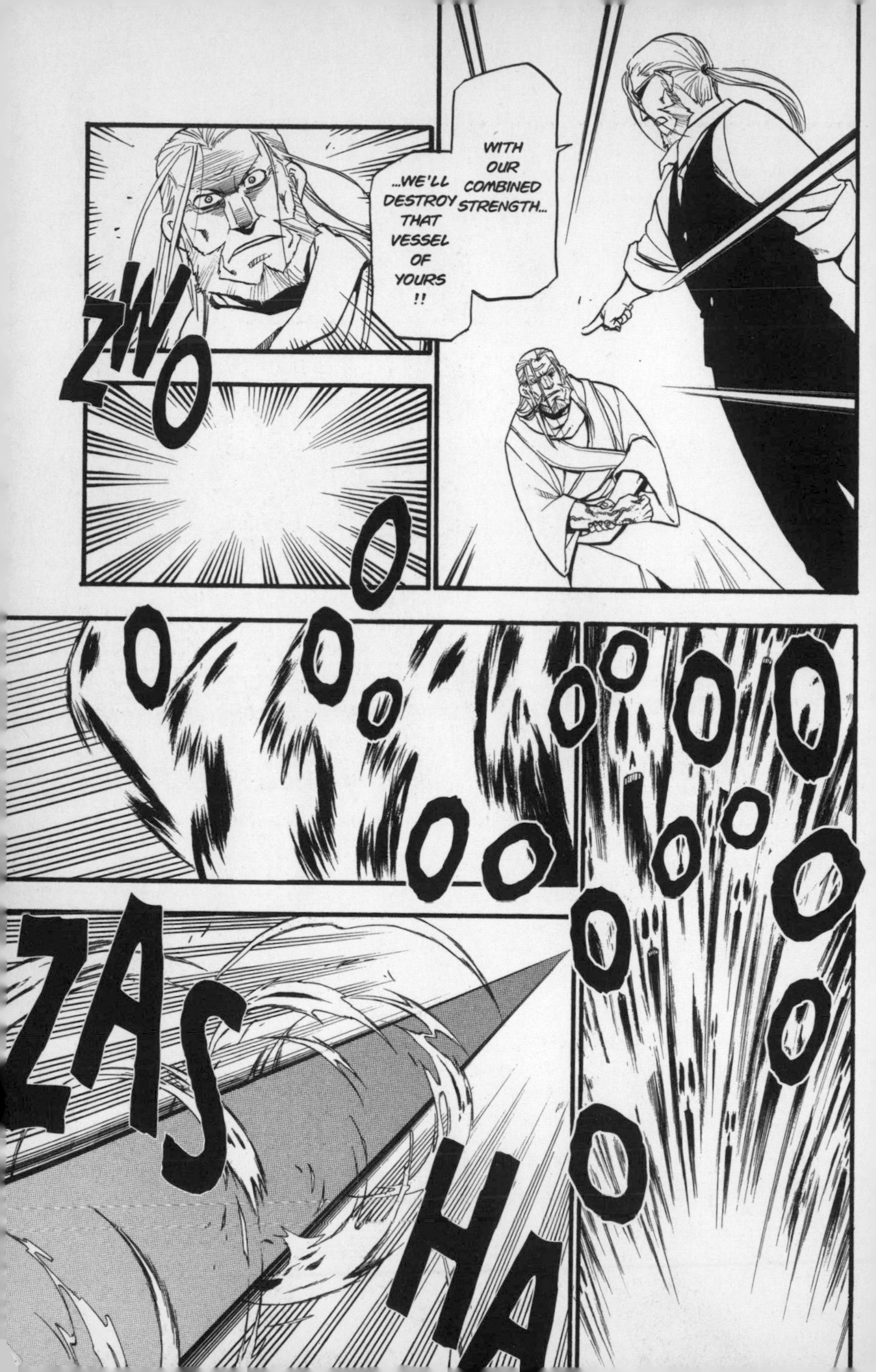
WITH OUR COMBINED STRENGTH...
...WE'LL DESTROY THAT VESSEL OF YOURS !!
ZWOOOOOOOOOOOOOOOOOOOOO
ZASHAA

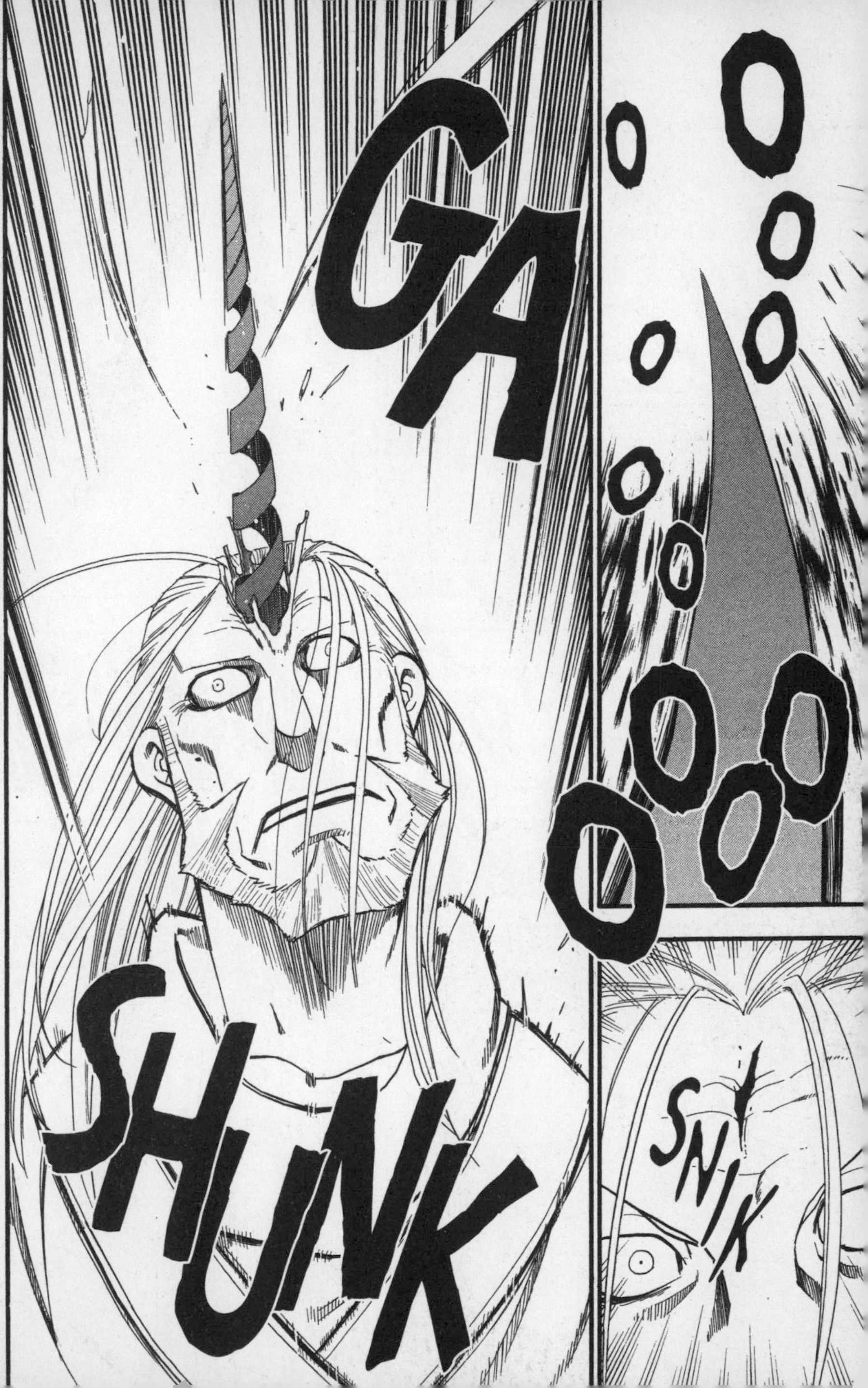
OOOOOOOOOOOO
SNIK
GA
SHUNK

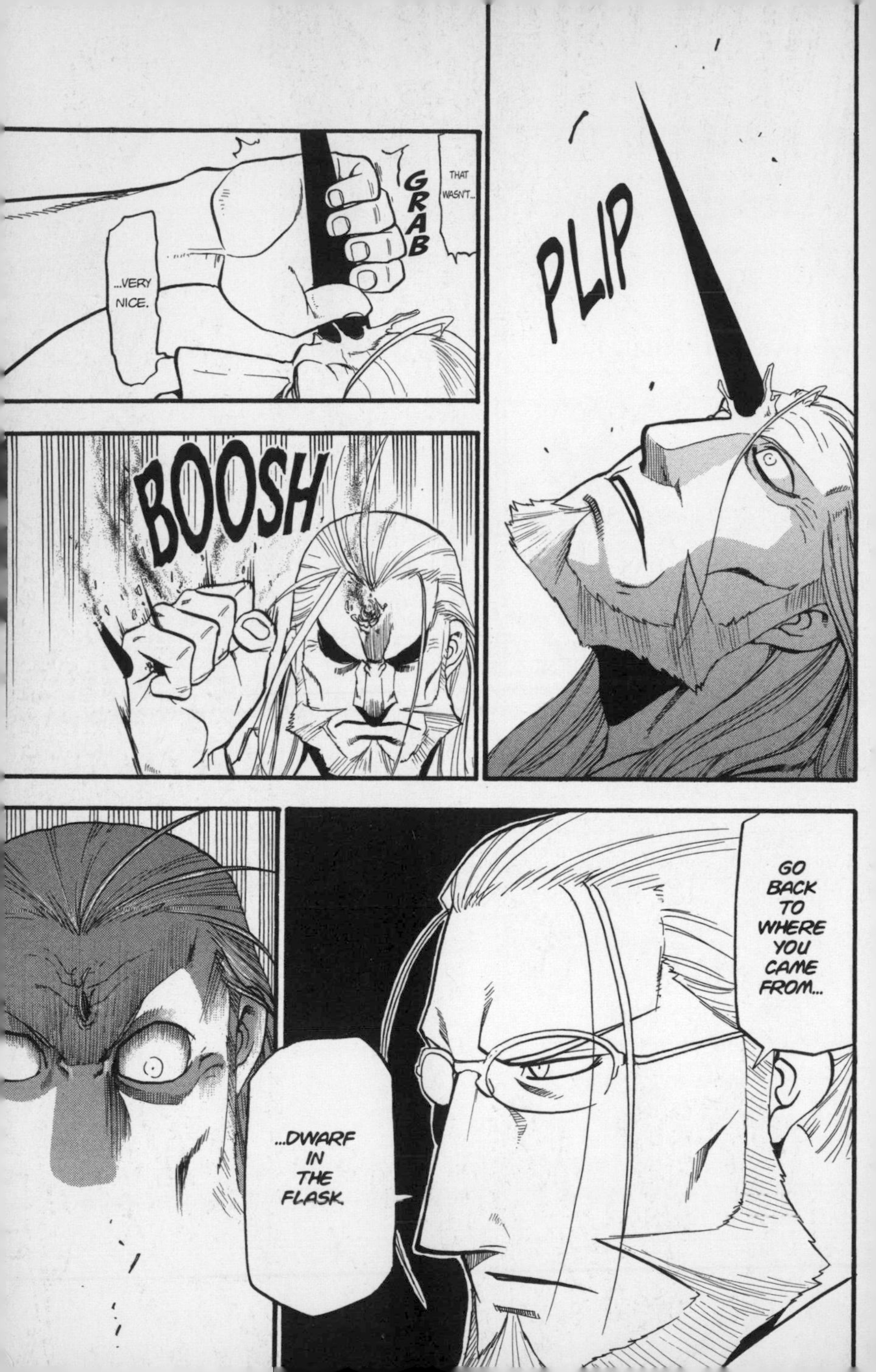
PLIP
THAT WASN'T...
GRAB
...VERY NICE.
BOOSH
GO BACK TO WHERE YOU CAME FROM...
...DWARF IN THE FLASK.

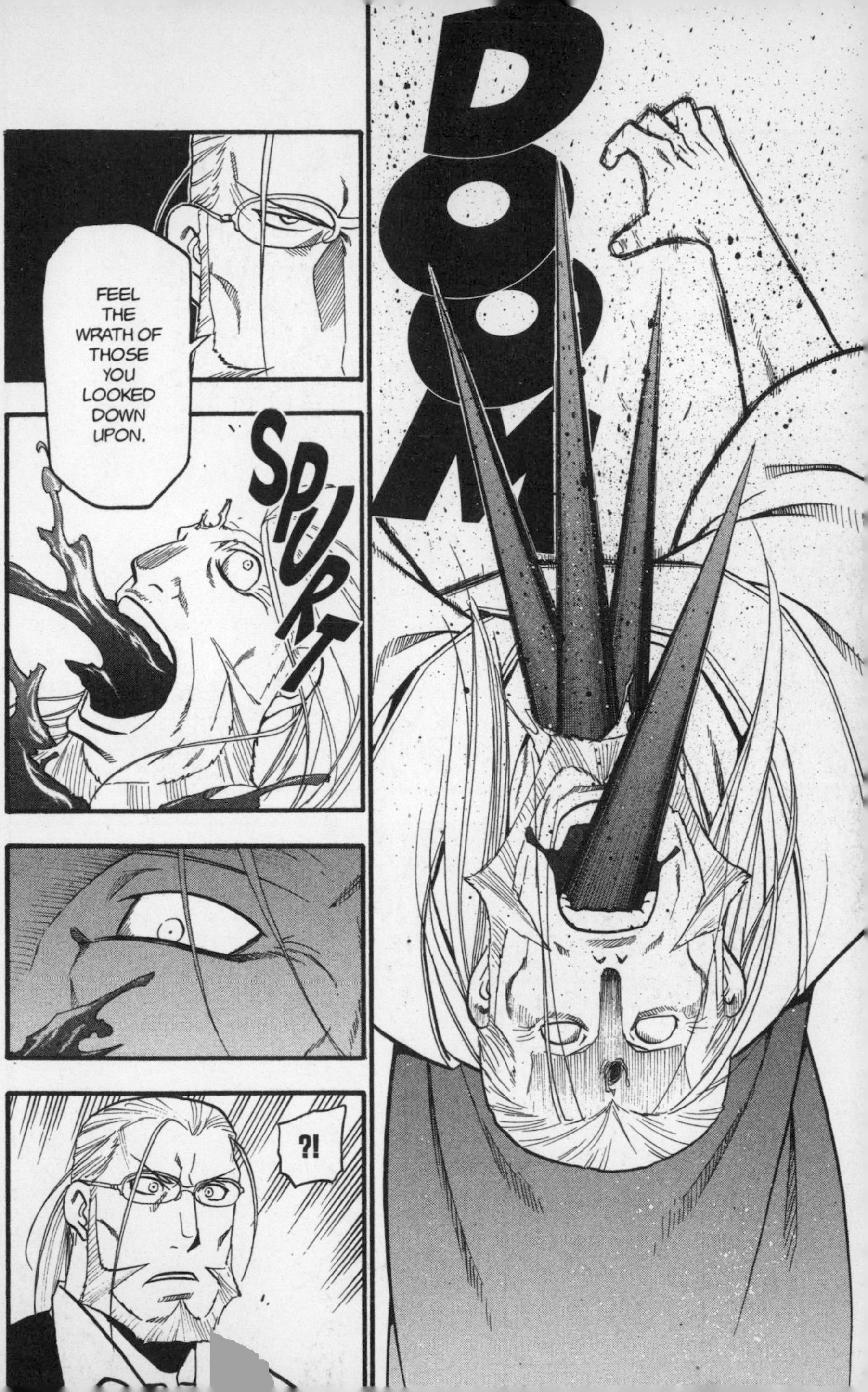
DOOM
FEEL THE WRATH OF THOSE YOU LOOKED DOWN UPON.
SPURT
?!

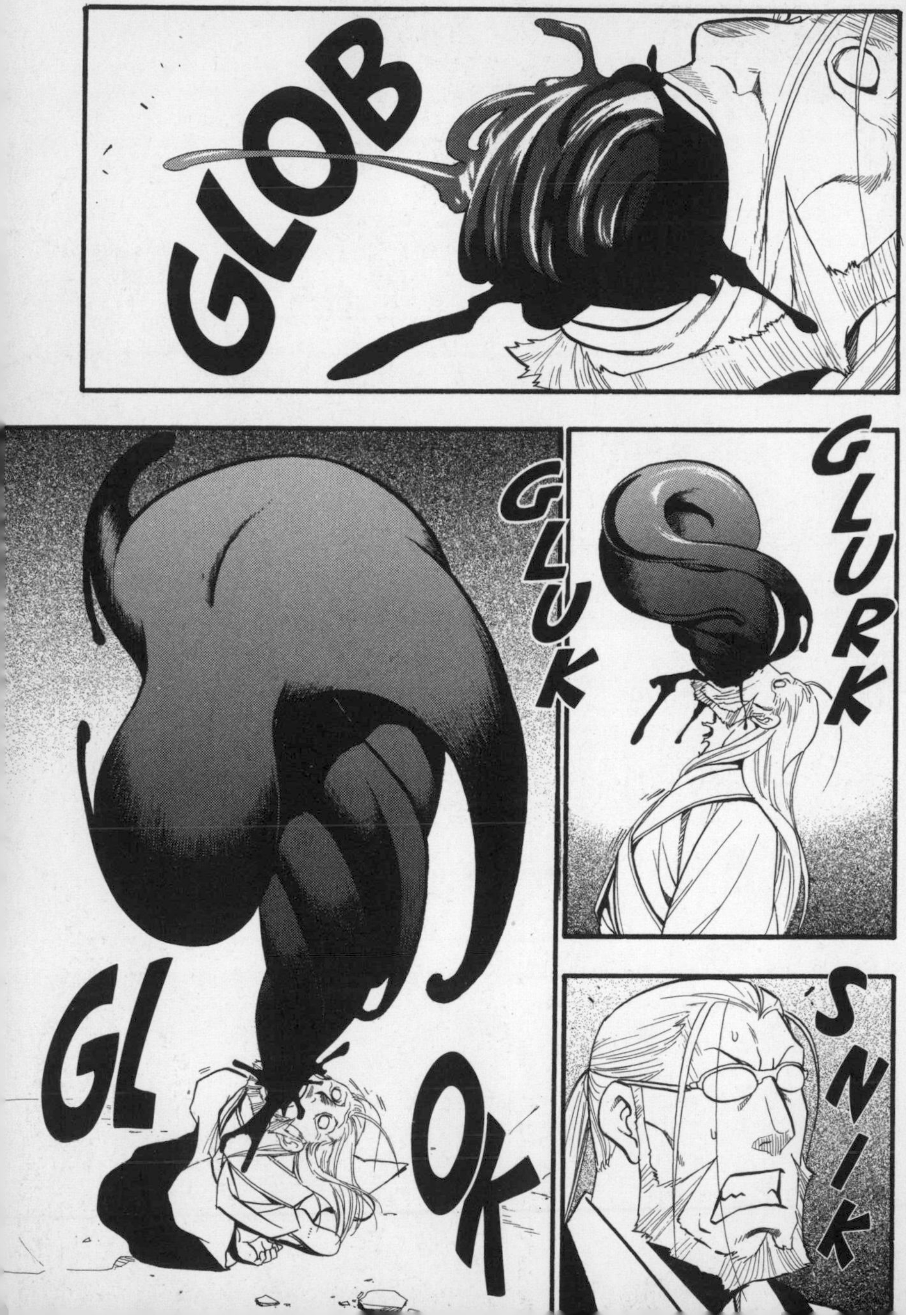
GLOB
GLURK
GLUK
SNIK
GLOK

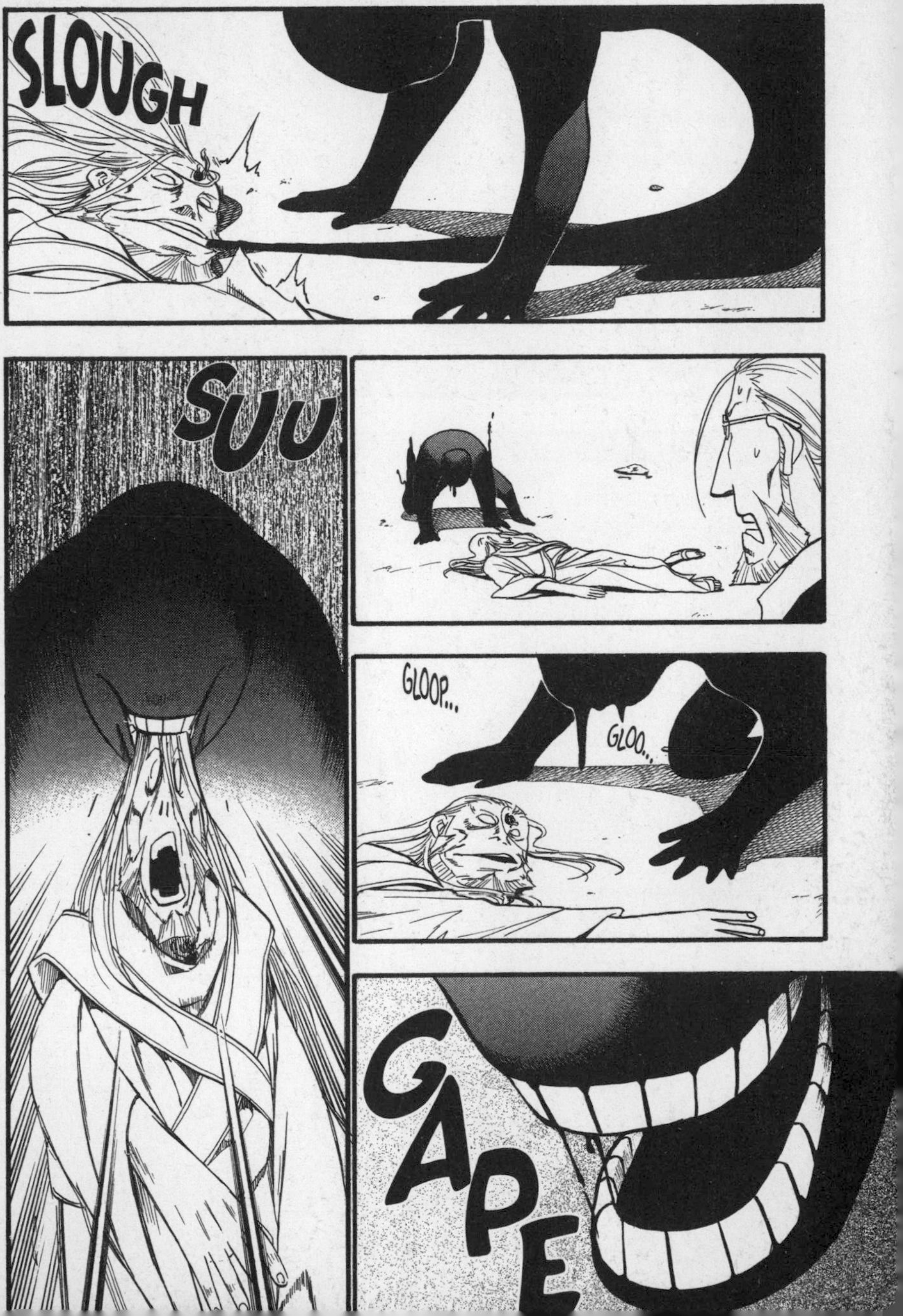
SLOUGH
GLOOP...
GLOO...
GAPE
SUU

VIP

SLUUURP

ZU

...HOHEN-HEIM.

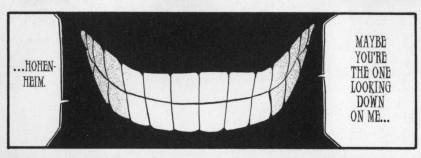

MAYBE YOU'RE THE ONE LOOKING DOWN ON ME...

ZU ZU ZU ZU ZU ZU ZU ZU ZU ZU

YOU HUMANS AREN'T THE ONLY ONES WHO HAVE EVOLVED!

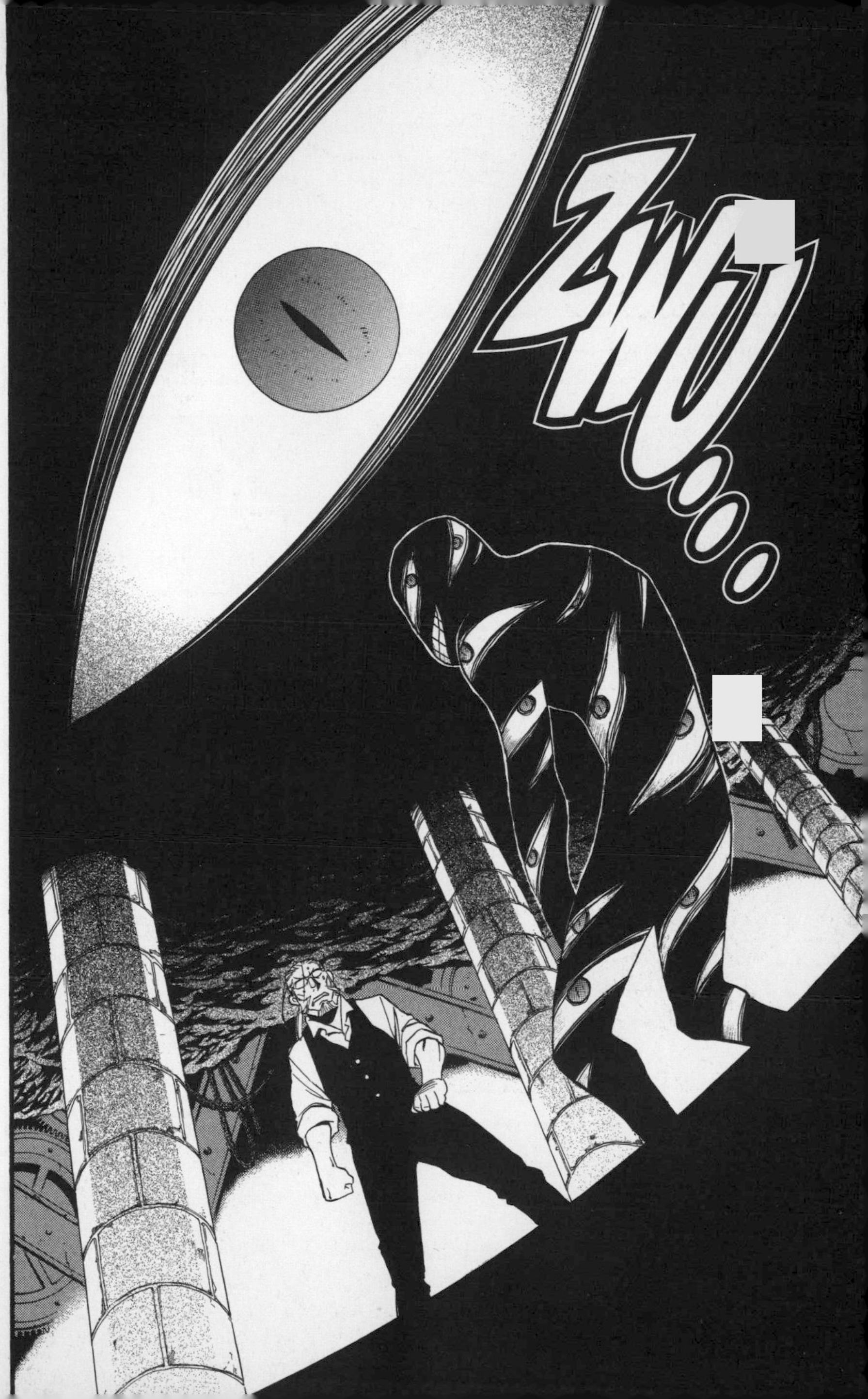
ZWOOO...

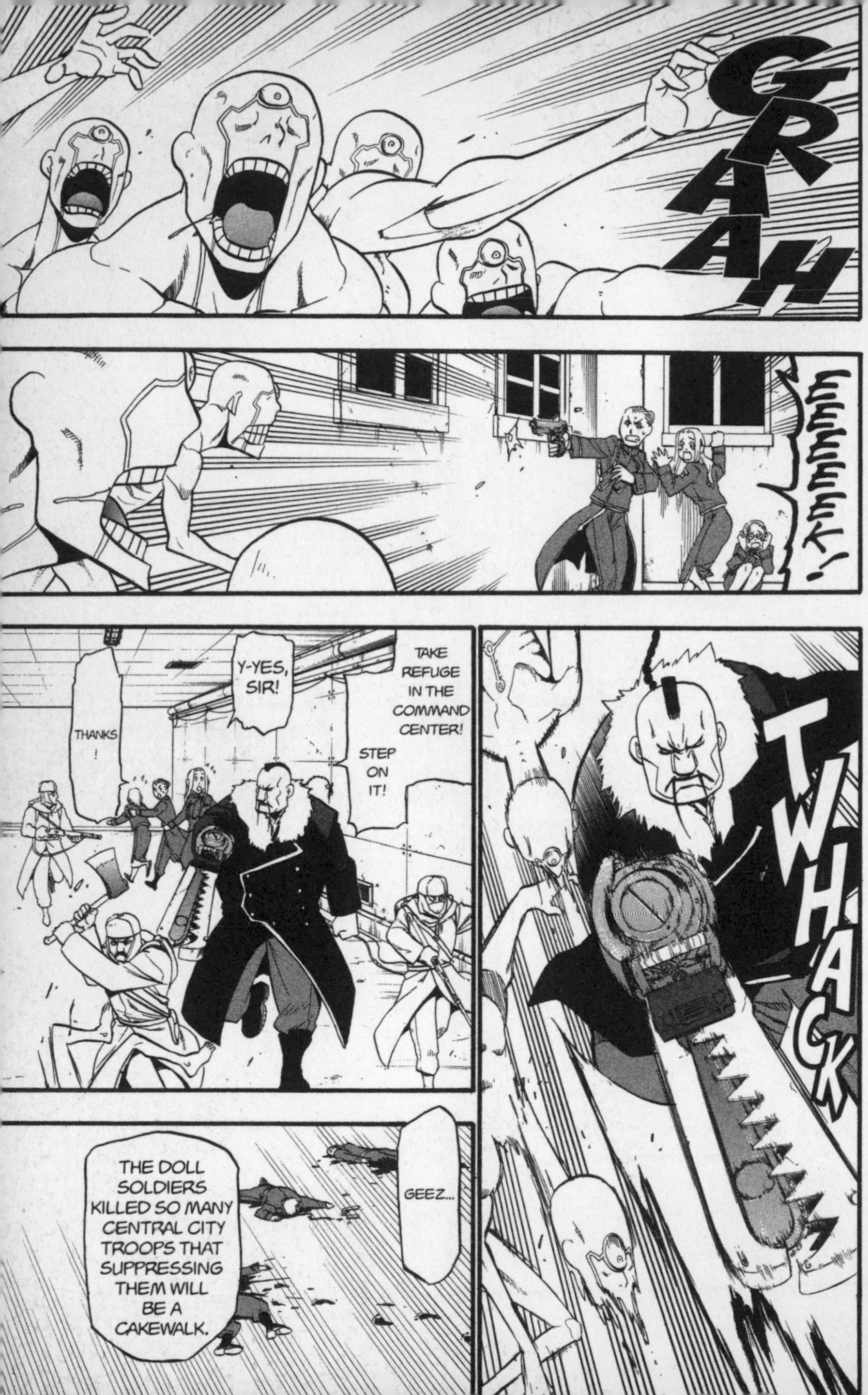
GRAAH
EEEEEEEK!
TWHACK
TAKE REFUGE IN THE COMMAND CENTER!
STEP ON IT!
Y-YES, SIR!
THANKS!
GEEZ...
THE DOLL SOLDIERS KILLED SO MANY CENTRAL CITY TROOPS THAT SUPPRESSING THEM WILL BE A CAKEWALK.

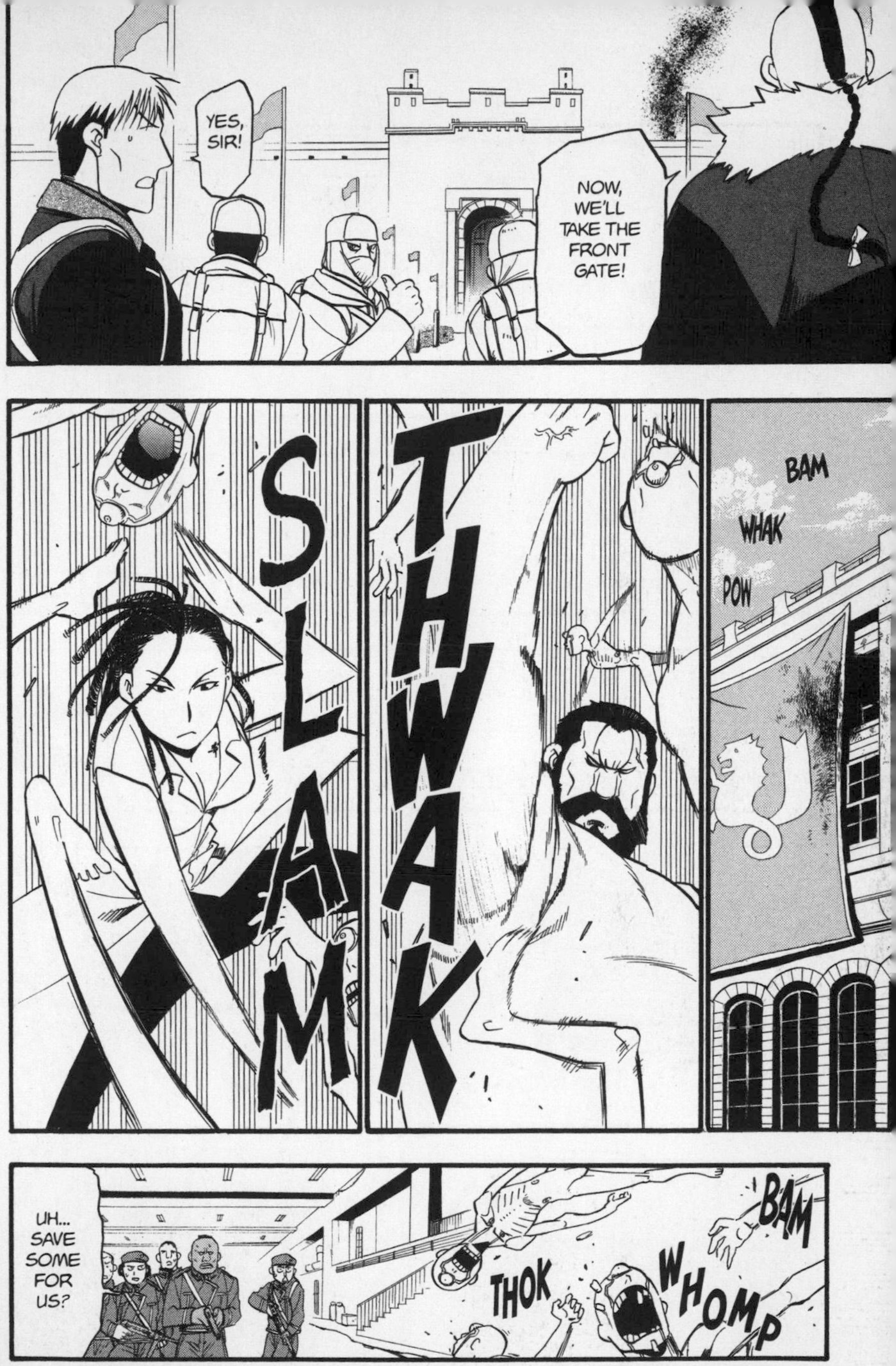
NOW, WE'LL TAKE THE FRONT GATE!
YES, SIR!
BAM
WHAK
POW
THWAK
SLAM
BAM
WHOMP
THOK
UH... SAVE SOME FOR US?

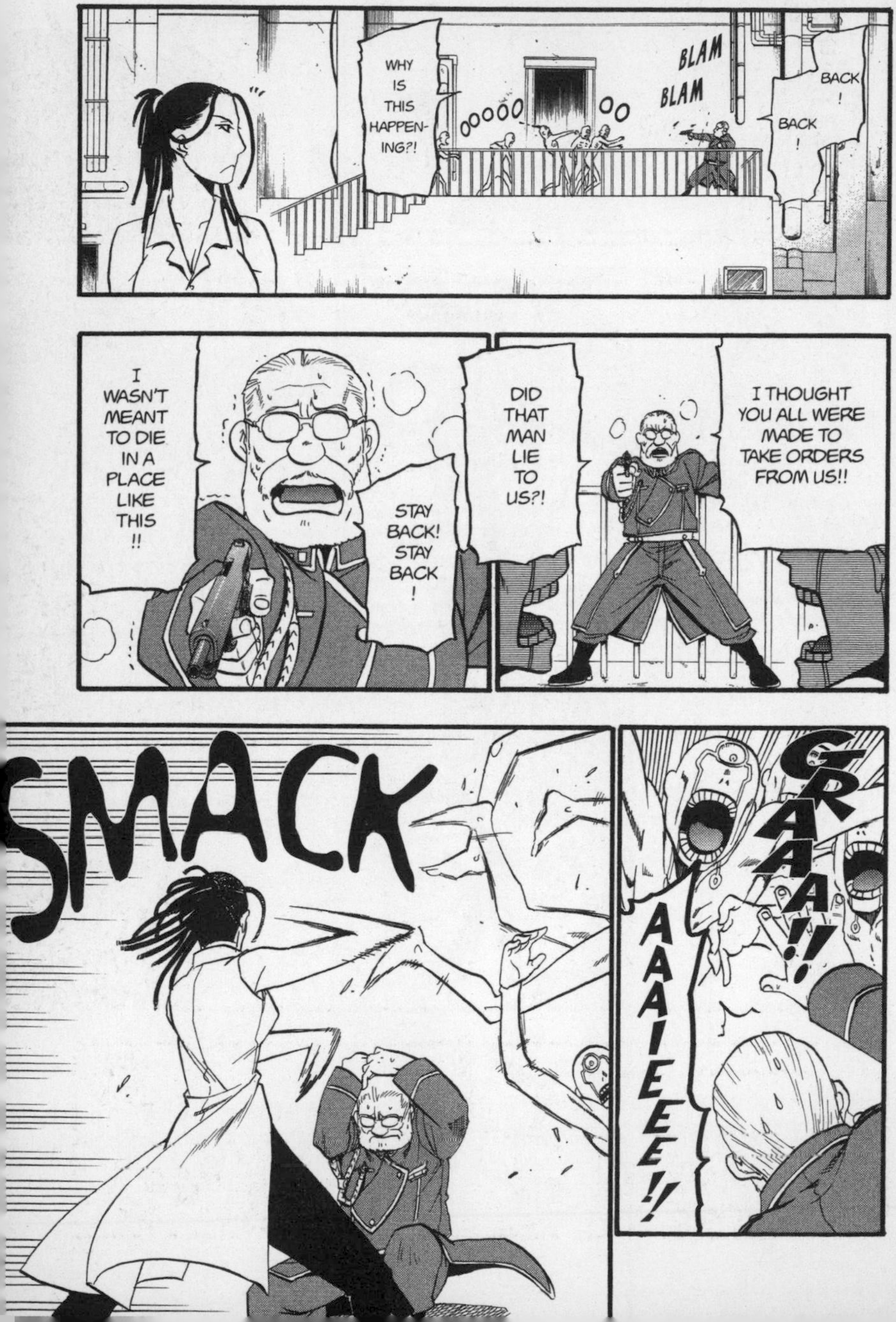
BACK! BACK!
BLAM BLAM
OO
OOOOO
WHY IS THIS HAPPENING?!
I THOUGHT YOU ALL WERE MADE TO TAKE ORDERS FROM US!!
DID THAT MAN LIE TO US?!
STAY BACK! STAY BACK!
I WASN'T MEANT TO DIE IN A PLACE LIKE THIS!!
GRAAAA!!
AAAIEEEE!!
SMACK

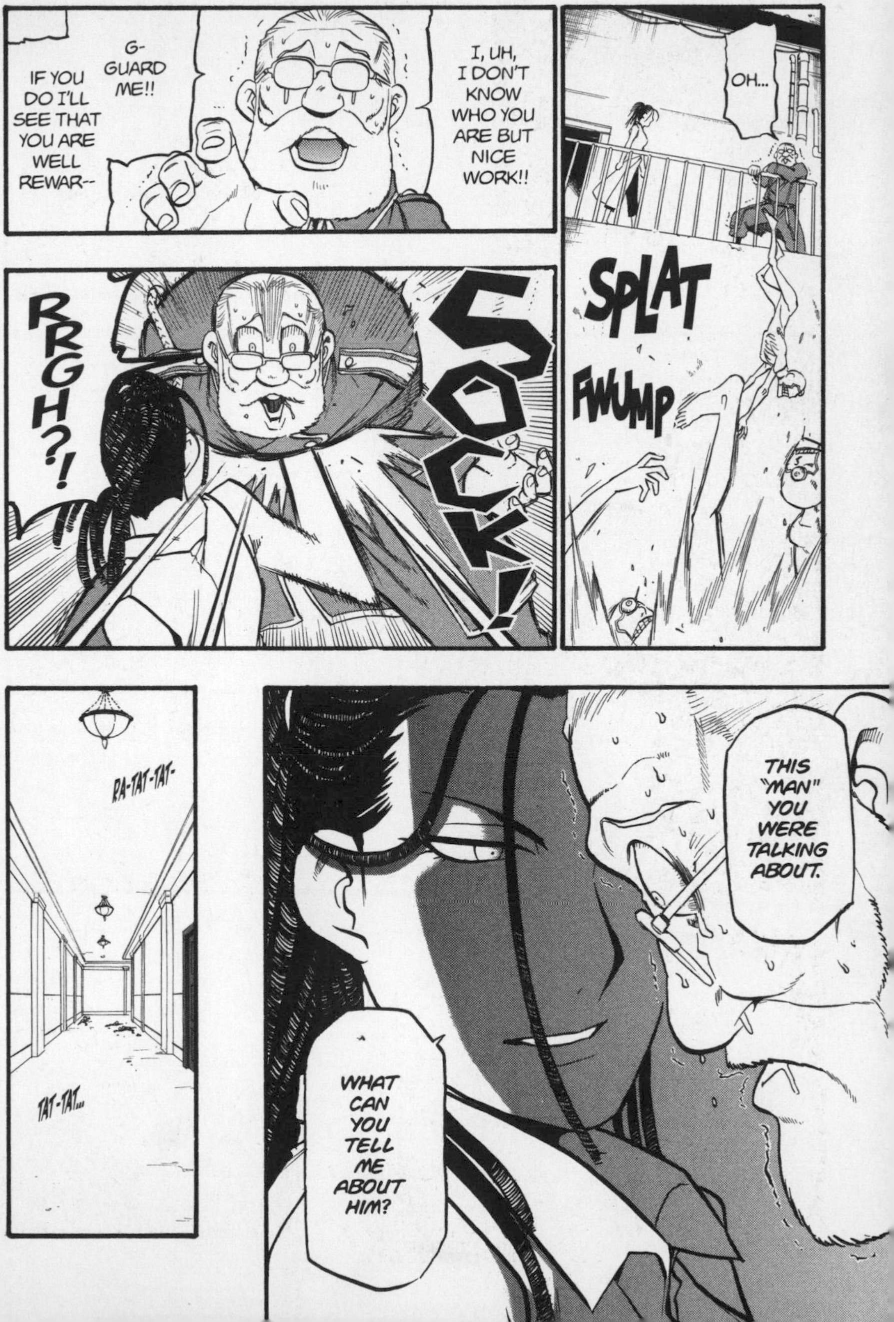
OH...
SPLAT
FWUMP
I, UH, I DON'T KNOW WHO YOU ARE BUT NICE WORK!!
G-GUARD ME!!
IF YOU DO I'LL SEE THAT YOU ARE WELL REWAR--
SOCK!
RRGH?!
THIS "MAN" YOU WERE TALKING ABOUT.
WHAT CAN YOU TELL ME ABOUT HIM?
RA-TAT-TAT-
TAT-TAT...

MAJOR GENERAL. HAVE A LOOK.

WHAT A MESS THE PRESIDENTIAL OFFICE IS IN.

WHOA...

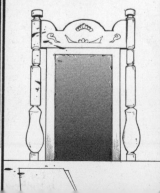

SHALL WE SET UP YOUR COMMAND CENTER HERE, MA'AM?

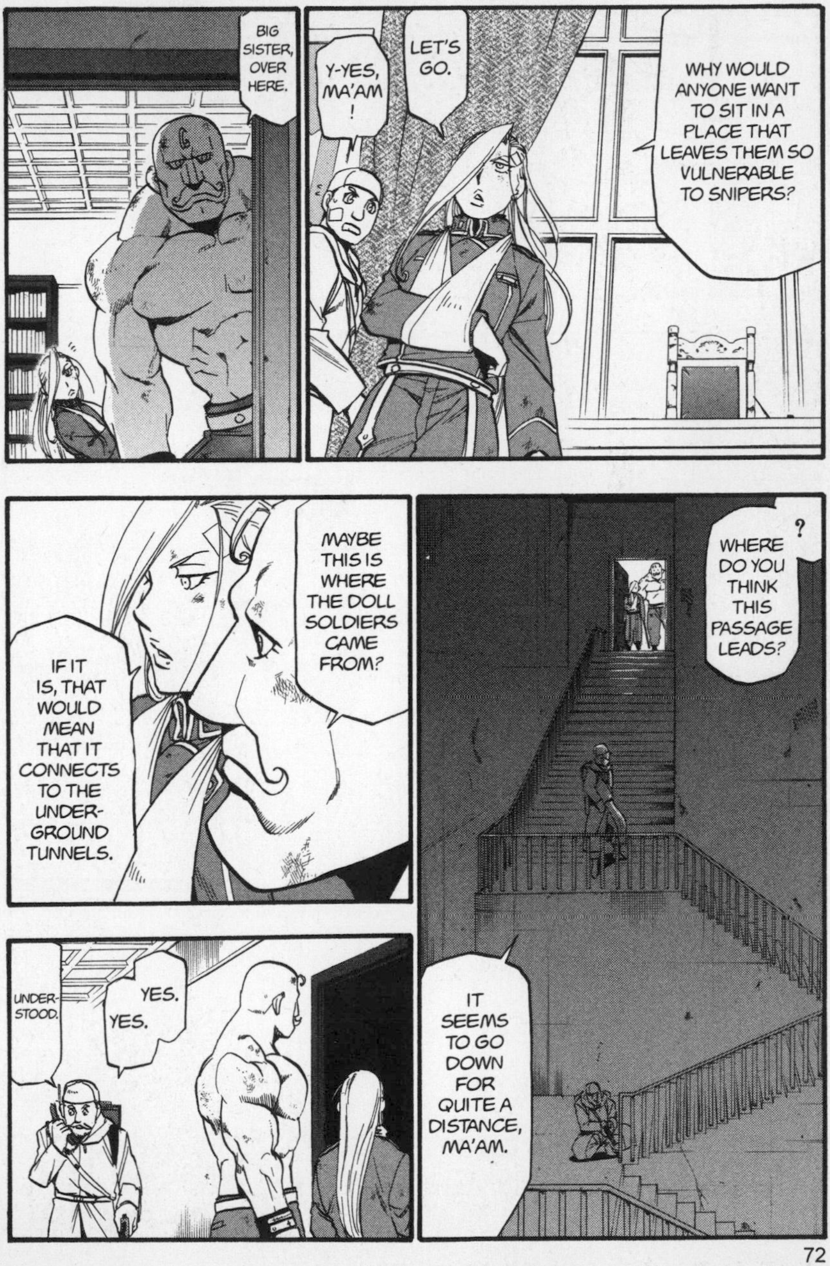
WHY WOULD ANYONE WANT TO SIT IN A PLACE THAT LEAVES THEM SO VULNERABLE TO SNIPERS?
LET'S GO.
Y-YES, MA'AM!
BIG SISTER, OVER HERE.
?
WHERE DO YOU THINK THIS PASSAGE LEADS?
IT SEEMS TO GO DOWN FOR QUITE A DISTANCE, MA'AM.
MAYBE THIS IS WHERE THE DOLL SOLDIERS CAME FROM?
IF IT IS, THAT WOULD MEAN THAT IT CONNECTS TO THE UNDER-GROUND TUNNELS.
YES. YES.
UNDER-STOOD.

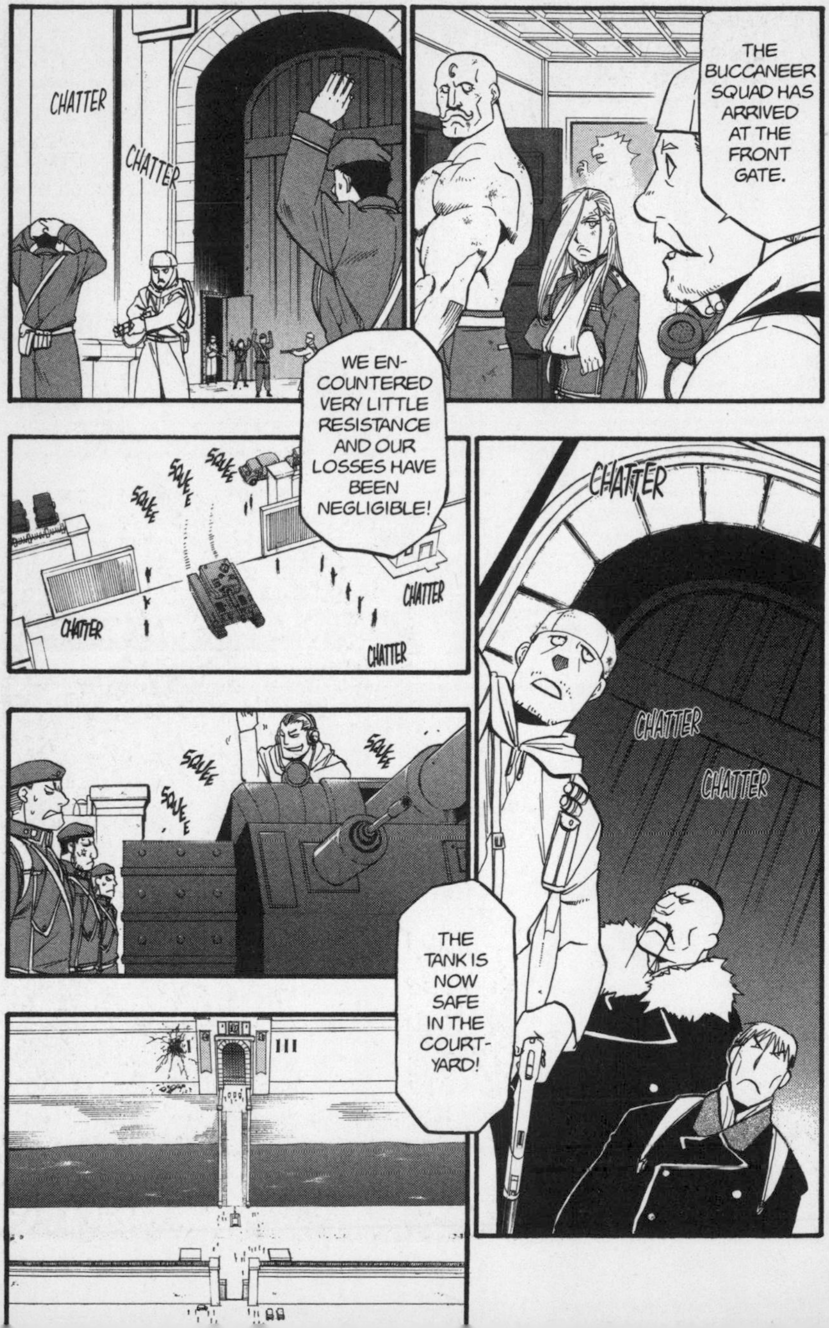
THE BUCCANEER SQUAD HAS ARRIVED AT THE FRONT GATE.
CHATTER
CHATTER
WE ENCOUNTERED VERY LITTLE RESISTANCE AND OUR LOSSES HAVE BEEN NEGLIGIBLE!
CHATTER
CHATTER
CHATTER
THE TANK IS NOW SAFE IN THE COURTYARD!
SQUEE
SQUEE
CHATTER
CHATTER
CHATTER
SQUEE
SQUEE
SQUEE

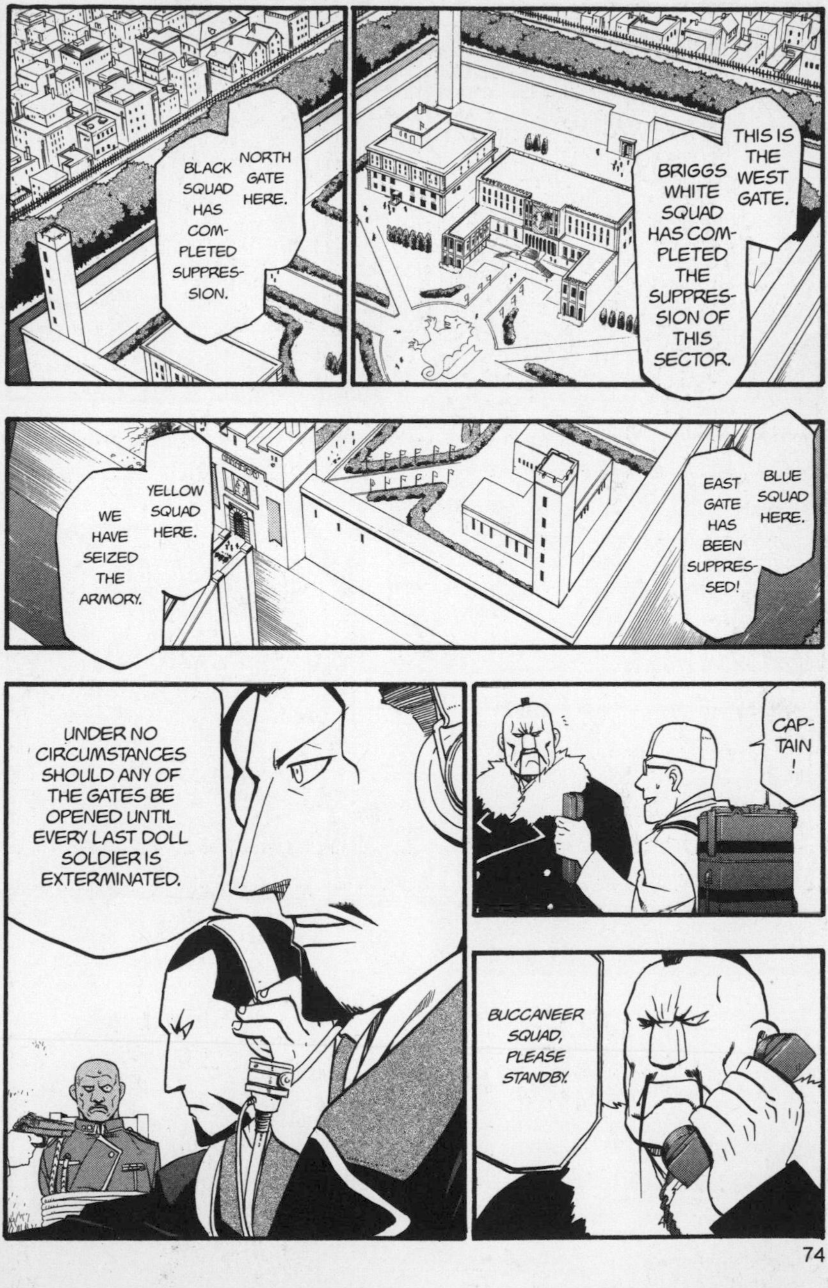
THIS IS THE WEST GATE.
BRIGGS WHITE SQUAD HAS COMPLETED THE SUPPRESSION OF THIS SECTOR.
NORTH GATE HERE.
BLACK SQUAD HAS COMPLETED SUPPRESSION.
BLUE SQUAD HERE.
EAST GATE HAS BEEN SUPPRESSED!
YELLOW SQUAD HERE.
WE HAVE SEIZED THE ARMORY.
CAPTAIN!
BUCCANEER SQUAD, PLEASE STANDBY.
UNDER NO CIRCUMSTANCES SHOULD ANY OF THE GATES BE OPENED UNTIL EVERY LAST DOLL SOLDIER IS EXTERMINATED.

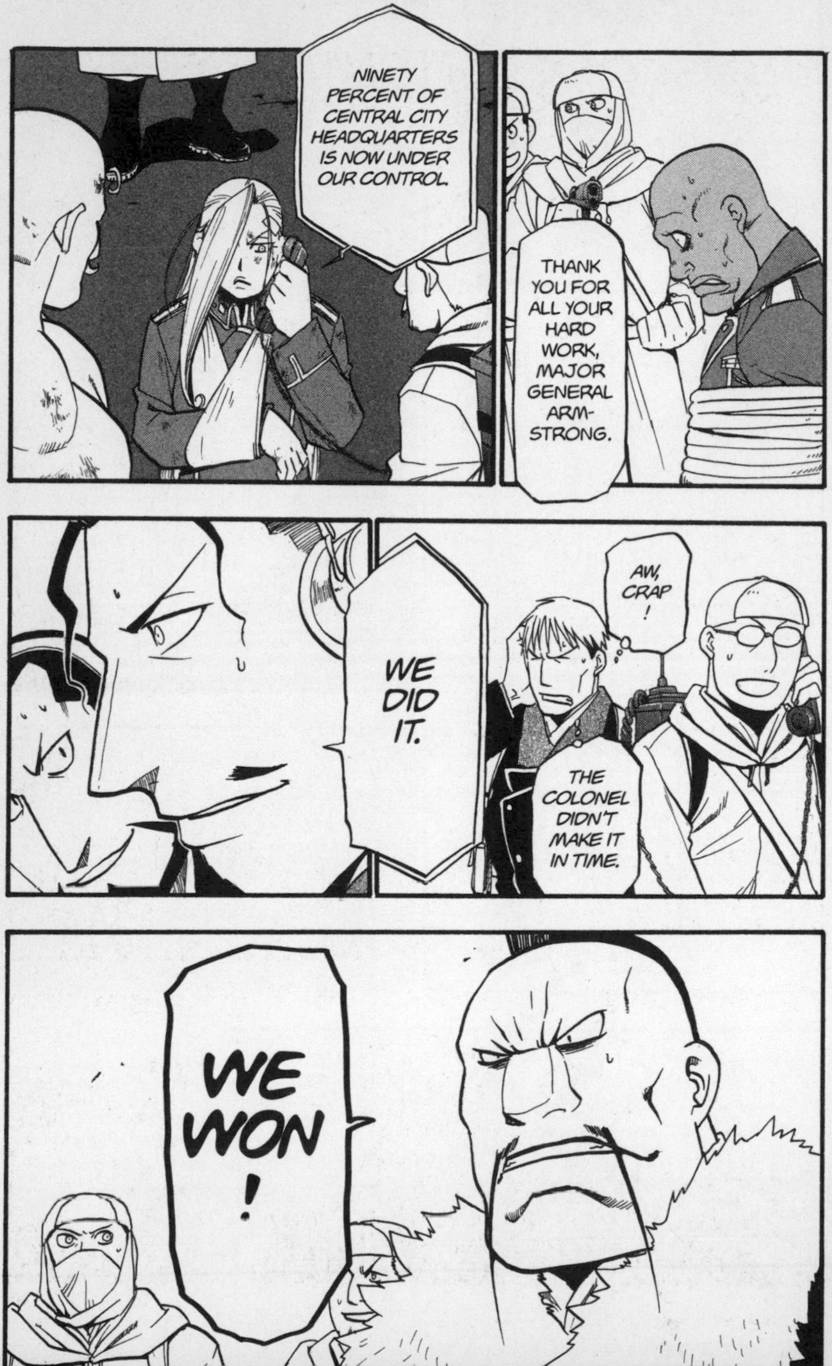
NINETY PERCENT OF CENTRAL CITY HEADQUARTERS IS NOW UNDER OUR CONTROL.
THANK YOU FOR ALL YOUR HARD WORK, MAJOR GENERAL ARM-STRONG.
AW, CRAP!
THE COLONEL DIDN'T MAKE IT IN TIME.
WE DID IT.
WE WON!

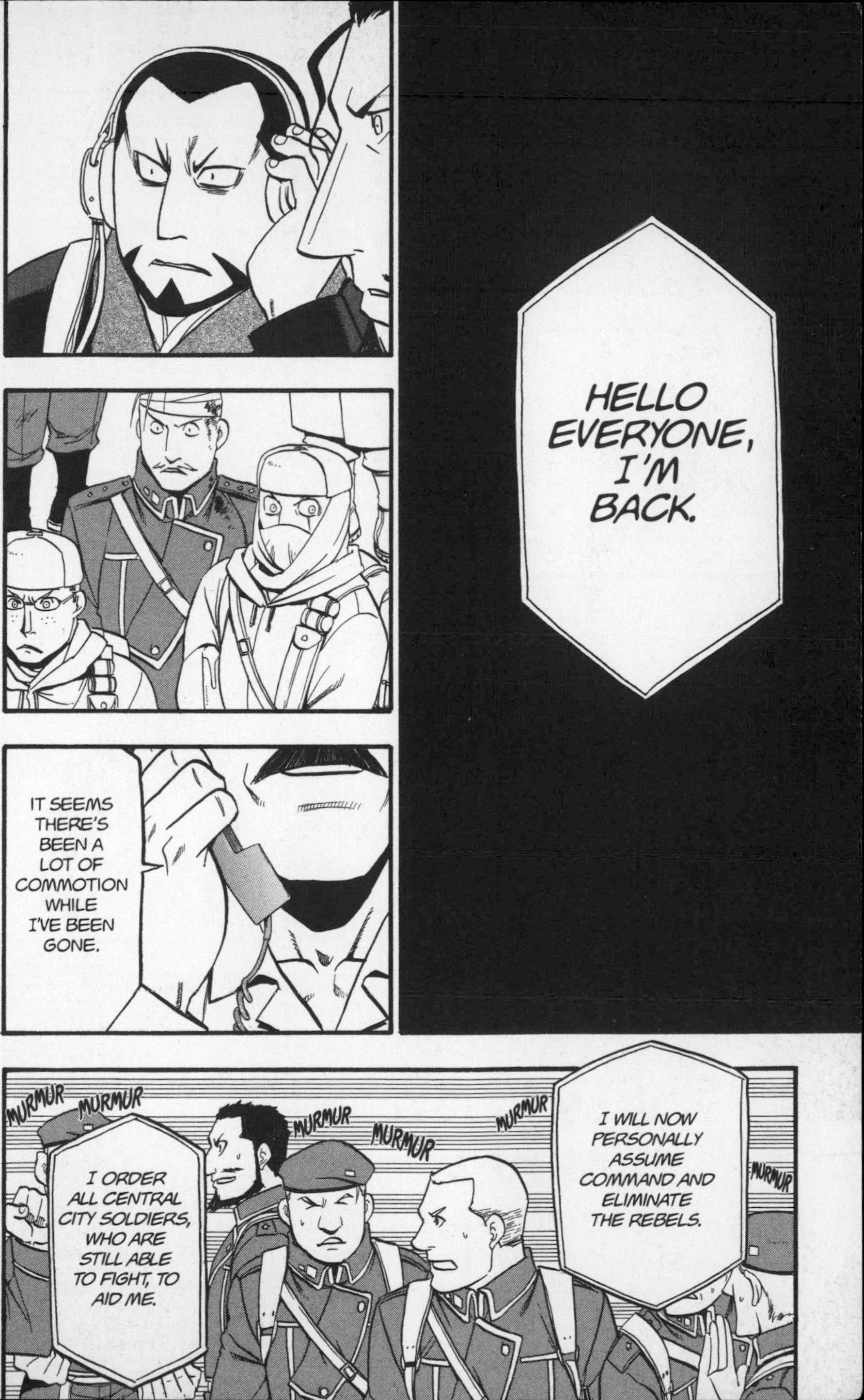
HELLO EVERYONE, I'M BACK.
IT SEEMS THERE'S BEEN A LOT OF COMMOTION WHILE I'VE BEEN GONE.
MURMUR
MURMUR
I WILL NOW PERSONALLY ASSUME COMMAND AND ELIMINATE THE REBELS.
MURMUR
MURMUR
MURMUR
MURMUR
I ORDER ALL CENTRAL CITY SOLDIERS, WHO ARE STILL ABLE TO FIGHT, TO AID ME.

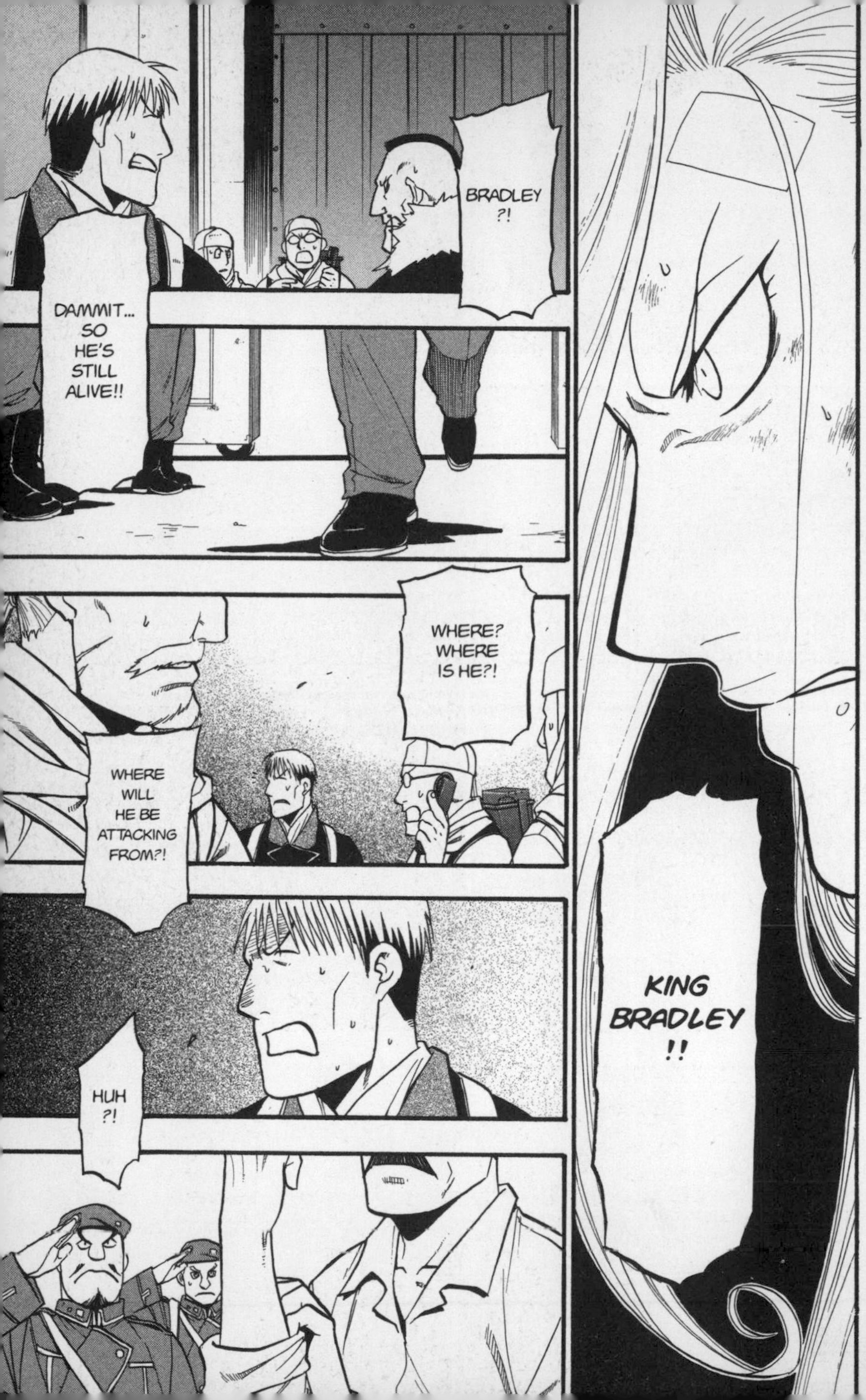
KING BRADLEY !!
BRADLEY ?!
DAMMIT... SO HE'S STILL ALIVE!!
WHERE? WHERE IS HE?!
WHERE WILL HE BE ATTACKING FROM?!
HUH ?!

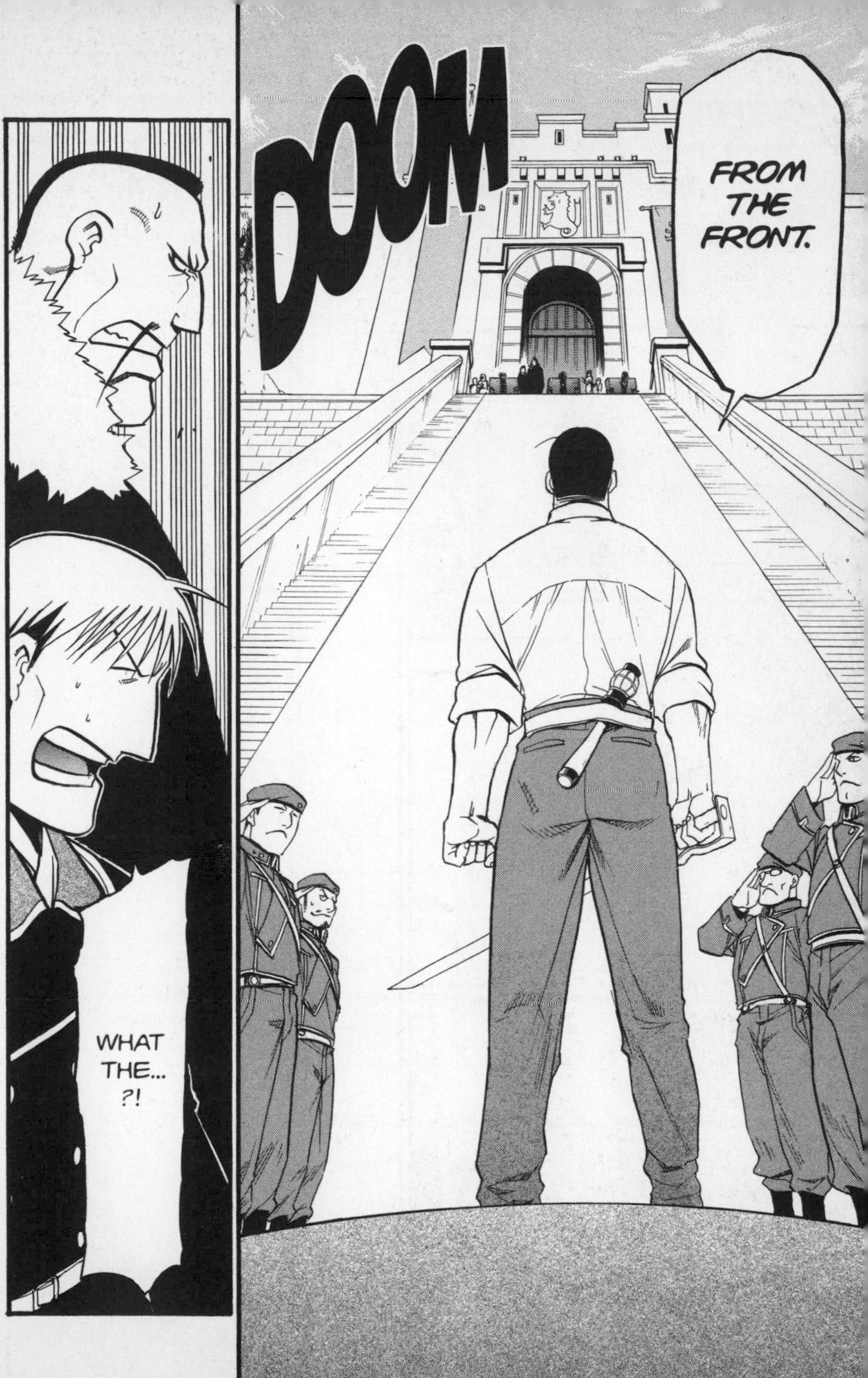
DOOM
FROM THE FRONT.
WHAT THE... ?!

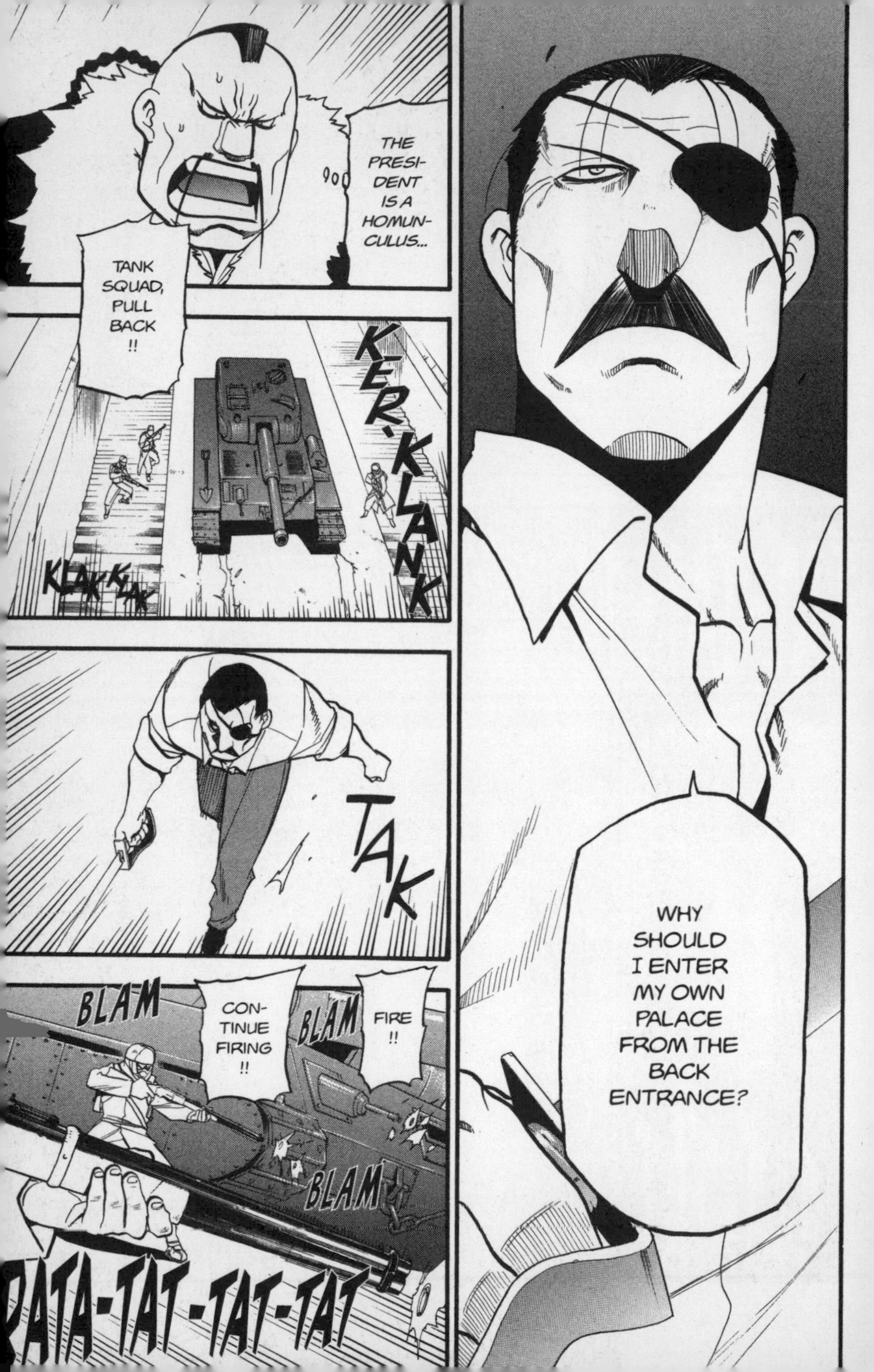
WHY SHOULD I ENTER MY OWN PALACE FROM THE BACK ENTRANCE?
THE PRESIDENT IS A HOMUNCULUS...
TANK SQUAD, PULL BACK !!
KER-KLANK
KLAK KLAK
TAK
FIRE !!
BLAM
BLAM
CONTINUE FIRING !!
BLAM
RATA-TAT-TAT-TAT

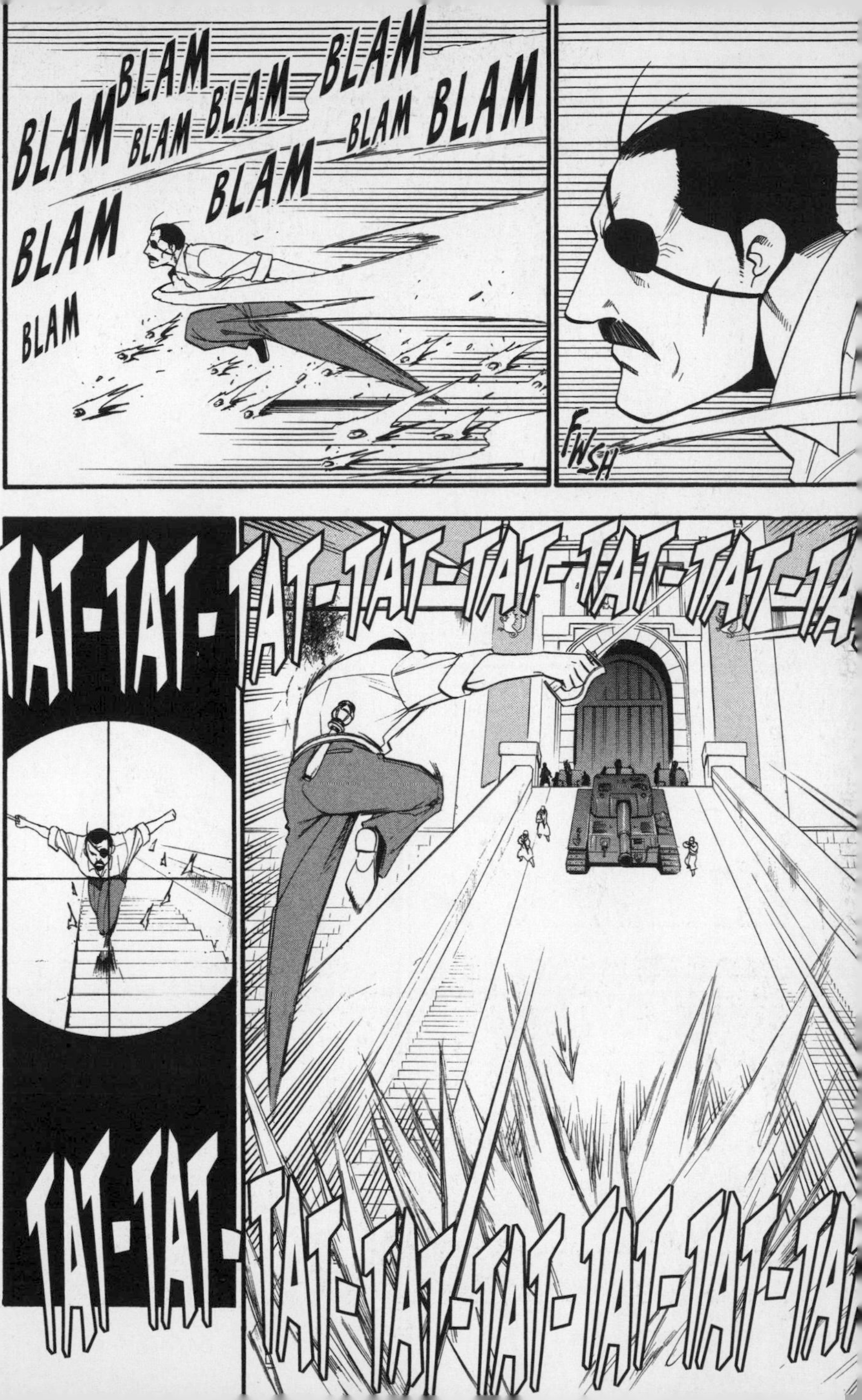
FWSH
BLAM BLAM BLAM BLAM BLAM BLAM BLAM BLAM BLAM BLAM BLAM
TAT-TAT-TAT-TAT-TAT-TAT-TAT-TA
TAT-TAT-TAT-TAT-TAT-TAT-TAT-TA

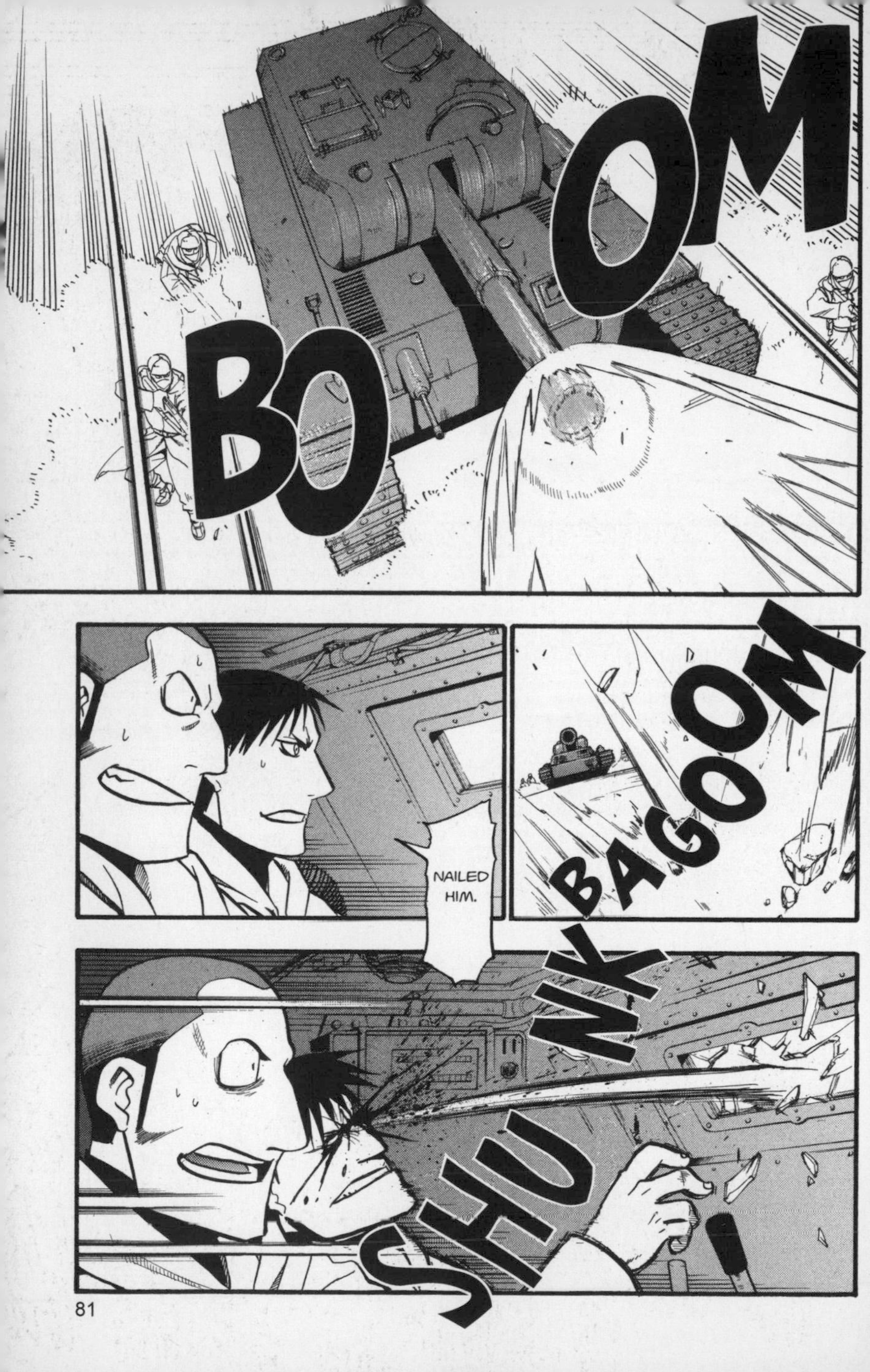
BOOM
BAGOOM
NAILED HIM.
SHUNK

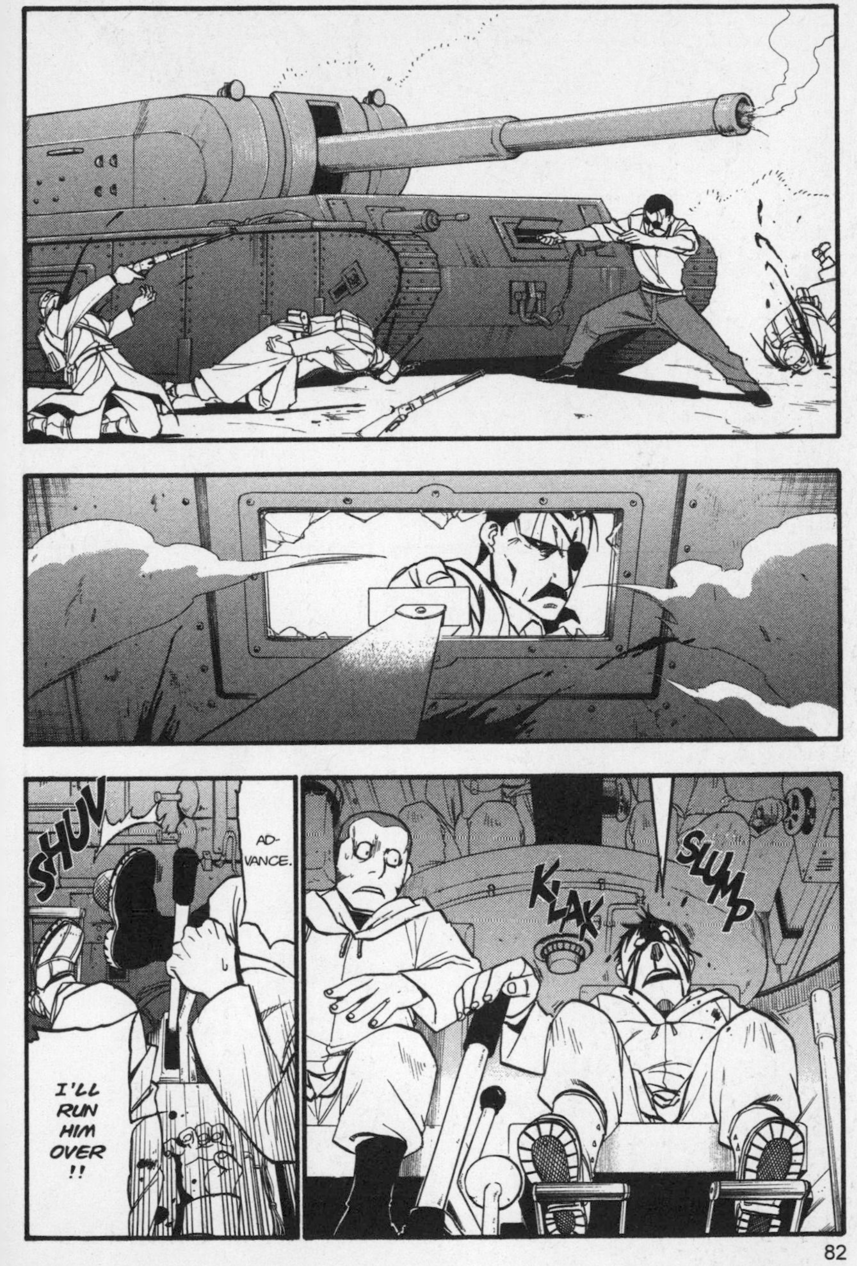
SLUMP
KLAK
ADVANCE.
SHUV
I'LL RUN HIM OVER !!

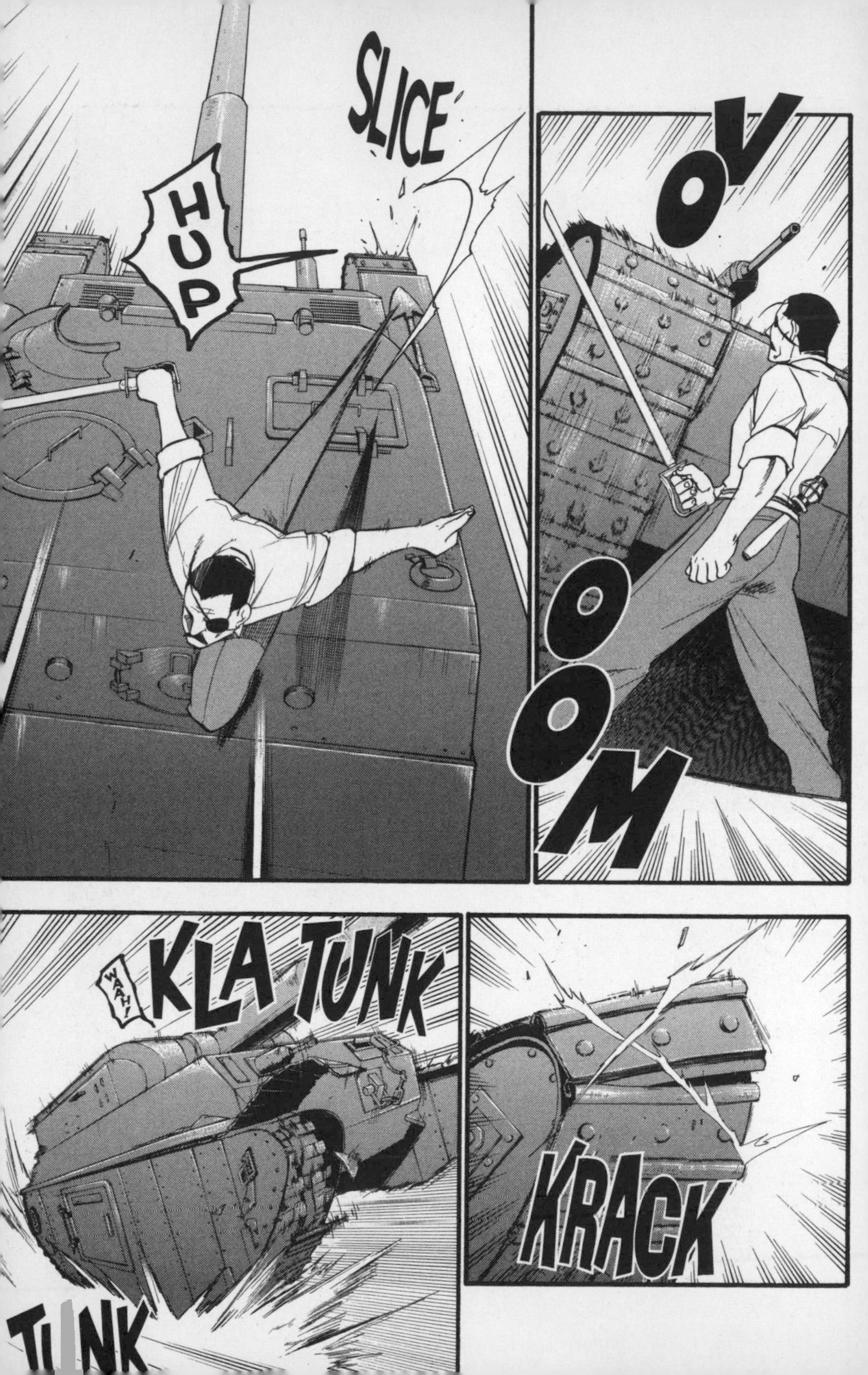
VOOOOM
SLICE
HUP
KRACK
WAAH!
KLA TUNK

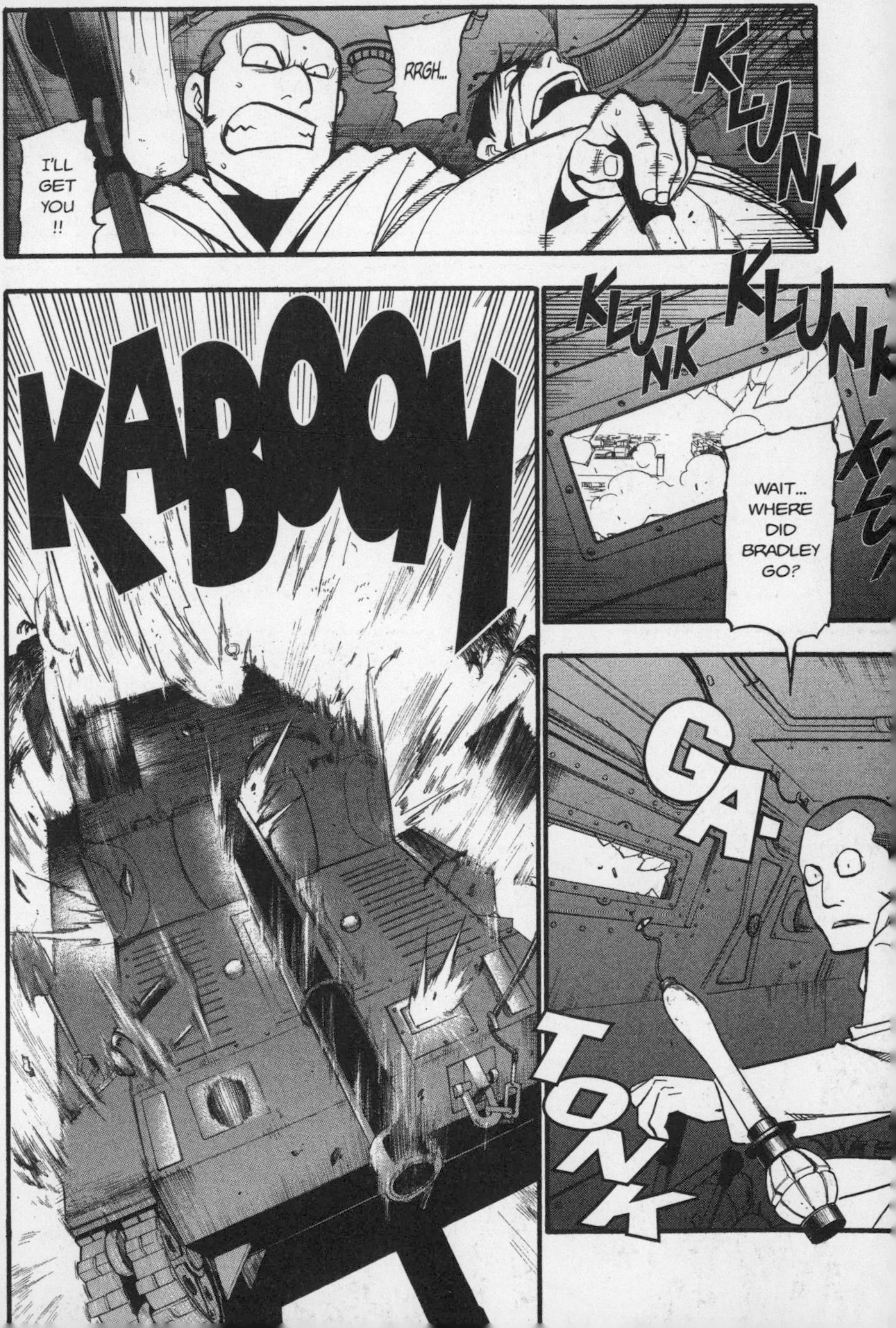
KLUNK
RRGH...
I'LL GET YOU!!
KLUNK
KLUNK
WAIT... WHERE DID BRADLEY GO?
GA-
TONK
KABOOM

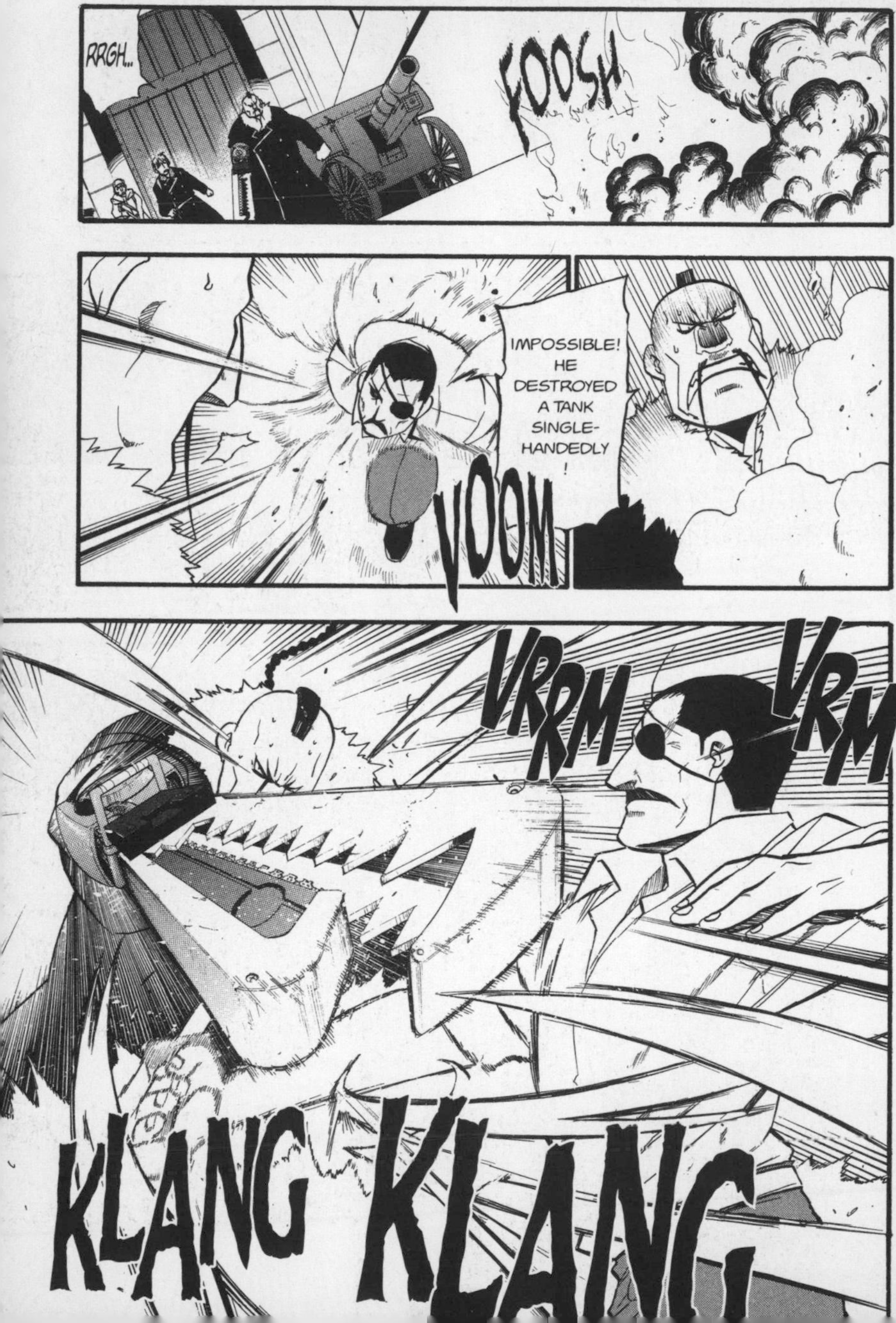
FOOSH
RRGH...
IMPOSSIBLE! HE DESTROYED A TANK SINGLE-HANDEDLY!
VOOM
VRM
VRRM
KLANG
KLANG

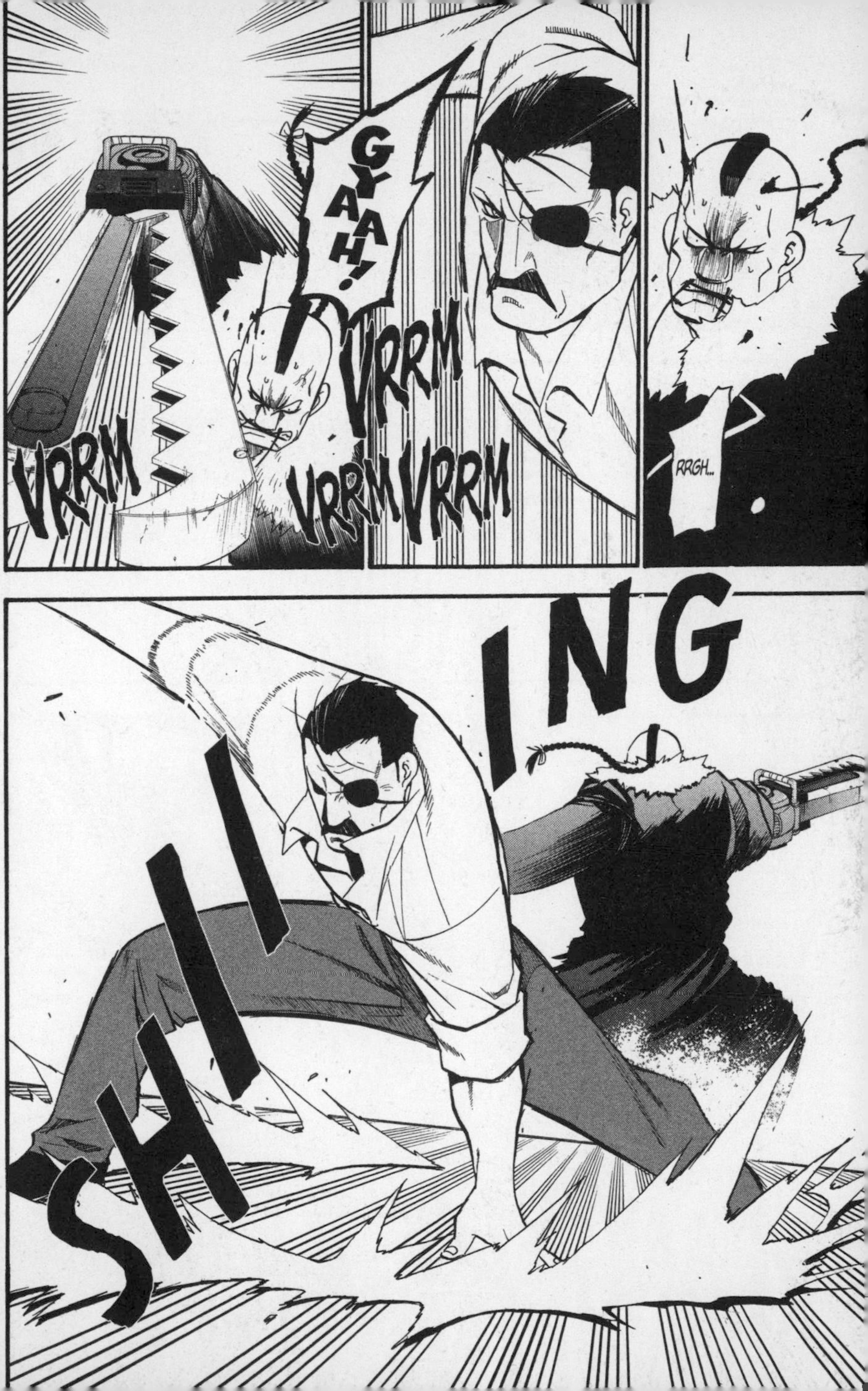
RRGH...
GYAAH!
VRRM
VRRM VRRM
VRRM
SHIIING

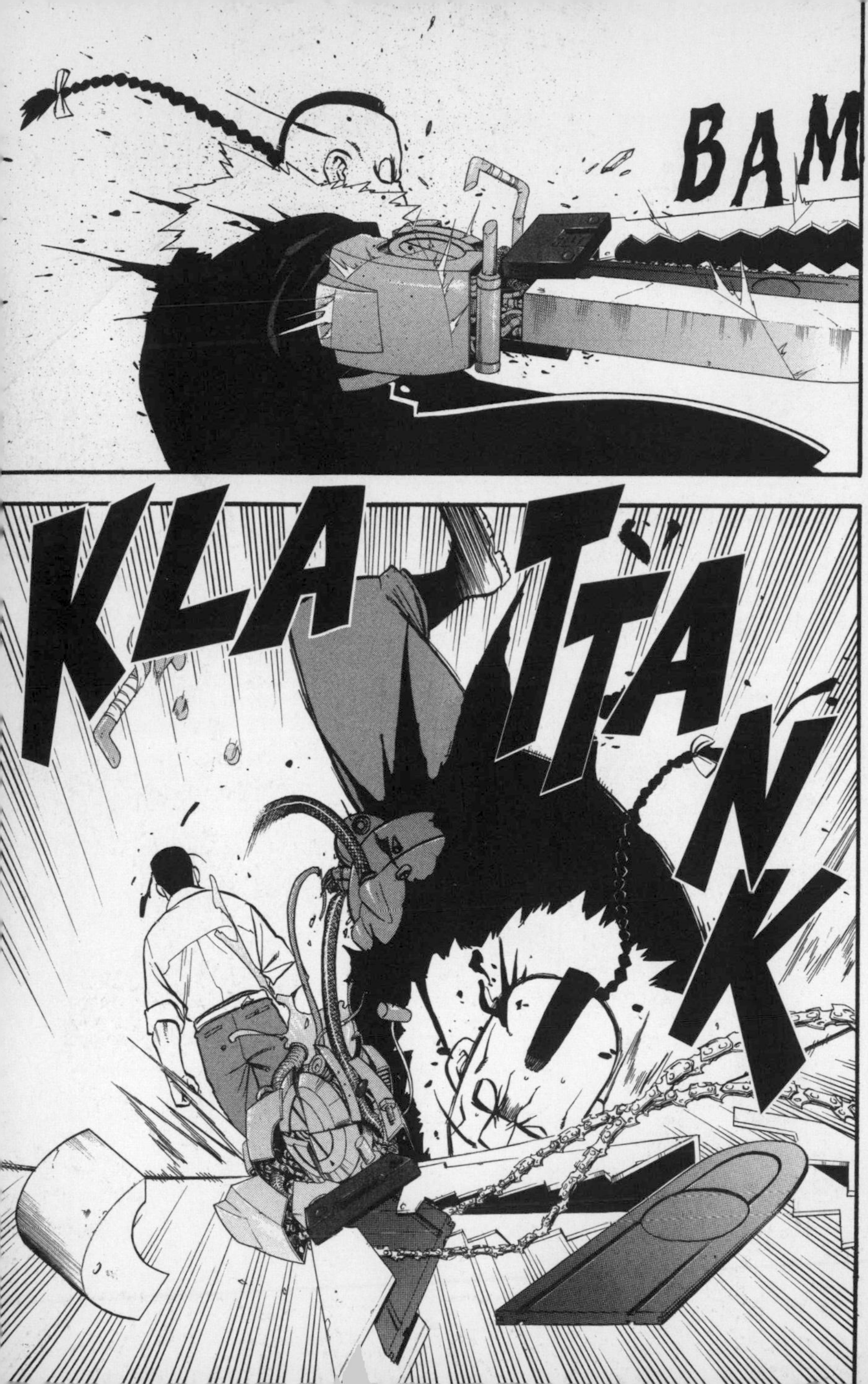
BAM
KLATTANK

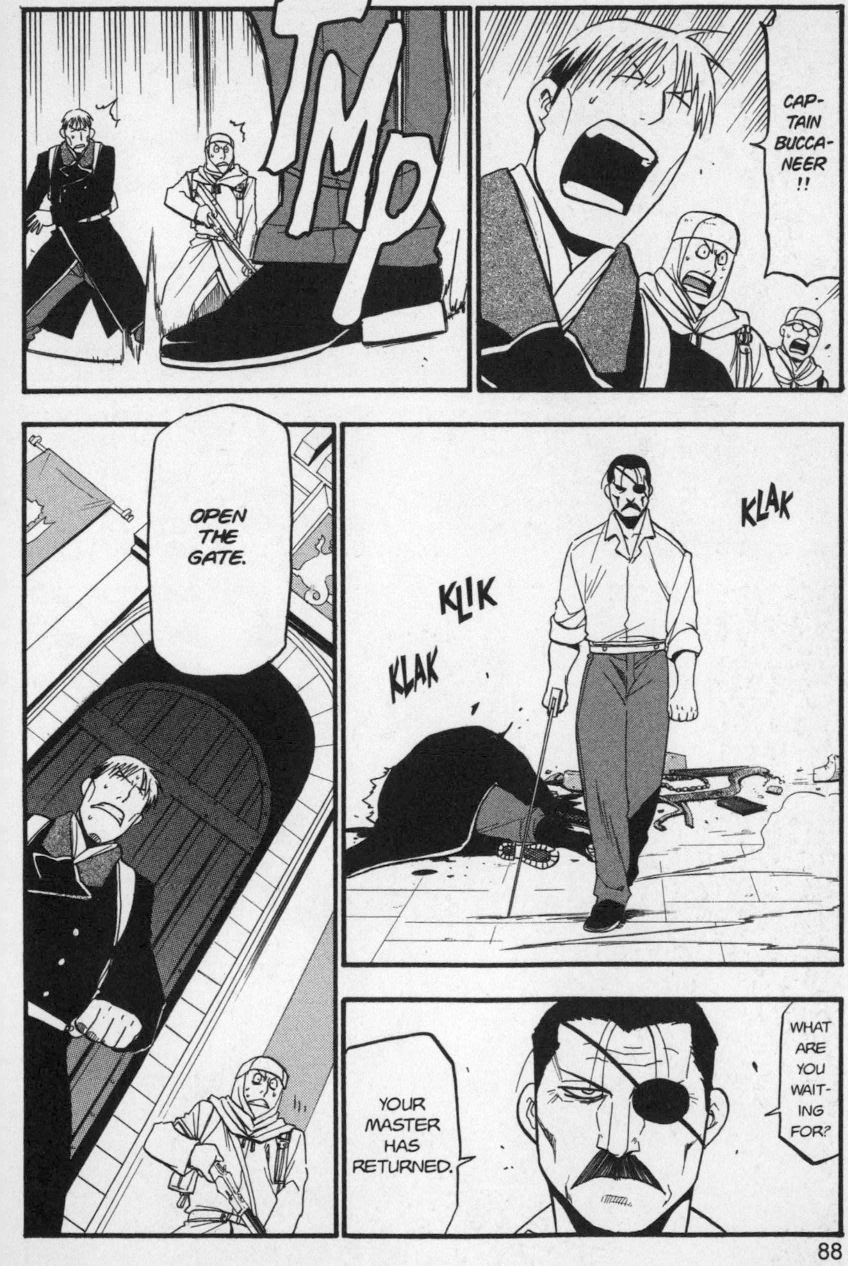
CAP-TAIN BUCCA-NEER!!
TMP
KLAK
KLIK
KLAK
WHAT ARE YOU WAIT-ING FOR?
YOUR MASTER HAS RETURNED.
OPEN THE GATE.

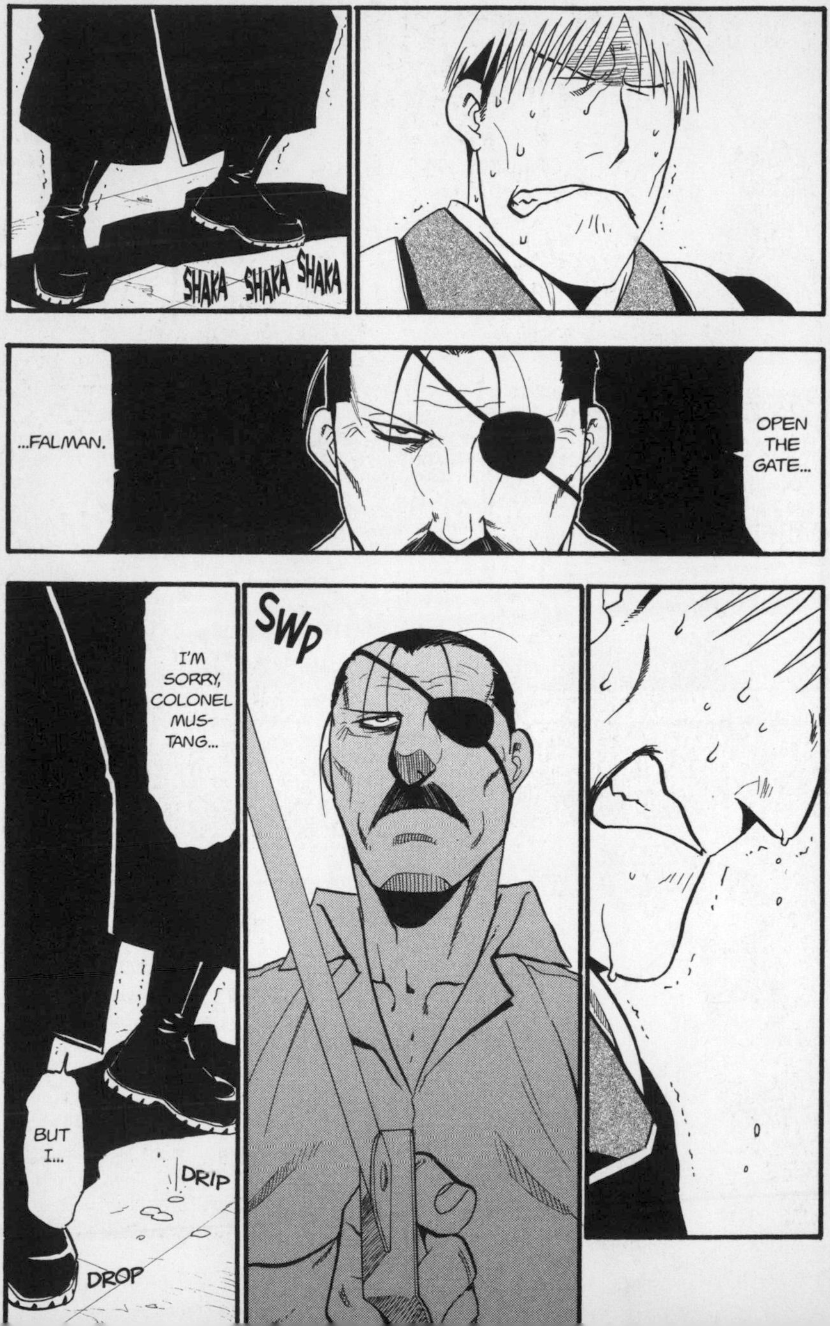
SHAKA SHAKA SHAKA
OPEN THE GATE...
...FALMAN.
SWP
I'M SORRY, COLONEL MUS-TANG...
BUT I...
DRIP
DROP

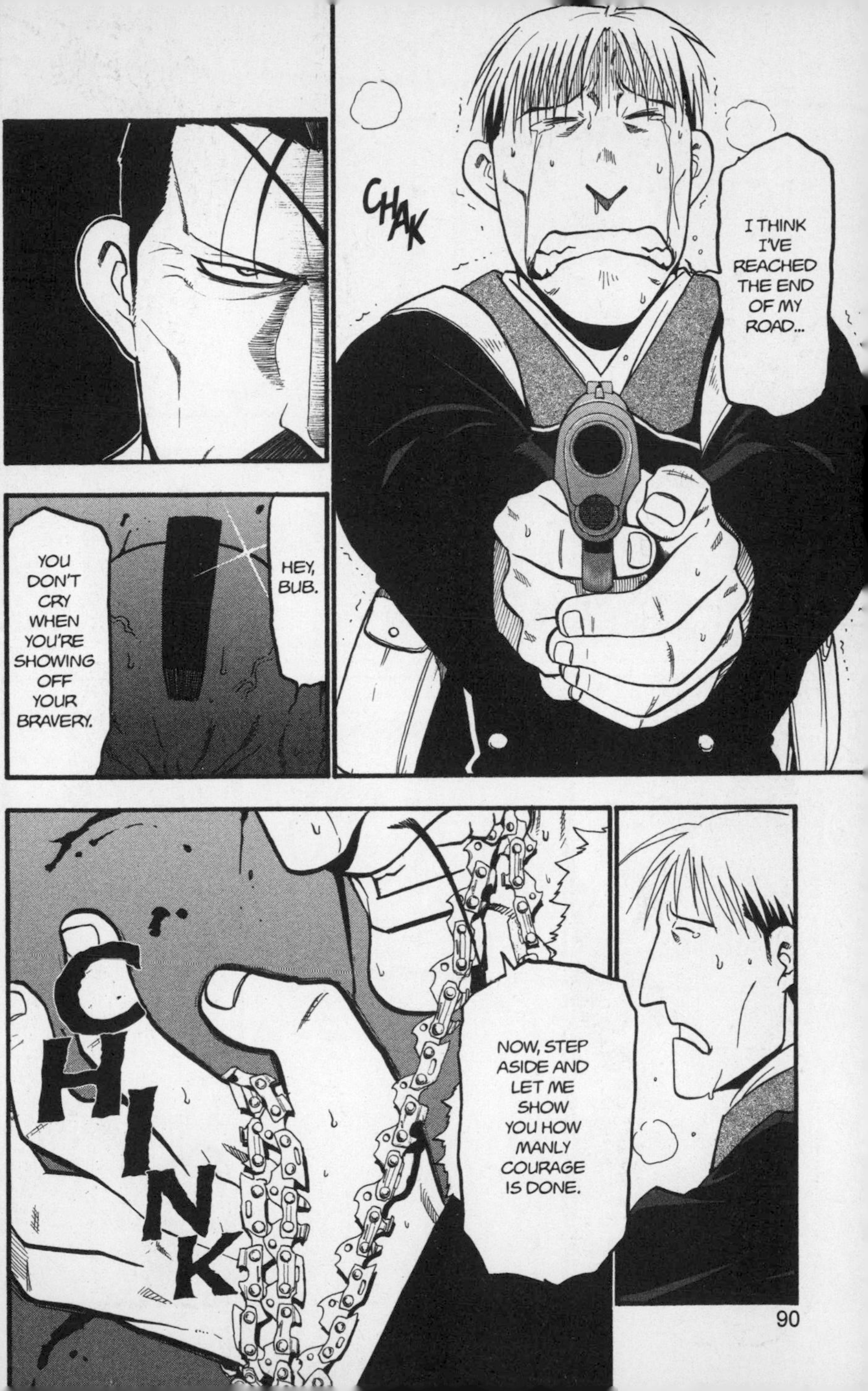
CHAK
I THINK I'VE REACHED THE END OF MY ROAD...
HEY, BUB.
YOU DON'T CRY WHEN YOU'RE SHOWING OFF YOUR BRAVERY.
NOW, STEP ASIDE AND LET ME SHOW YOU HOW MANLY COURAGE IS DONE.
CHINK

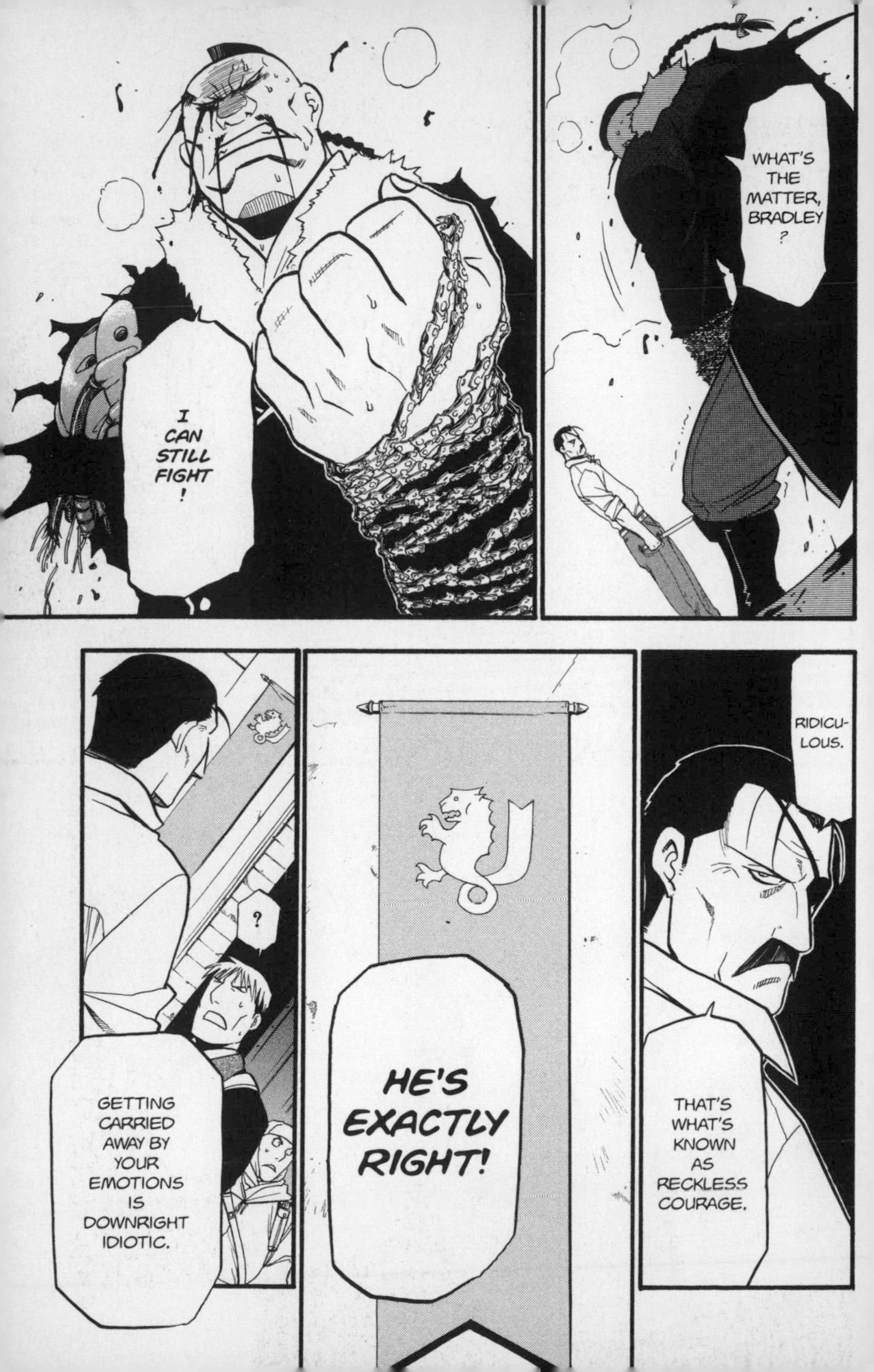
WHAT'S THE MATTER, BRADLEY?
I CAN STILL FIGHT!
RIDICULOUS.
THAT'S WHAT'S KNOWN AS RECKLESS COURAGE.
HE'S EXACTLY RIGHT!
?
GETTING CARRIED AWAY BY YOUR EMOTIONS IS DOWNRIGHT IDIOTIC.

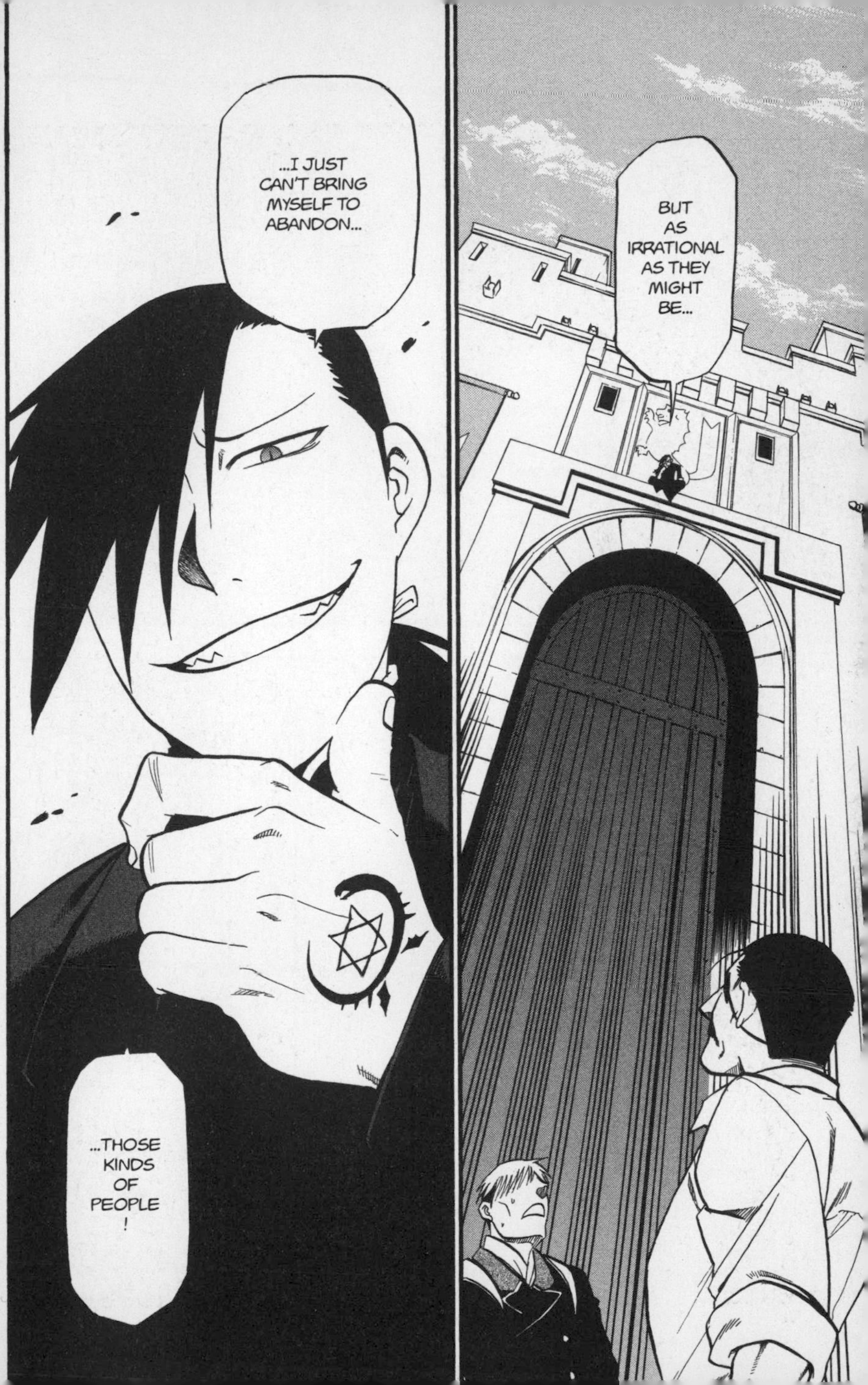
BUT AS IRRATIONAL AS THEY MIGHT BE...
...I JUST CAN'T BRING MYSELF TO ABANDON...
...THOSE KINDS OF PEOPLE!

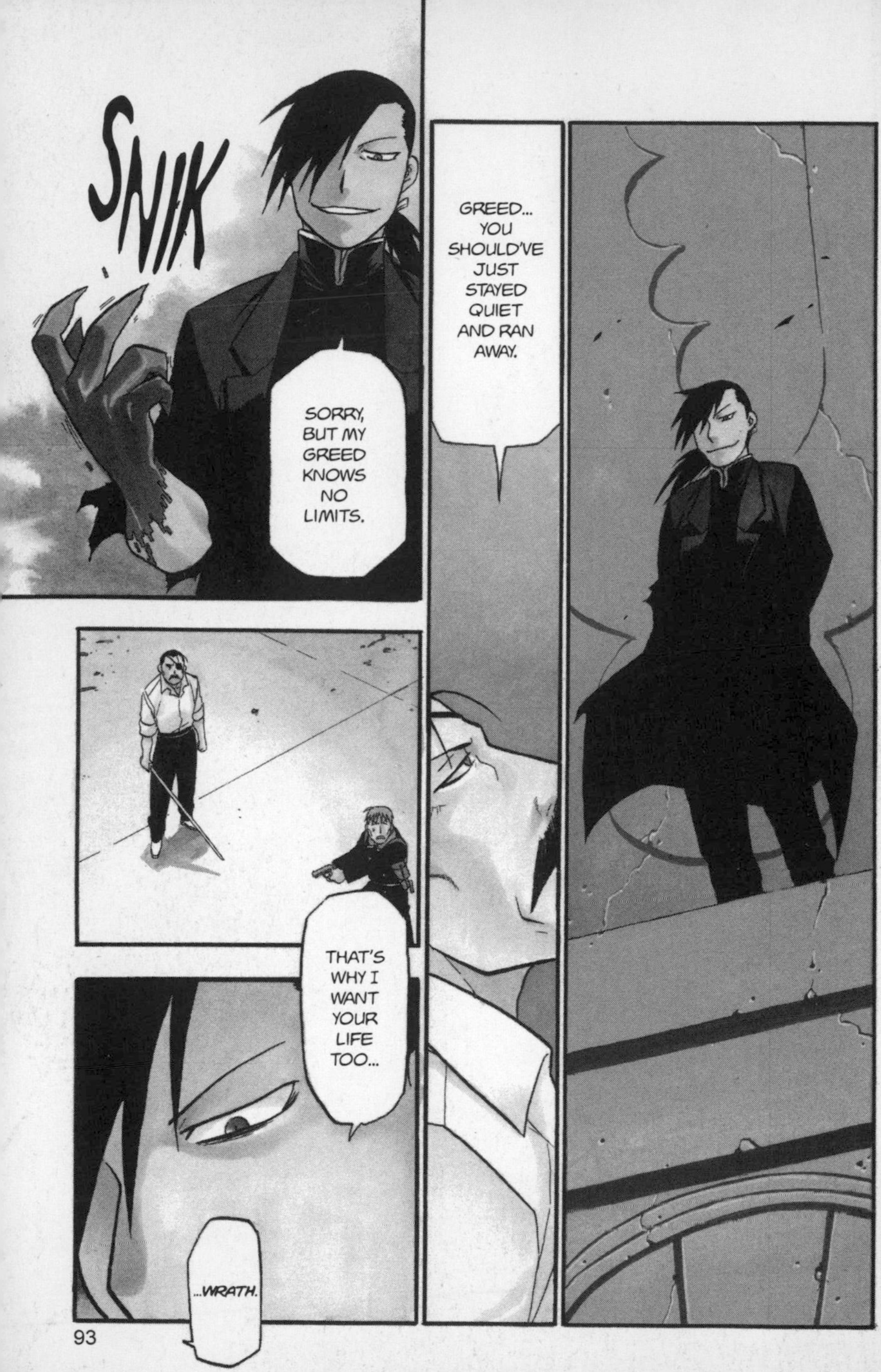
GREED... YOU SHOULD'VE JUST STAYED QUIET AND RAN AWAY.
SNIK
SORRY, BUT MY GREED KNOWS NO LIMITS.
THAT'S WHY I WANT YOUR LIFE TOO...
...WRATH.

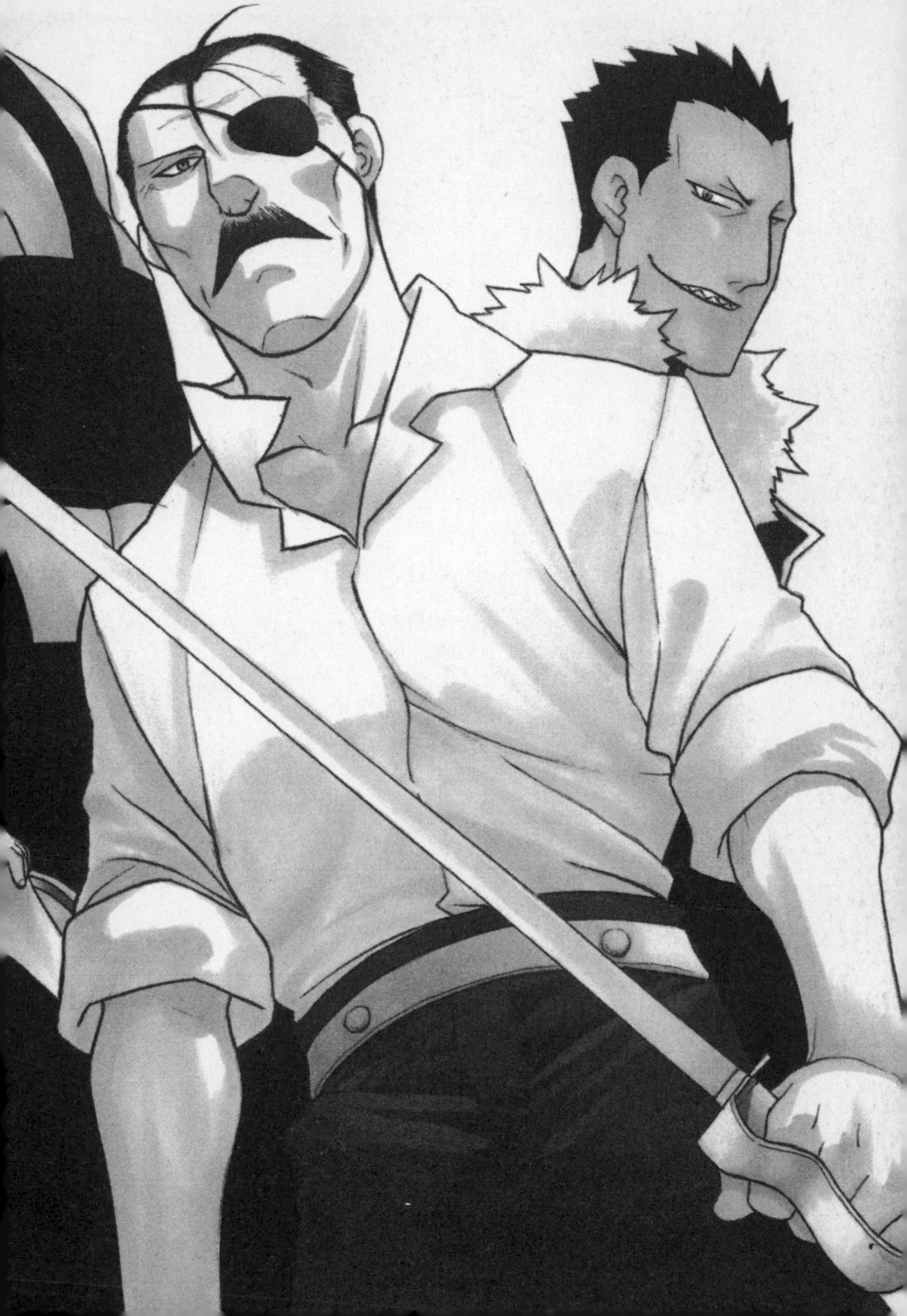

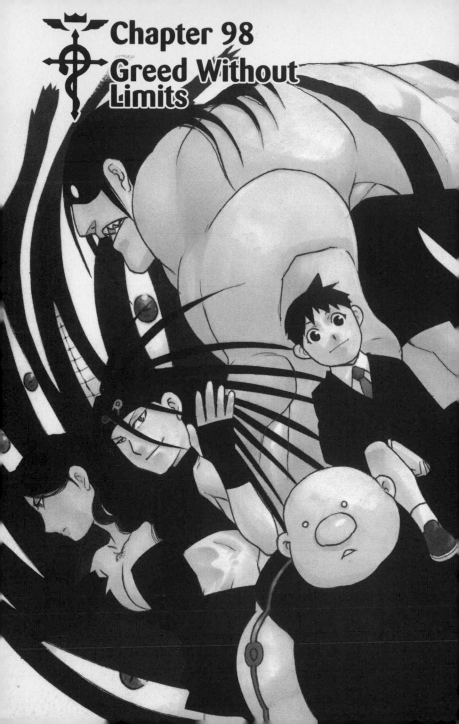

# Chapter 98
## Greed Without Limits

FULLMETAL
ALCHEMIST

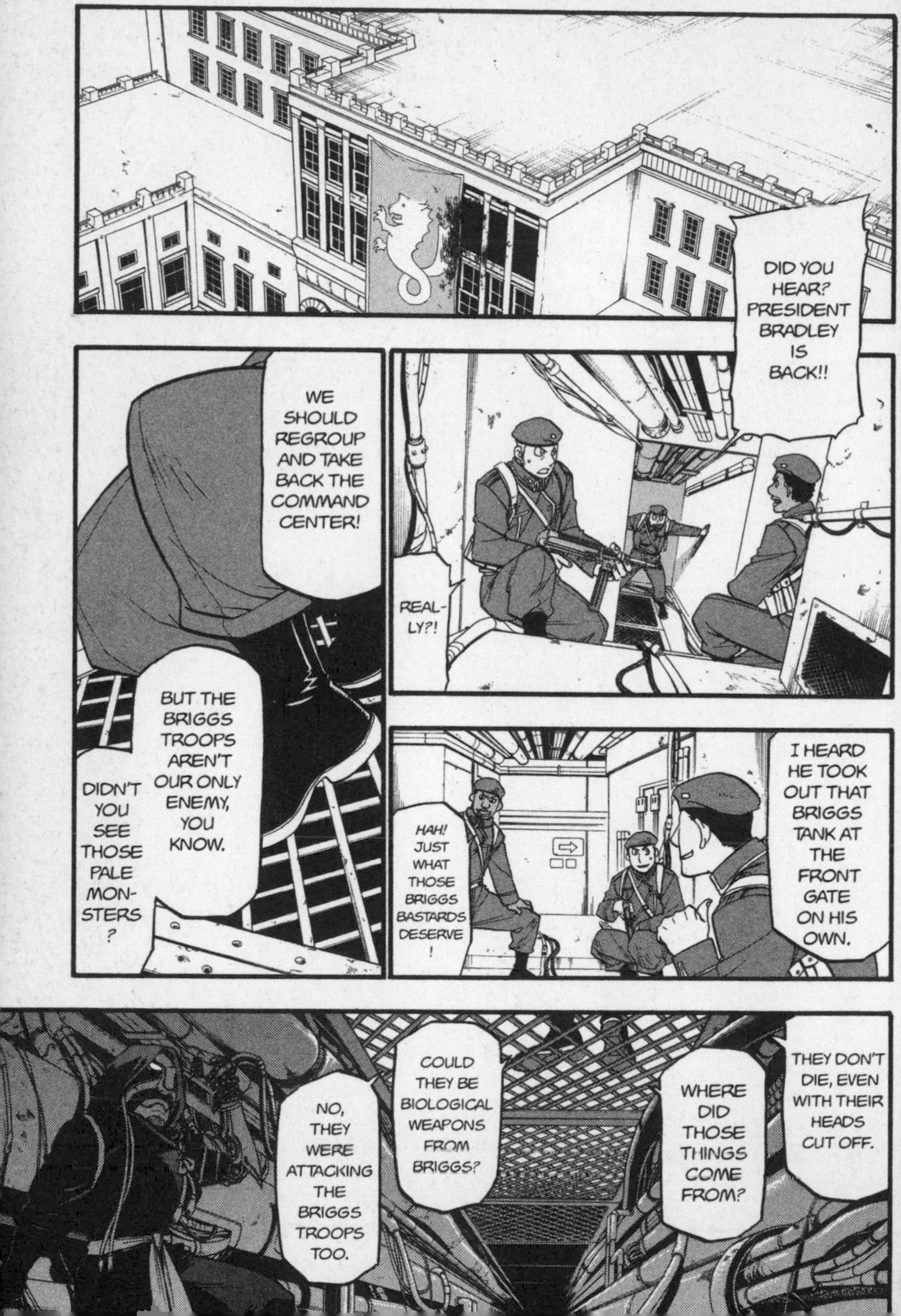
DID YOU HEAR? PRESIDENT BRADLEY IS BACK!!
REAL-LY?!
I HEARD HE TOOK OUT THAT BRIGGS TANK AT THE FRONT GATE ON HIS OWN.
HAH! JUST WHAT THOSE BRIGGS BASTARDS DESERVE!
WE SHOULD REGROUP AND TAKE BACK THE COMMAND CENTER!
BUT THE BRIGGS TROOPS AREN'T OUR ONLY ENEMY, YOU KNOW.
DIDN'T YOU SEE THOSE PALE MONSTERS?
THEY DON'T DIE, EVEN WITH THEIR HEADS CUT OFF.
WHERE DID THOSE THINGS COME FROM?
COULD THEY BE BIOLOGICAL WEAPONS FROM BRIGGS?
NO, THEY WERE ATTACKING THE BRIGGS TROOPS TOO.

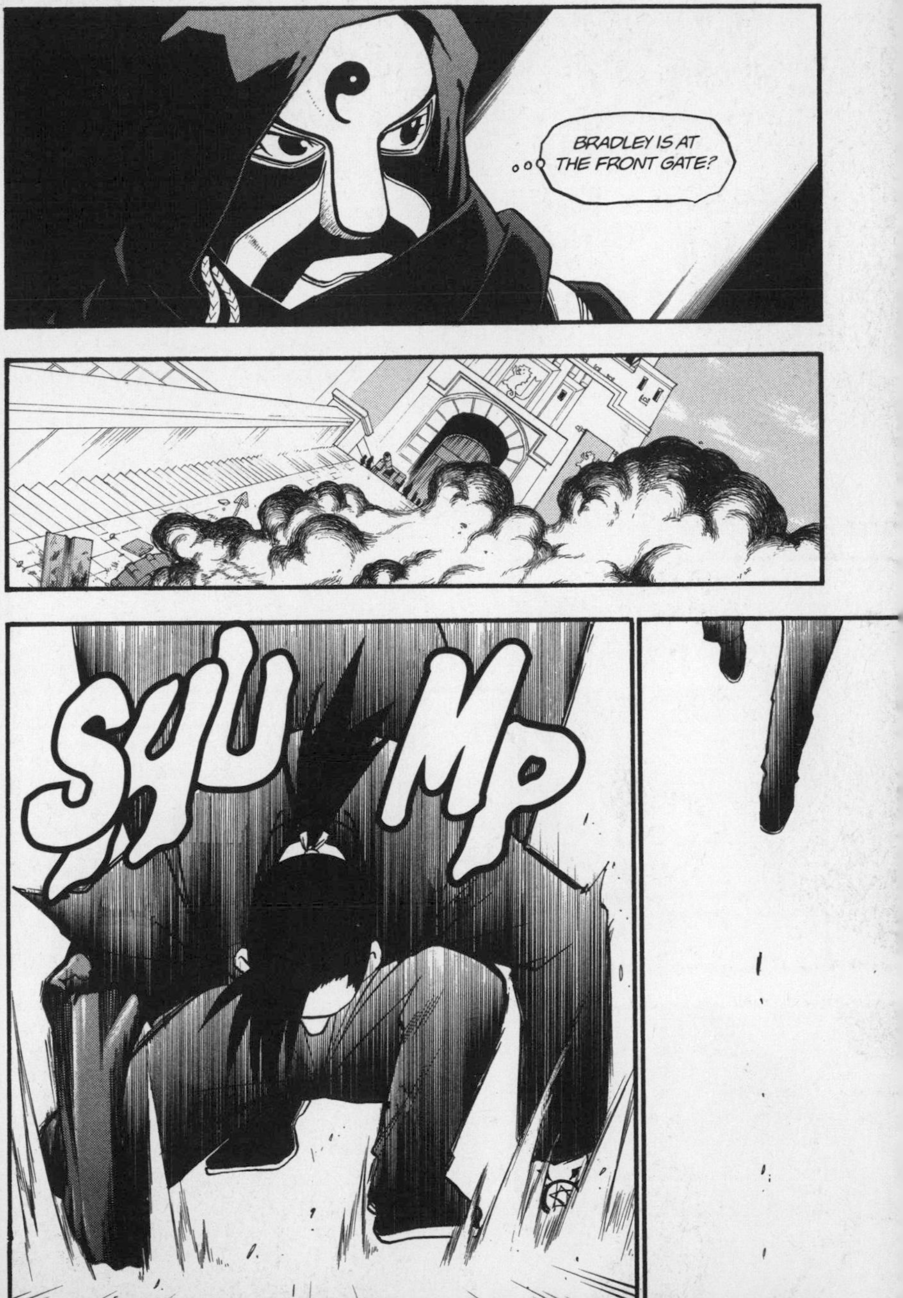
BRADLEY IS AT THE FRONT GATE?
SHUMP

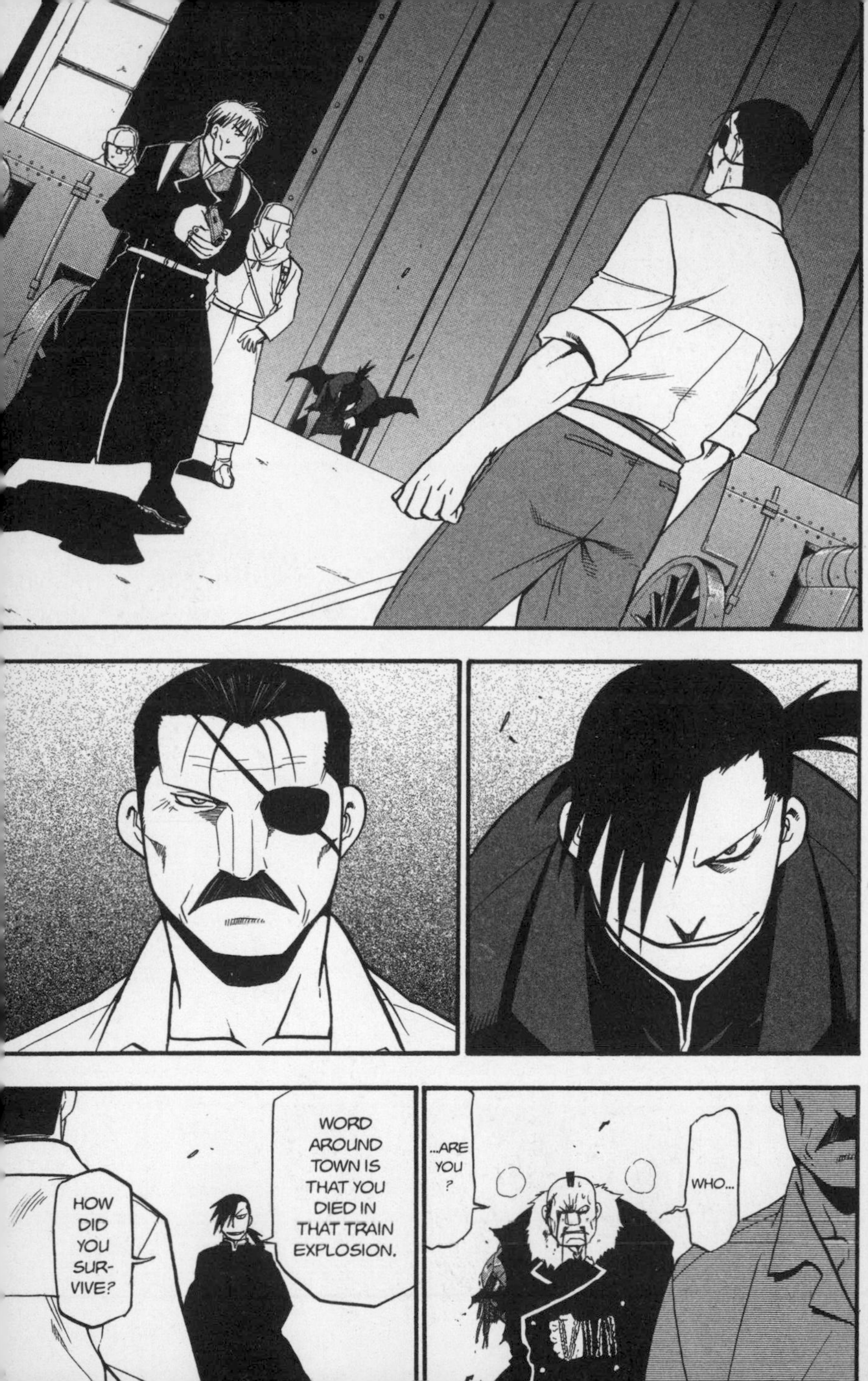
WHO...
...ARE YOU?
WORD AROUND TOWN IS THAT YOU DIED IN THAT TRAIN EXPLOSION.
HOW DID YOU SURVIVE?

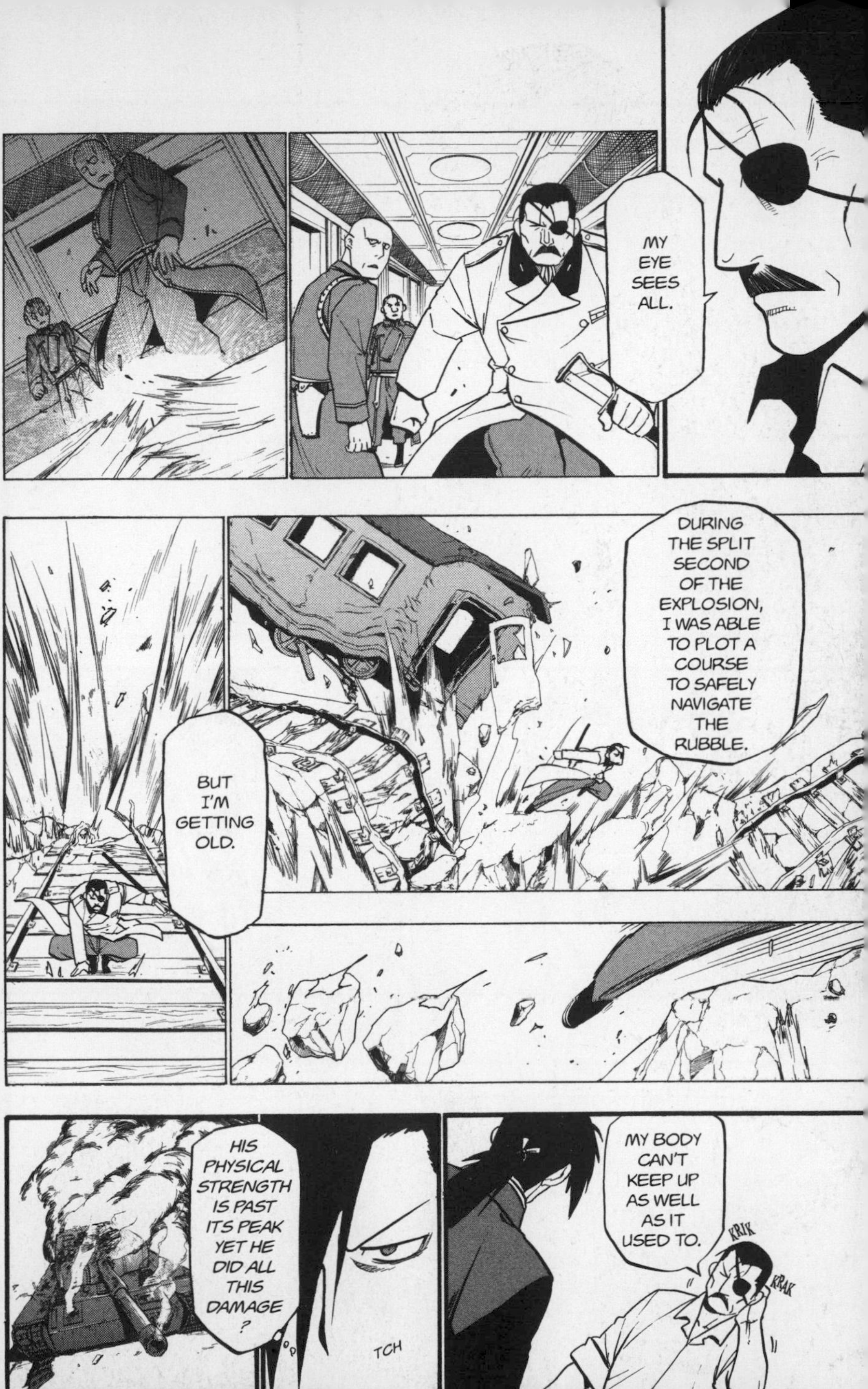
MY EYE SEES ALL.
DURING THE SPLIT SECOND OF THE EXPLOSION, I WAS ABLE TO PLOT A COURSE TO SAFELY NAVIGATE THE RUBBLE.
BUT I'M GETTING OLD.
MY BODY CAN'T KEEP UP AS WELL AS IT USED TO.
KRIK
KRAK
HIS PHYSICAL STRENGTH IS PAST ITS PEAK YET HE DID ALL THIS DAMAGE?
TCH

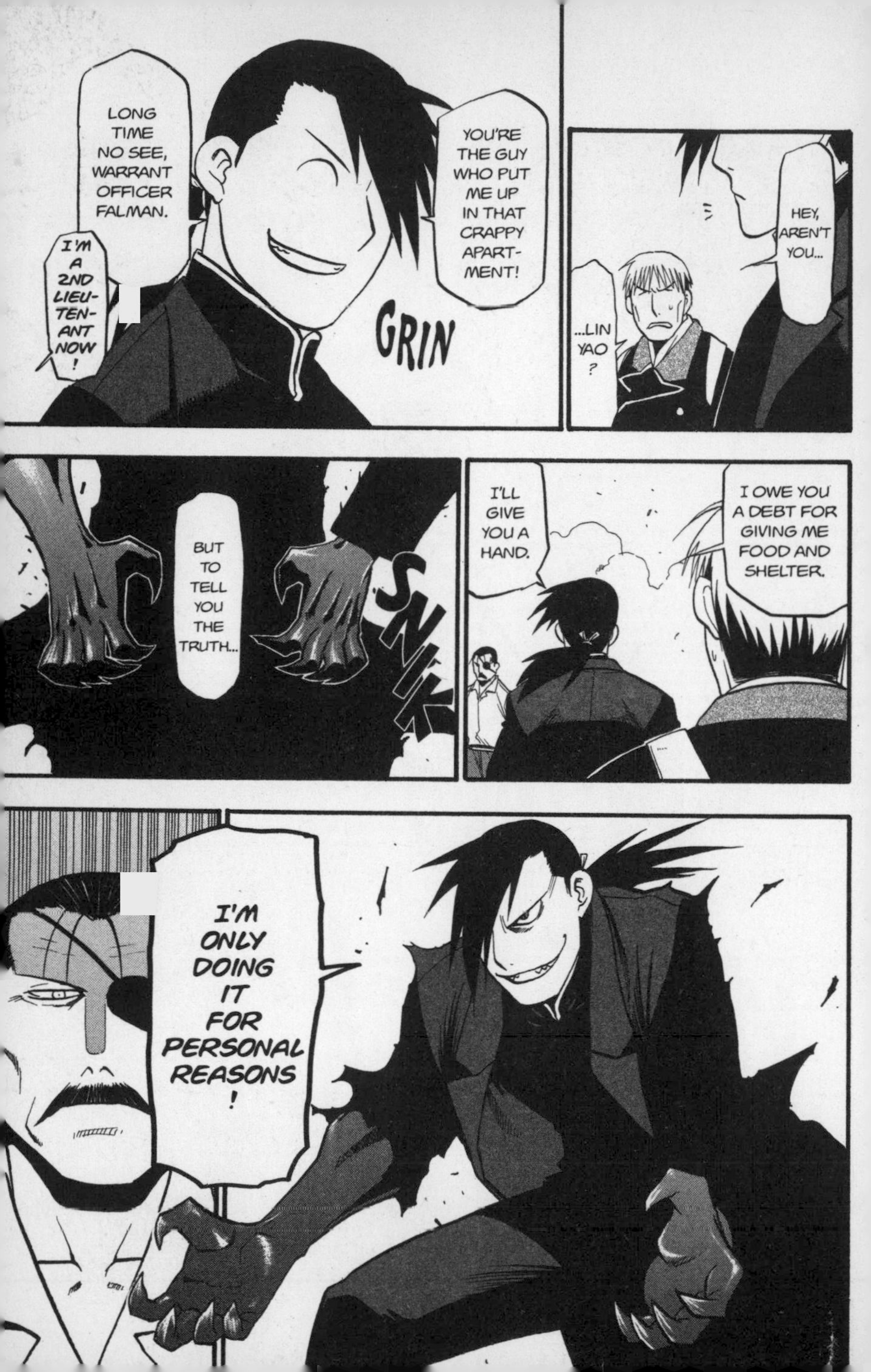
HEY, AREN'T YOU...
...LIN YAO?
YOU'RE THE GUY WHO PUT ME UP IN THAT CRAPPY APARTMENT!
LONG TIME NO SEE, WARRANT OFFICER FALMAN.
I'M A 2ND LIEUTENANT NOW!
GRIN
I OWE YOU A DEBT FOR GIVING ME FOOD AND SHELTER.
I'LL GIVE YOU A HAND.
SNIK
BUT TO TELL YOU THE TRUTH...
I'M ONLY DOING IT FOR PERSONAL REASONS!

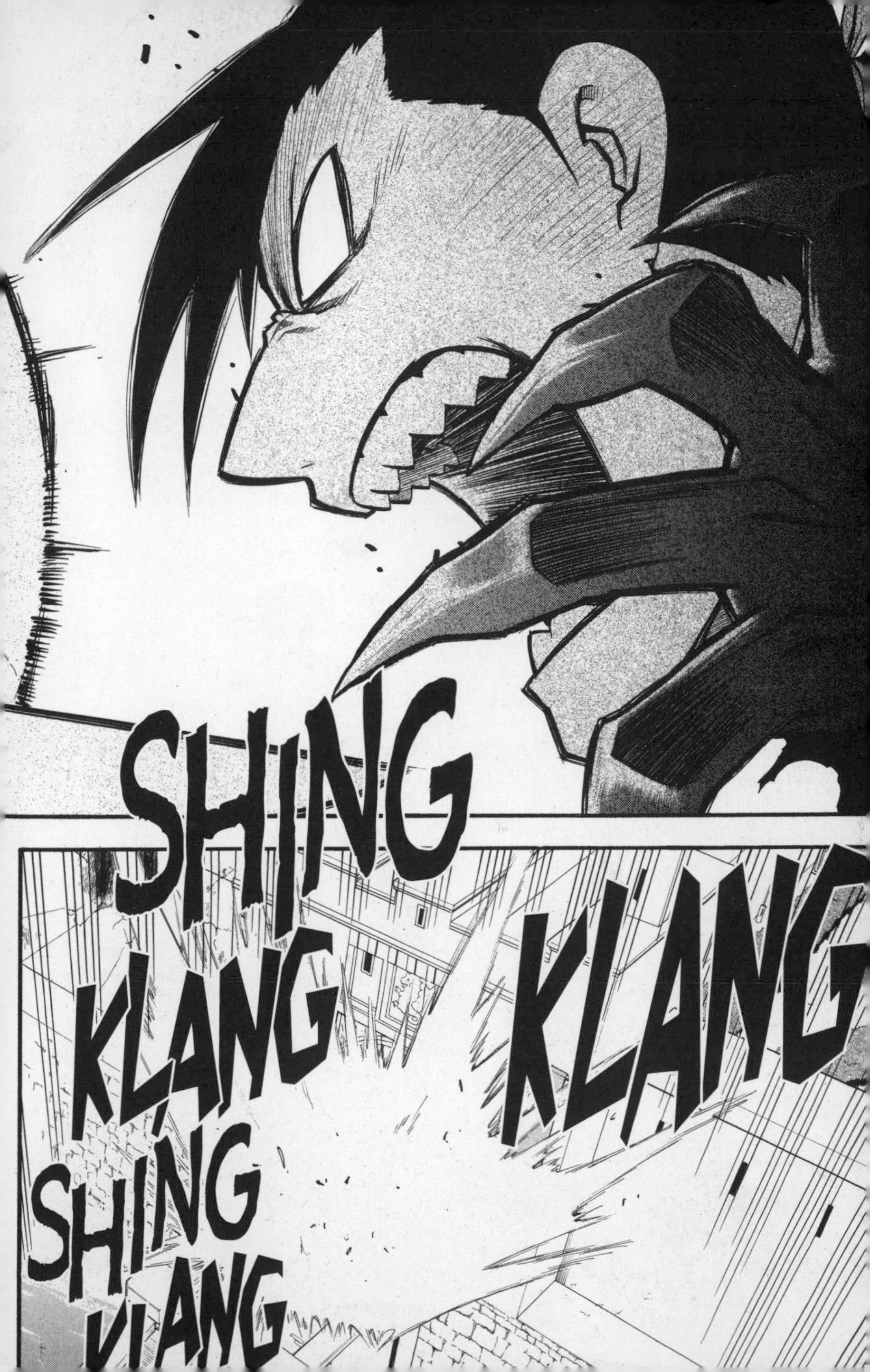
SHING
KLANG
KLANG
SHING

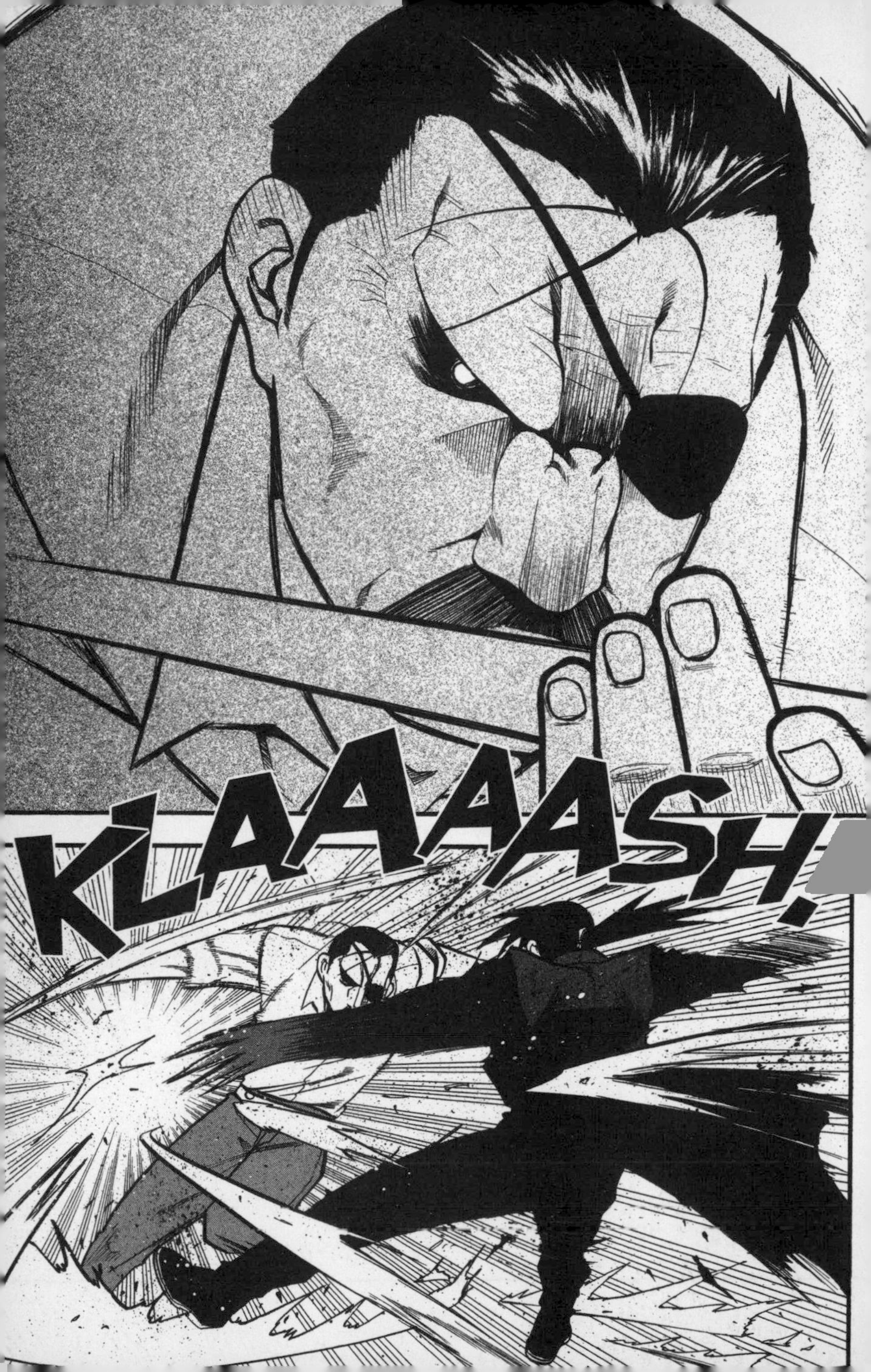
KLAAAASH!

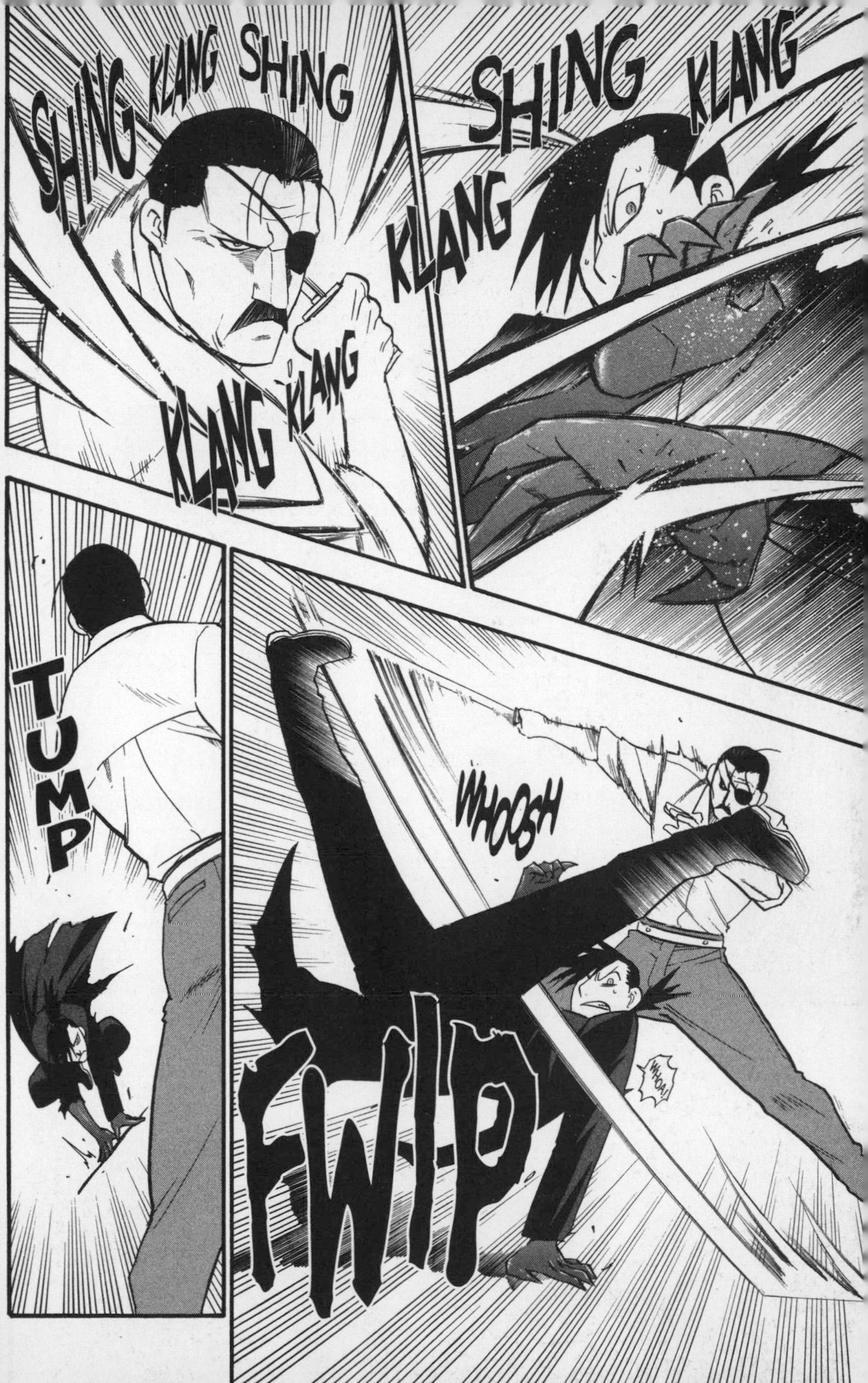
SHING
KLANG
KLANG
SHING
KLANG
SHING
KLANG
KLANG
WHOOSH
WHOA!
FWIP
TUMP

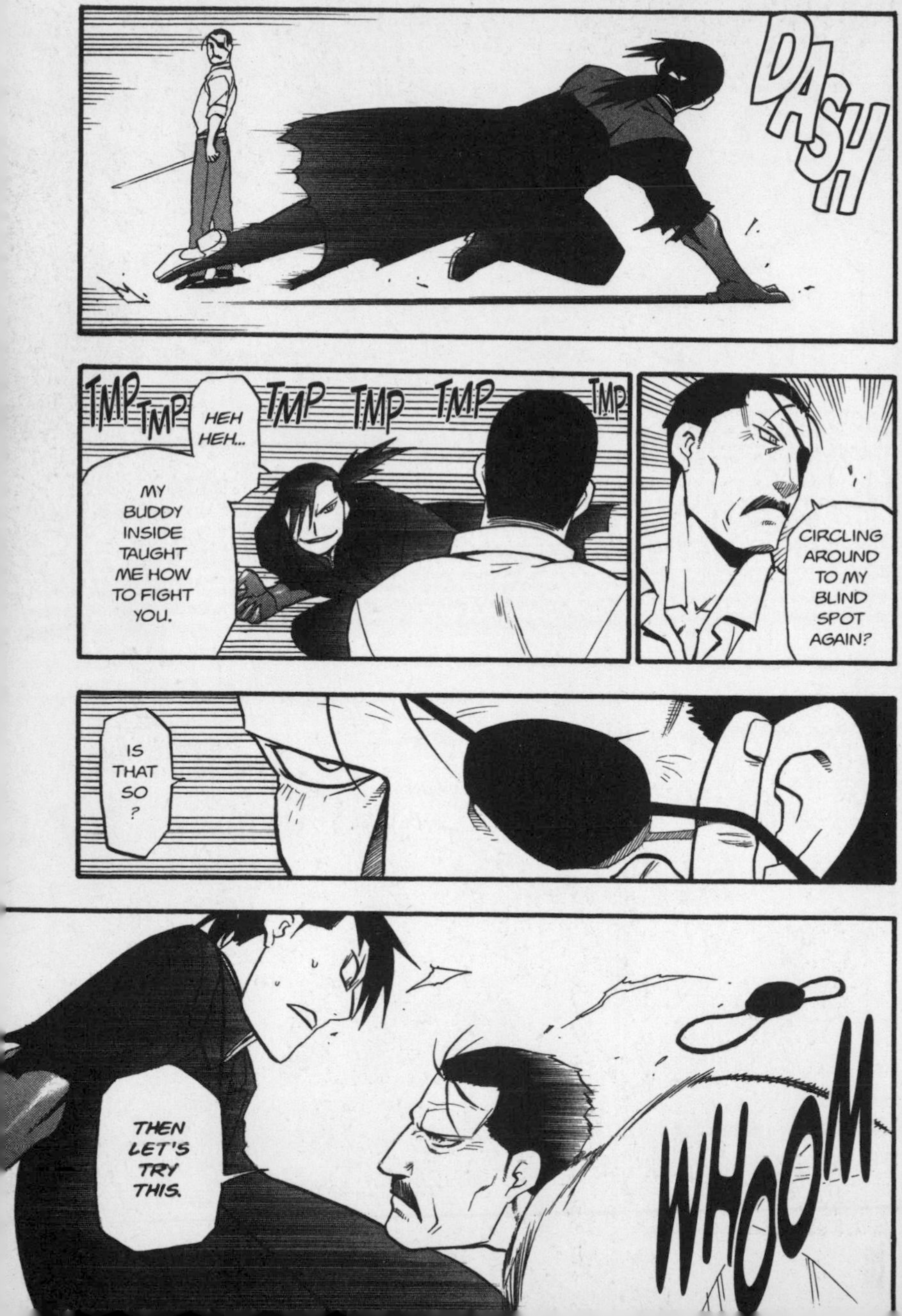
DASH
CIRCLING AROUND TO MY BLIND SPOT AGAIN?
TMP TMP TMP TMP
HEH HEH...
TMP TMP
MY BUDDY INSIDE TAUGHT ME HOW TO FIGHT YOU.
IS THAT SO?
WHOOM
THEN LET'S TRY THIS.

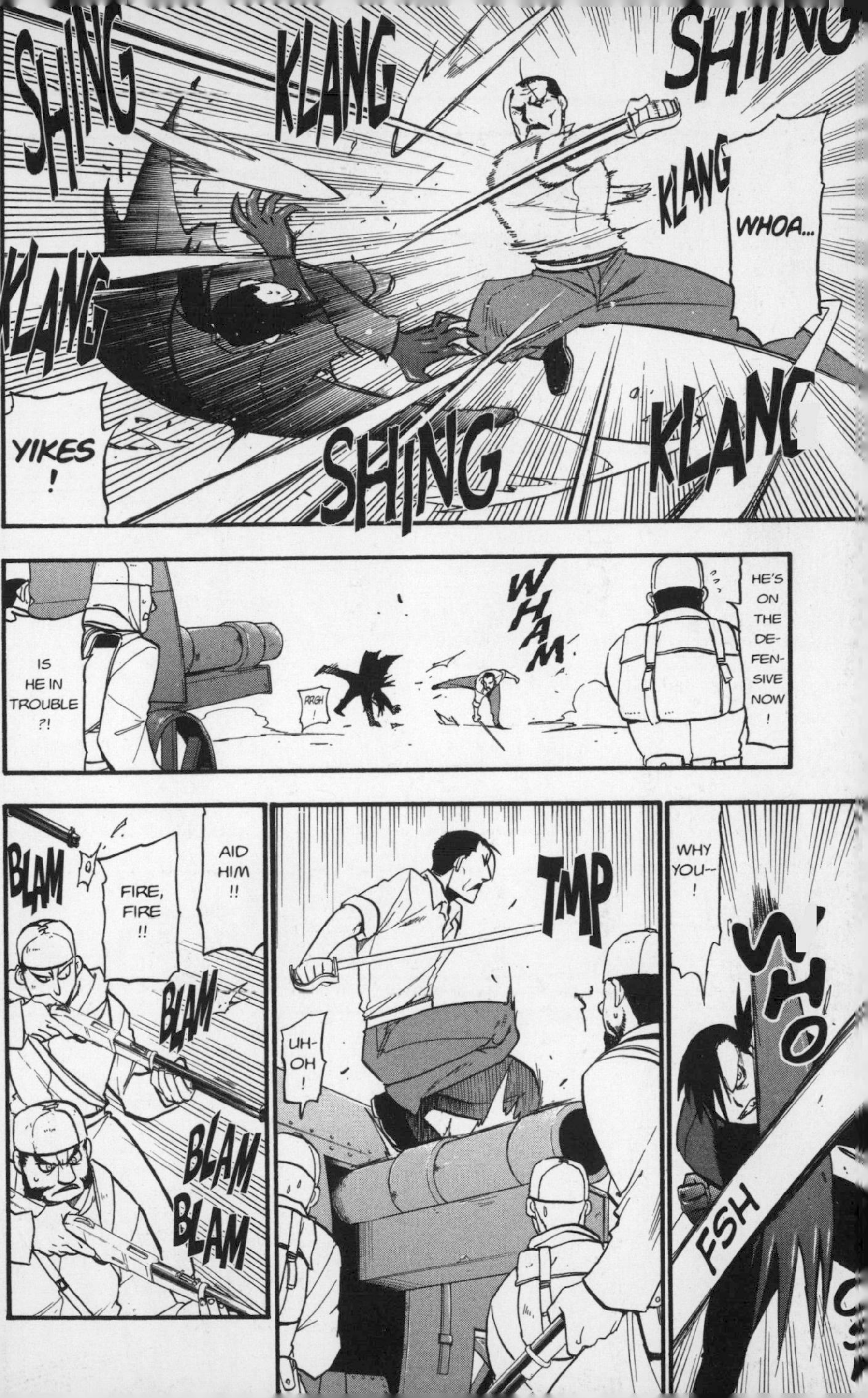
SHING
KLANG
WHOA...
KLANG
SHING
KLANG
KLANG
SHING
YIKES!
HE'S ON THE DE-FEN-SIVE NOW!
WHAM
RRGH!
IS HE IN TROUBLE?!
WHY YOU--!
FSH
TMP
UH-OH!
AID HIM!!
FIRE, FIRE!!
BLAM
BLAM
BLAM
BLAM

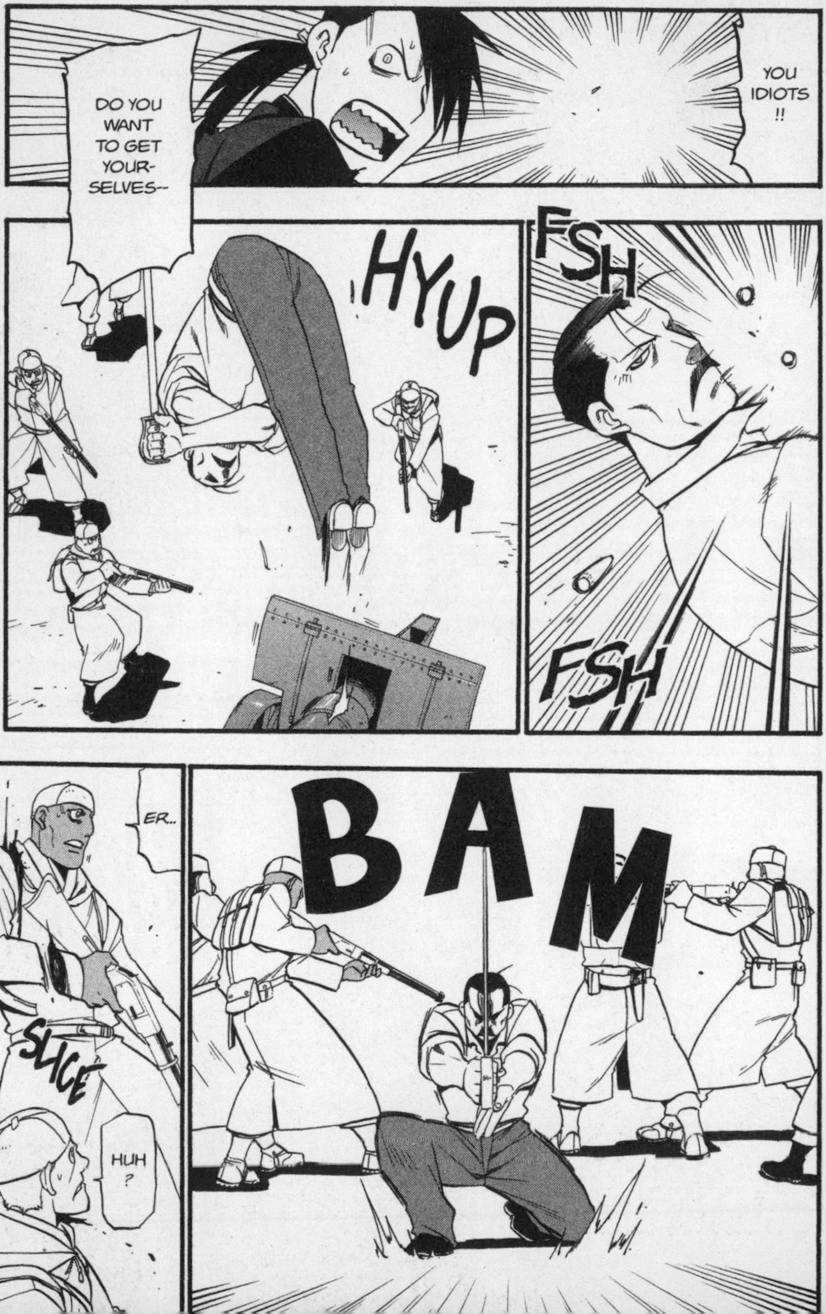
YOU IDIOTS !!
DO YOU WANT TO GET YOUR-SELVES--
FSH
FSH
HYUP
BAM
ER...
SLICE
HUH ?

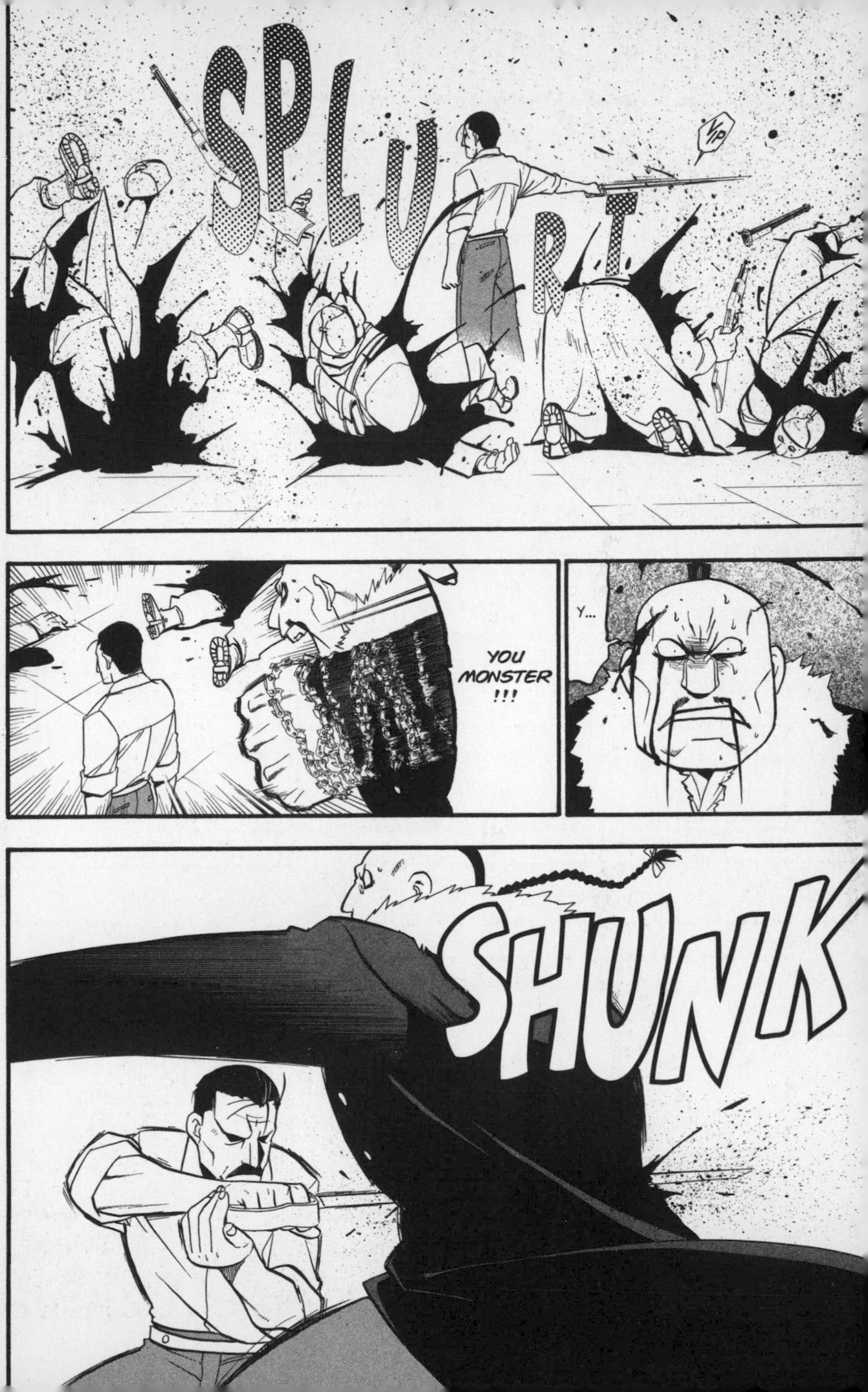
YIP
SPLURT
Y...
YOU MONSTER !!!
SHUNK

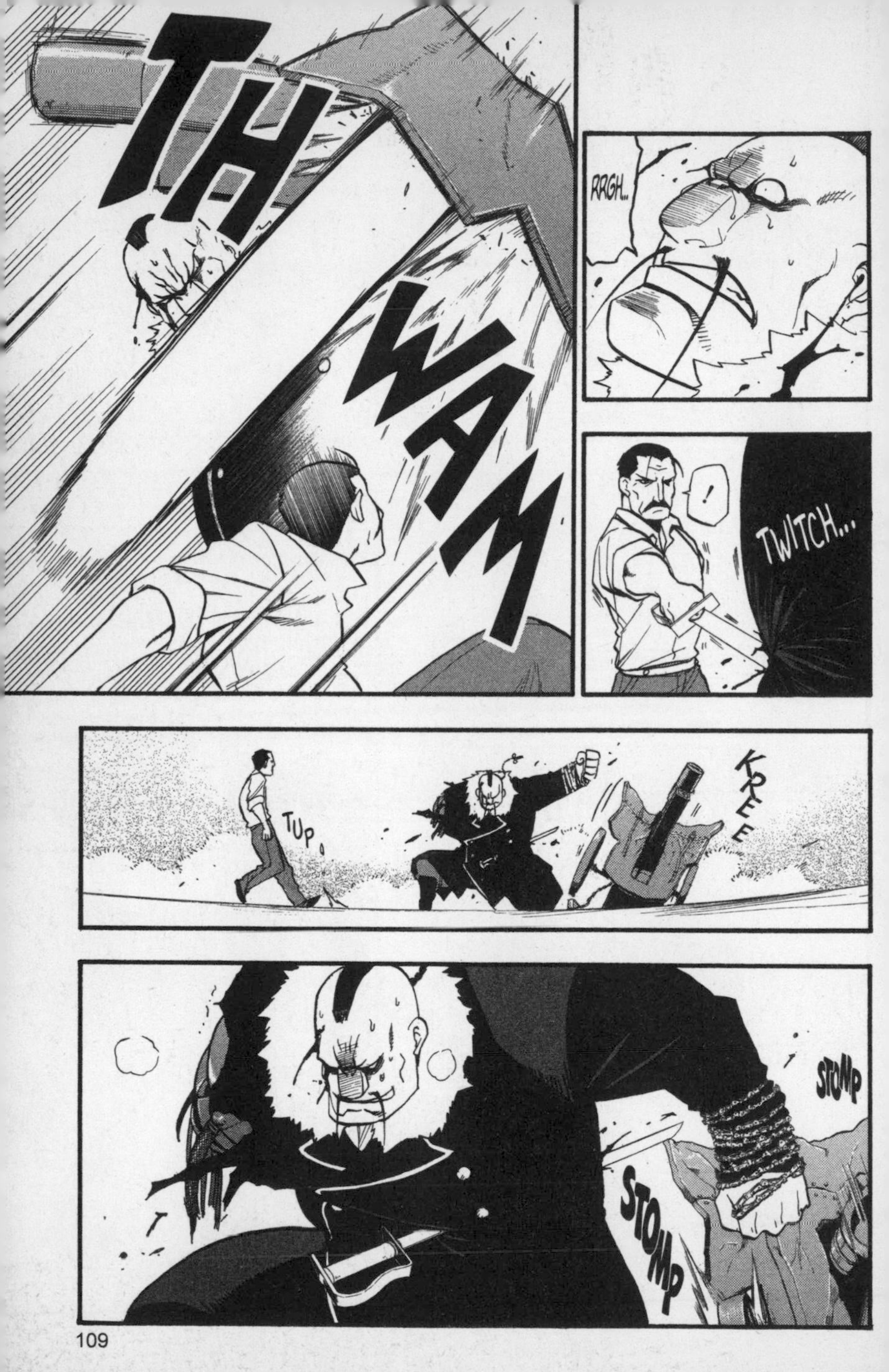
RRGH...
!
TWITCH...
TH-
WAM
KREE
TUP
STOMP
STOMP

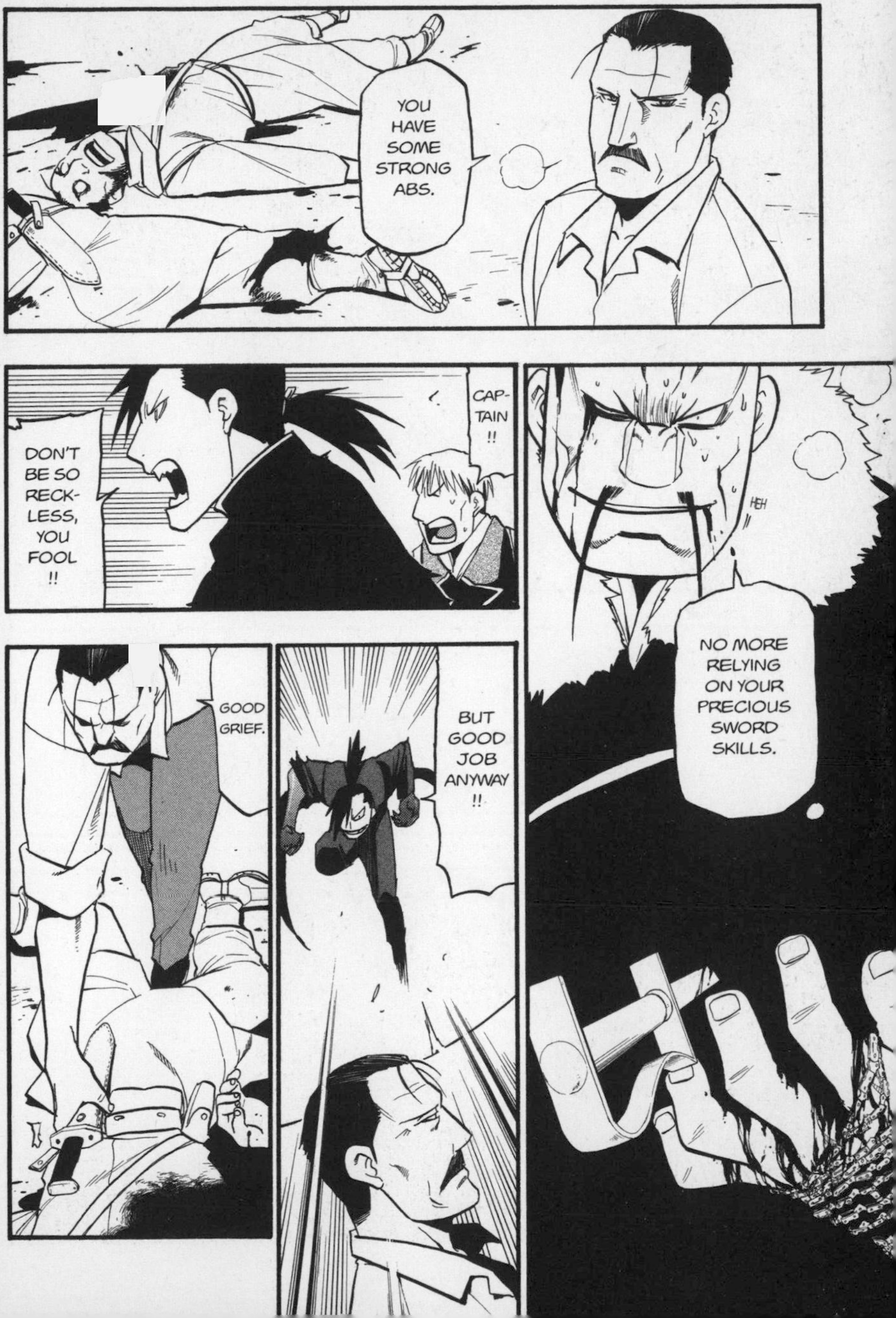
YOU HAVE SOME STRONG ABS.
HEH
NO MORE RELYING ON YOUR PRECIOUS SWORD SKILLS.
CAPTAIN!!
DON'T BE SO RECKLESS, YOU FOOL!!
BUT GOOD JOB ANYWAY!!
GOOD GRIEF.

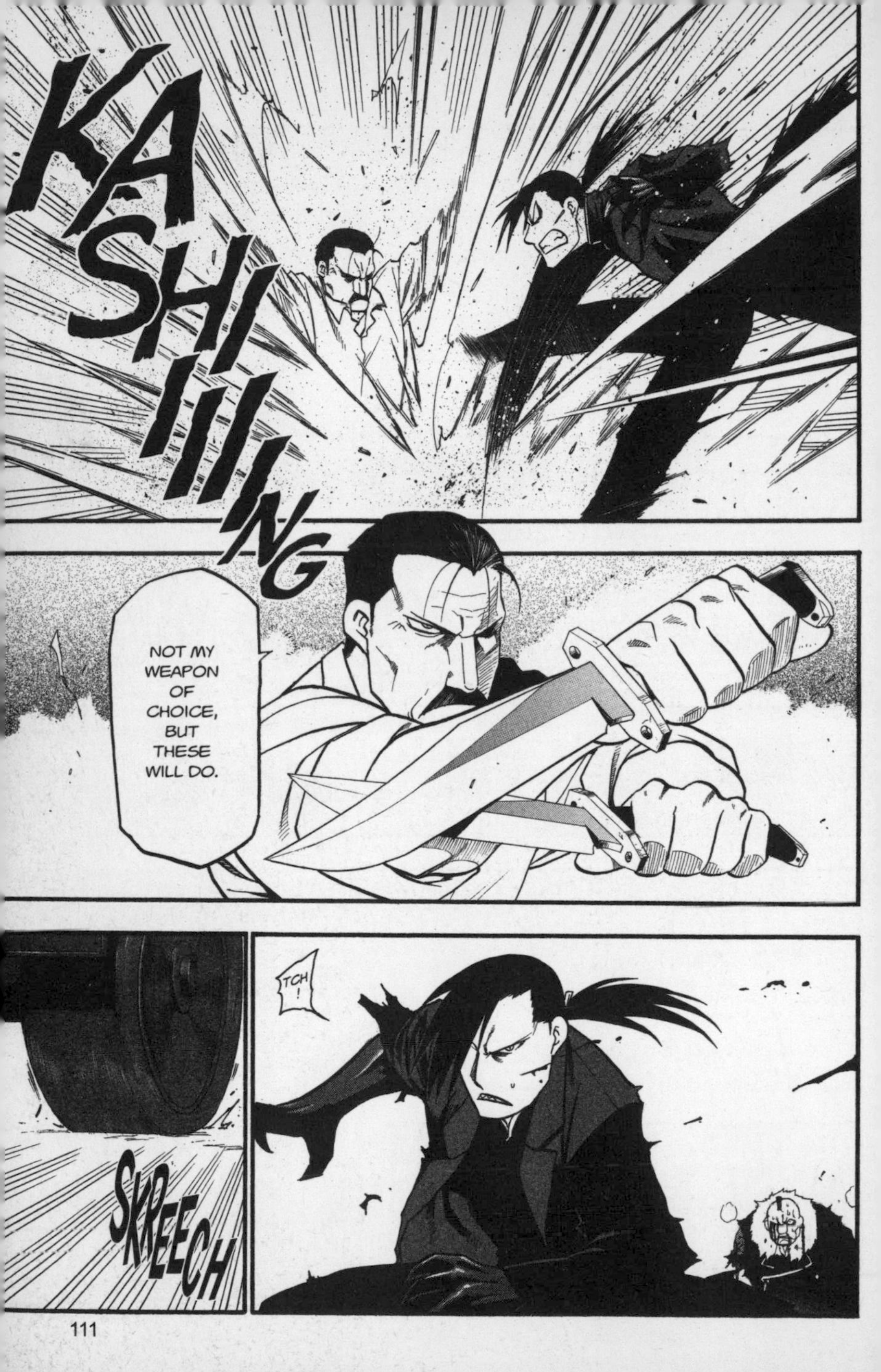
KASHIIIING
NOT MY WEAPON OF CHOICE, BUT THESE WILL DO.
TCH!
SKREECH

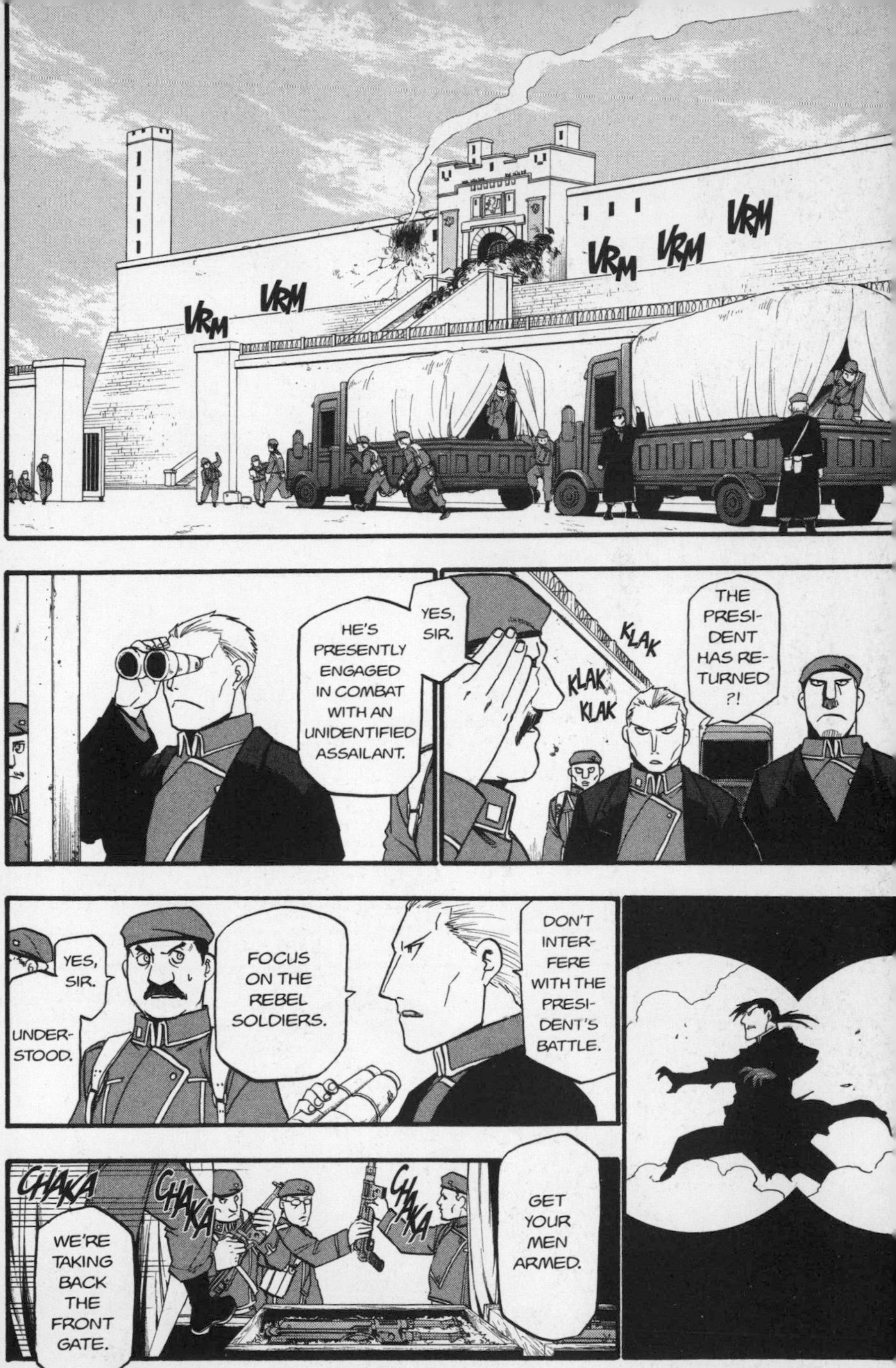
VRM
VRM
VRM
VRM
VRM
THE PRESIDENT HAS RETURNED?!
KLAK
KLAK
KLAK
YES, SIR.
HE'S PRESENTLY ENGAGED IN COMBAT WITH AN UNIDENTIFIED ASSAILANT.
DON'T INTERFERE WITH THE PRESIDENT'S BATTLE.
FOCUS ON THE REBEL SOLDIERS.
YES, SIR.
UNDERSTOOD.
GET YOUR MEN ARMED.
CHAKA
CHAKA
CHAKA
WE'RE TAKING BACK THE FRONT GATE.

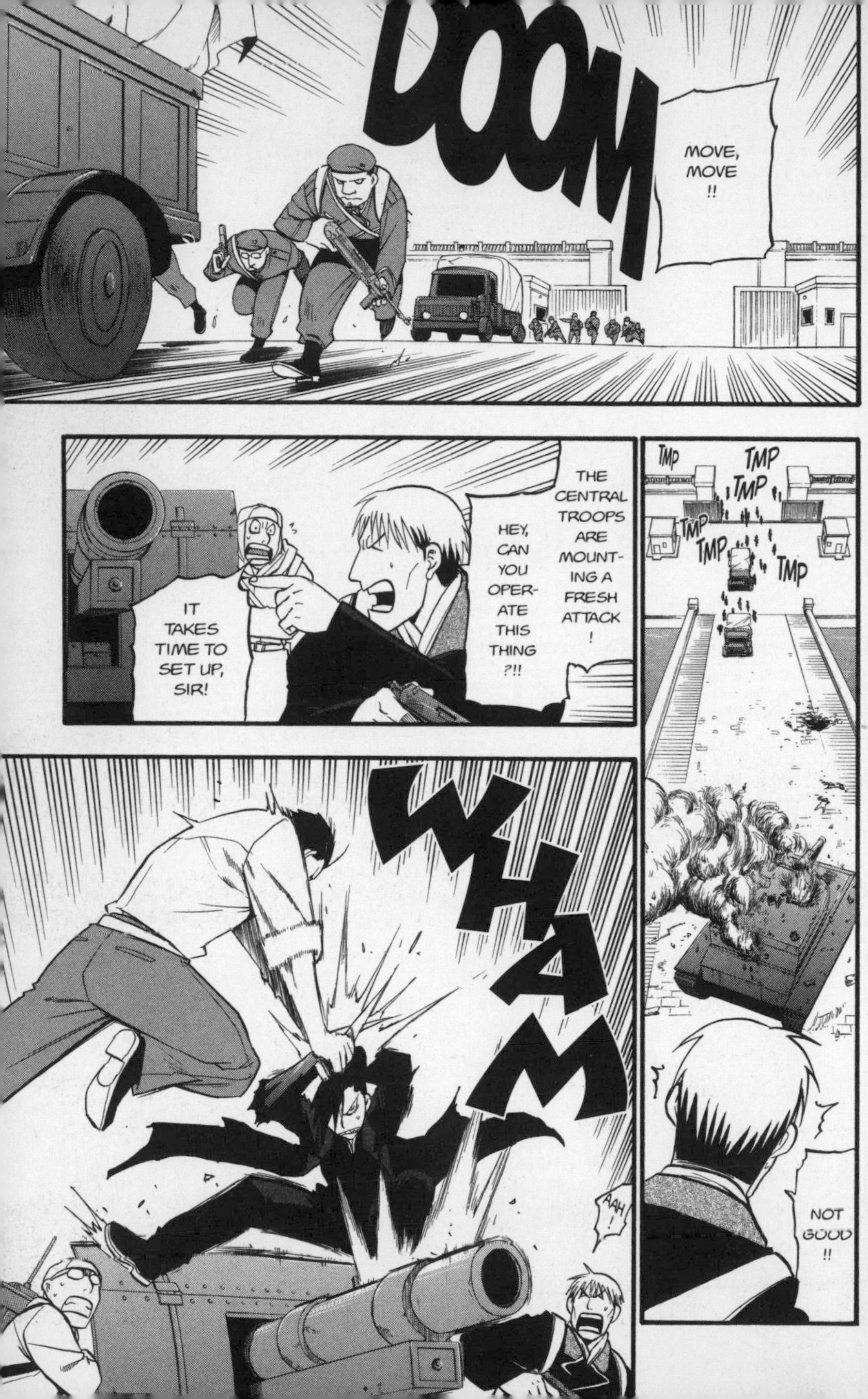
DOOM
MOVE, MOVE !!
TMP TMP TMP TMP TMP TMP
NOT GOOD !!
THE CENTRAL TROOPS ARE MOUNTING A FRESH ATTACK !
HEY, CAN YOU OPERATE THIS THING ?!!
IT TAKES TIME TO SET UP, SIR!
WHAM
AAH !

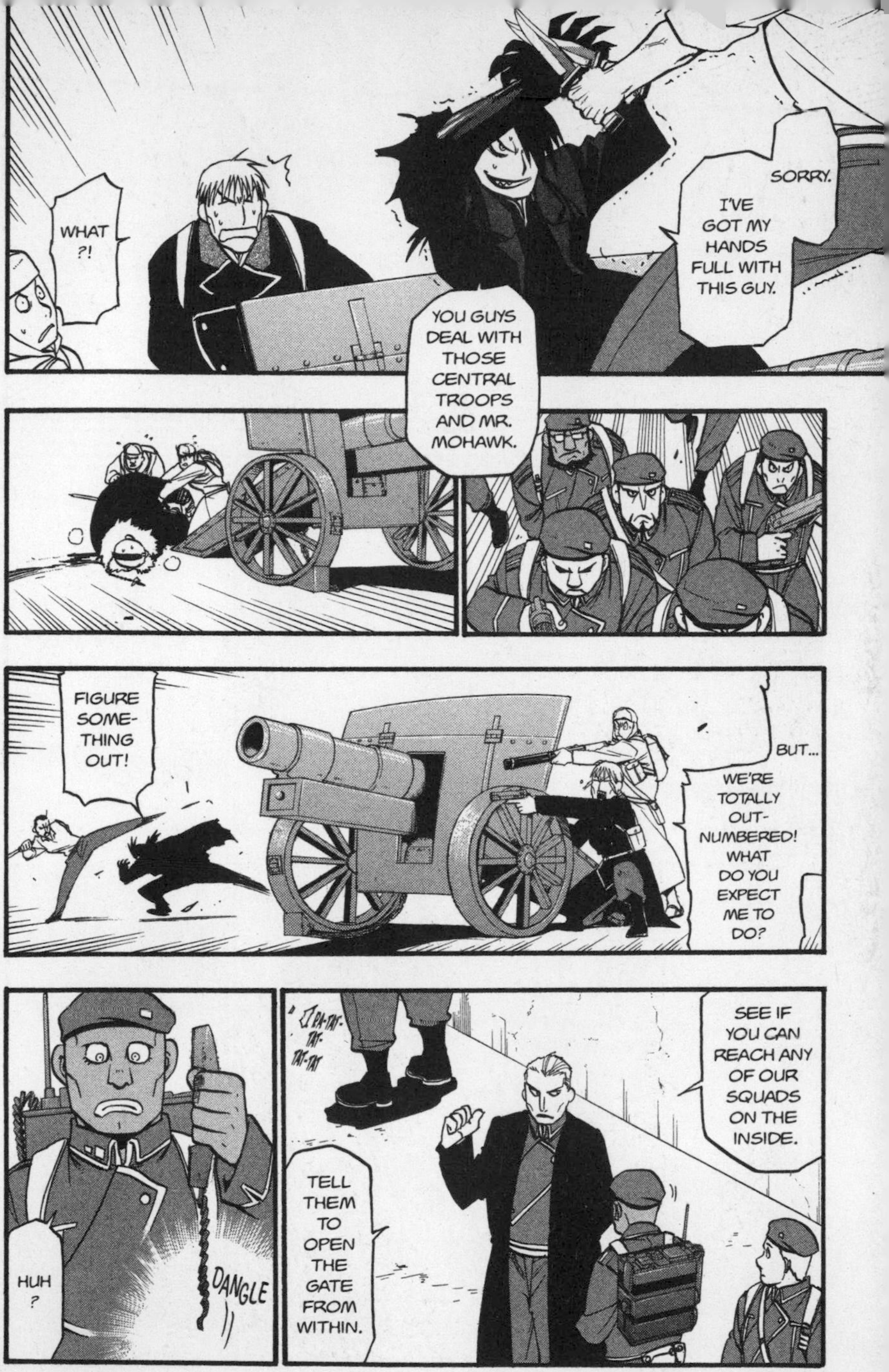
SORRY.
I'VE GOT MY HANDS FULL WITH THIS GUY.
YOU GUYS DEAL WITH THOSE CENTRAL TROOPS AND MR. MOHAWK.
WHAT ?!
BUT... WE'RE TOTALLY OUT-NUMBERED! WHAT DO YOU EXPECT ME TO DO?
FIGURE SOME-THING OUT!
SEE IF YOU CAN REACH ANY OF OUR SQUADS ON THE INSIDE.
TELL THEM TO OPEN THE GATE FROM WITHIN.
BA-TAT-TAT-TAT
DANGLE
HUH ?

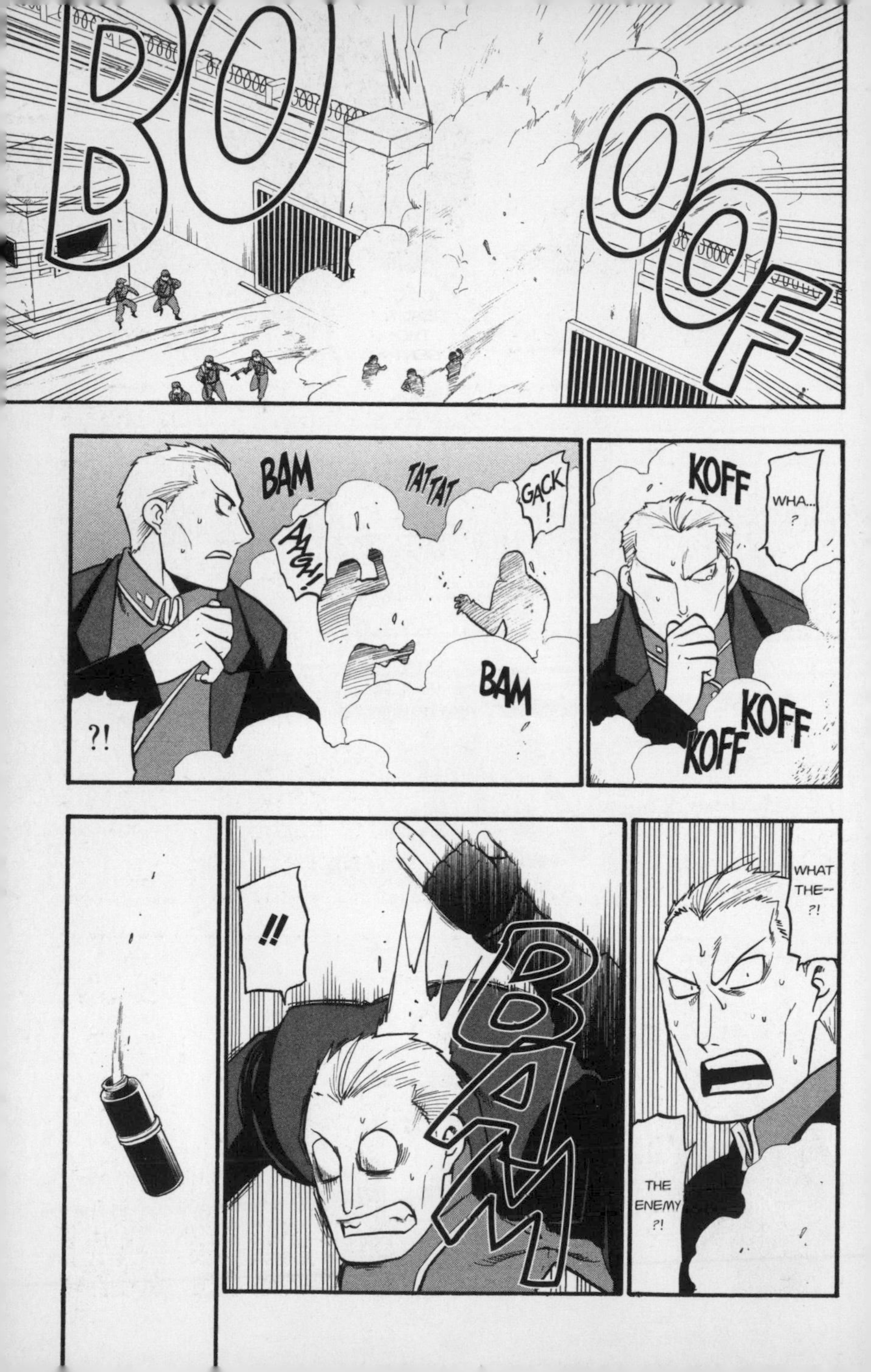
BOOOF
KOFF
WHA...?
KOFF
KOFF
GACK!
TAT TAT
BAM
AAGH!
BAM
?!
WHAT THE--?!
THE ENEMY?!
!!
BAM

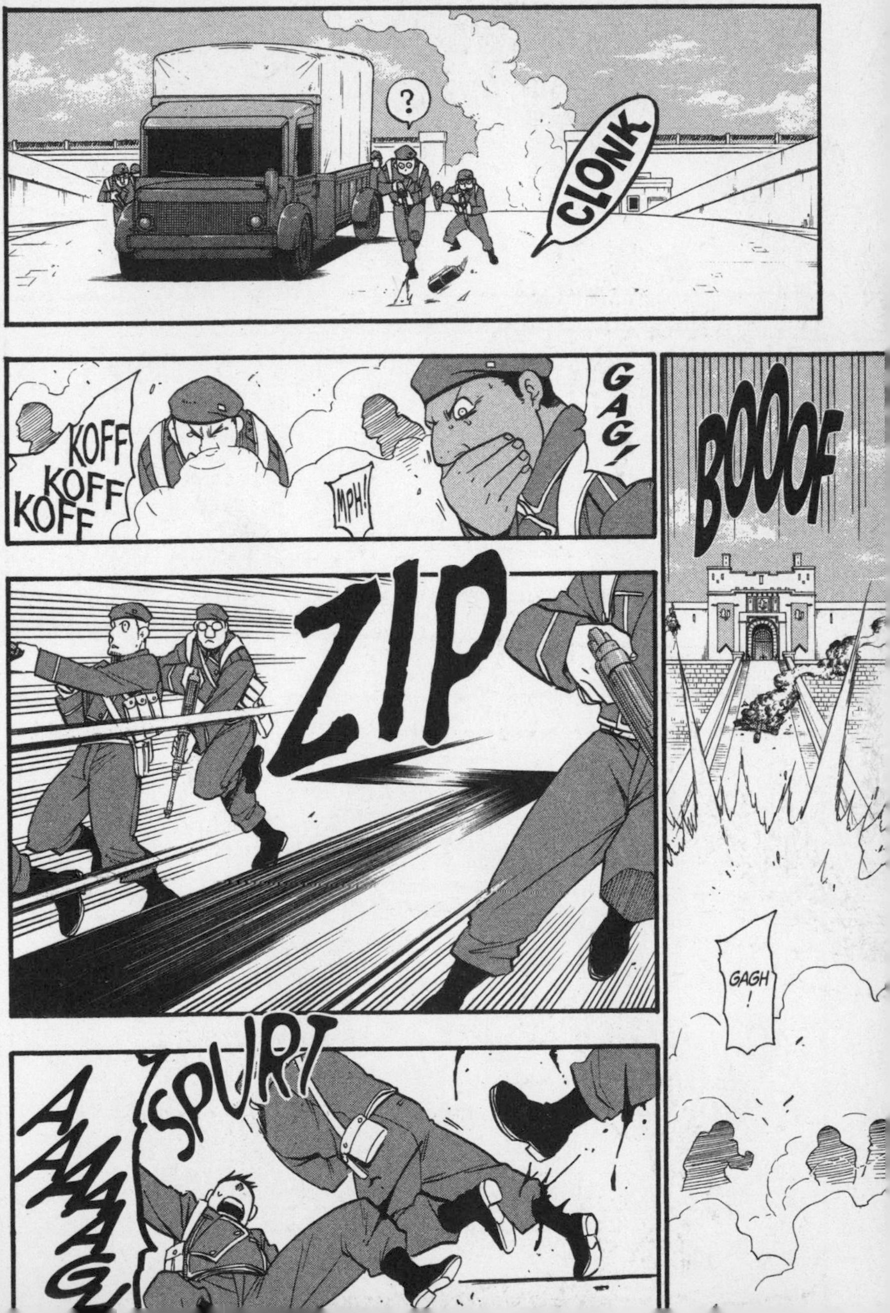
?
CLONK
BOOOF
GAGH!
GAG!
MPH!
KOFF KOFF KOFF
ZIP
SPURT

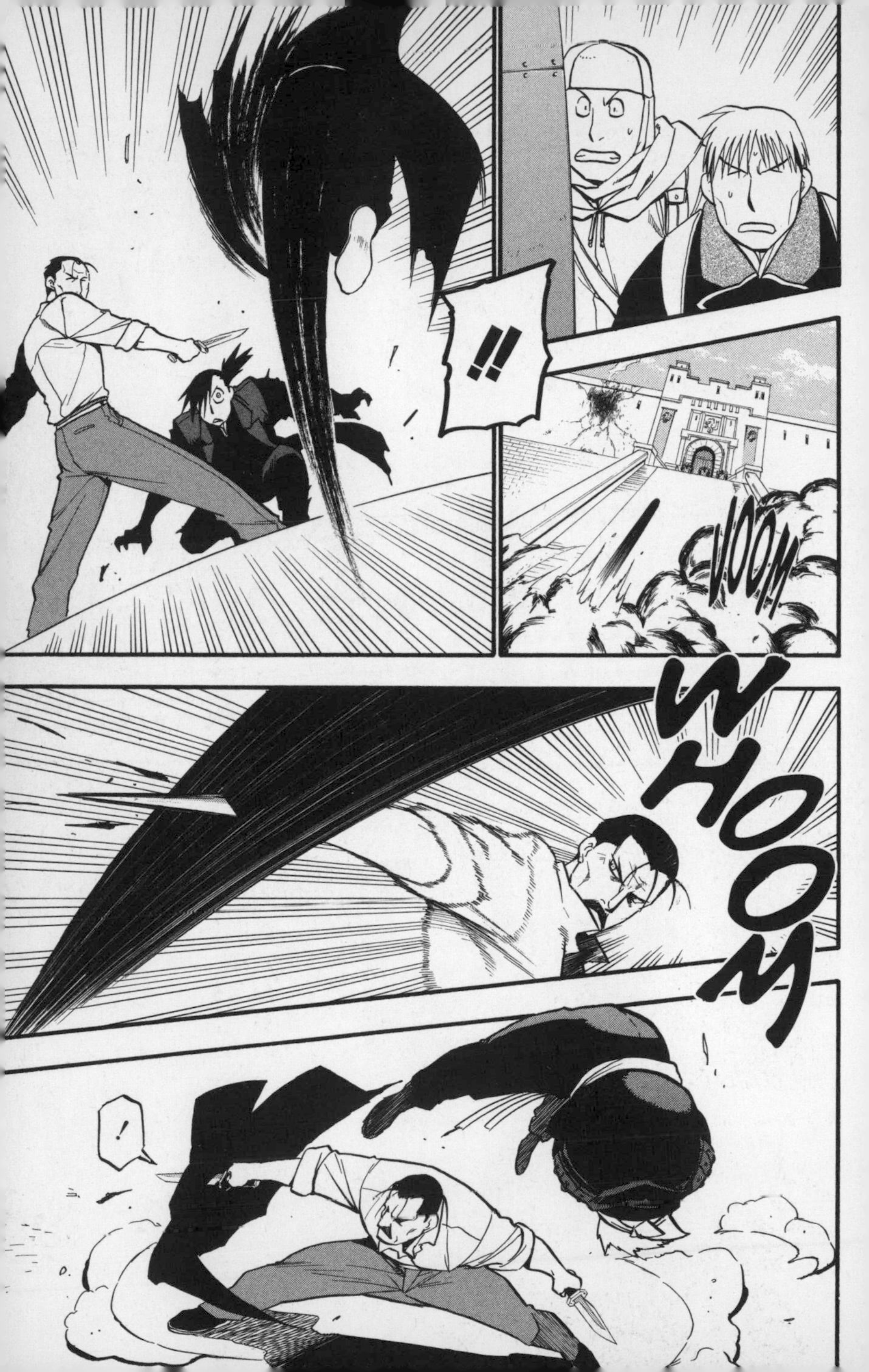
!!
VOOM
WHOOM
!

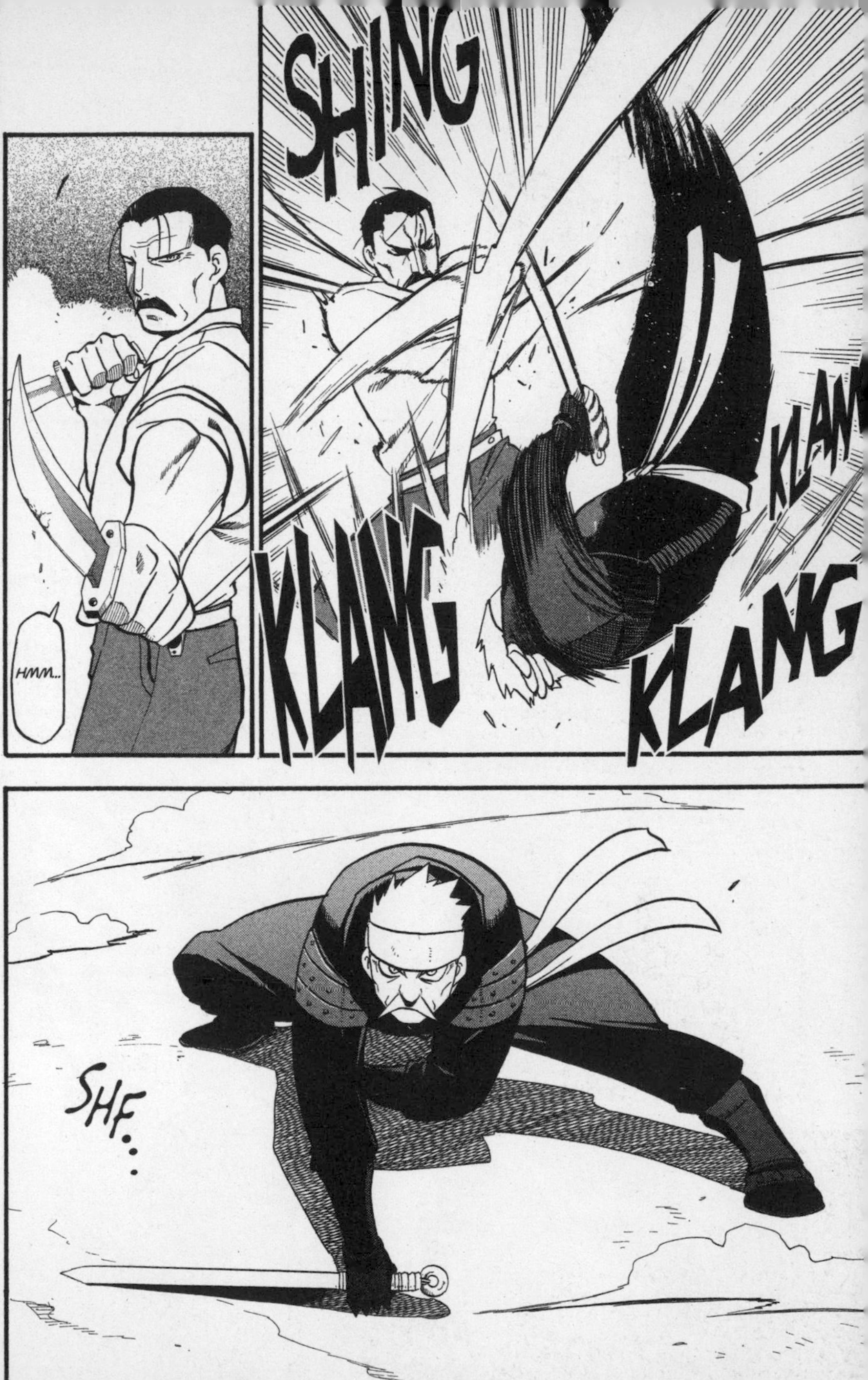
SHING
KLANG
KLAM
KLANG
HMM..
SHF...

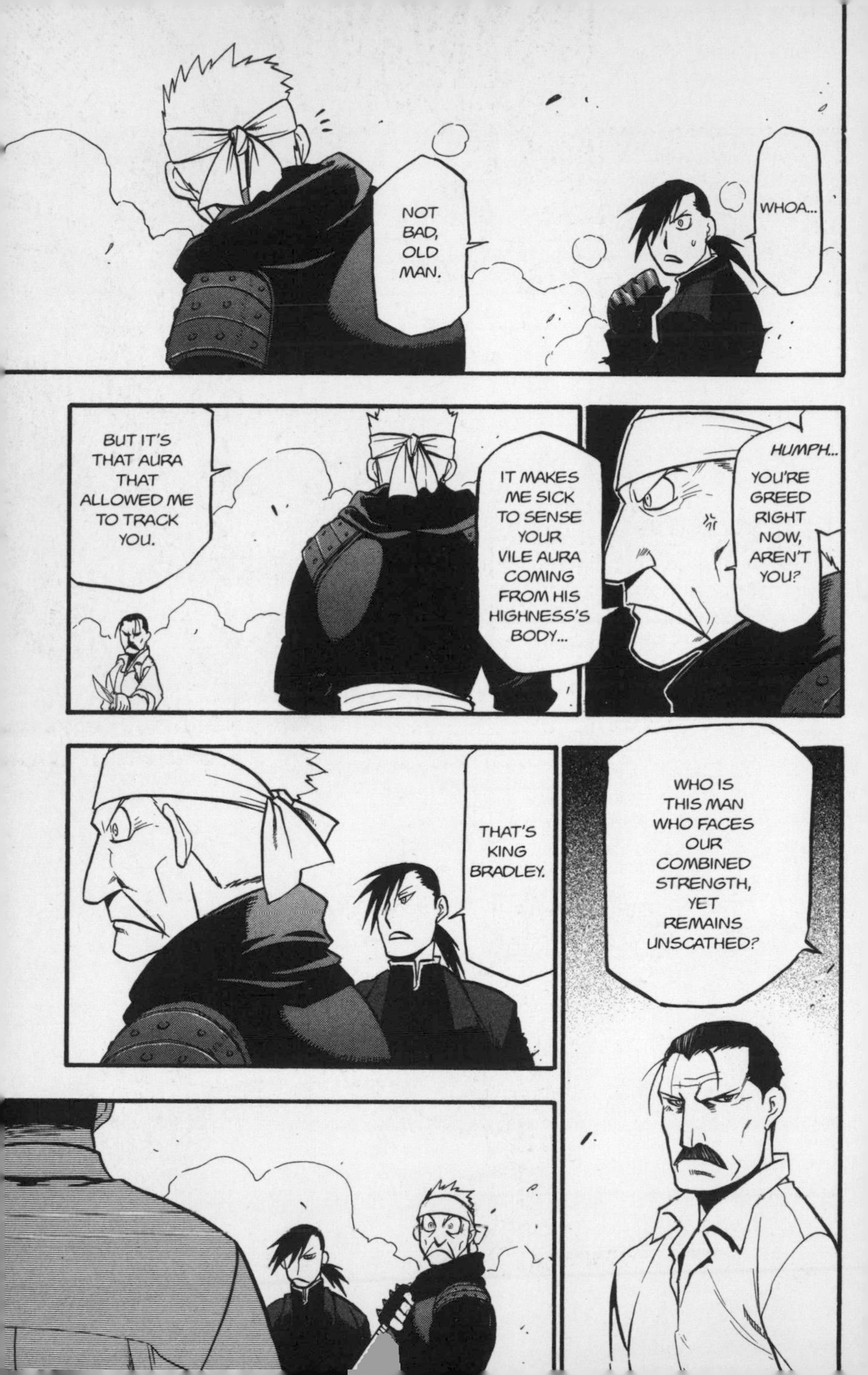
WHOA...
NOT BAD, OLD MAN.
HUMPH... YOU'RE GREED RIGHT NOW, AREN'T YOU?
IT MAKES ME SICK TO SENSE YOUR VILE AURA COMING FROM HIS HIGHNESS'S BODY...
BUT IT'S THAT AURA THAT ALLOWED ME TO TRACK YOU.
WHO IS THIS MAN WHO FACES OUR COMBINED STRENGTH, YET REMAINS UNSCATHED?
THAT'S KING BRADLEY.

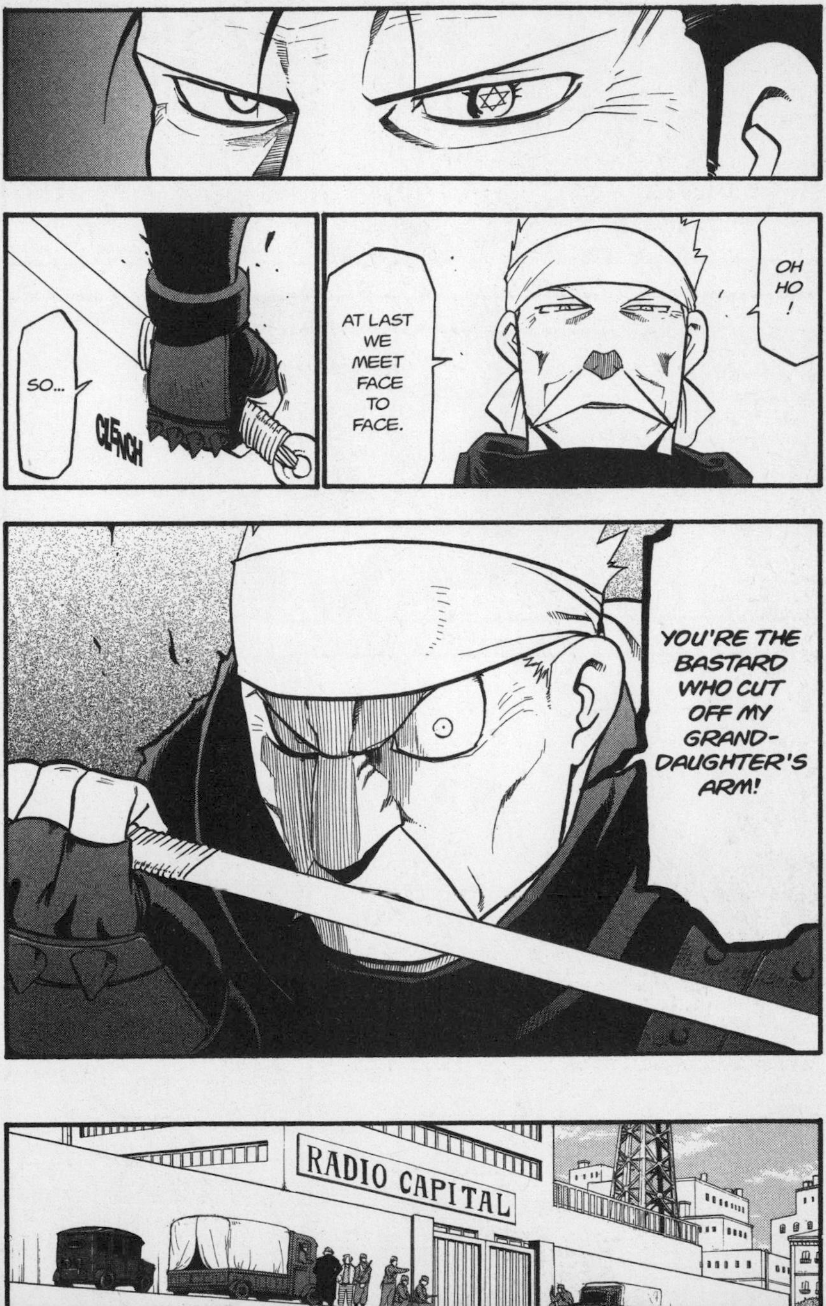
OH HO!
AT LAST WE MEET FACE TO FACE.
SO...
CLENCH
YOU'RE THE BASTARD WHO CUT OFF MY GRAND-DAUGHTER'S ARM!
RADIO CAPITAL

FIRST LADY BRADLEY!

REALLY?!

UH HUH...

!!

THE PRESIDENT HAS RETURNED!

HE'S ALIVE!

TCH!

IS SELIM SAFE?!

HE'S NOT HURT, IS HE?!

THAT WE DON'T KNOW YET.

OH... OH!

I'M SO GLAD...

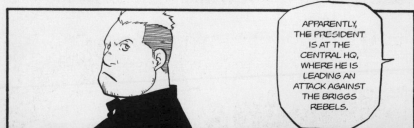

APPARENTLY, THE PRESIDENT IS AT THE CENTRAL HQ, WHERE HE IS LEADING AN ATTACK AGAINST THE BRIGGS REBELS.

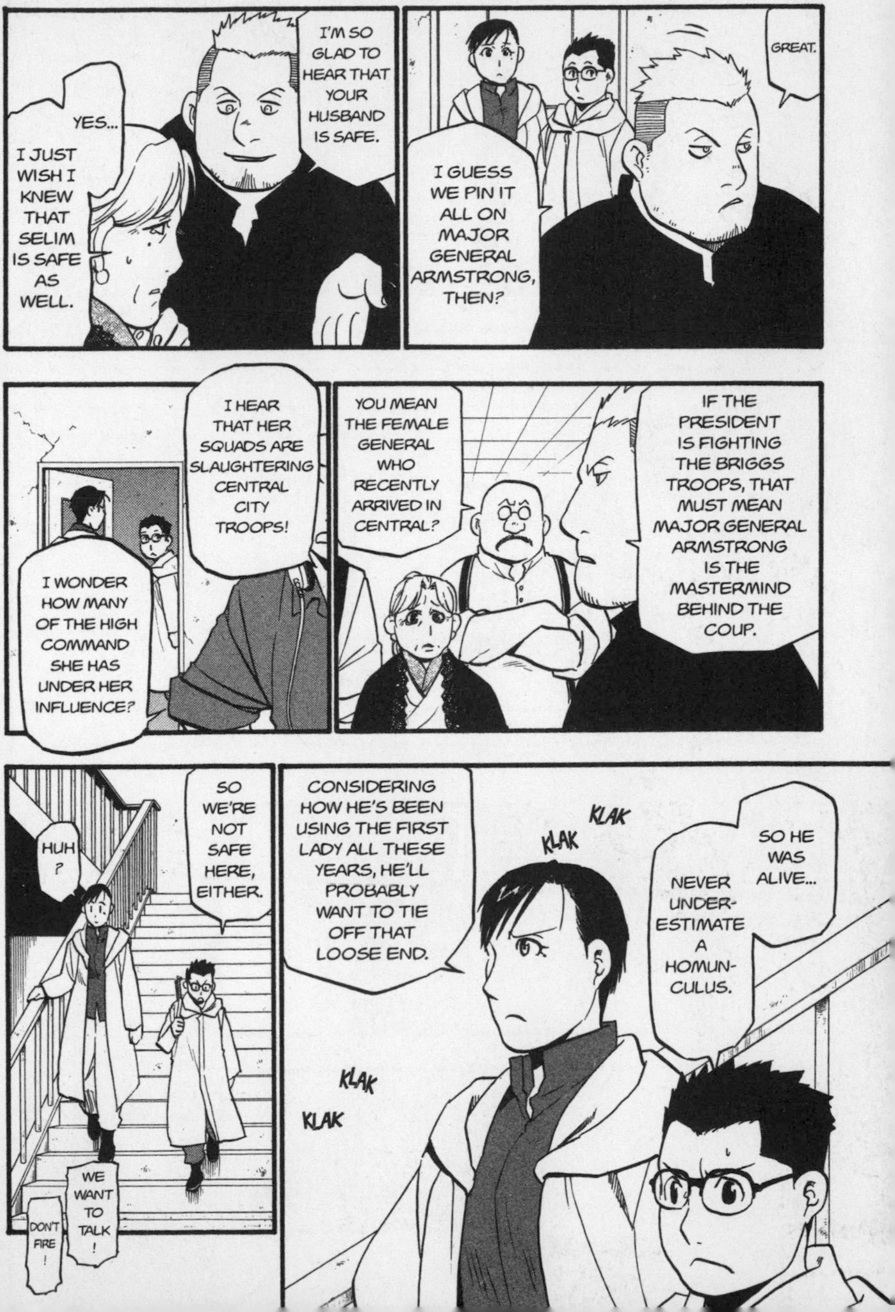
GREAT.
I GUESS WE PIN IT ALL ON MAJOR GENERAL ARMSTRONG, THEN?
I'M SO GLAD TO HEAR THAT YOUR HUSBAND IS SAFE.
YES... I JUST WISH I KNEW THAT SELIM IS SAFE AS WELL.
IF THE PRESIDENT IS FIGHTING THE BRIGGS TROOPS, THAT MUST MEAN MAJOR GENERAL ARMSTRONG IS THE MASTERMIND BEHIND THE COUP.
YOU MEAN THE FEMALE GENERAL WHO RECENTLY ARRIVED IN CENTRAL?
I HEAR THAT HER SQUADS ARE SLAUGHTERING CENTRAL CITY TROOPS!
I WONDER HOW MANY OF THE HIGH COMMAND SHE HAS UNDER HER INFLUENCE?
SO HE WAS ALIVE...
KLAK
KLAK
NEVER UNDER-ESTIMATE A HOMUN-CULUS.
CONSIDERING HOW HE'S BEEN USING THE FIRST LADY ALL THESE YEARS, HE'LL PROBABLY WANT TO TIE OFF THAT LOOSE END.
KLAK
KLAK
SO WE'RE NOT SAFE HERE, EITHER.
HUH?
WE WANT TO TALK!
DON'T FIRE!

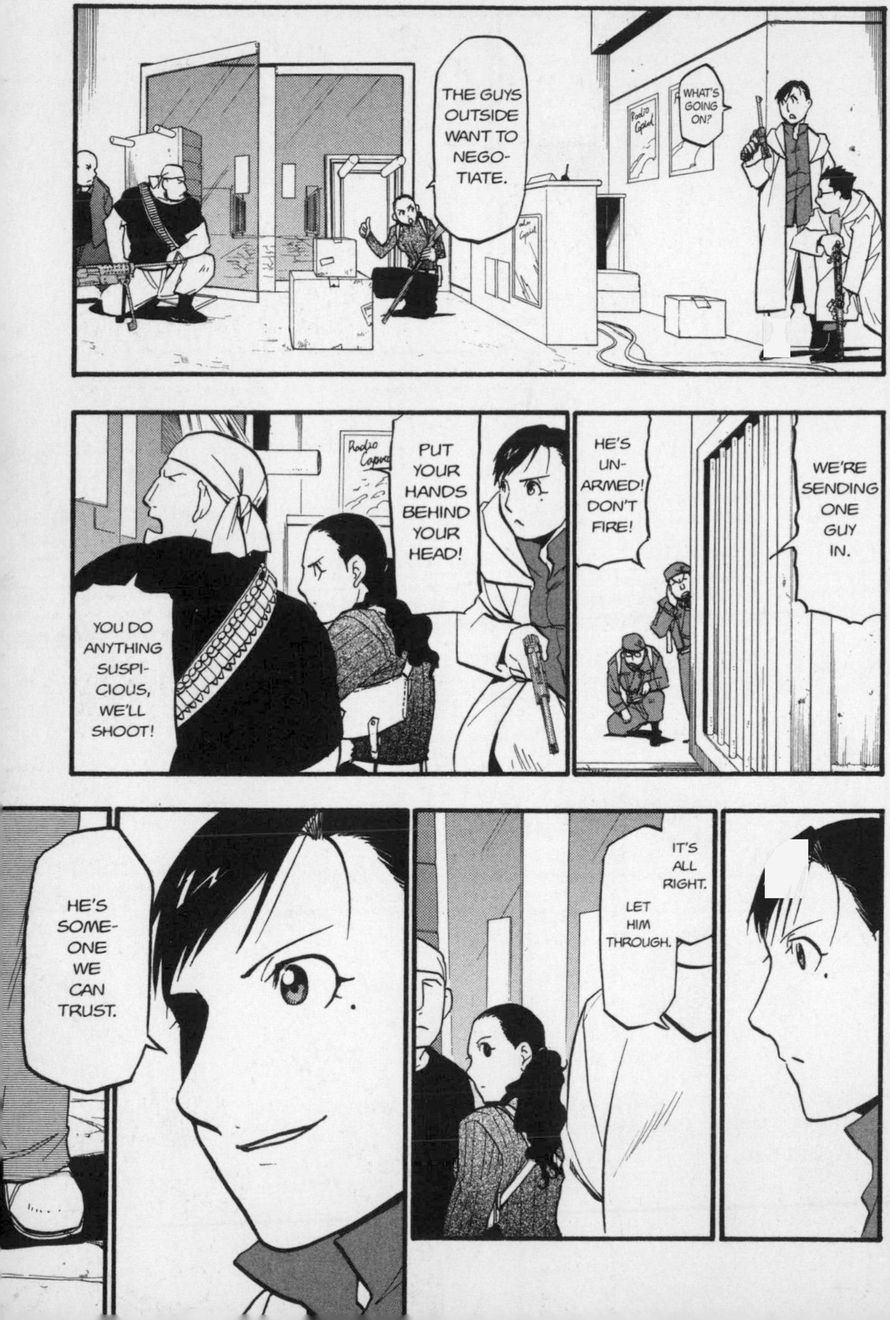
WHAT'S GOING ON?
THE GUYS OUTSIDE WANT TO NEGOTIATE.
WE'RE SENDING ONE GUY IN.
HE'S UNARMED! DON'T FIRE!
PUT YOUR HANDS BEHIND YOUR HEAD!
YOU DO ANYTHING SUSPICIOUS, WE'LL SHOOT!
IT'S ALL RIGHT.
LET HIM THROUGH.
HE'S SOMEONE WE CAN TRUST.

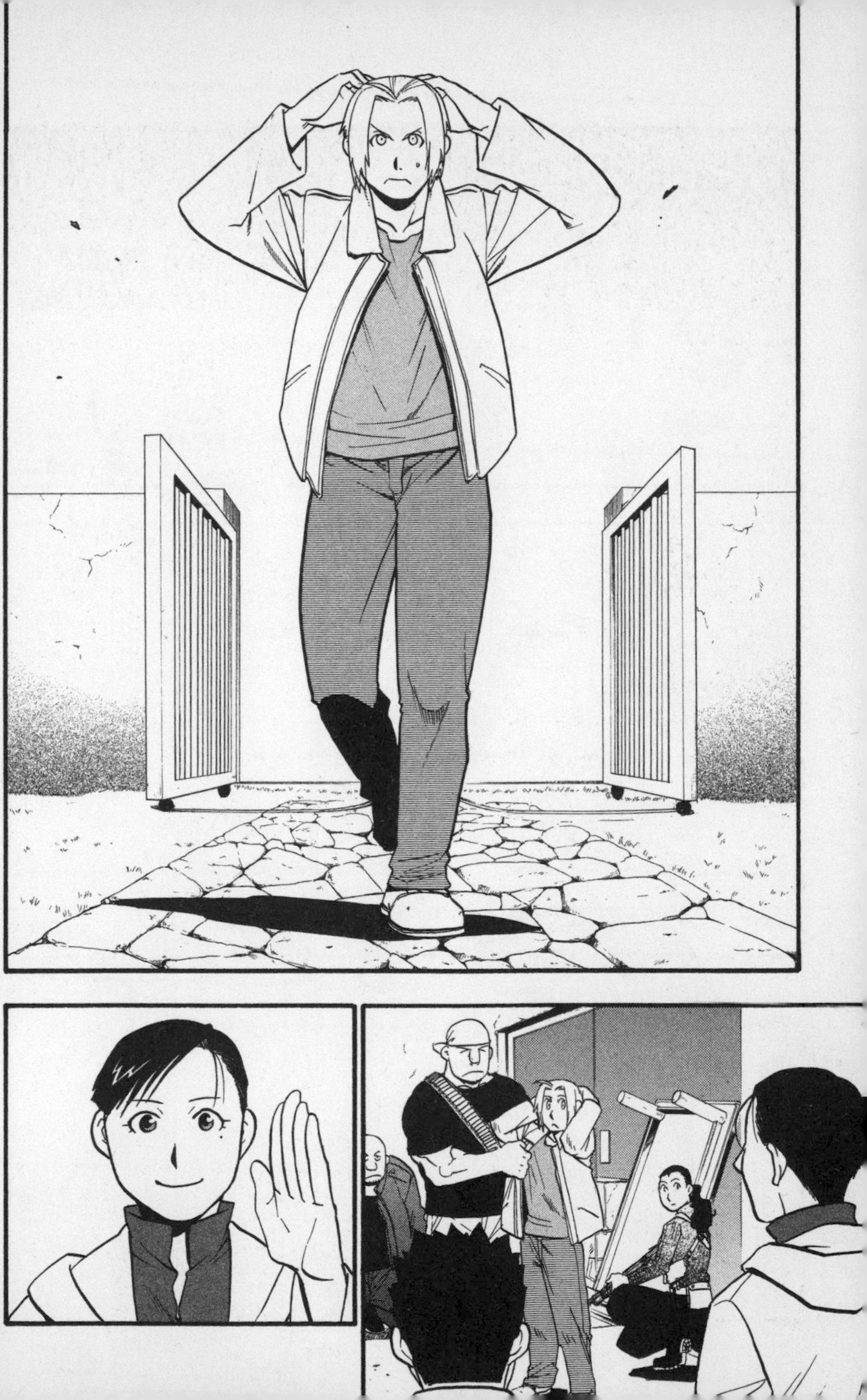

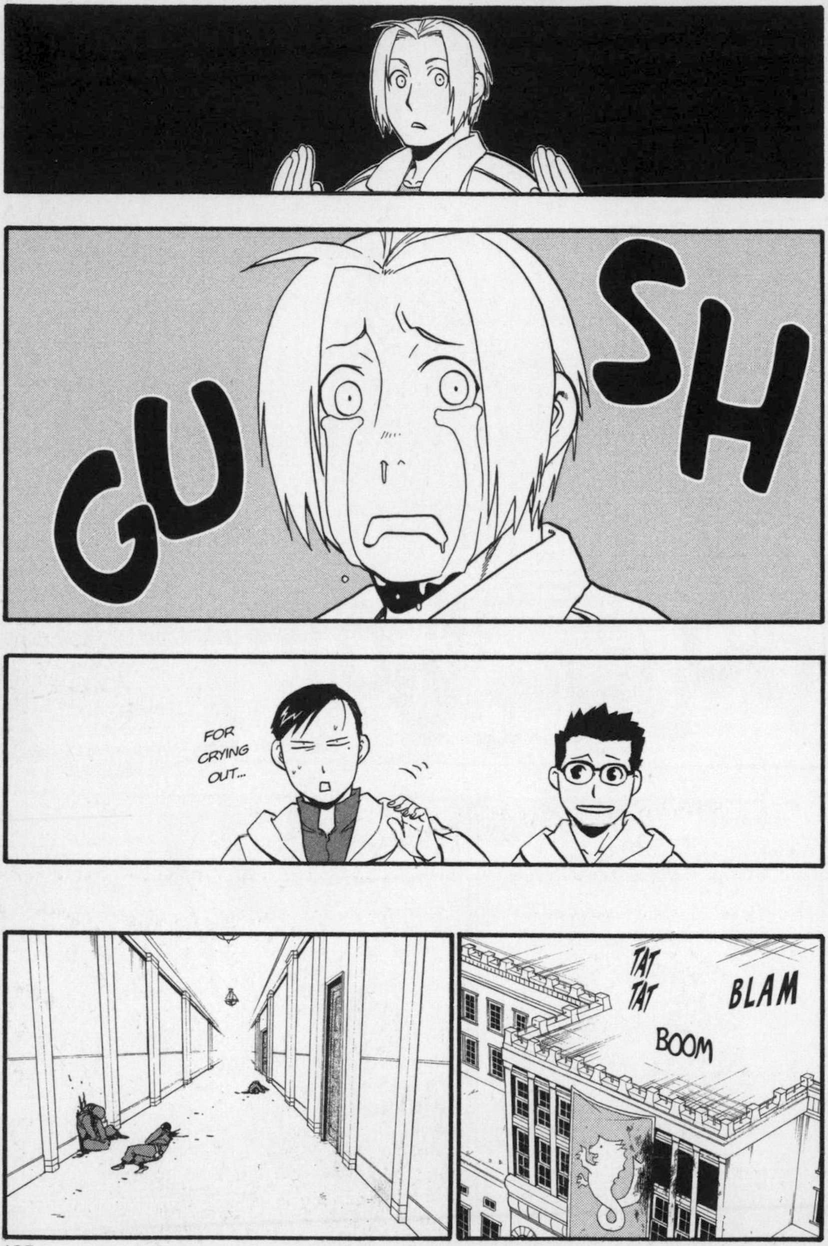
GUSH
FOR CRYING OUT...
BLAM
TAT TAT
BOOM

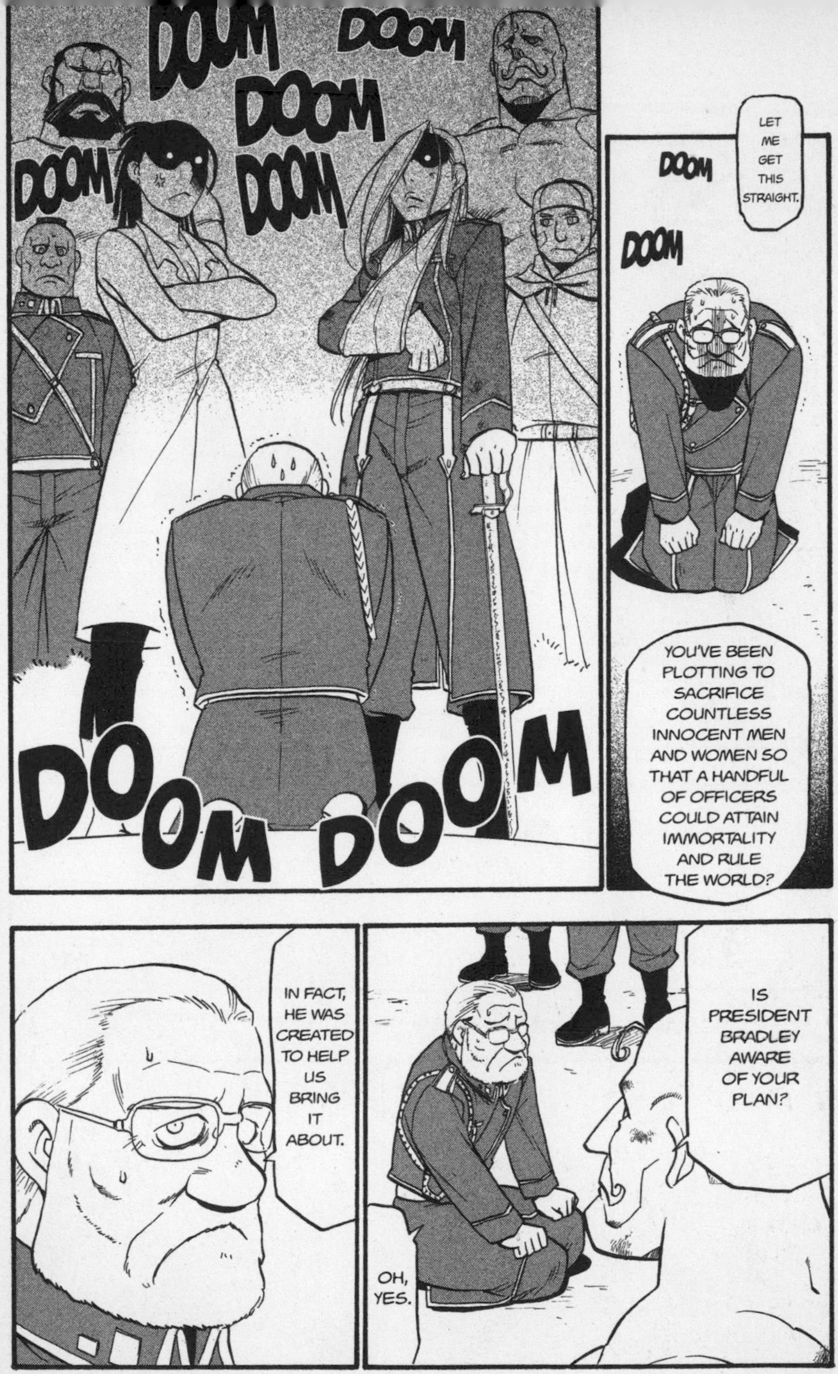
LET ME GET THIS STRAIGHT.
DOOM
DOOM
YOU'VE BEEN PLOTTING TO SACRIFICE COUNTLESS INNOCENT MEN AND WOMEN SO THAT A HANDFUL OF OFFICERS COULD ATTAIN IMMORTALITY AND RULE THE WORLD?
DOOM
DOOM
DOOM
DOOM
DOOM
DOOM
DOOOM DOOOM
IS PRESIDENT BRADLEY AWARE OF YOUR PLAN?
OH, YES.
IN FACT, HE WAS CREATED TO HELP US BRING IT ABOUT.

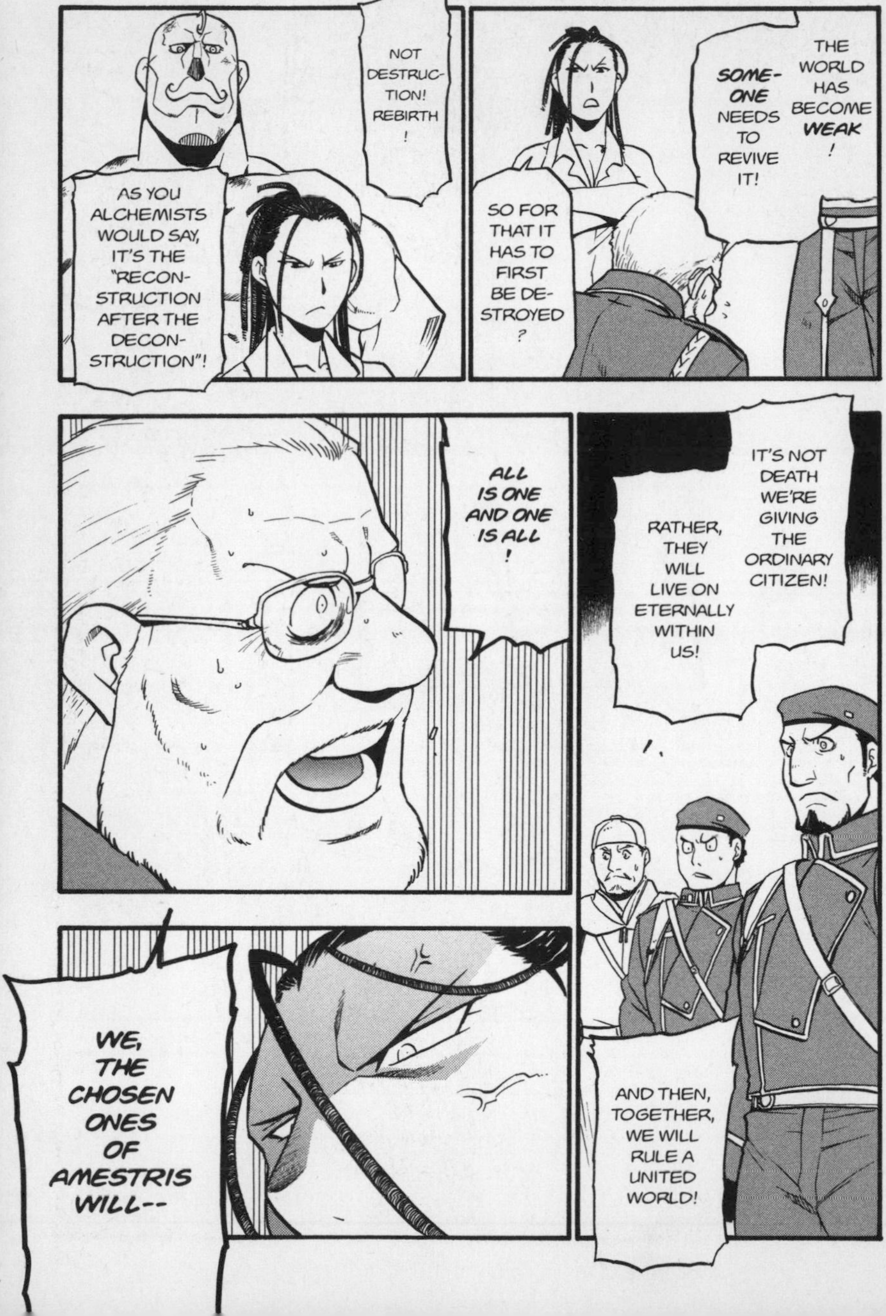
THE WORLD HAS BECOME WEAK!
SOME-ONE NEEDS TO REVIVE IT!
SO FOR THAT IT HAS TO FIRST BE DE-STROYED?
NOT DESTRUC-TION! REBIRTH!
AS YOU ALCHEMISTS WOULD SAY, IT'S THE "RECON-STRUCTION AFTER THE DECON-STRUCTION"!
IT'S NOT DEATH WE'RE GIVING THE ORDINARY CITIZEN!
RATHER, THEY WILL LIVE ON ETERNALLY WITHIN US!
AND THEN, TOGETHER, WE WILL RULE A UNITED WORLD!
ALL IS ONE AND ONE IS ALL!
WE, THE CHOSEN ONES OF AMESTRIS WILL--

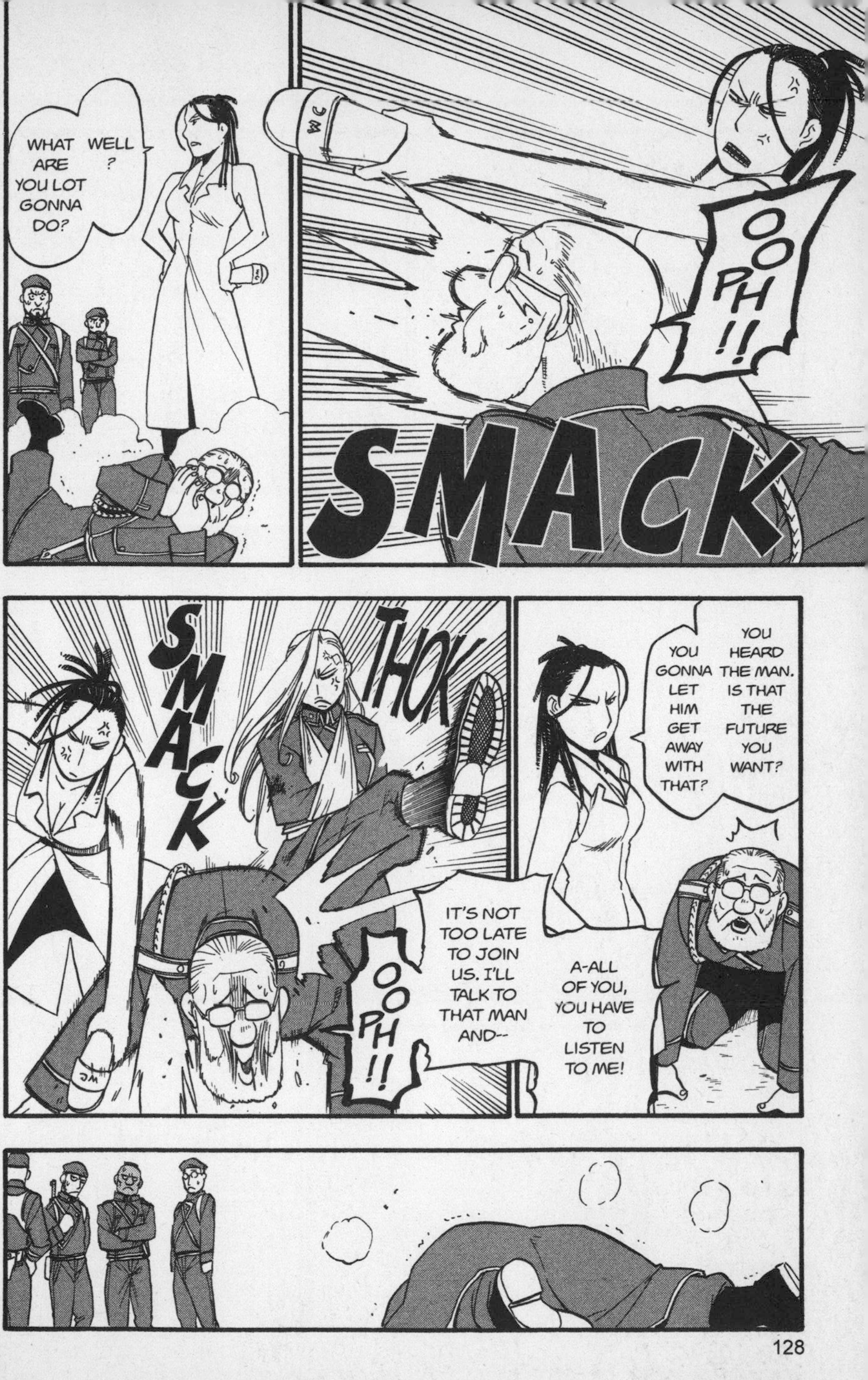
OOPH!!
SMACK
WELL?
WHAT ARE YOU LOT GONNA DO?
YOU HEARD THE MAN. IS THAT THE FUTURE YOU WANT?
YOU GONNA LET HIM GET AWAY WITH THAT?
A-ALL OF YOU, YOU HAVE TO LISTEN TO ME!
IT'S NOT TOO LATE TO JOIN US. I'LL TALK TO THAT MAN AND--
OOPH!!
THOK
SMACK

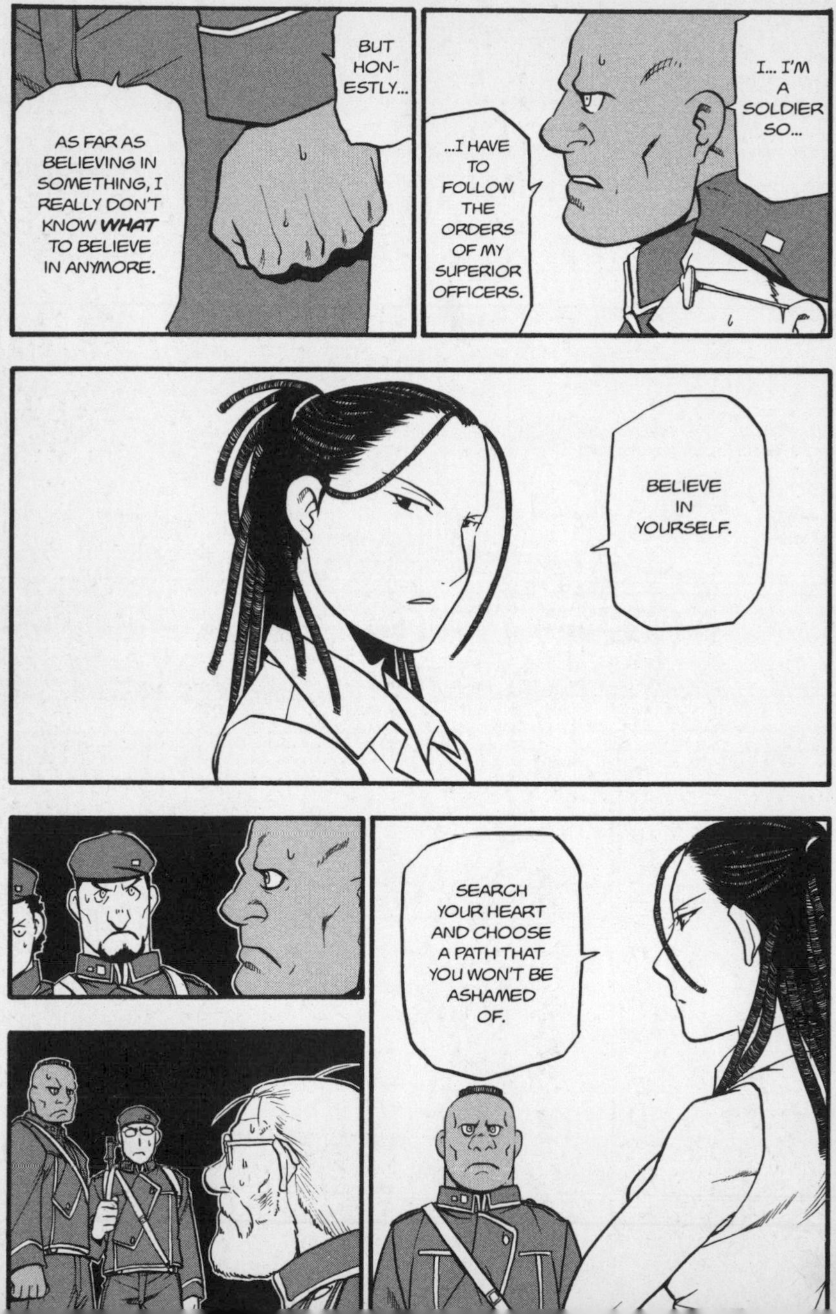
I... I'M A SOLDIER SO...
...I HAVE TO FOLLOW THE ORDERS OF MY SUPERIOR OFFICERS.
BUT HON-ESTLY...
AS FAR AS BELIEVING IN SOMETHING, I REALLY DON'T KNOW WHAT TO BELIEVE IN ANYMORE.
BELIEVE IN YOURSELF.
SEARCH YOUR HEART AND CHOOSE A PATH THAT YOU WON'T BE ASHAMED OF.

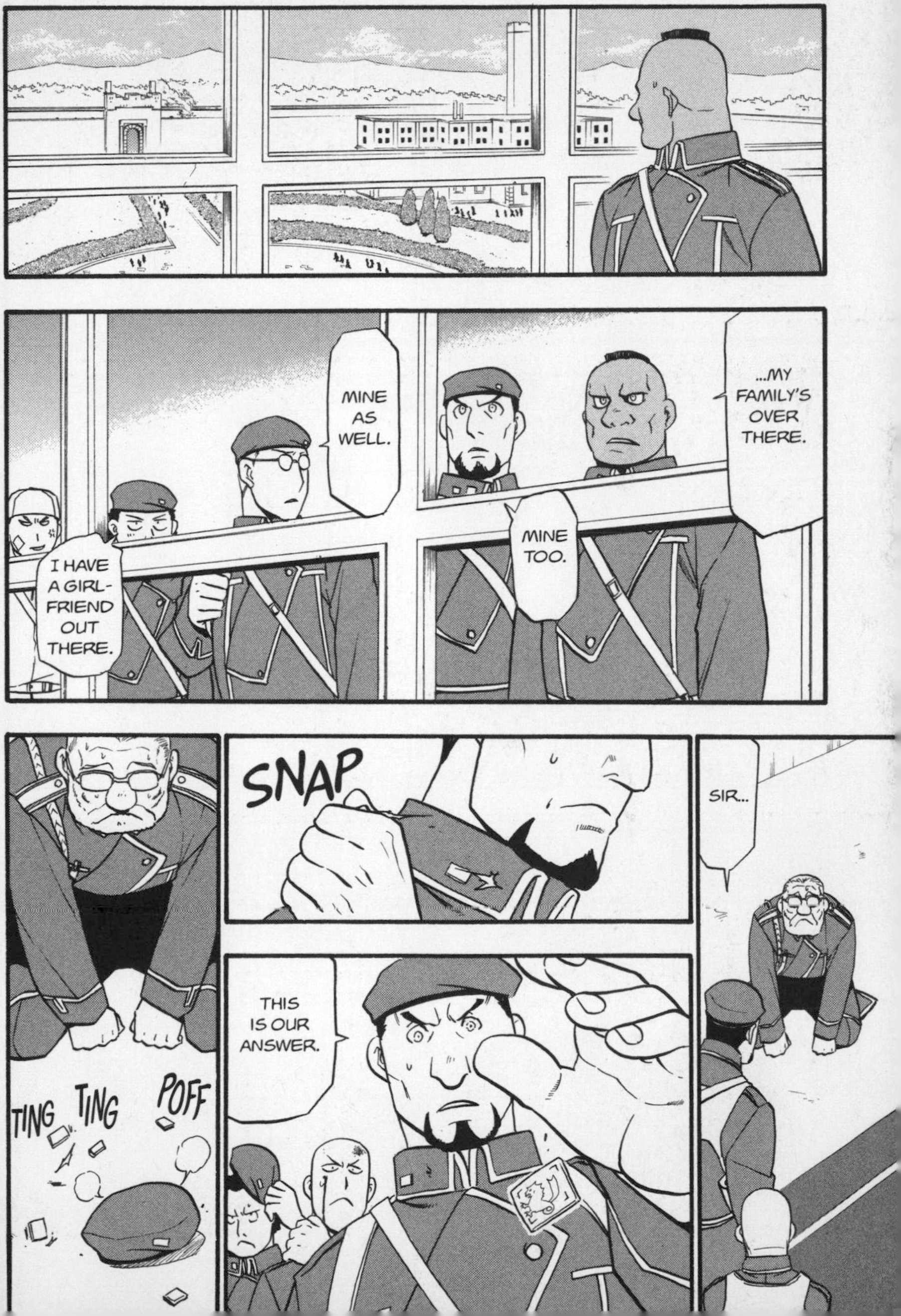
...MY FAMILY'S OVER THERE.
MINE AS WELL.
MINE TOO.
I HAVE A GIRL-FRIEND OUT THERE.
SIR...
SNAP
THIS IS OUR ANSWER.
TING
TING
POFF

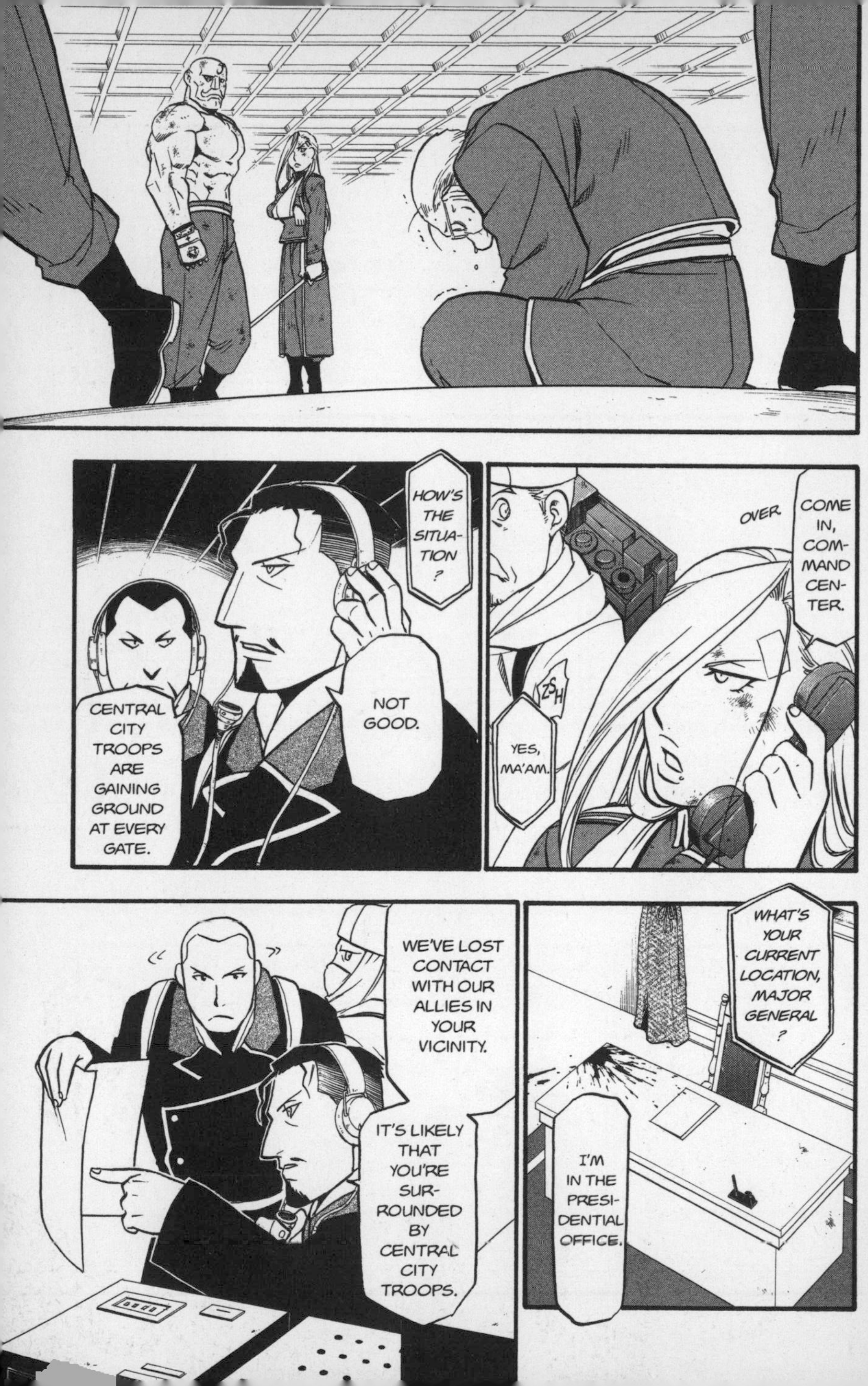
COME IN, COMMAND CENTER.
OVER
ZSH
YES, MA'AM.
HOW'S THE SITUATION?
NOT GOOD.
CENTRAL CITY TROOPS ARE GAINING GROUND AT EVERY GATE.
WHAT'S YOUR CURRENT LOCATION, MAJOR GENERAL?
I'M IN THE PRESIDENTIAL OFFICE.
WE'VE LOST CONTACT WITH OUR ALLIES IN YOUR VICINITY.
IT'S LIKELY THAT YOU'RE SURROUNDED BY CENTRAL CITY TROOPS.

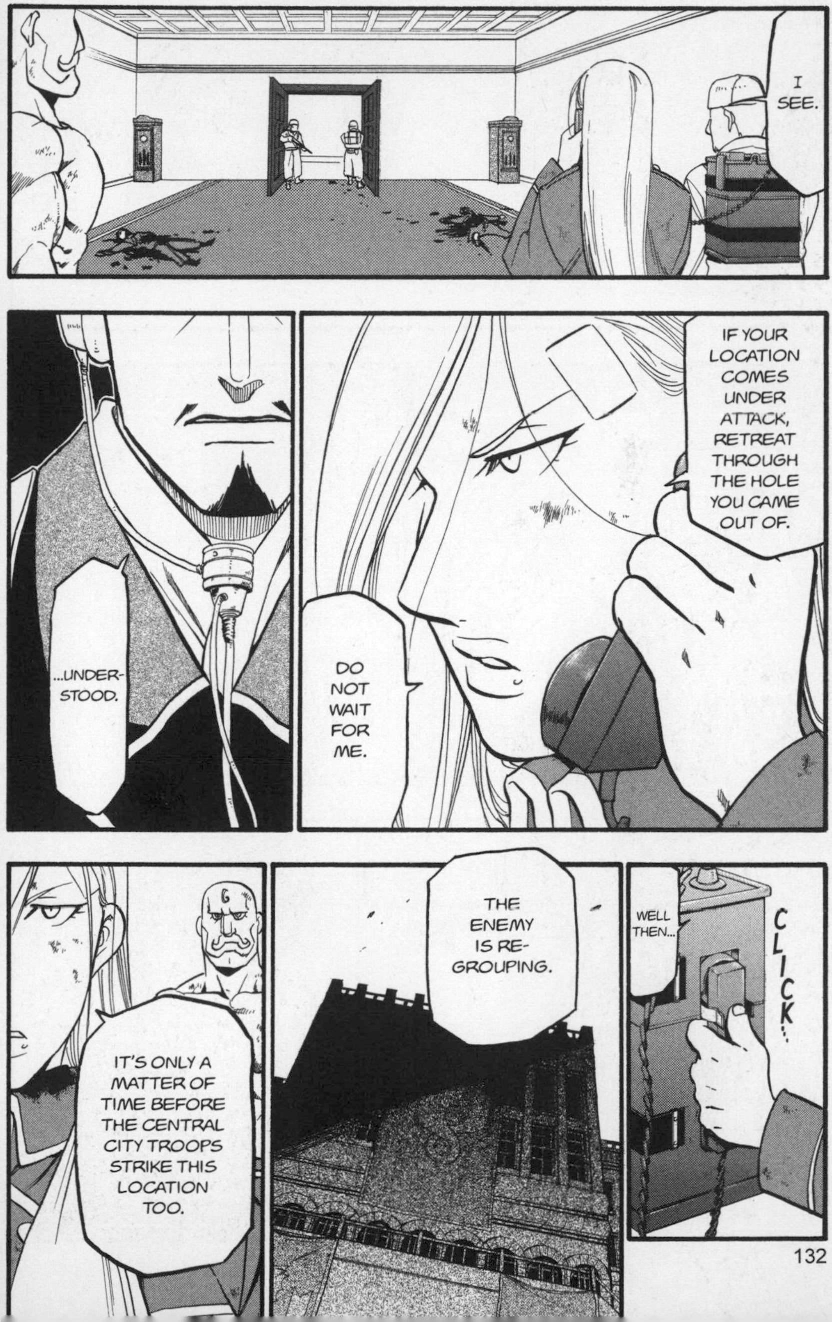
I SEE.
IF YOUR LOCATION COMES UNDER ATTACK, RETREAT THROUGH THE HOLE YOU CAME OUT OF.
DO NOT WAIT FOR ME.
...UNDER-STOOD.
WELL THEN...
CLICK...
THE ENEMY IS RE-GROUPING.
IT'S ONLY A MATTER OF TIME BEFORE THE CENTRAL CITY TROOPS STRIKE THIS LOCATION TOO.

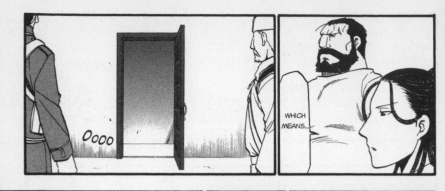

OOOO

WHICH MEANS...

THAT'S STRANGE.

GWOOM

DOWN IT IS.

I COULDA SWORN IT WAS THIS WAY...

OR WAS IT THAT WAY...?

GWOOM

GWOOM

HMM...

GWOOM

GWOOM

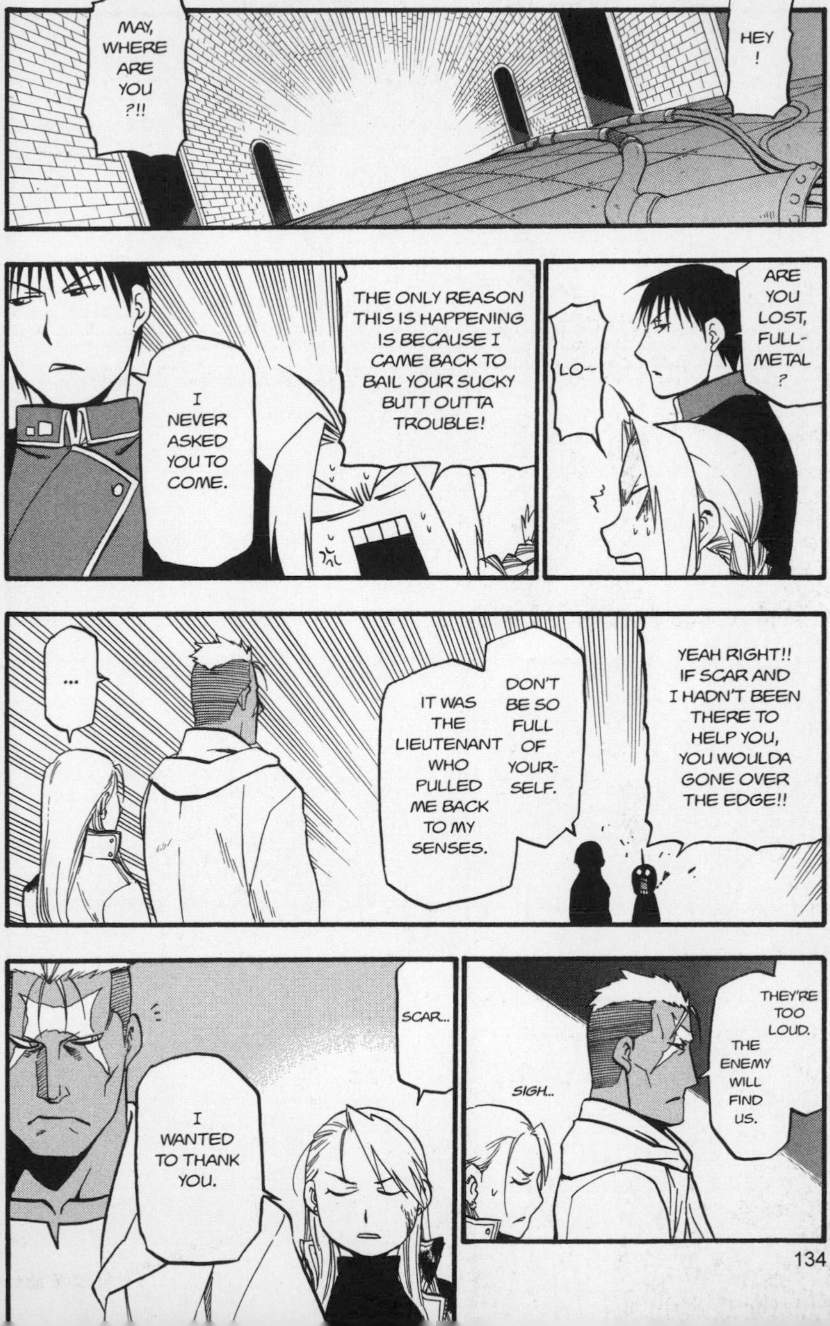
HEY!
MAY, WHERE ARE YOU?!!
ARE YOU LOST, FULL-METAL?
LO--
THE ONLY REASON THIS IS HAPPENING IS BECAUSE I CAME BACK TO BAIL YOUR SUCKY BUTT OUTTA TROUBLE!
I NEVER ASKED YOU TO COME.
YEAH RIGHT!! IF SCAR AND I HADN'T BEEN THERE TO HELP YOU, YOU WOULDA GONE OVER THE EDGE!!
DON'T BE SO FULL OF YOUR-SELF.
IT WAS THE LIEUTENANT WHO PULLED ME BACK TO MY SENSES.
...
THEY'RE TOO LOUD.
THE ENEMY WILL FIND US.
SIGH...
SCAR...
I WANTED TO THANK YOU.

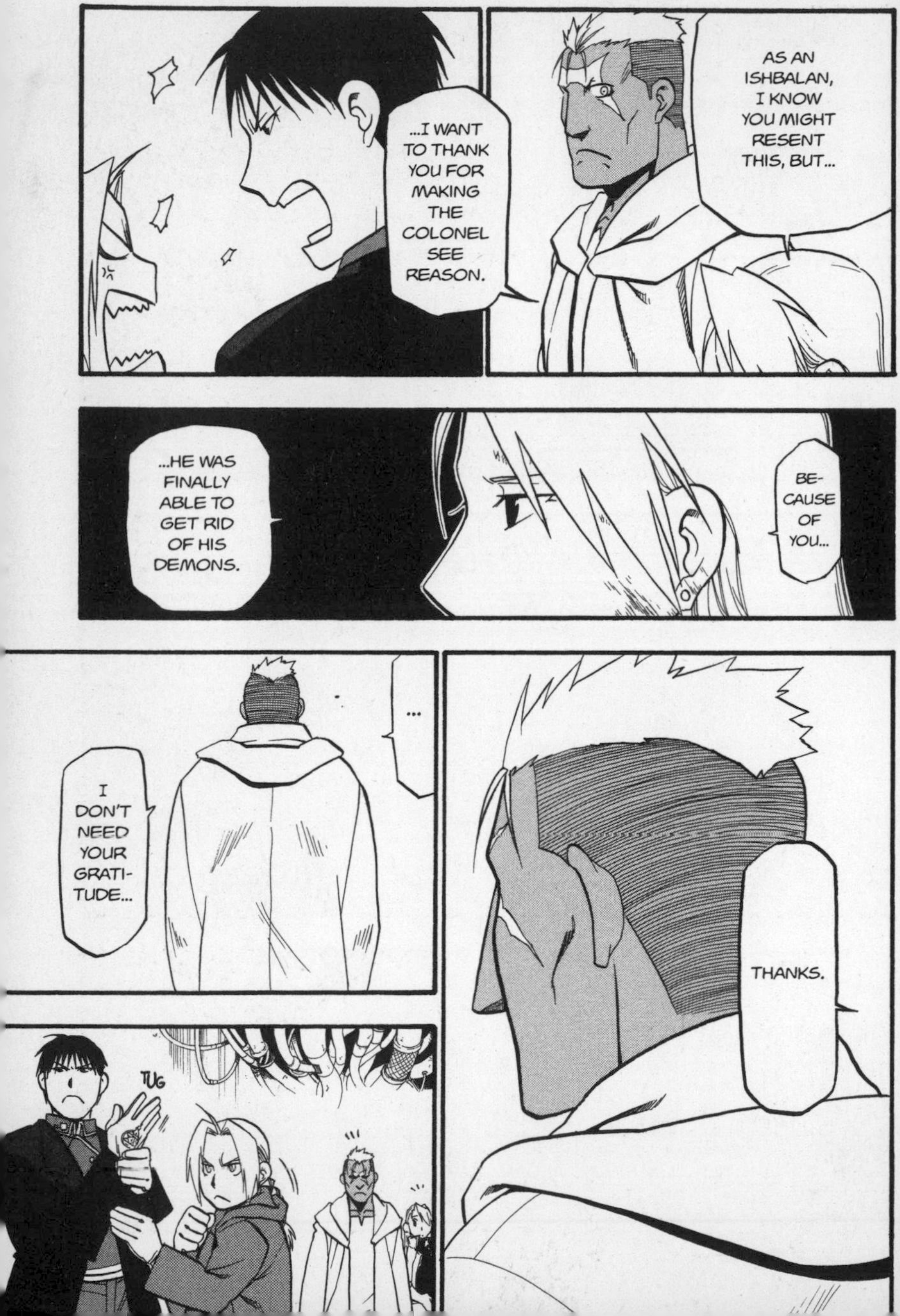
AS AN ISHBALAN, I KNOW YOU MIGHT RESENT THIS, BUT...
...I WANT TO THANK YOU FOR MAKING THE COLONEL SEE REASON.
BE-CAUSE OF YOU...
...HE WAS FINALLY ABLE TO GET RID OF HIS DEMONS.
THANKS.
...
I DON'T NEED YOUR GRATI-TUDE...
TUG

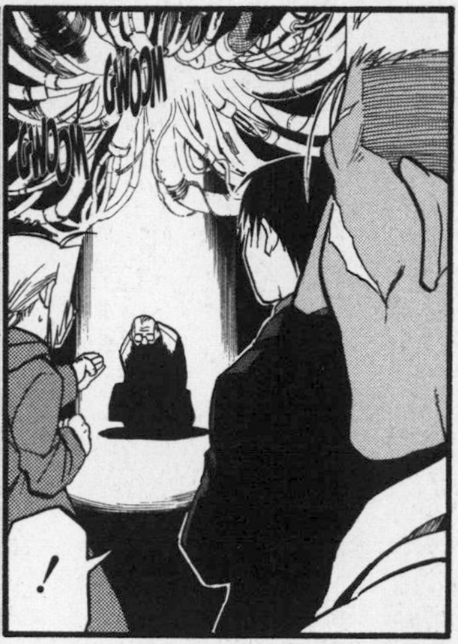
GWOOM
GWOOM
GWOOM
!
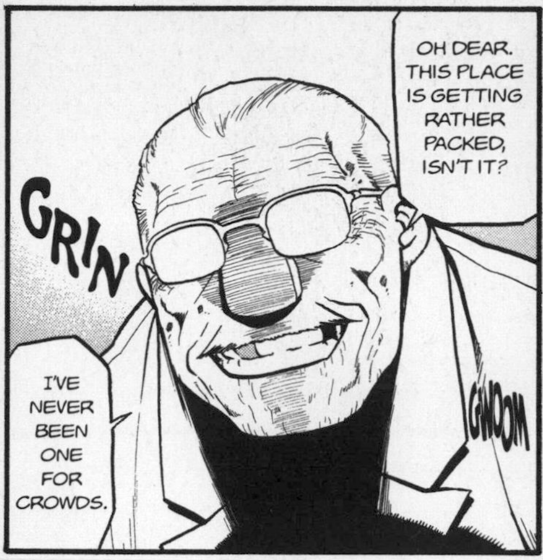
OH DEAR. THIS PLACE IS GETTING RATHER PACKED, ISN'T IT?
GRIN
I'VE NEVER BEEN ONE FOR CROWDS.
GWOOM
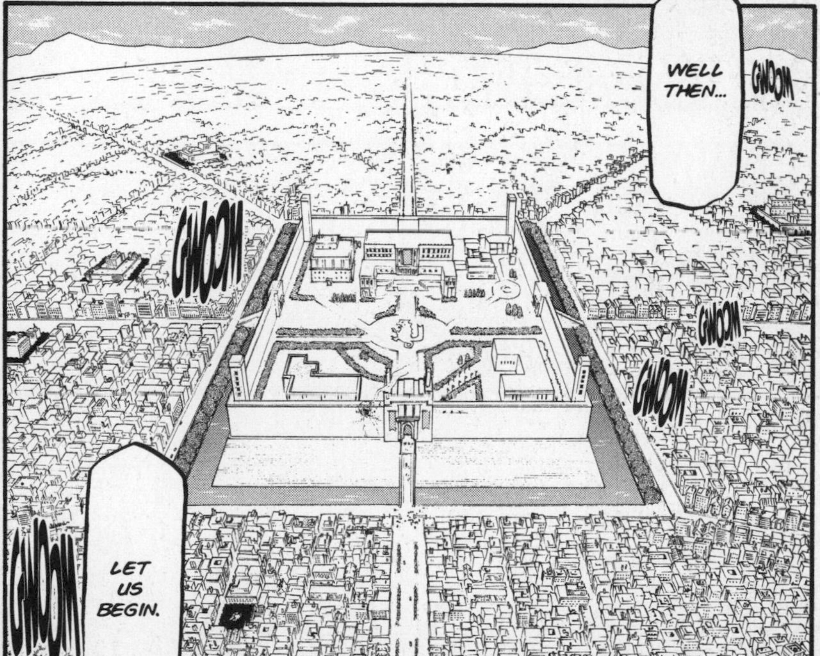
WELL THEN...
GWOOM
GWOOM
GWOOM
GWOOM
GWOOM
LET US BEGIN.

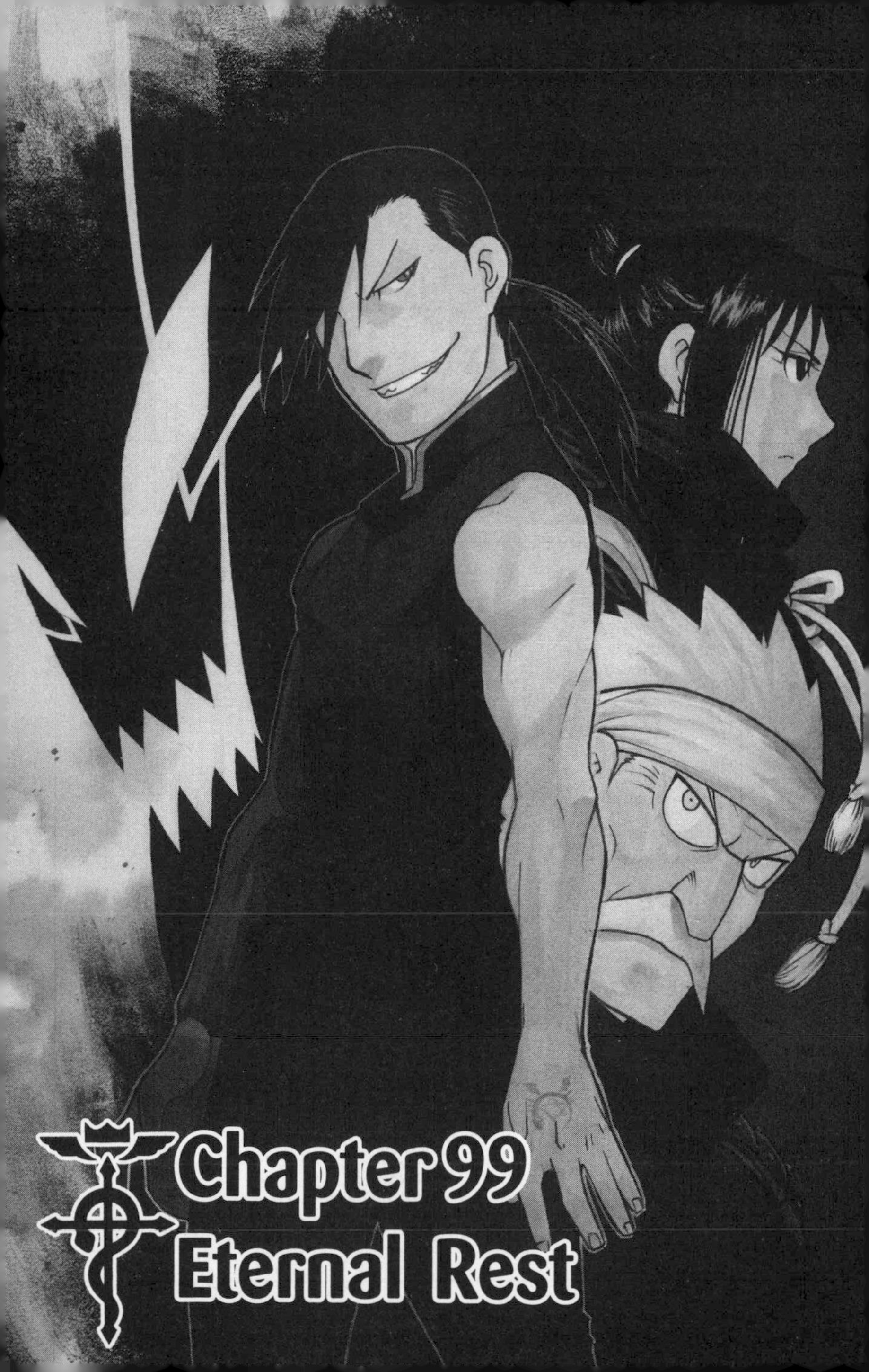
Chapter 99
Eternal Rest

FULLMETAL
ALCHEMIST

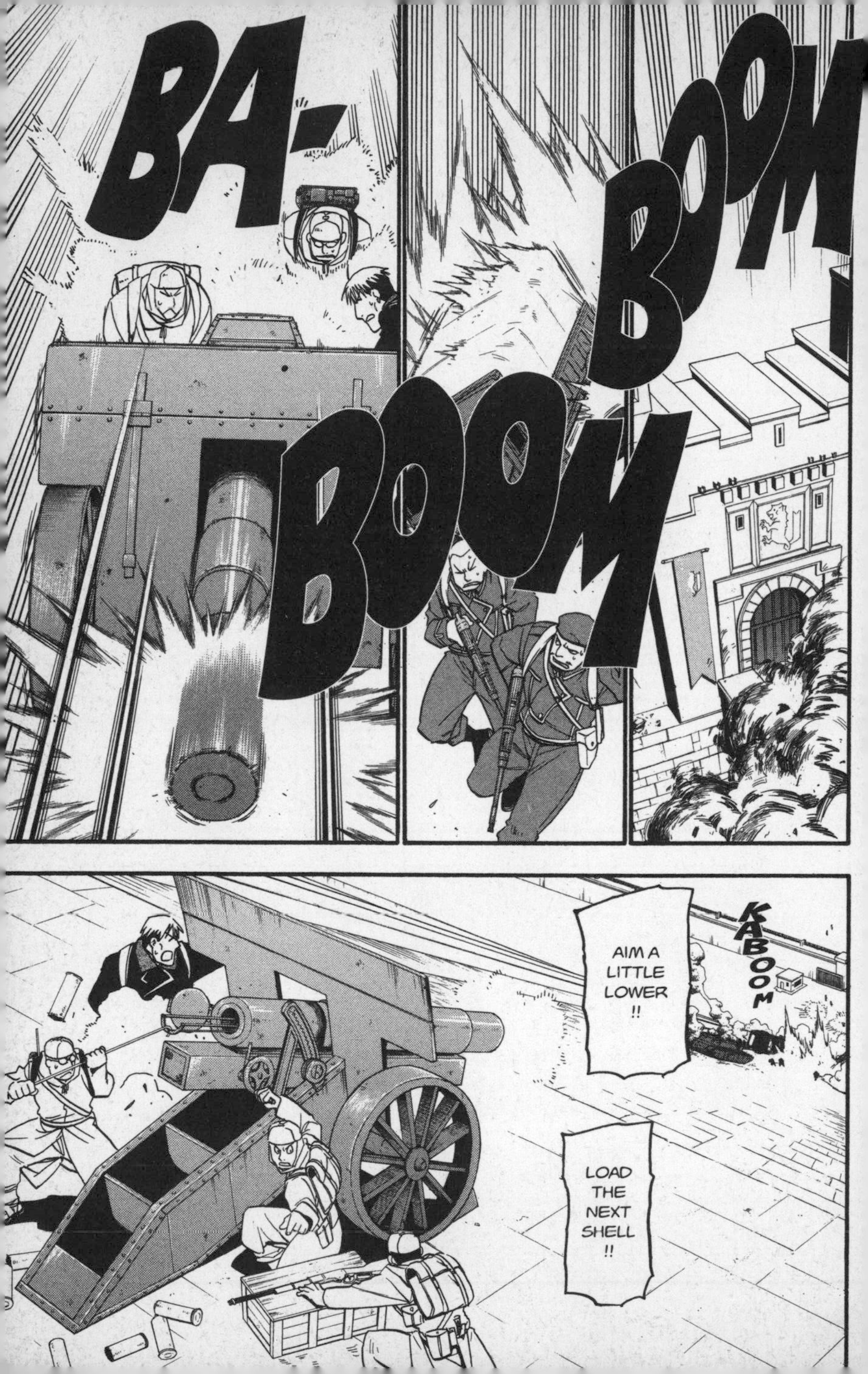
BA-
BOOM
BOOM
KABOOM
AIM A LITTLE LOWER !!
LOAD THE NEXT SHELL !!

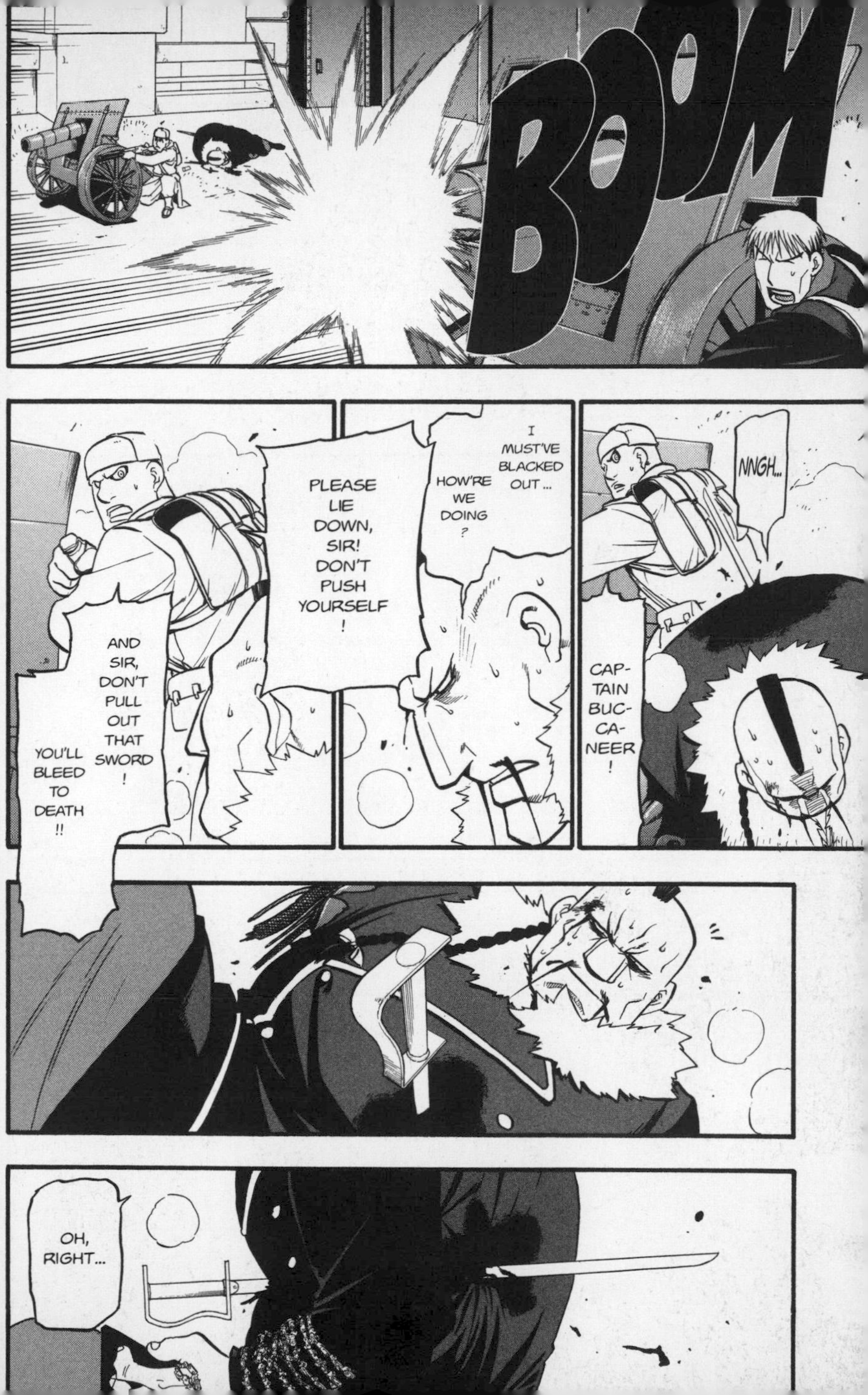
BOOOM
NNGH...
CAPTAIN BUCCANEER!
I MUST'VE BLACKED OUT...
HOW'RE WE DOING?
PLEASE LIE DOWN, SIR! DON'T PUSH YOURSELF!
AND SIR, DON'T PULL OUT THAT SWORD!
YOU'LL BLEED TO DEATH!!
OH, RIGHT...

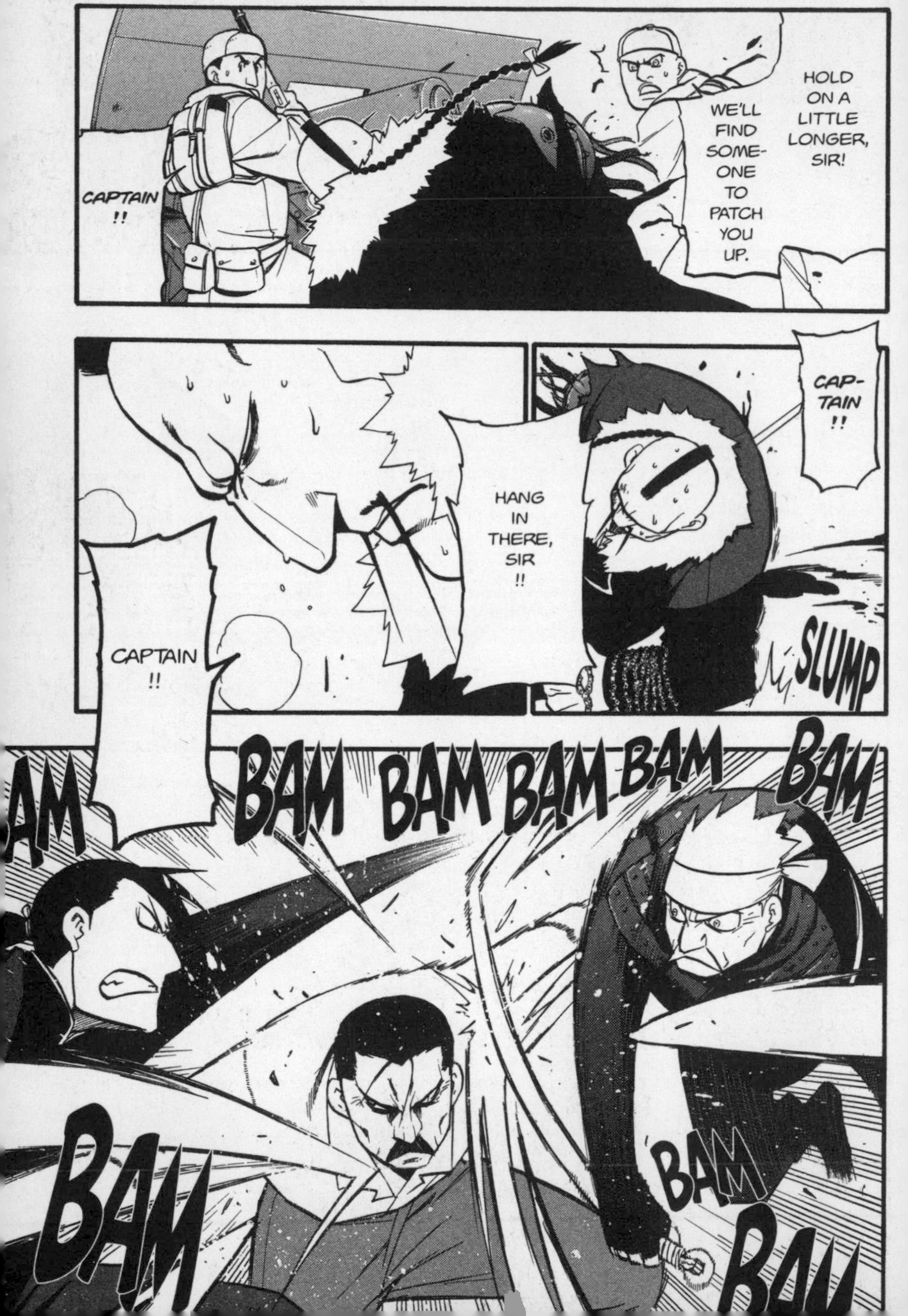
HOLD ON A LITTLE LONGER, SIR!
WE'LL FIND SOMEONE TO PATCH YOU UP.
CAPTAIN !!
CAP-TAIN !!
HANG IN THERE, SIR !!
SLUMP
CAPTAIN !!
BAM
BAM
BAM BAM
BAM
BAM
AM
BAM
BAM
BAM

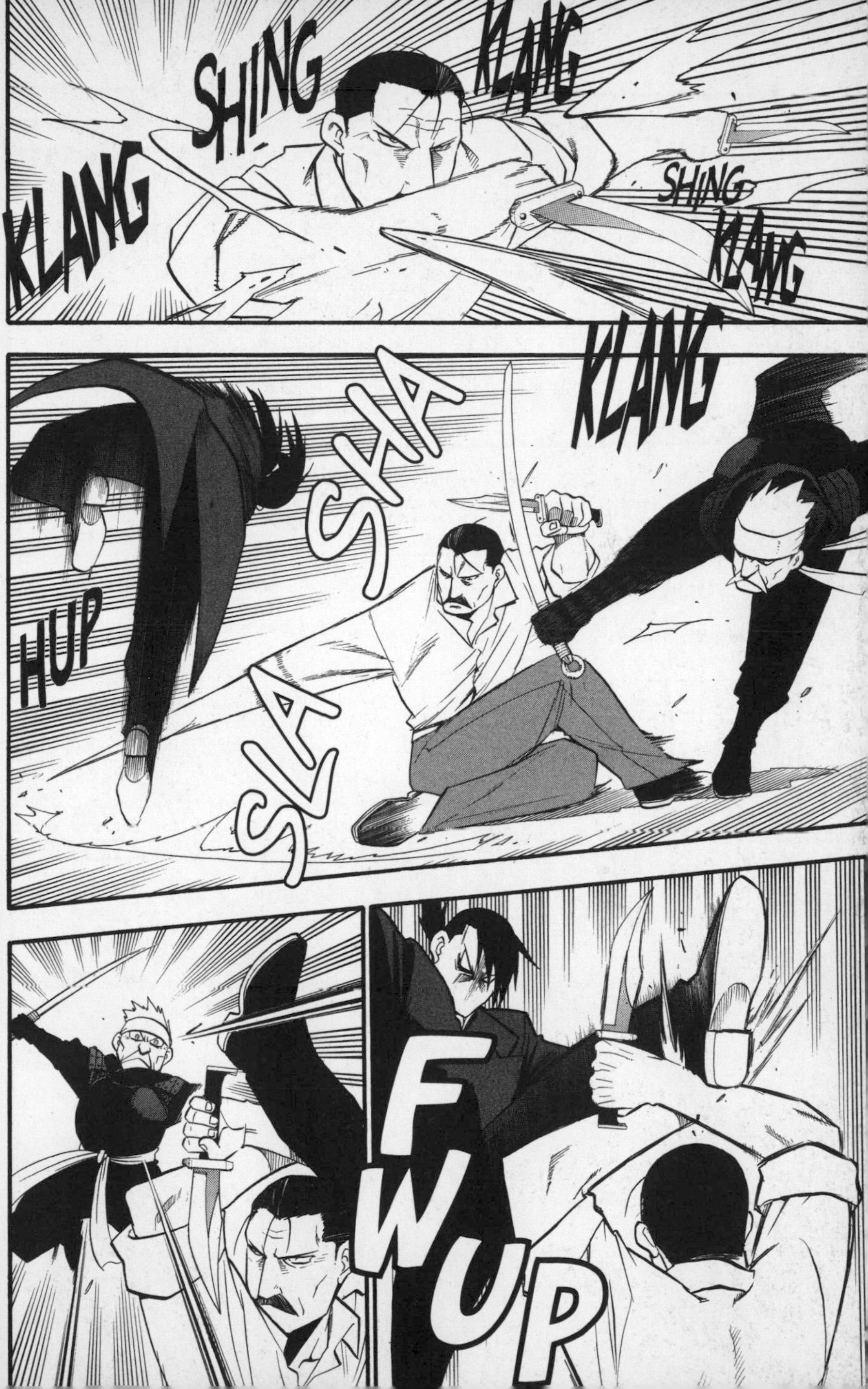
KLANG
SHING
KLANG
SHING
KLANG
KLANG
KLANG
SLA SHA
HUP
FWUP

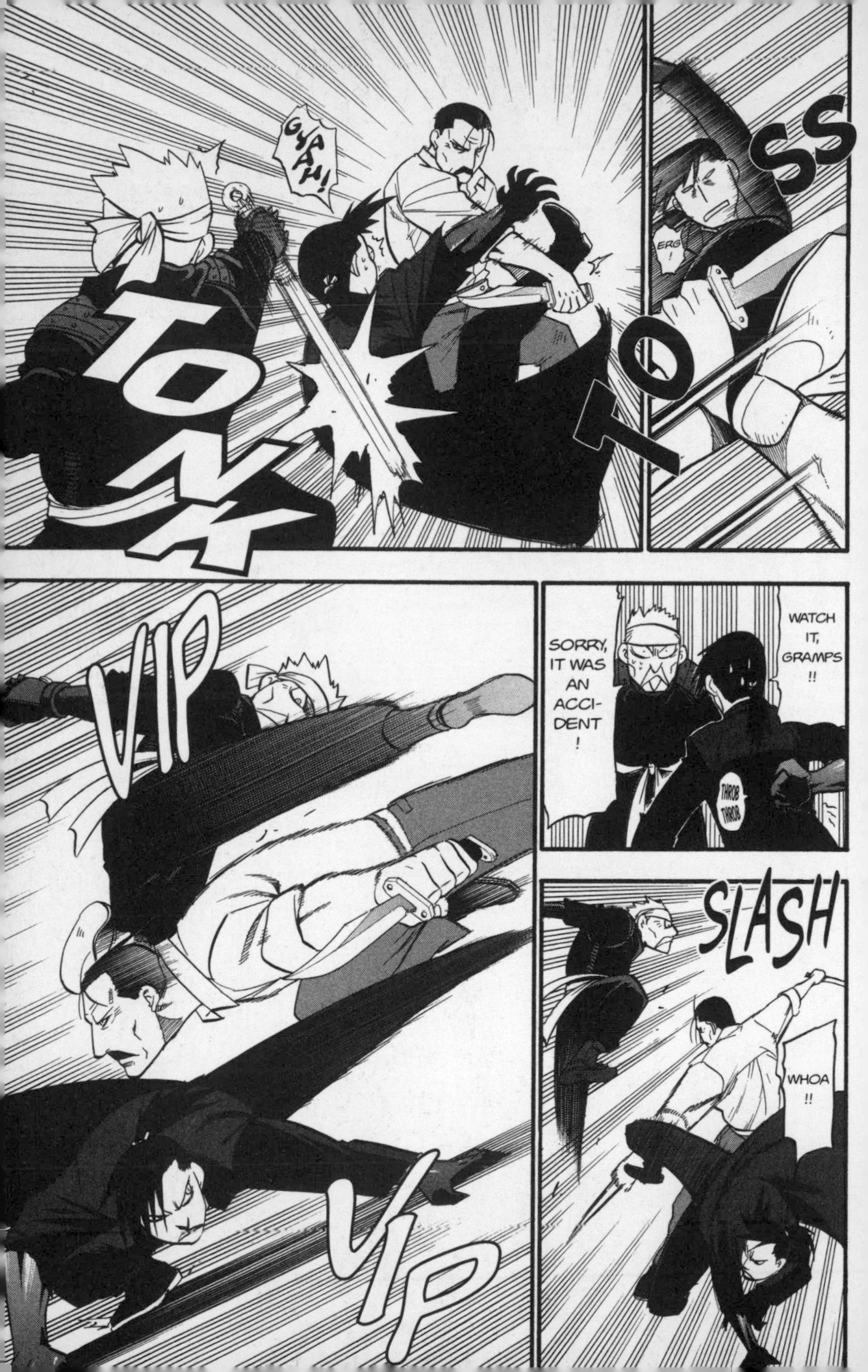
TOSS
ERG!
GYAAH!
TONK
WATCH IT, GRAMPS!!
SORRY, IT WAS AN ACCIDENT!
THROB THROB
SLASH
WHOA!!
VIP
VIP

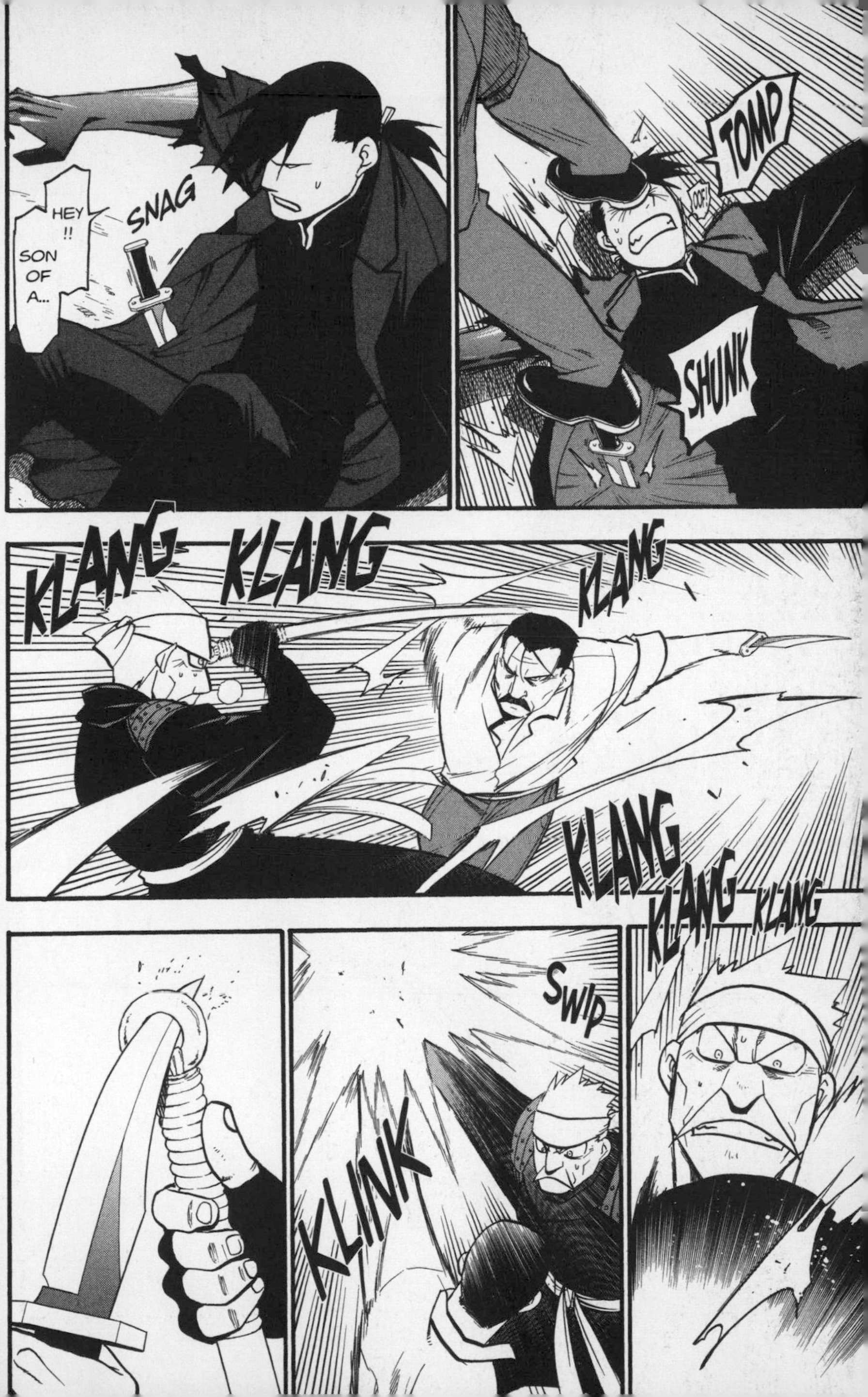
TOMP
OOF!
SHUNK
SNAG
HEY!! SON OF A...
KLANG
KLANG
KLANG
KLANG
KLANG
KLANG
SWIP
KLINK

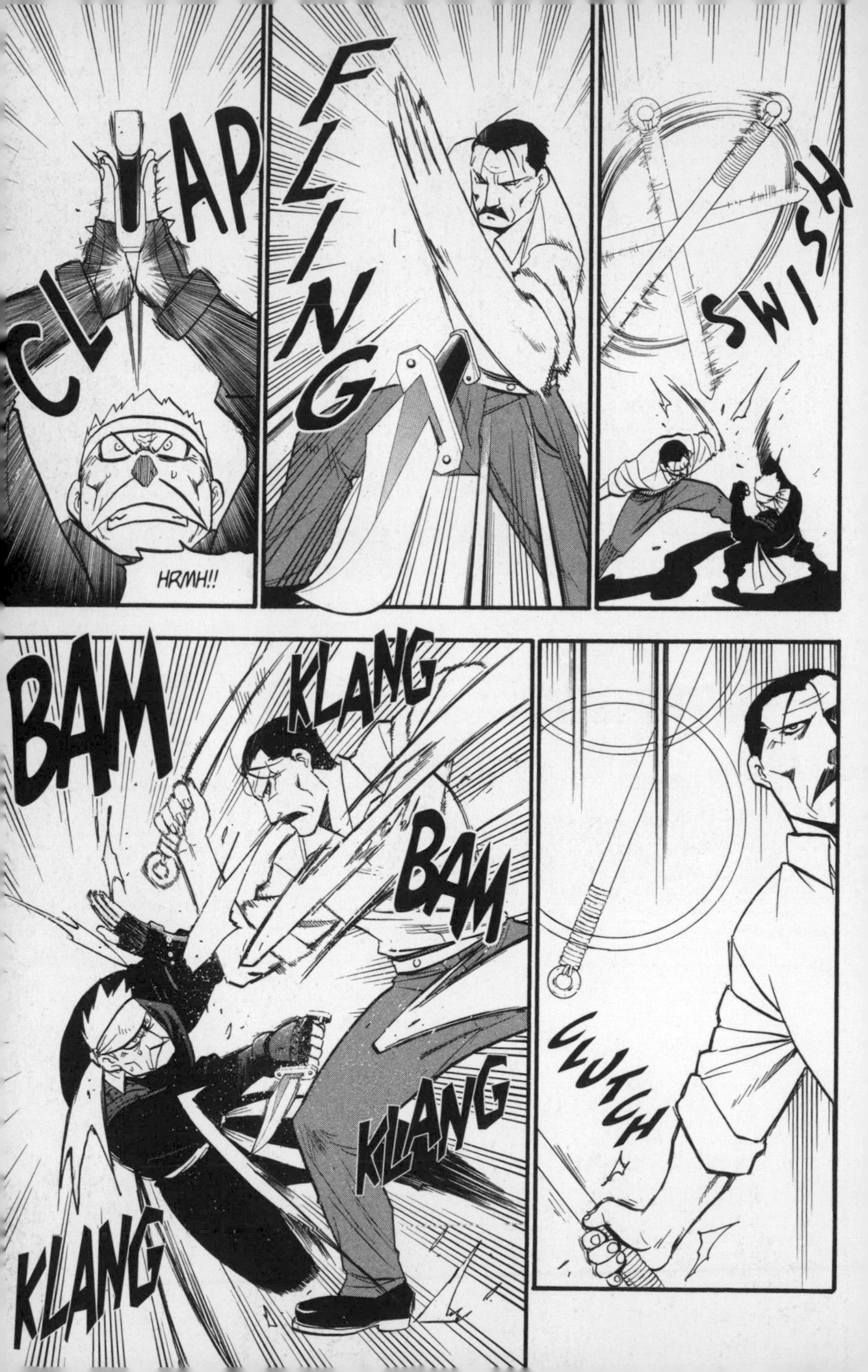
SWISH
FLING
CLAP
HRMH!!
CLUTCH
KLANG
BAM
BAM
KLANG
KLANG

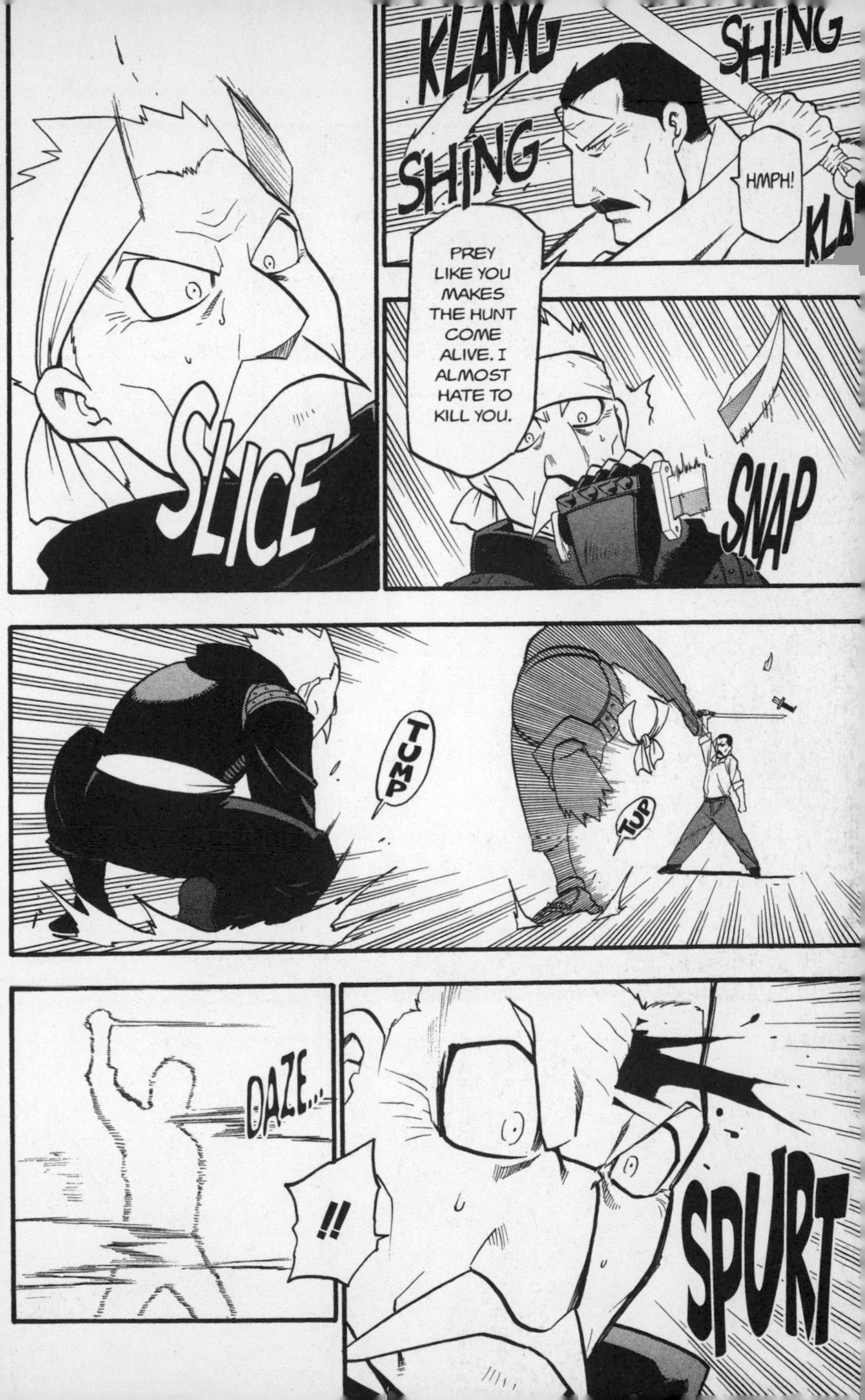
SHING
HMPH!
KLA
KLANG
SHING
PREY LIKE YOU MAKES THE HUNT COME ALIVE. I ALMOST HATE TO KILL YOU.
SNAP
SLICE
TUP
TUMP
SPURT
!!
DAZE...

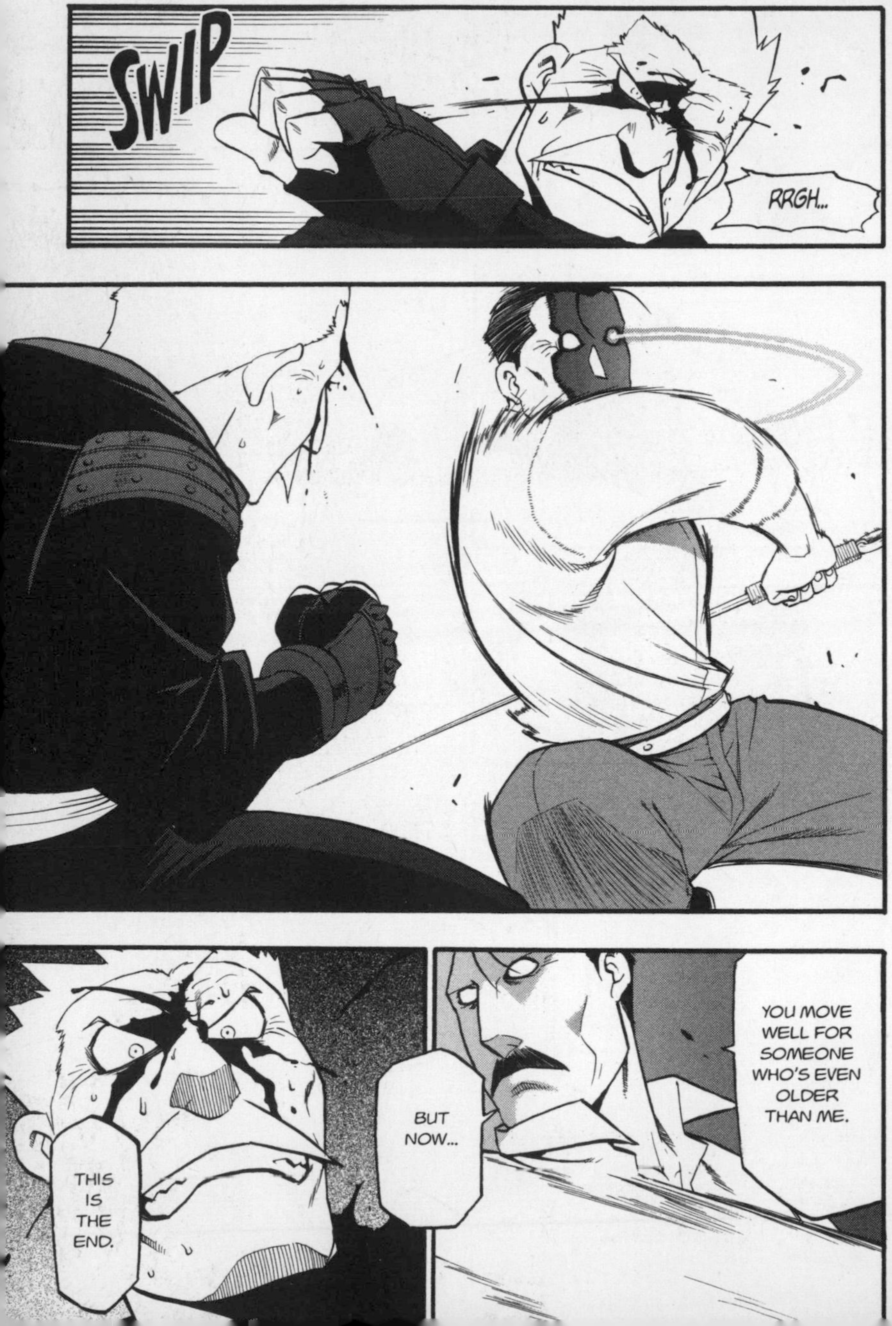
SWIP
RRGH...
YOU MOVE WELL FOR SOMEONE WHO'S EVEN OLDER THAN ME.
BUT NOW...
THIS IS THE END.

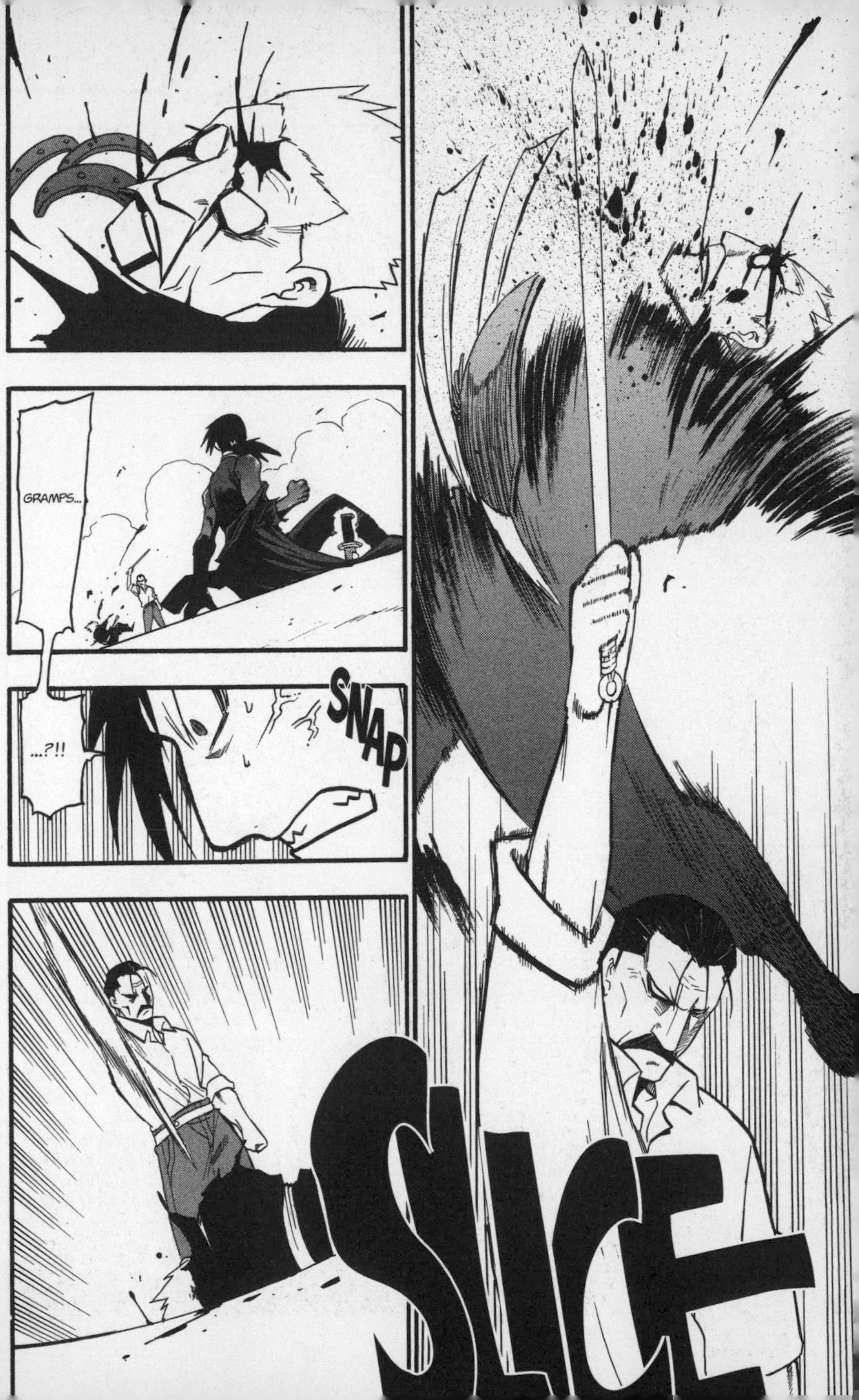
SLICE
GRAMPS...
SNAP
...?!!

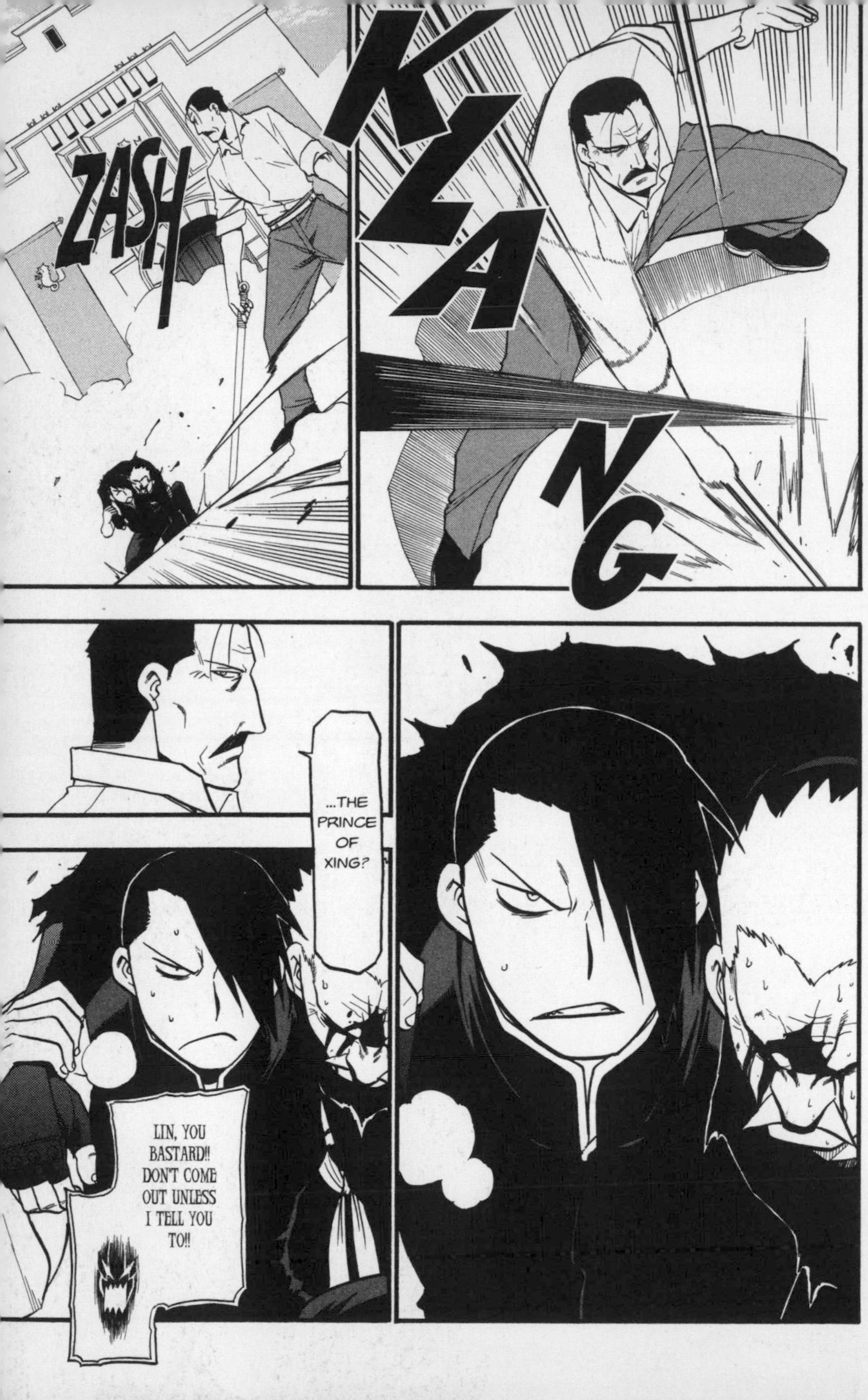
KLANG
ZASH
...THE PRINCE OF XING?
LIN, YOU BASTARD!! DON'T COME OUT UNLESS I TELL YOU TO!!

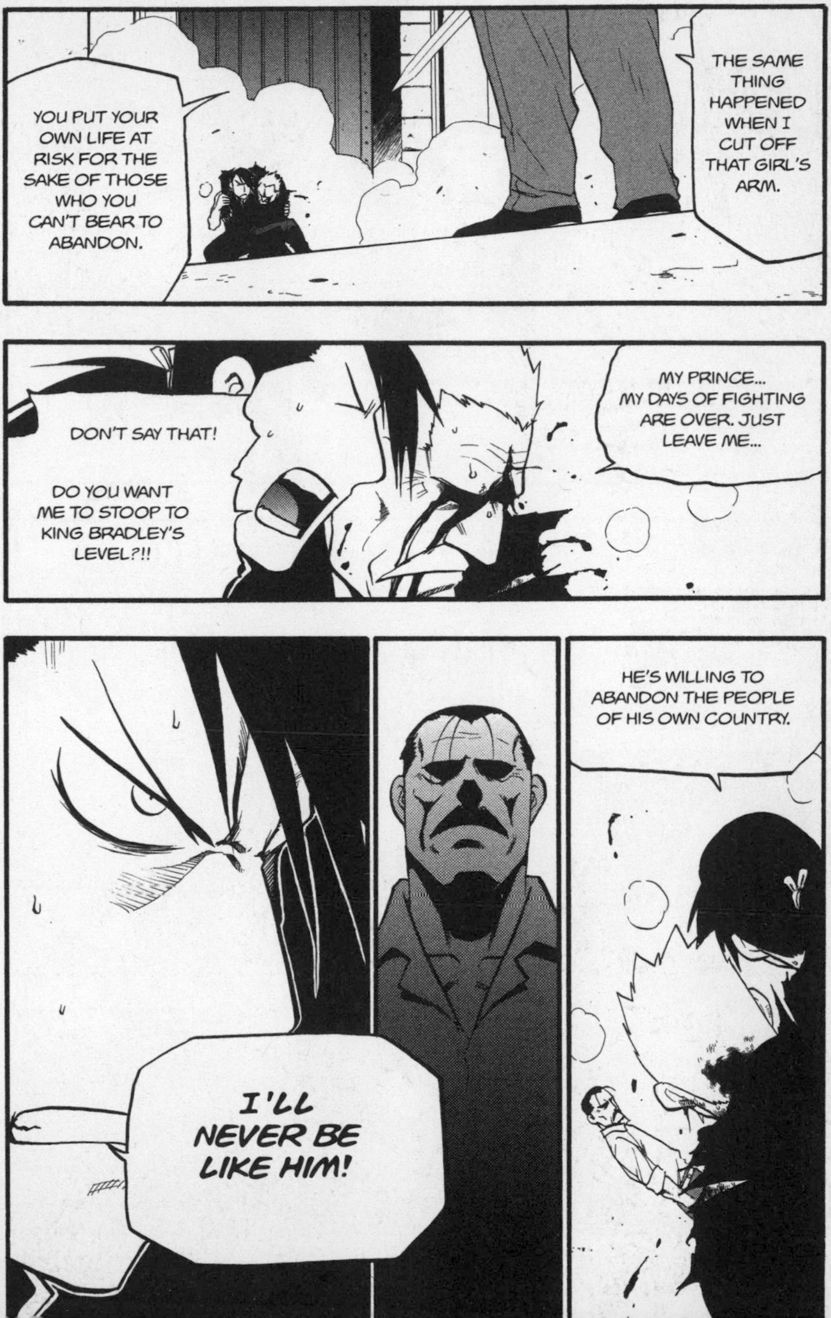
THE SAME THING HAPPENED WHEN I CUT OFF THAT GIRL'S ARM.
YOU PUT YOUR OWN LIFE AT RISK FOR THE SAKE OF THOSE WHO YOU CAN'T BEAR TO ABANDON.
MY PRINCE... MY DAYS OF FIGHTING ARE OVER. JUST LEAVE ME...
DON'T SAY THAT!
DO YOU WANT ME TO STOOP TO KING BRADLEY'S LEVEL?!!
HE'S WILLING TO ABANDON THE PEOPLE OF HIS OWN COUNTRY.
I'LL NEVER BE LIKE HIM!

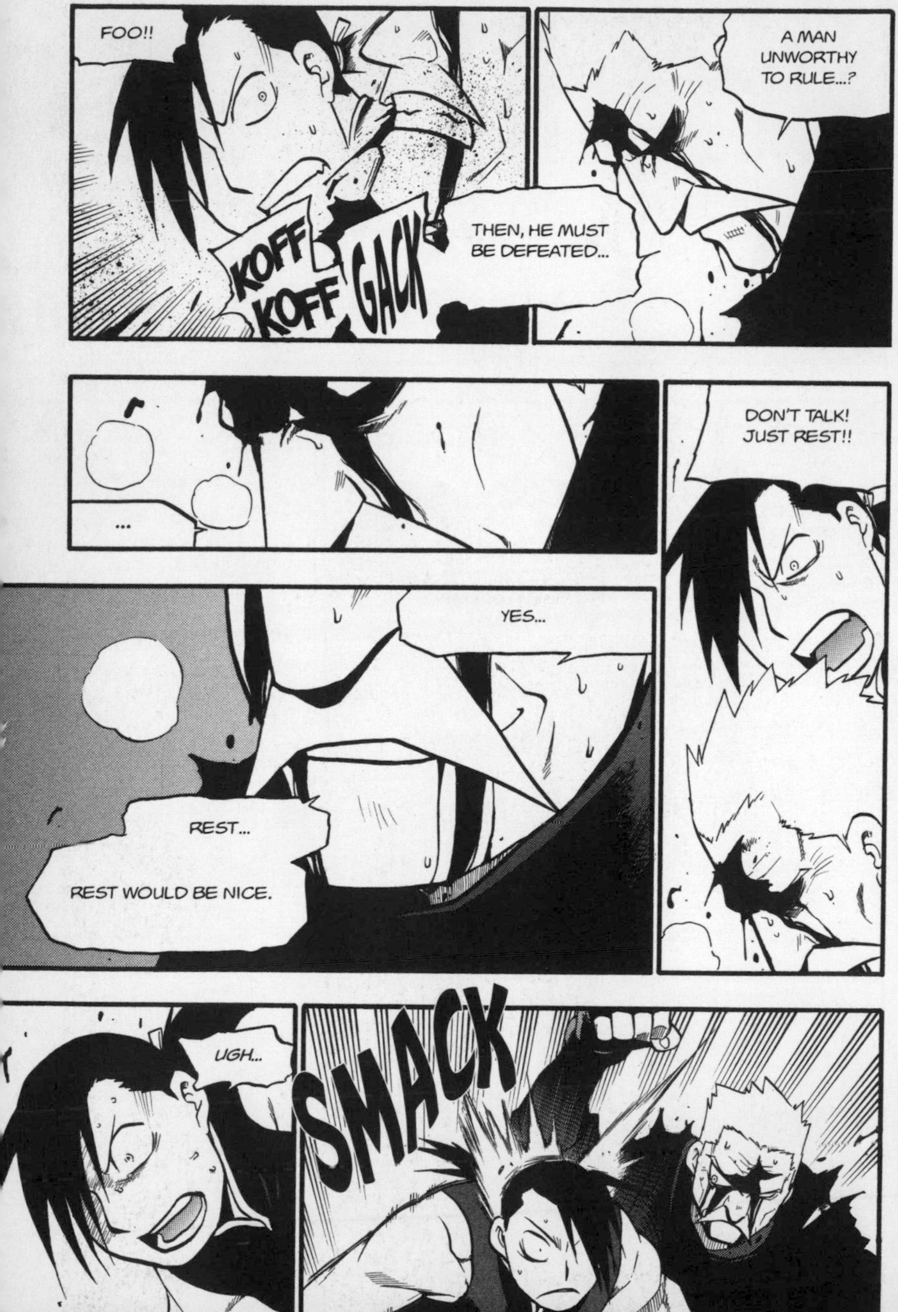
A MAN UNWORTHY TO RULE...?
THEN, HE MUST BE DEFEATED...
FOO!!
KOFF KOFF
GACK
DON'T TALK! JUST REST!!
...
YES...
REST...
REST WOULD BE NICE.
SMACK
UGH...

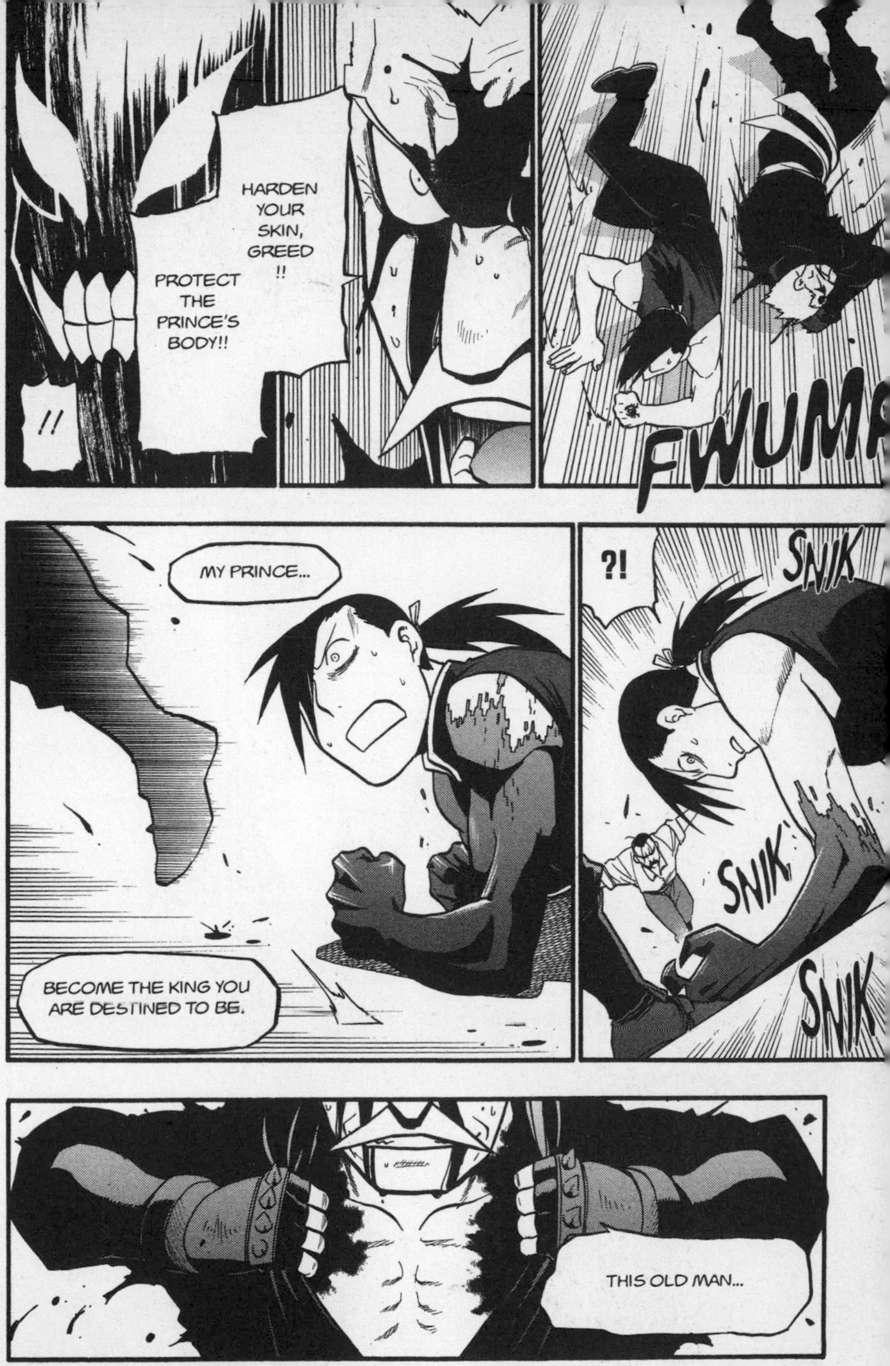
FWUM
HARDEN YOUR SKIN, GREED !!
PROTECT THE PRINCE'S BODY!!
!!
?!
SNIK
SNIK
SNIK
MY PRINCE...
BECOME THE KING YOU ARE DESTINED TO BE.
THIS OLD MAN...

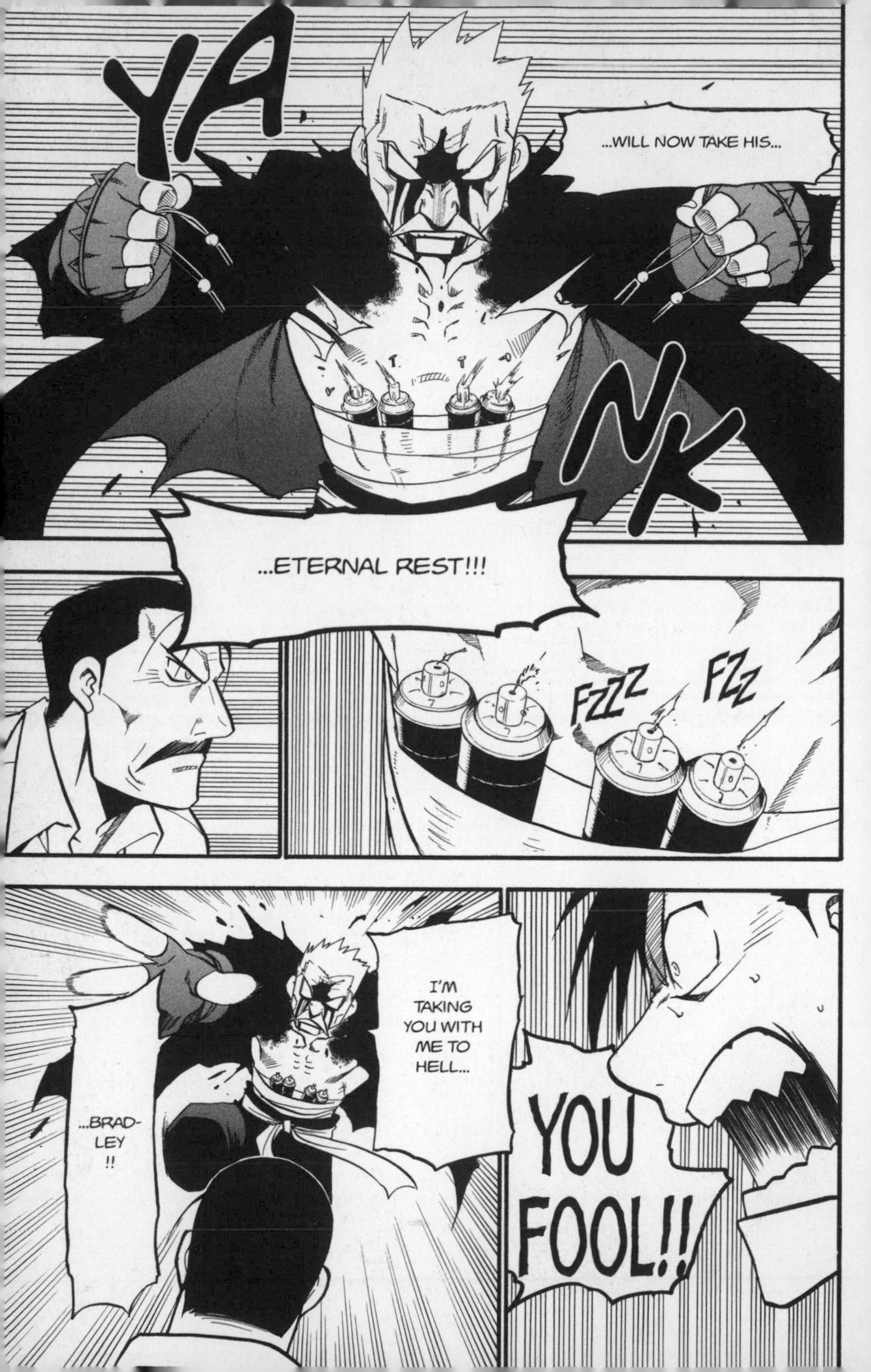
...WILL NOW TAKE HIS...
YA
NK
...ETERNAL REST!!!
FZZZ
FZZ
YOU FOOL!!
I'M TAKING YOU WITH ME TO HELL...
...BRAD-LEY !!

SLASH
FZZ

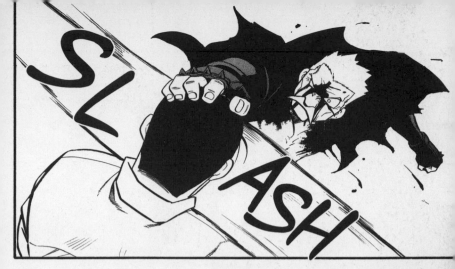

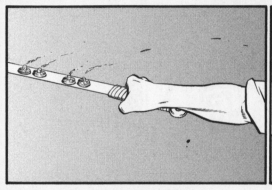

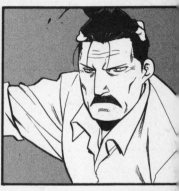

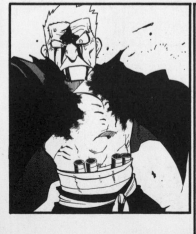

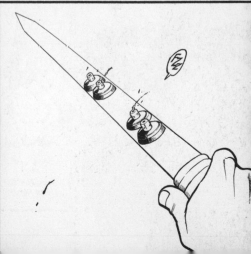

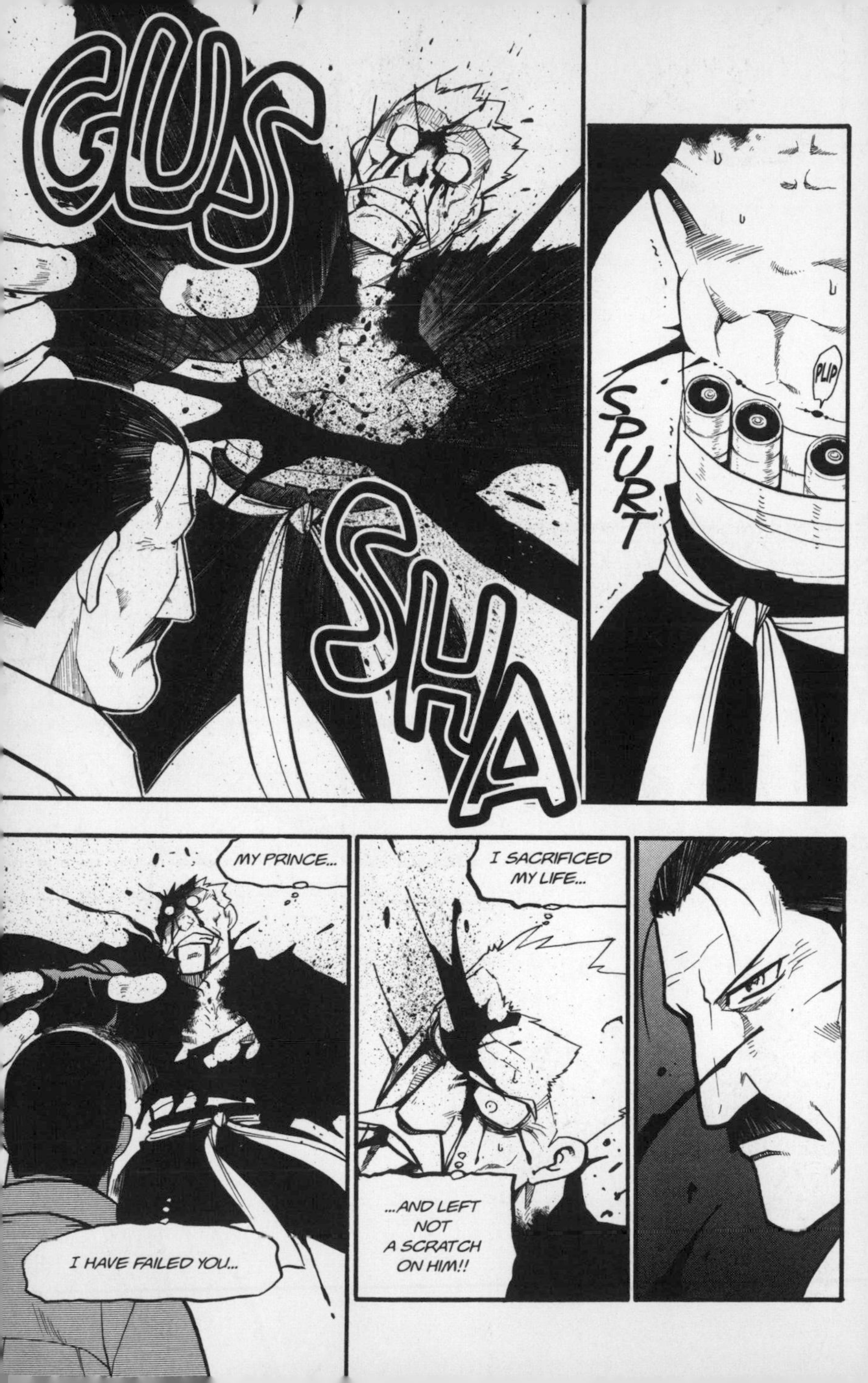
PLIP
SPURT
GUS
SHA
I SACRIFICED MY LIFE...
...AND LEFT NOT A SCRATCH ON HIM!!
MY PRINCE...
I HAVE FAILED YOU...

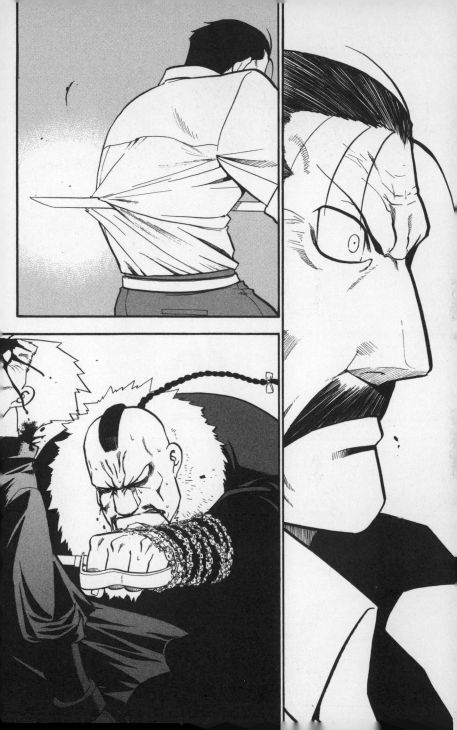

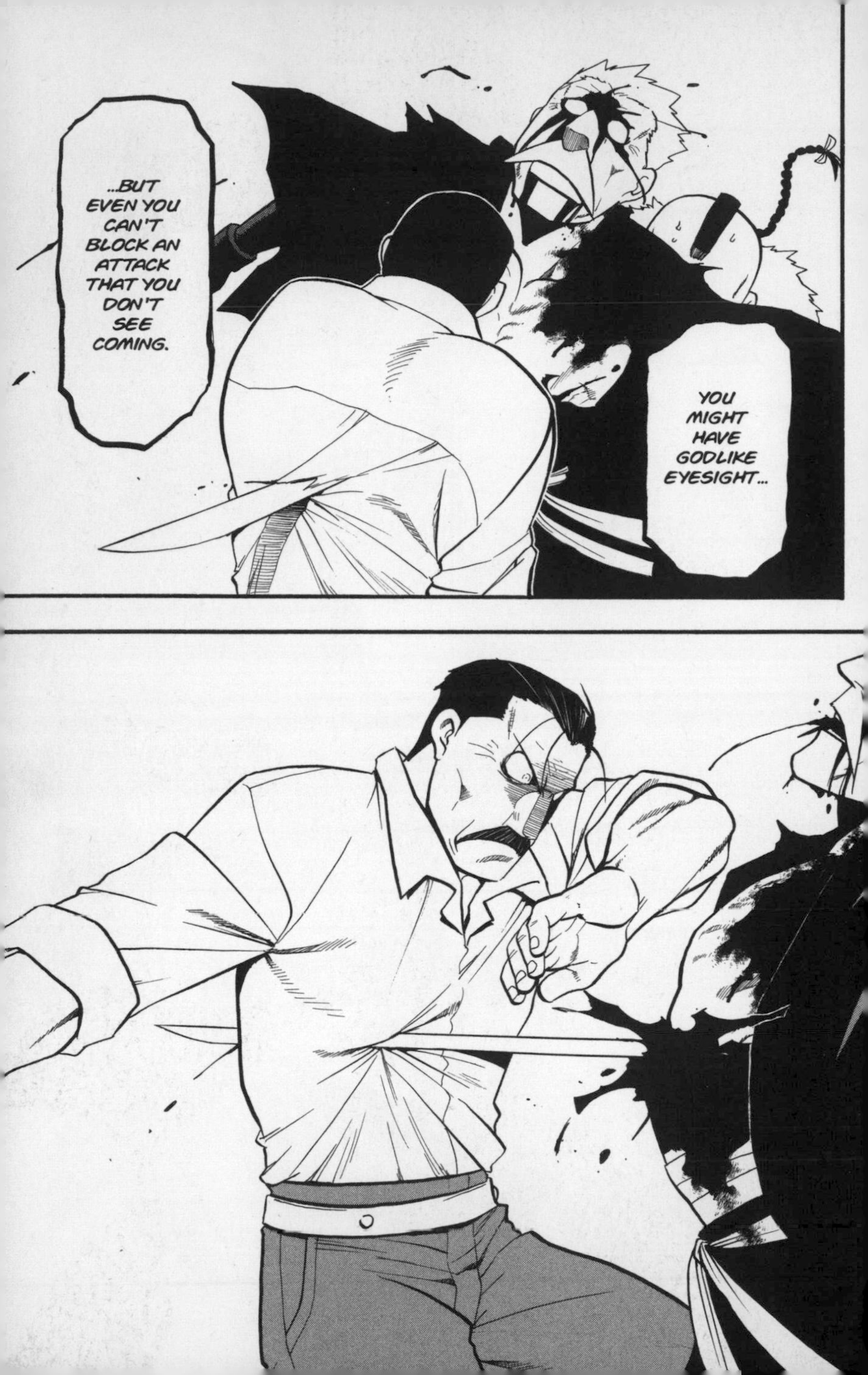
YOU MIGHT HAVE GODLIKE EYESIGHT...
...BUT EVEN YOU CAN'T BLOCK AN ATTACK THAT YOU DON'T SEE COMING.

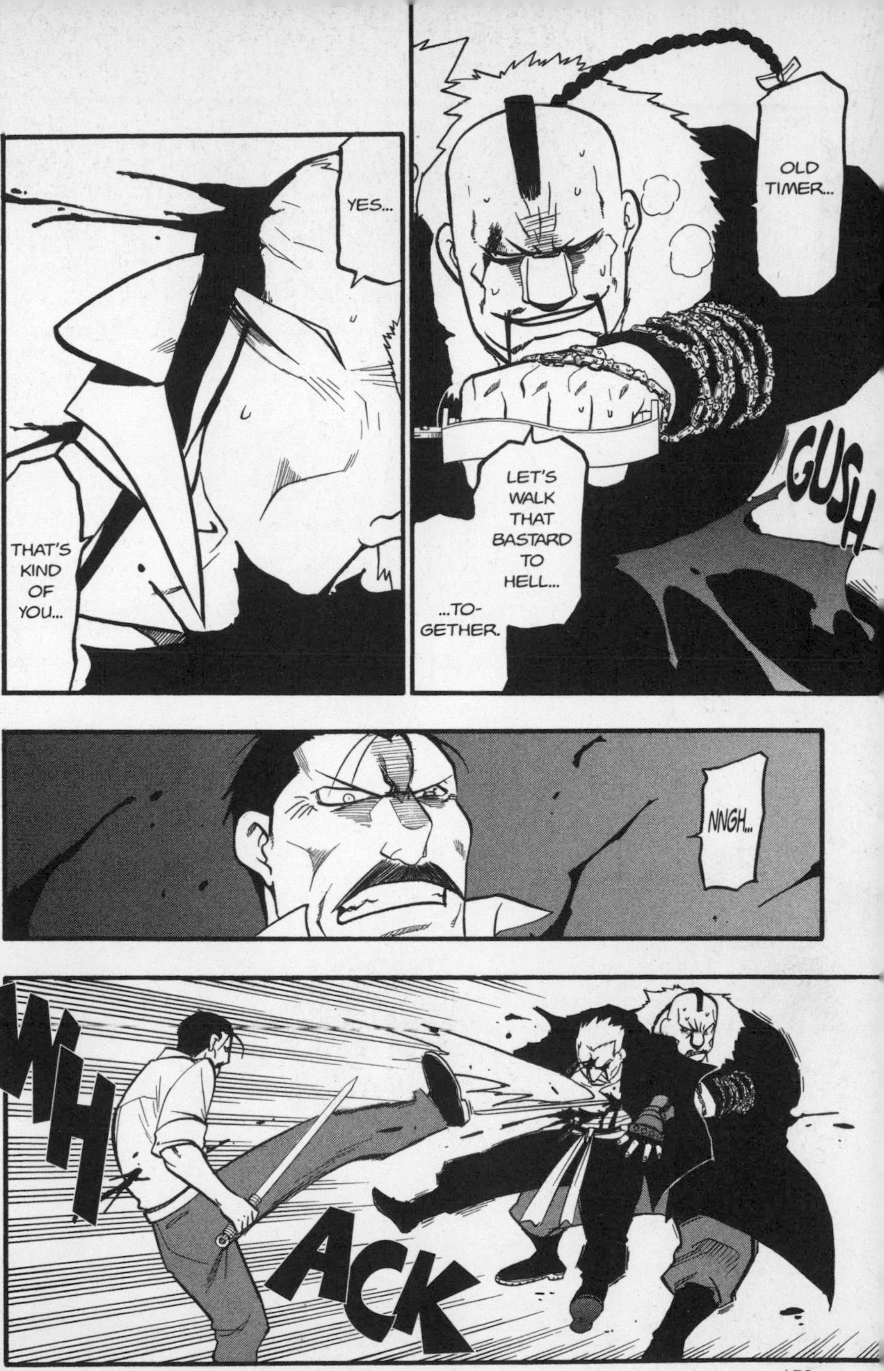
OLD TIMER...
LET'S WALK THAT BASTARD TO HELL...
...TO-GETHER.
GUSH
YES...
THAT'S KIND OF YOU...
NNGH...
WHACK

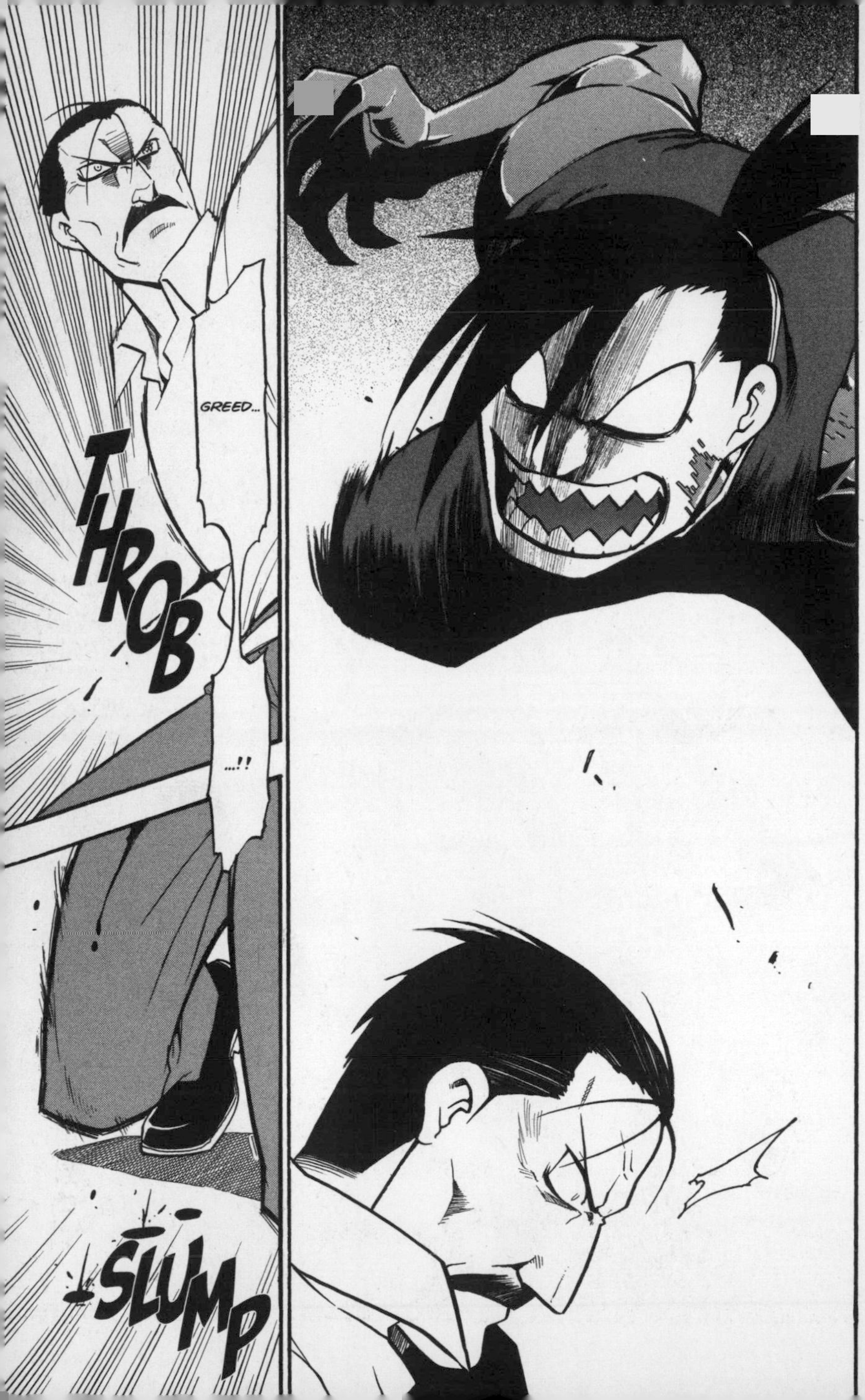
GREED...
THROB
...!!
SLUMP

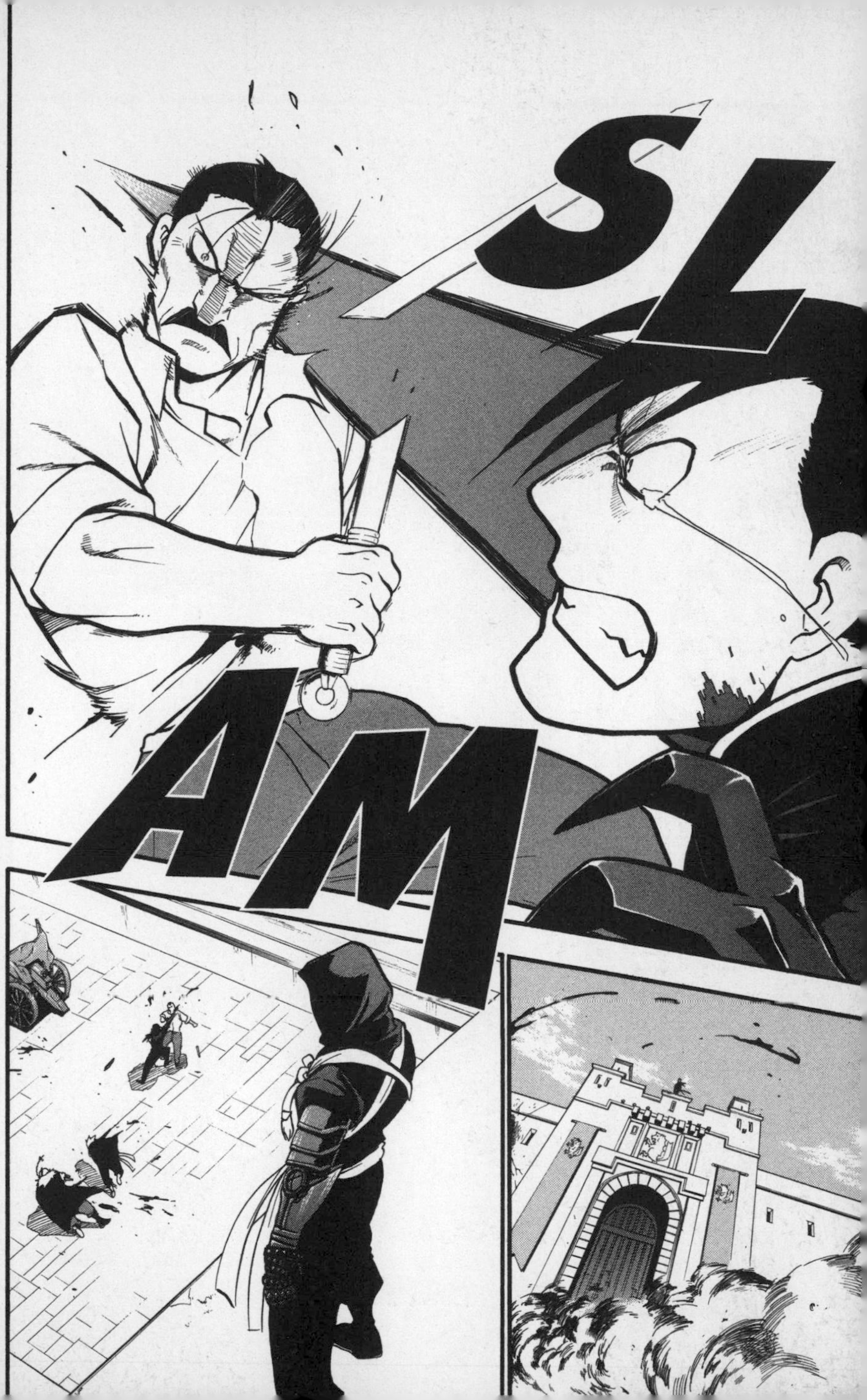
SLAM

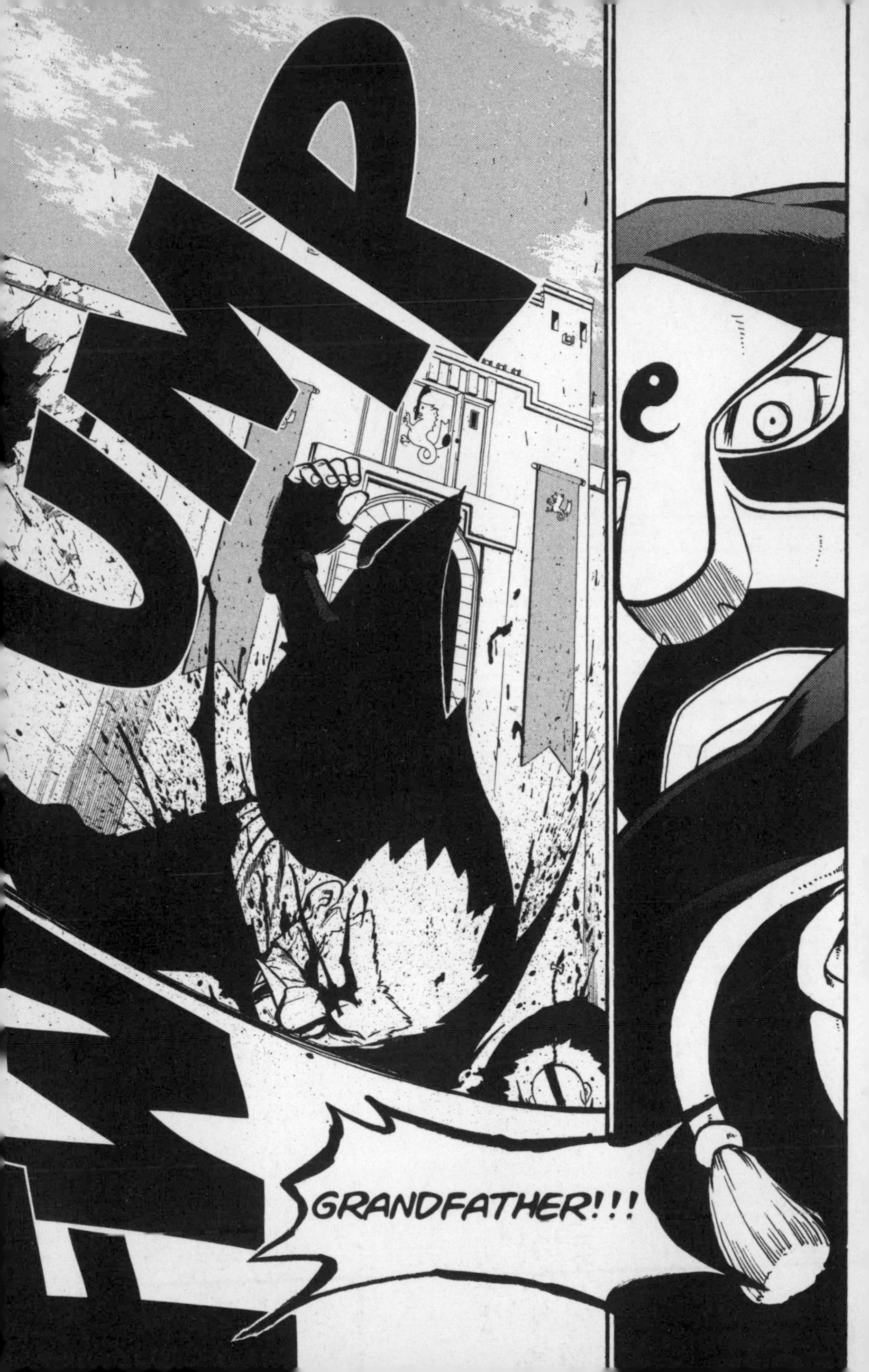
THUMP
GRANDFATHER!!!

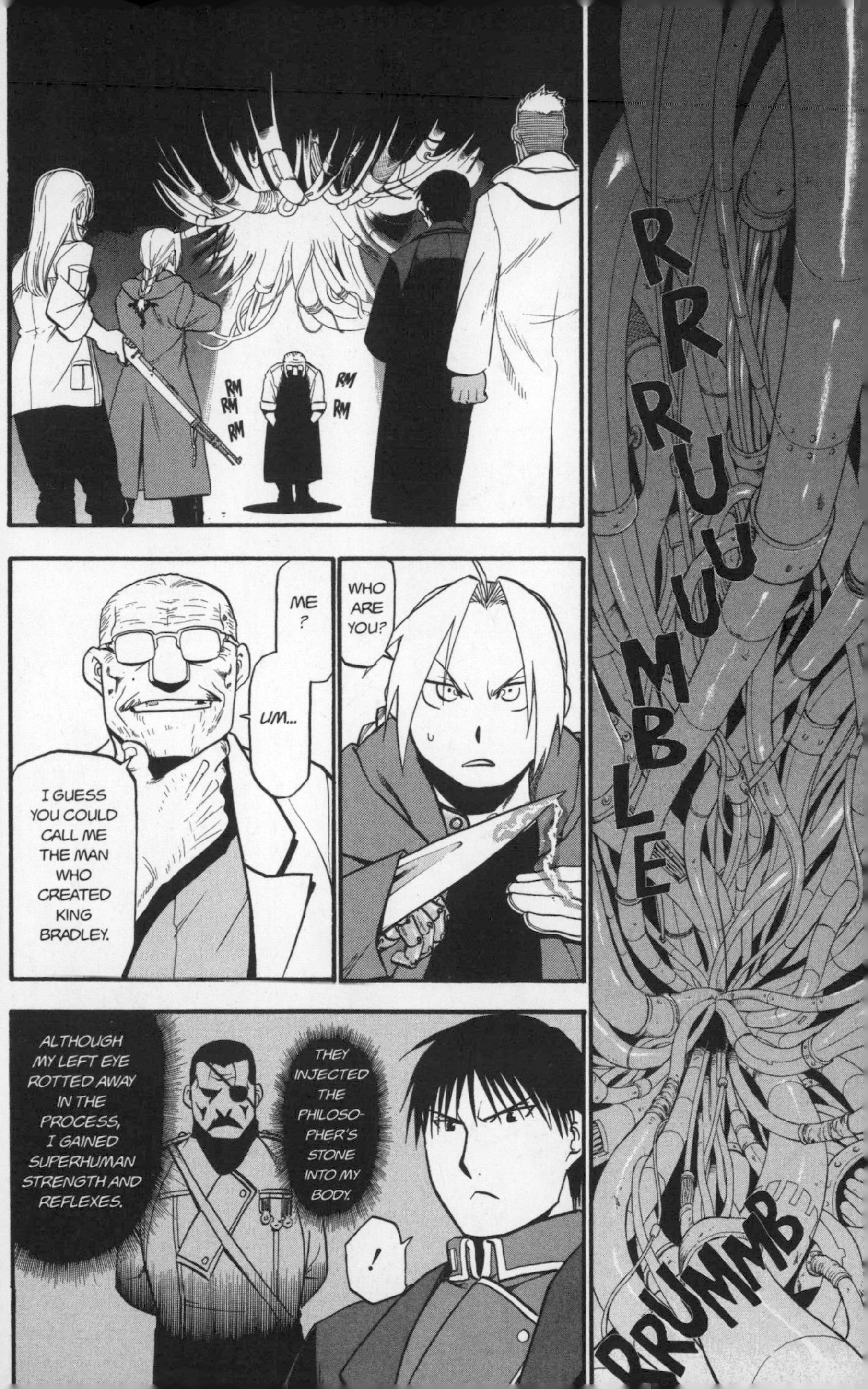
RRRRUUUMBLE
DRUMMB
RM RM RM
RM RM
WHO ARE YOU?
ME?
UM...
I GUESS YOU COULD CALL ME THE MAN WHO CREATED KING BRADLEY.
THEY INJECTED THE PHILOSOPHER'S STONE INTO MY BODY.
ALTHOUGH MY LEFT EYE ROTTED AWAY IN THE PROCESS, I GAINED SUPERHUMAN STRENGTH AND REFLEXES.
!

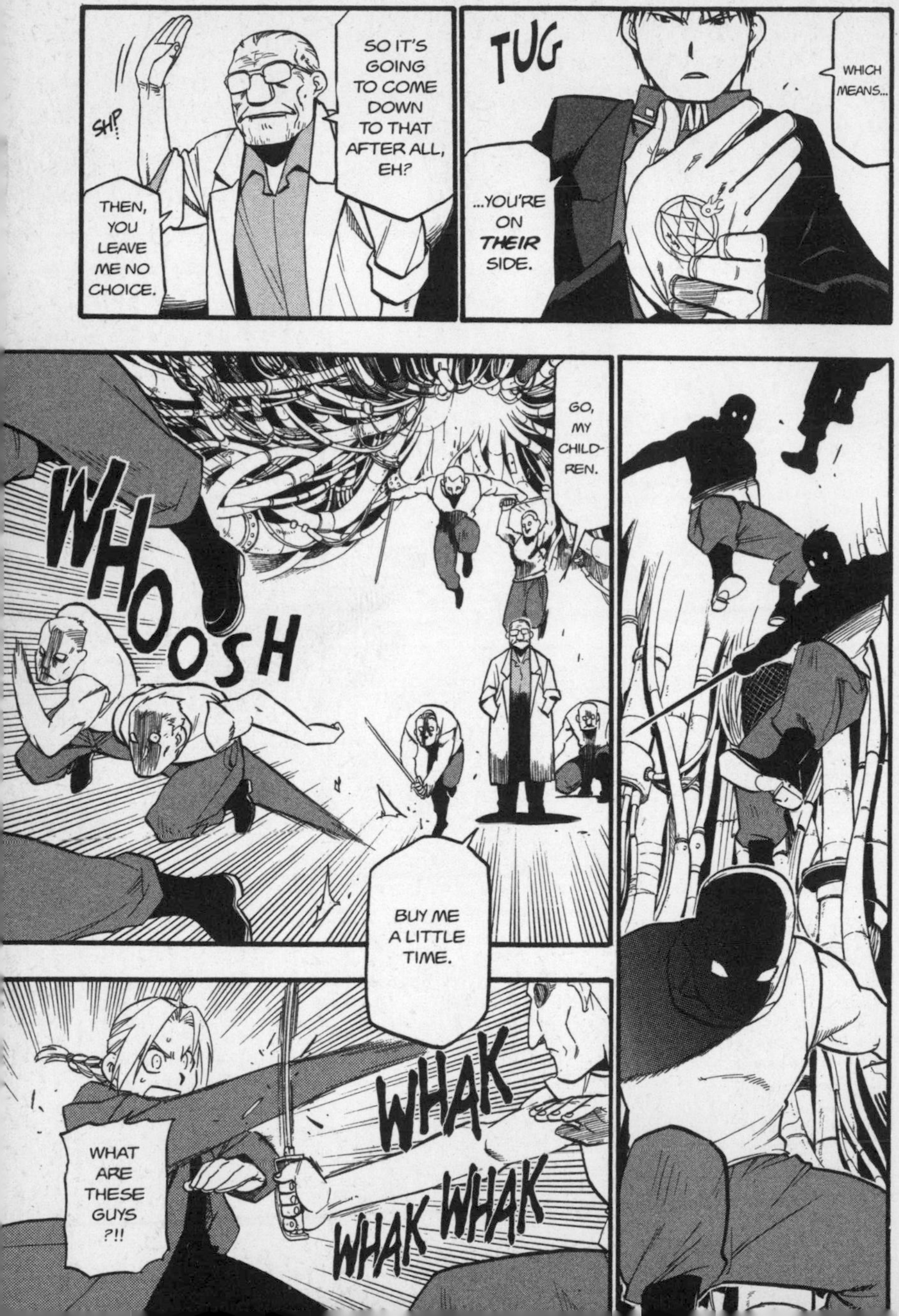
WHICH MEANS...
TUG
...YOU'RE ON *THEIR* SIDE.
SO IT'S GOING TO COME DOWN TO THAT AFTER ALL, EH?
SHP!
THEN, YOU LEAVE ME NO CHOICE.
GO, MY CHILDREN.
WHOOSH
BUY ME A LITTLE TIME.
WHAK
WHAK WHAK
WHAT ARE THESE GUYS?!!

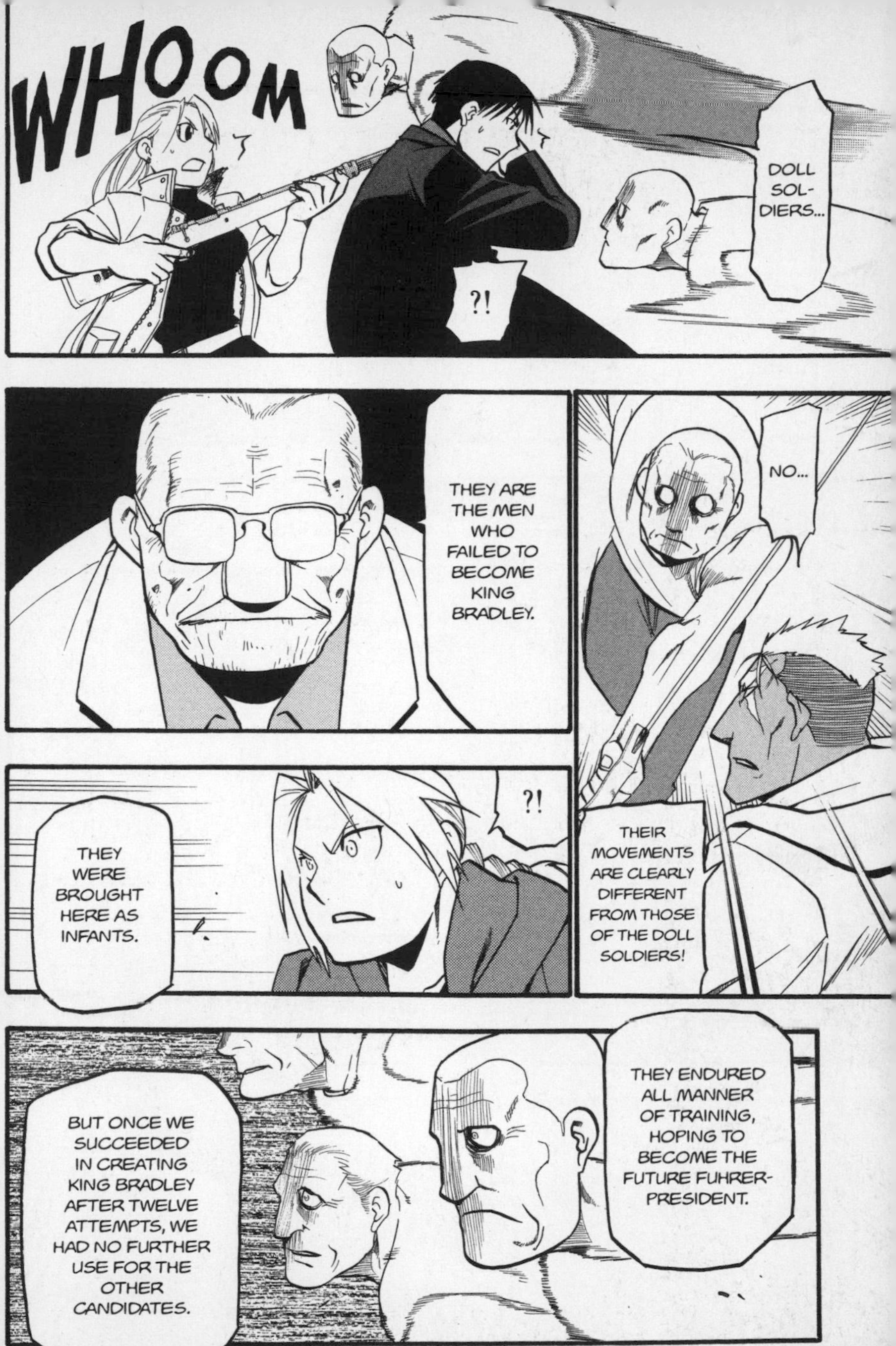
DOLL SOLDIERS...
WHOOM
?!
NO...
THEIR MOVEMENTS ARE CLEARLY DIFFERENT FROM THOSE OF THE DOLL SOLDIERS!
THEY ARE THE MEN WHO FAILED TO BECOME KING BRADLEY.
?!
THEY WERE BROUGHT HERE AS INFANTS.
THEY ENDURED ALL MANNER OF TRAINING, HOPING TO BECOME THE FUTURE FUHRER-PRESIDENT.
BUT ONCE WE SUCCEEDED IN CREATING KING BRADLEY AFTER TWELVE ATTEMPTS, WE HAD NO FURTHER USE FOR THE OTHER CANDIDATES.

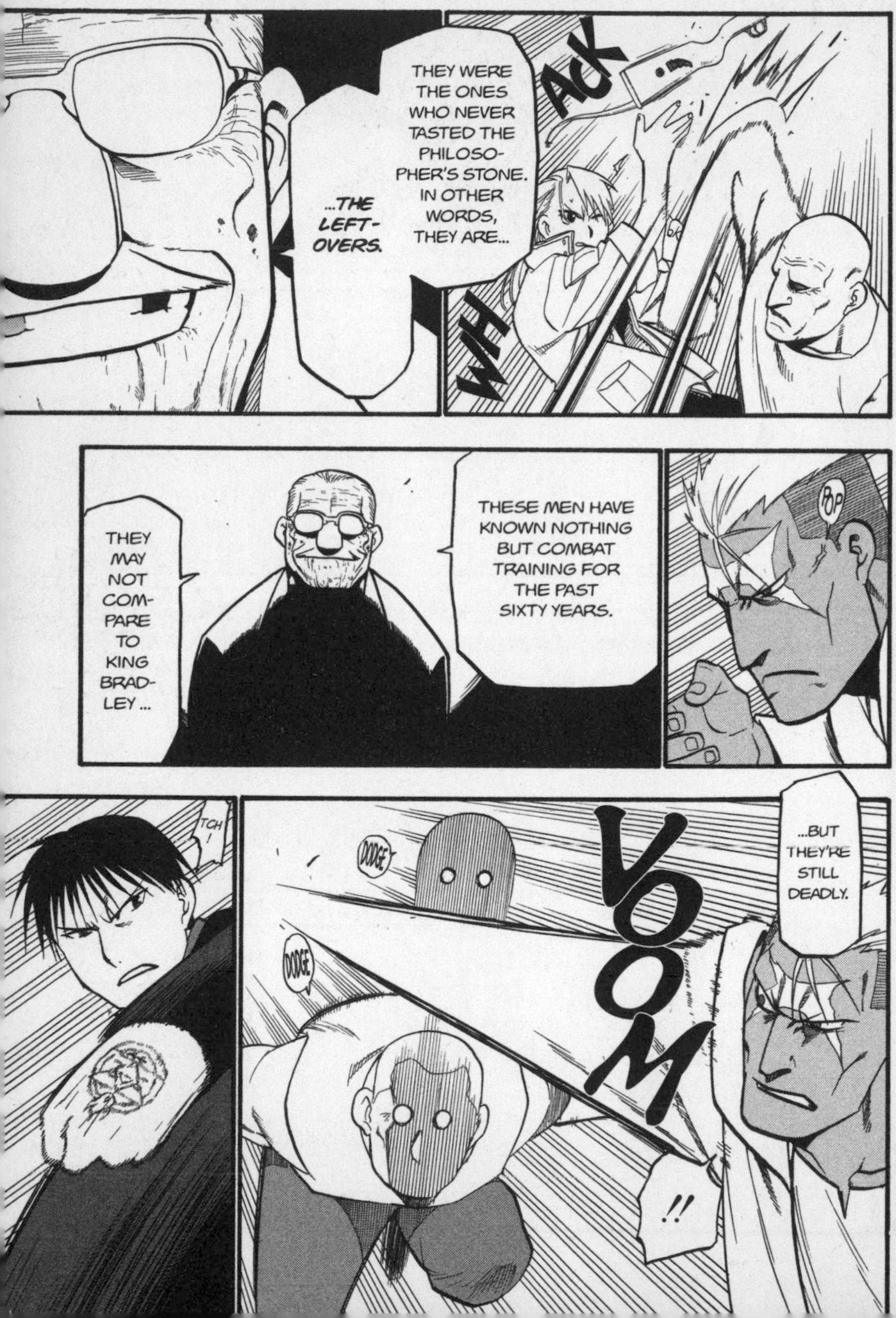
WHACK
THEY WERE THE ONES WHO NEVER TASTED THE PHILOSOPHER'S STONE. IN OTHER WORDS, THEY ARE...
...THE LEFTOVERS.
POP
THESE MEN HAVE KNOWN NOTHING BUT COMBAT TRAINING FOR THE PAST SIXTY YEARS.
THEY MAY NOT COMPARE TO KING BRADLEY...
...BUT THEY'RE STILL DEADLY.
VOOM
DODGE
DODGE
!!
TCH!

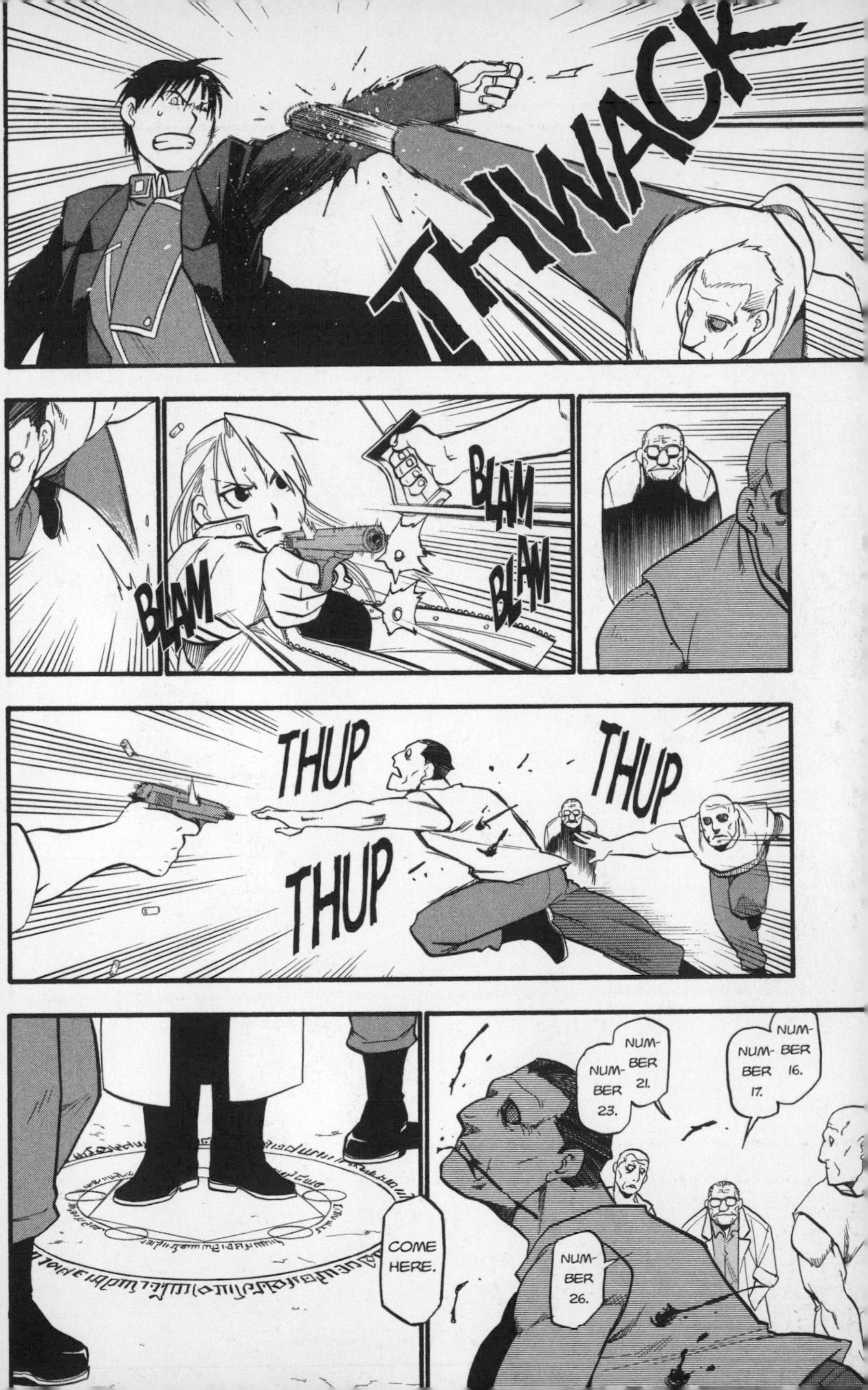
THWACK
BLAM
BLAM
BLAM
THUP
THUP
THUP
NUMBER 16.
NUMBER 17.
NUMBER 21.
NUMBER 23.
NUMBER 26.
COME HERE.

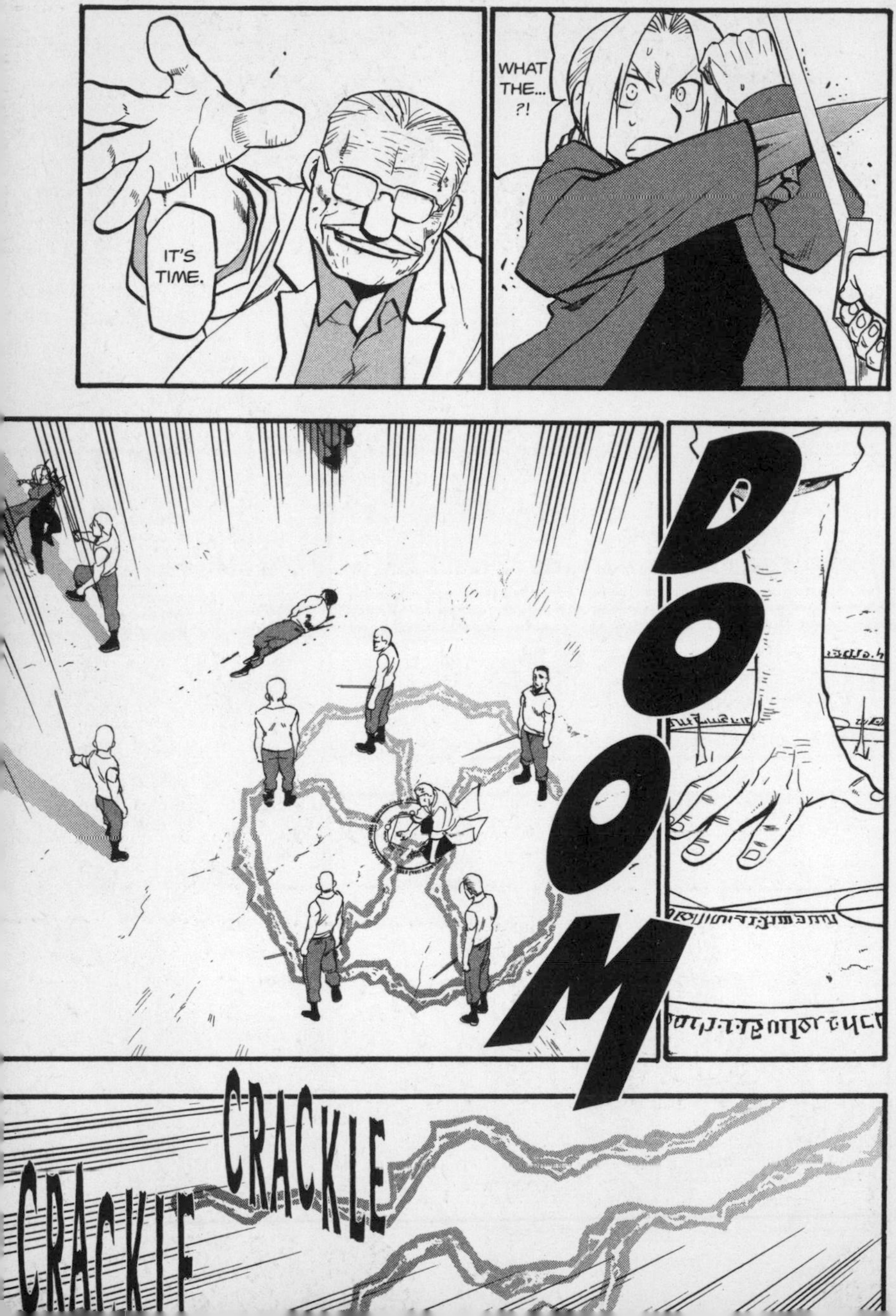

WHAT THE... ?!
IT'S TIME.
DOOM
CRACKLE
CRACKLE

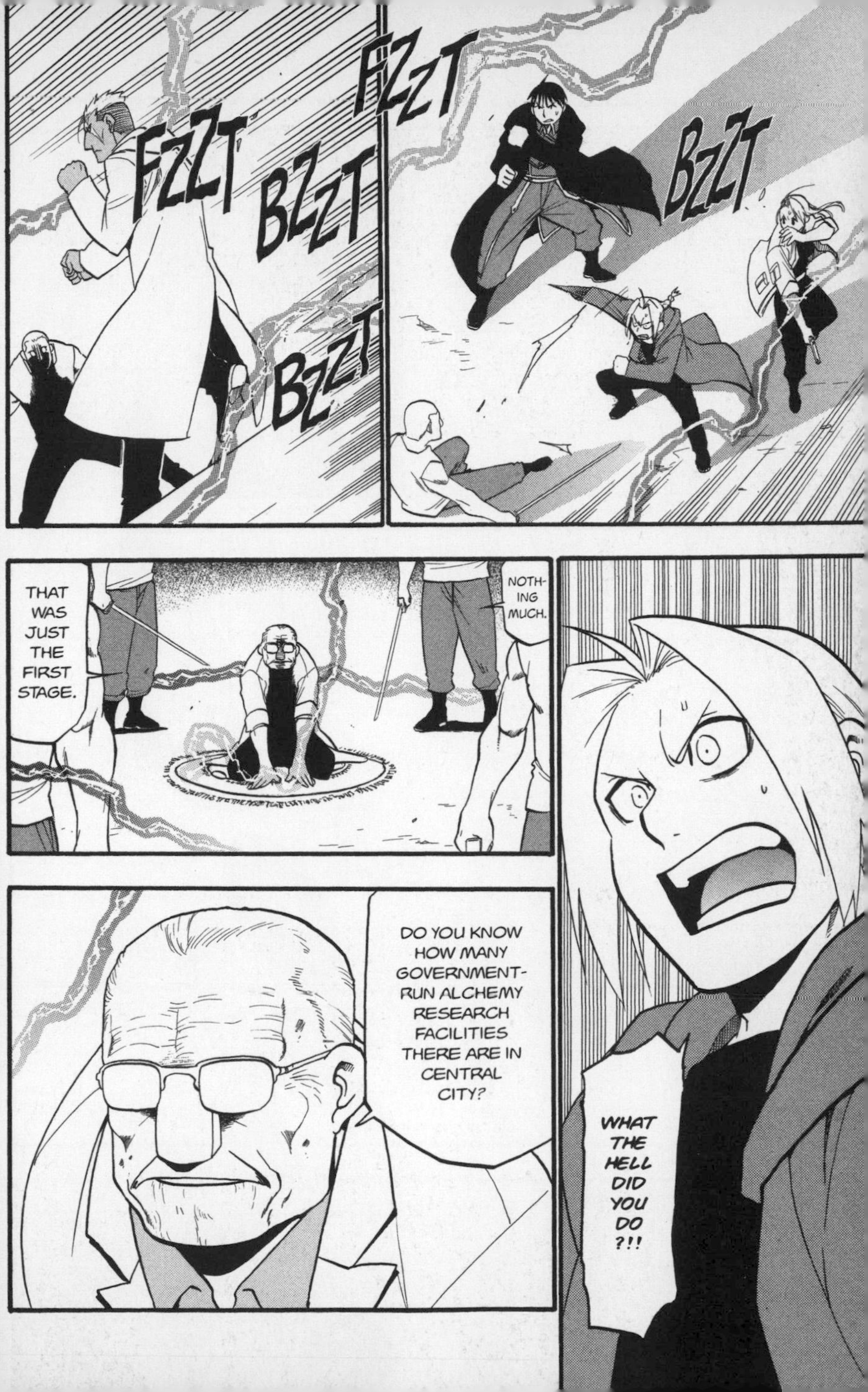
FZZT
BZZT
FZZT
BZZT
BZZT
WHAT THE HELL DID YOU DO?!!
NOTH-ING MUCH.
THAT WAS JUST THE FIRST STAGE.
DO YOU KNOW HOW MANY GOVERNMENT-RUN ALCHEMY RESEARCH FACILITIES THERE ARE IN CENTRAL CITY?

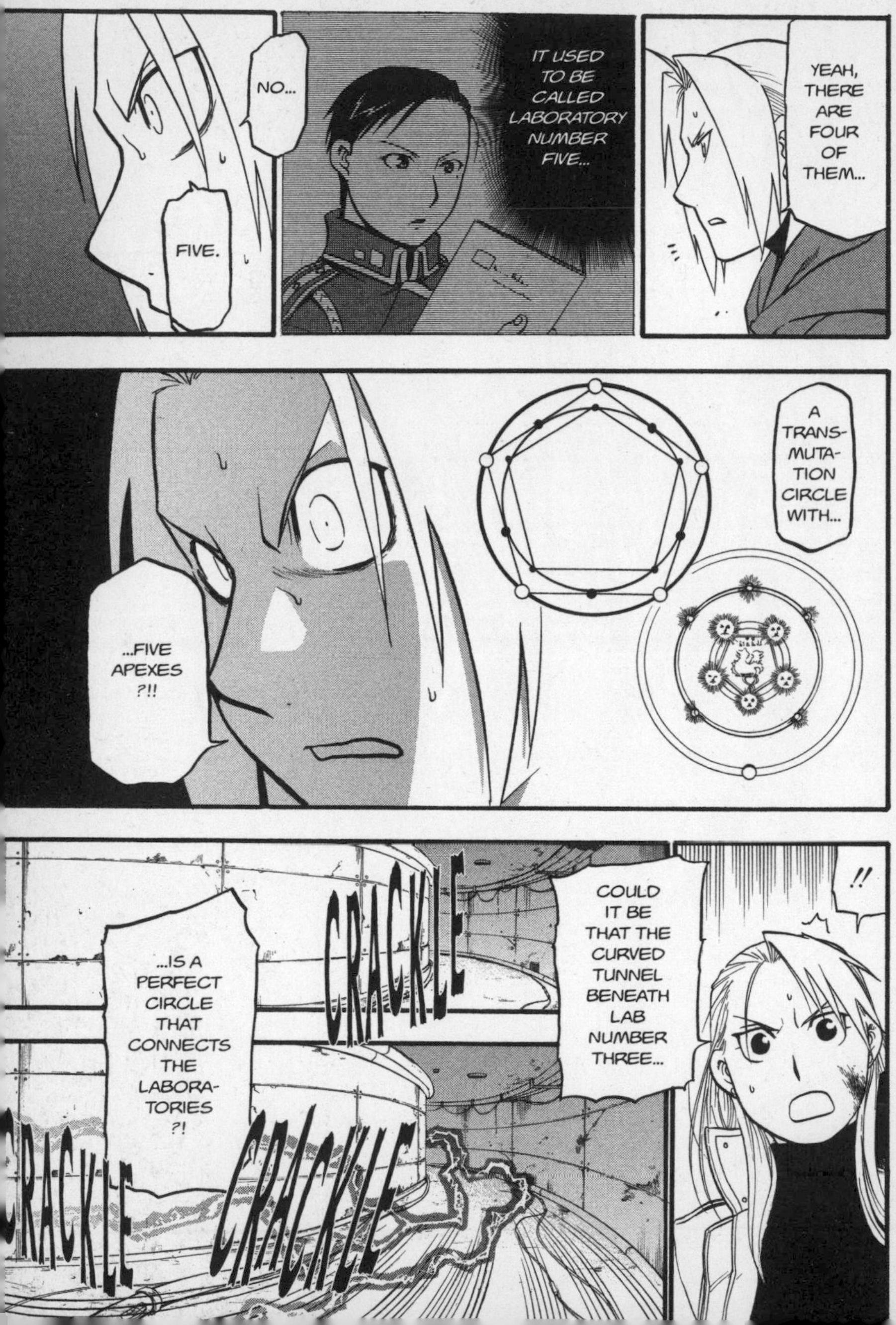
YEAH, THERE ARE FOUR OF THEM...
IT USED TO BE CALLED LABORATORY NUMBER FIVE...
NO...
FIVE.
A TRANSMUTATION CIRCLE WITH...
...FIVE APEXES ?!!
!!
COULD IT BE THAT THE CURVED TUNNEL BENEATH LAB NUMBER THREE...
CRACKLE
...IS A PERFECT CIRCLE THAT CONNECTS THE LABORATORIES ?!
CRACKLE
CRACKLE

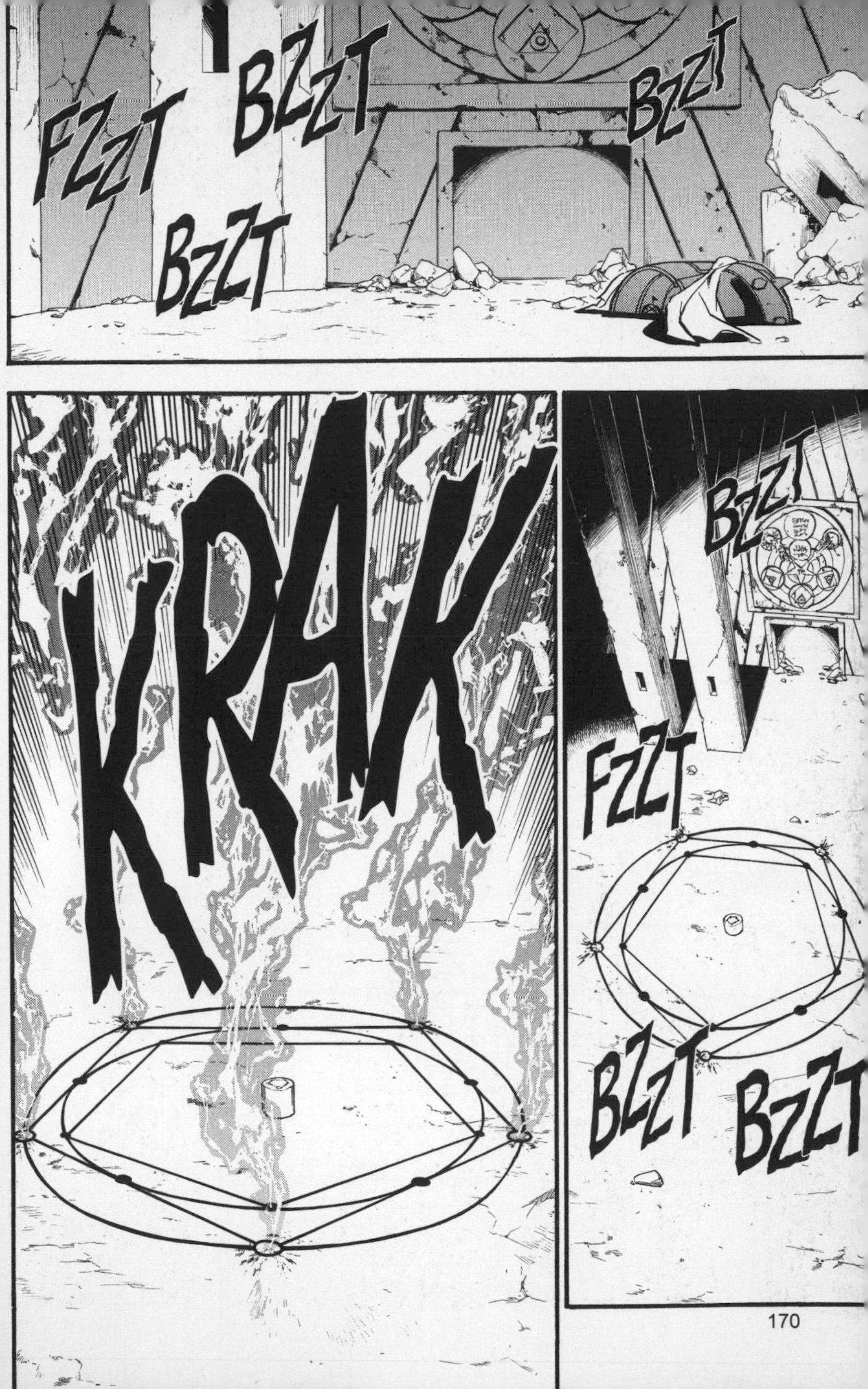
BZZT
BZZT
FZZT
BZZT
BZZT
FZZT
BZZT
BZZT
KRAK

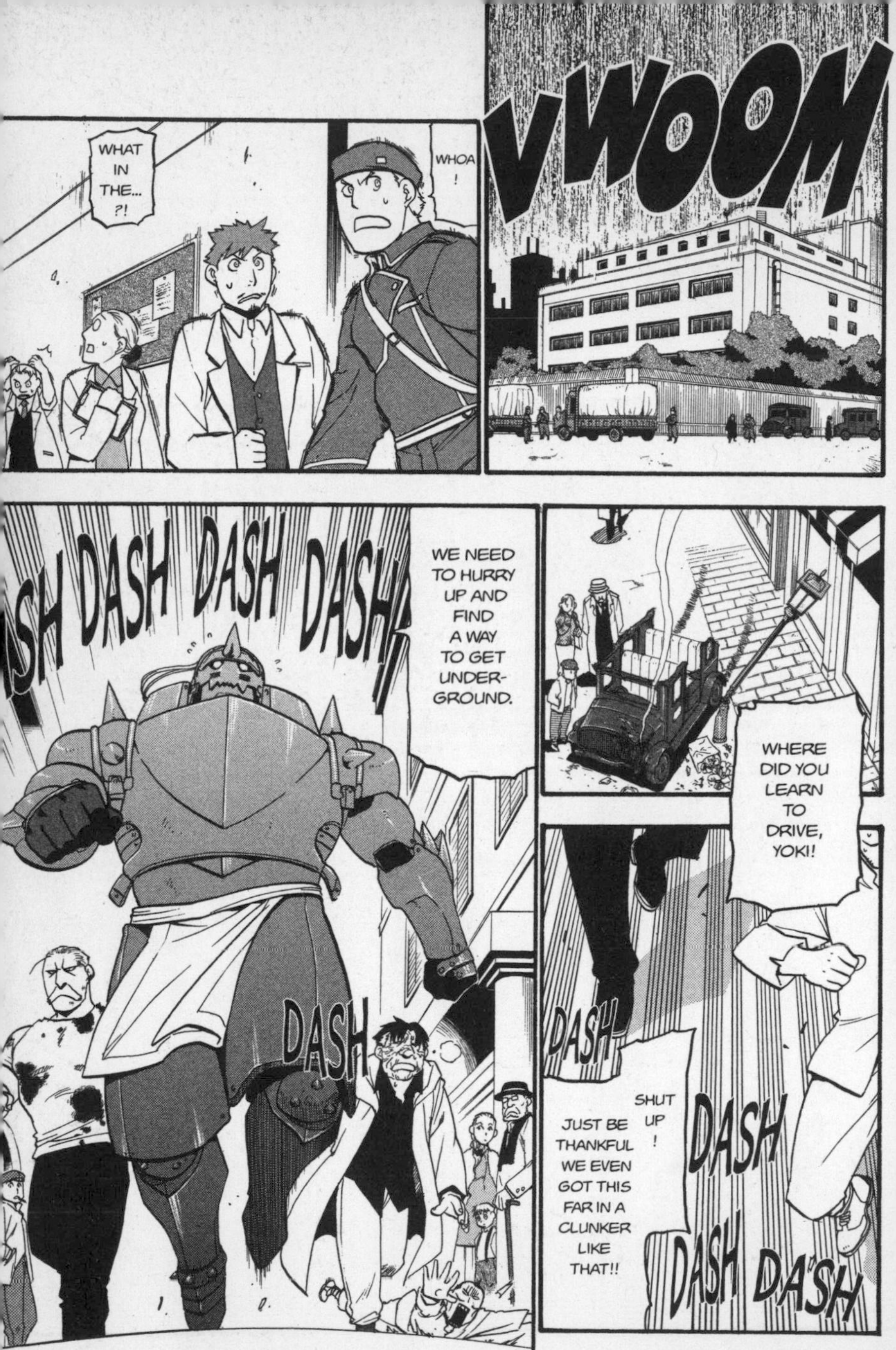
VWOOM
WHOA!
WHAT IN THE...?!
WHERE DID YOU LEARN TO DRIVE, YOKI!
DASH
SHUT UP!
JUST BE THANKFUL WE EVEN GOT THIS FAR IN A CLUNKER LIKE THAT!!
DASH
DASH DASH
WE NEED TO HURRY UP AND FIND A WAY TO GET UNDER-GROUND.
SH DASH DASH DASH
DASH

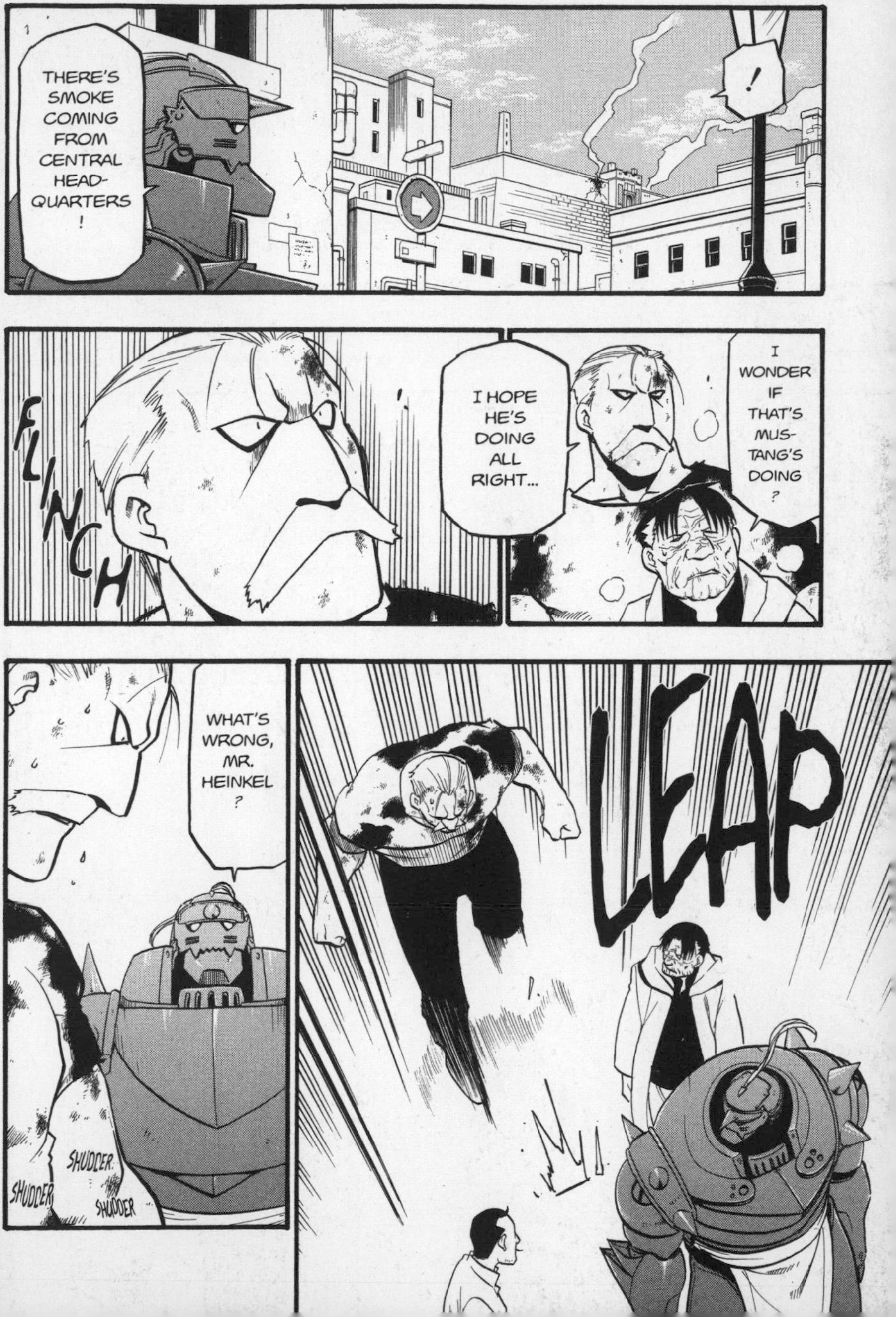
!
THERE'S SMOKE COMING FROM CENTRAL HEAD-QUARTERS!
I WONDER IF THAT'S MUS-TANG'S DOING?
I HOPE HE'S DOING ALL RIGHT...
FLINCH
LEAP
WHAT'S WRONG, MR. HEINKEL?
SHUDDER
SHUDDER
SHUDDER

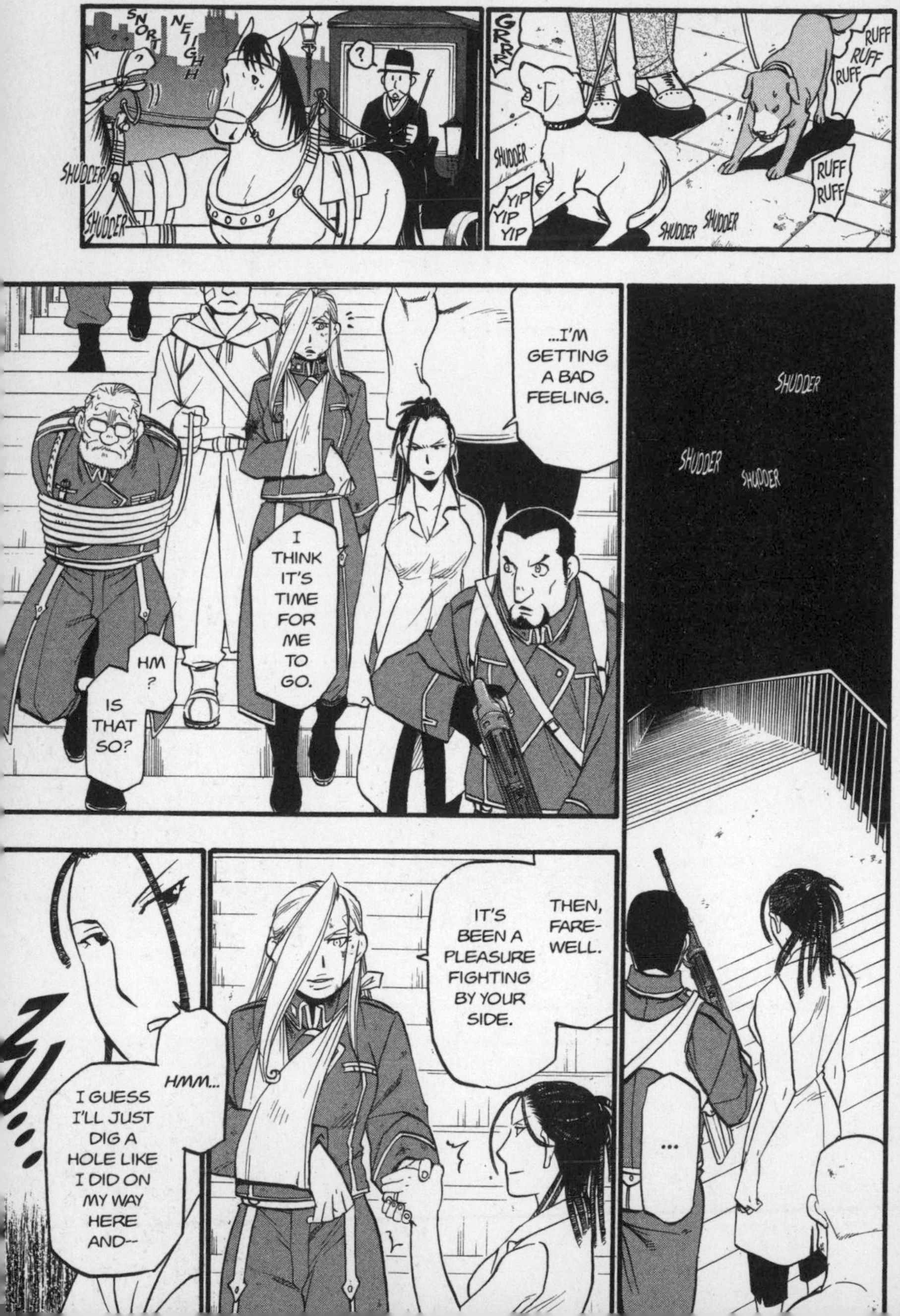
GRRR
RUFF RUFF RUFF
SHUDDER
YIP YIP YIP
RUFF RUFF
SHUDDER
SHUDDER
SNORT
NEIGH
?
SHUDDER
SHUDDER
SHUDDER
SHUDDER
SHUDDER
...I'M GETTING A BAD FEELING.
I THINK IT'S TIME FOR ME TO GO.
HM? IS THAT SO?
...
THEN, FARE-WELL.
IT'S BEEN A PLEASURE FIGHTING BY YOUR SIDE.
HMM...
I GUESS I'LL JUST DIG A HOLE LIKE I DID ON MY WAY HERE AND--

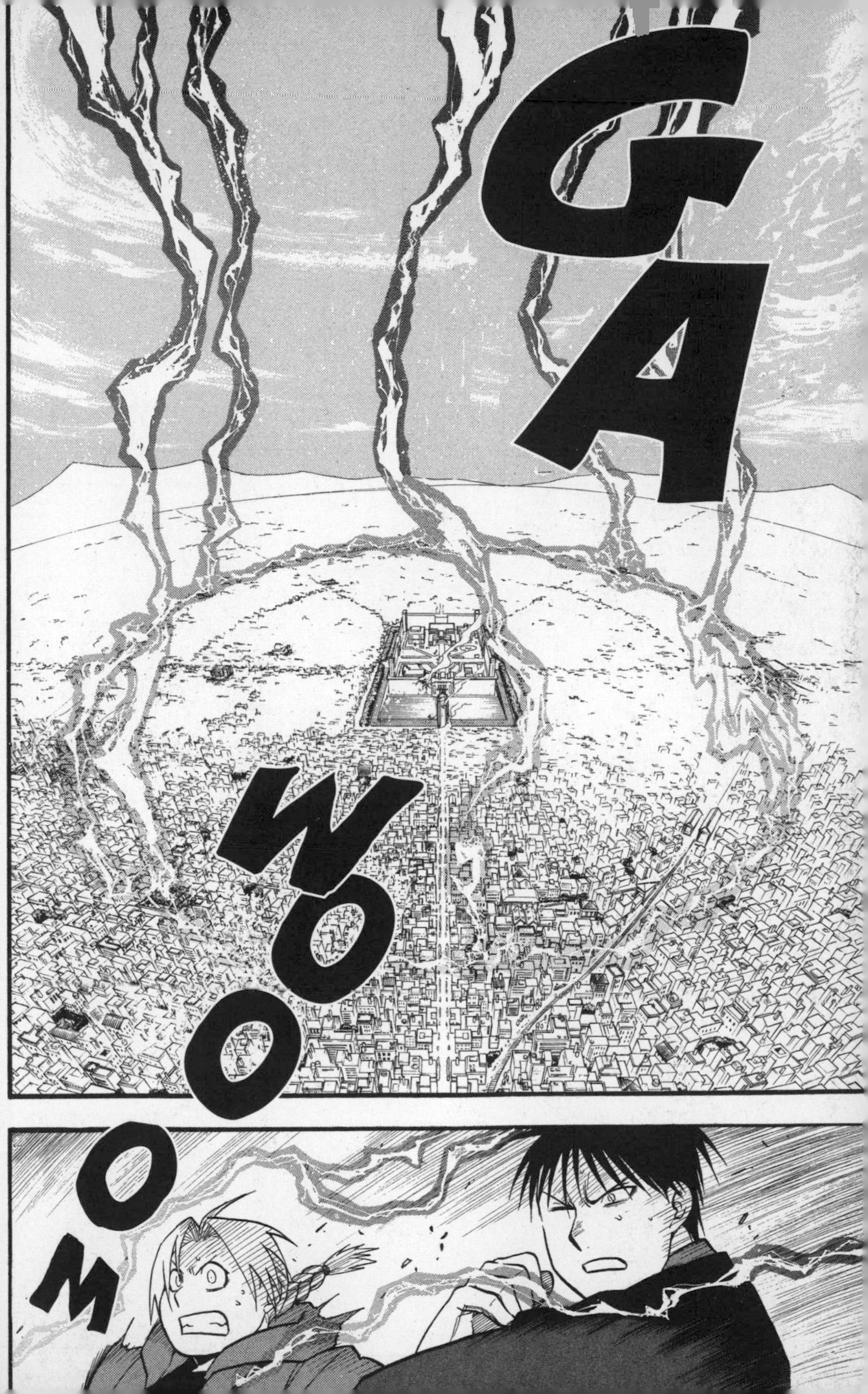
GAWOOOM

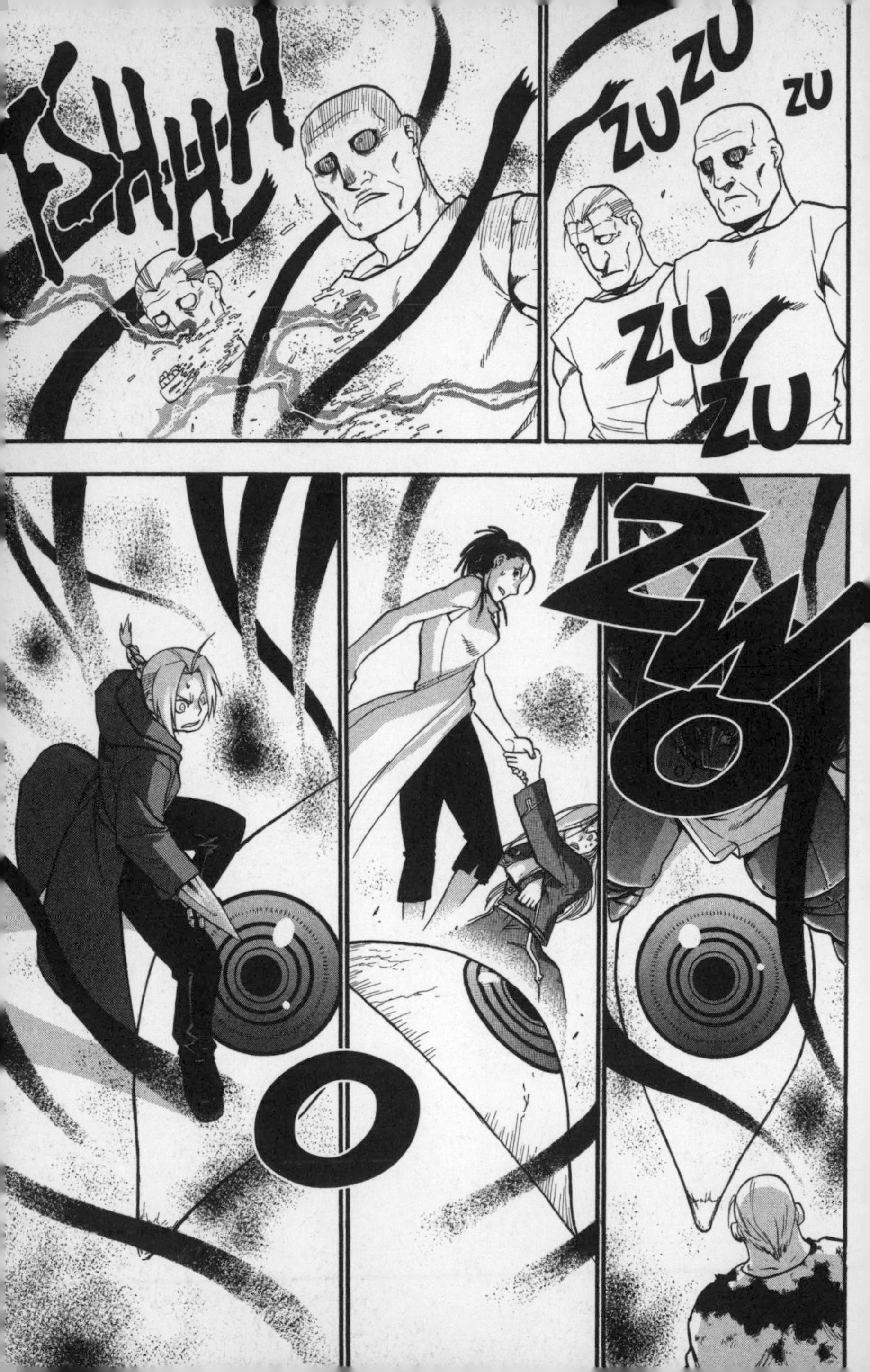
ZU ZU ZU
ZU ZU
FSH-H-H
ZWO
O

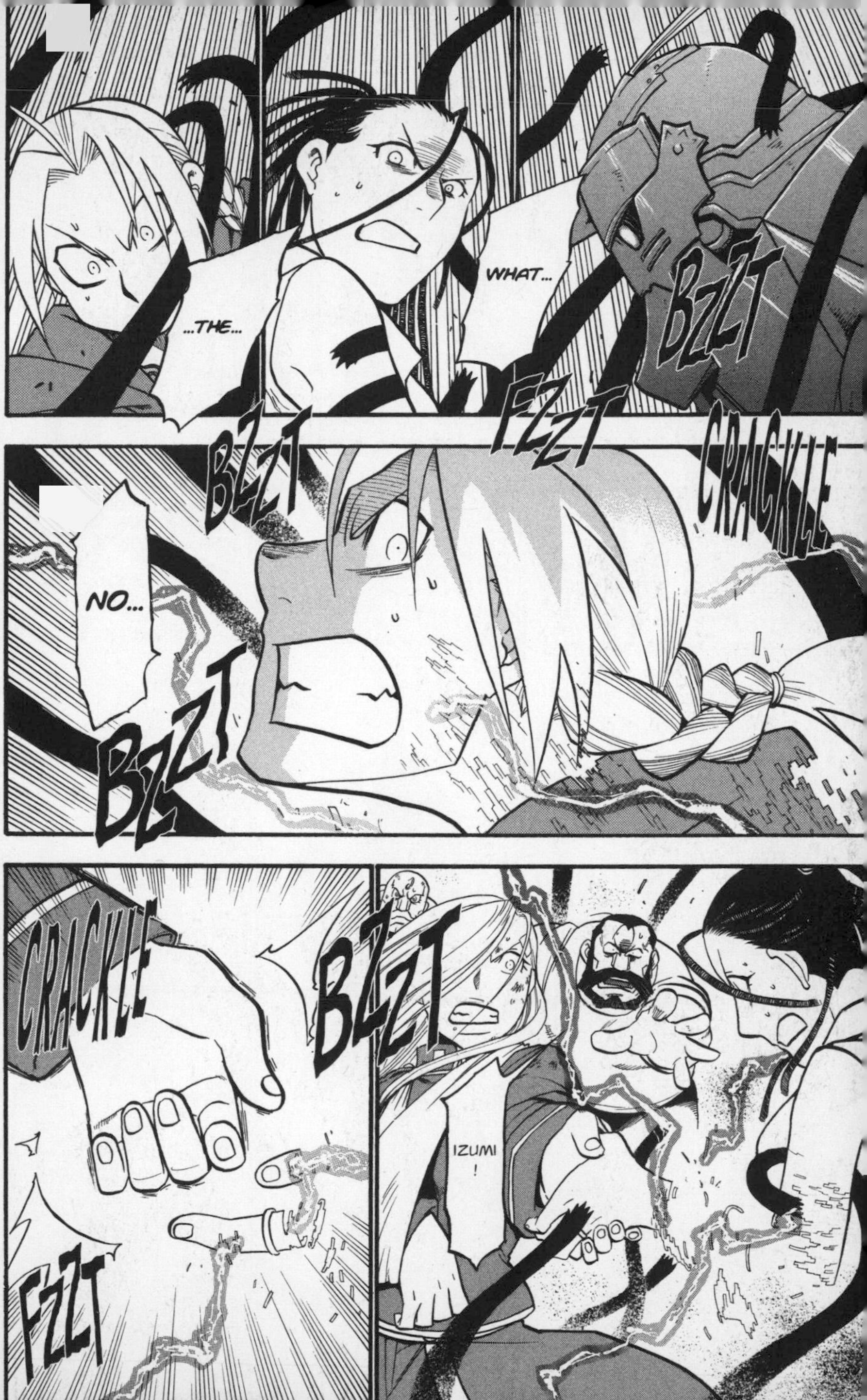
BZZT
WHAT...
...THE...
CRACKLE
FZZT
BZZT
NO...
BZZT
BZZT
IZUMI!
CRACKLE
FZZT

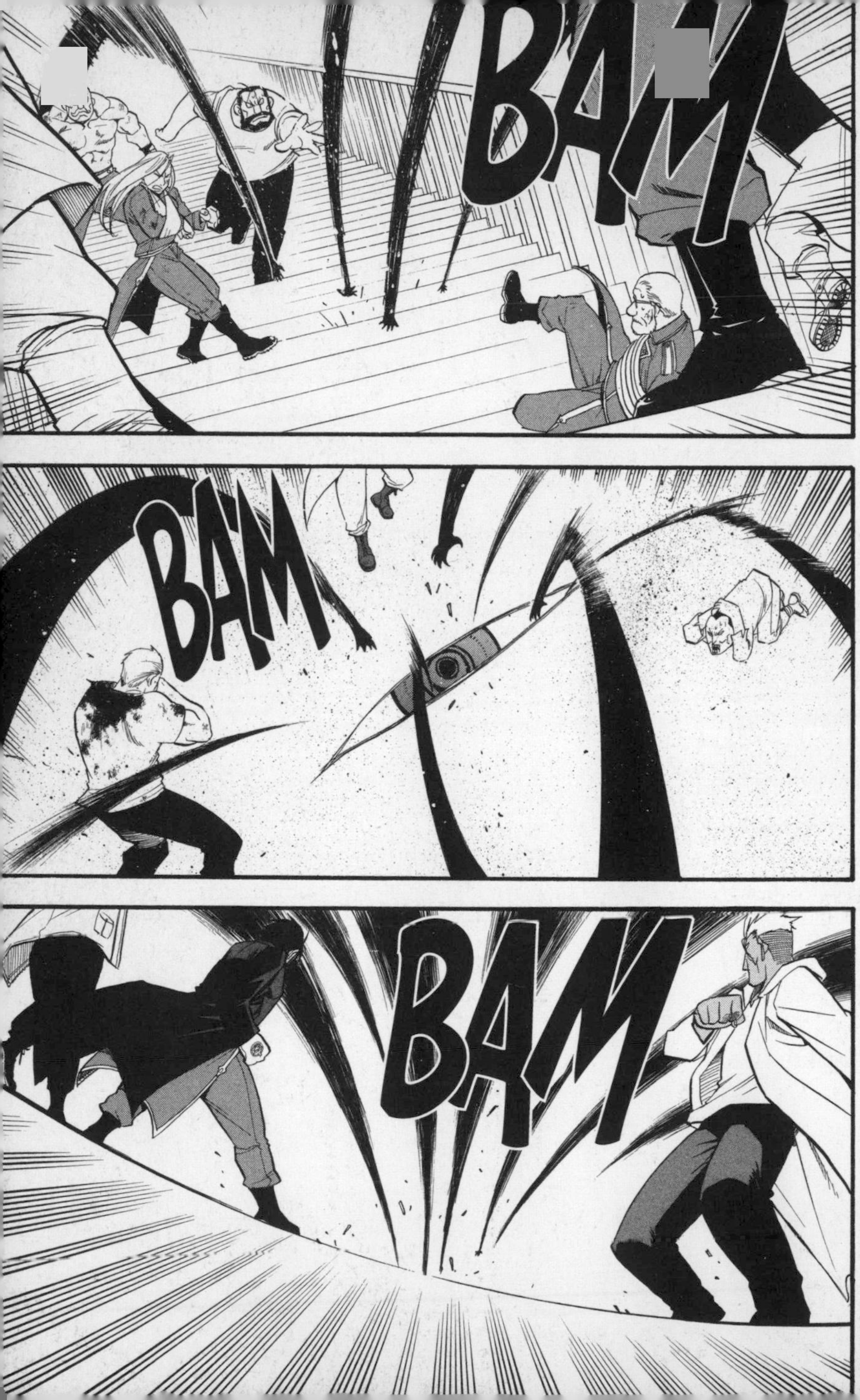
BAM
BAM
BAM

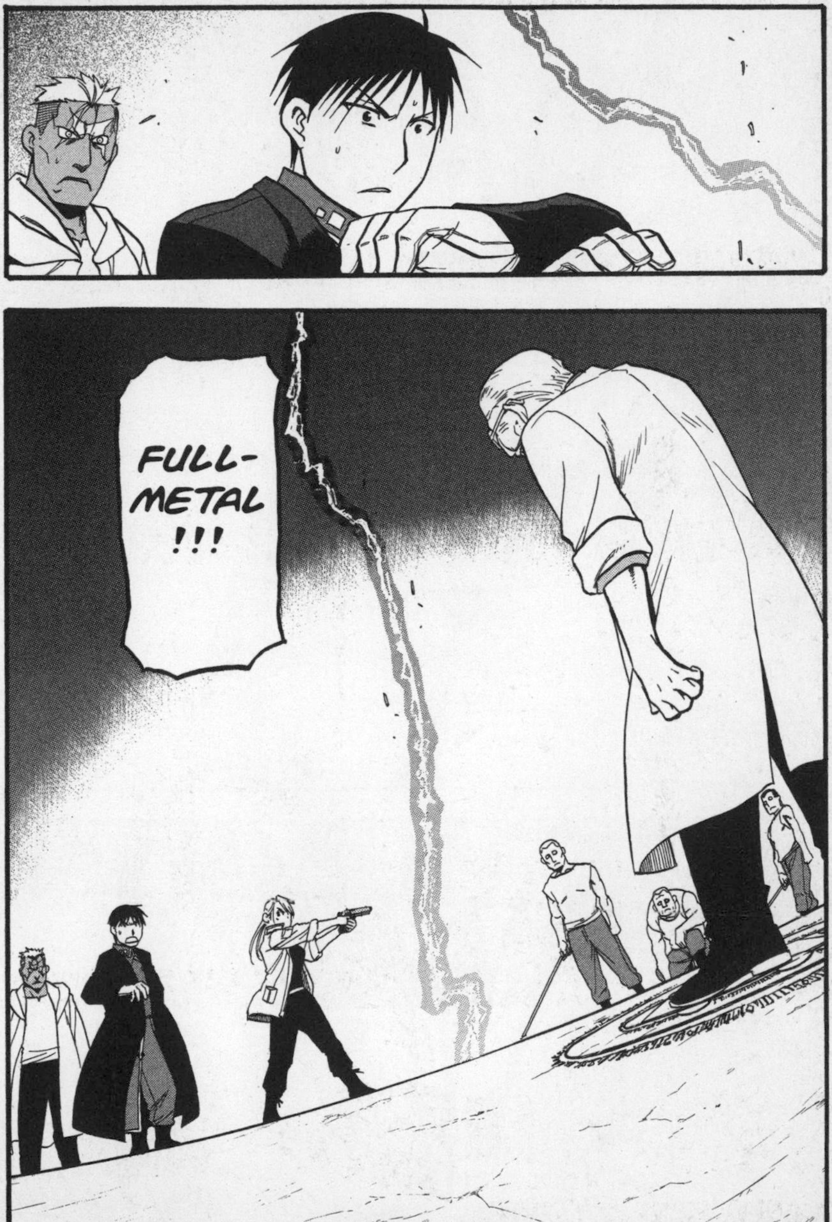
FULL-
METAL
!!!

# Special Episode:
# Fullmetal Alchemist, Wii: Daughter of the Dusk
## Prologue

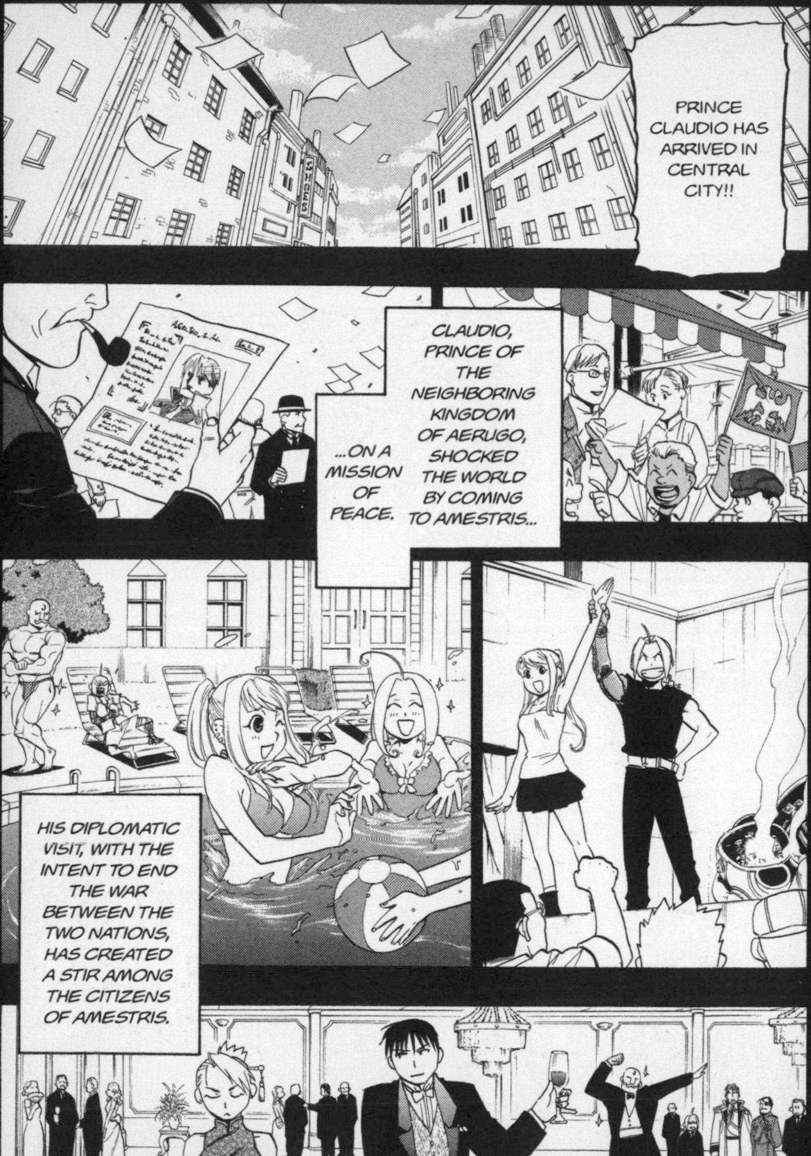

PRINCE CLAUDIO HAS ARRIVED IN CENTRAL CITY!!
CLAUDIO, PRINCE OF THE NEIGHBORING KINGDOM OF AERUGO, SHOCKED THE WORLD BY COMING TO AMESTRIS...
...ON A MISSION OF PEACE.
HIS DIPLOMATIC VISIT, WITH THE INTENT TO END THE WAR BETWEEN THE TWO NATIONS, HAS CREATED A STIR AMONG THE CITIZENS OF AMESTRIS.

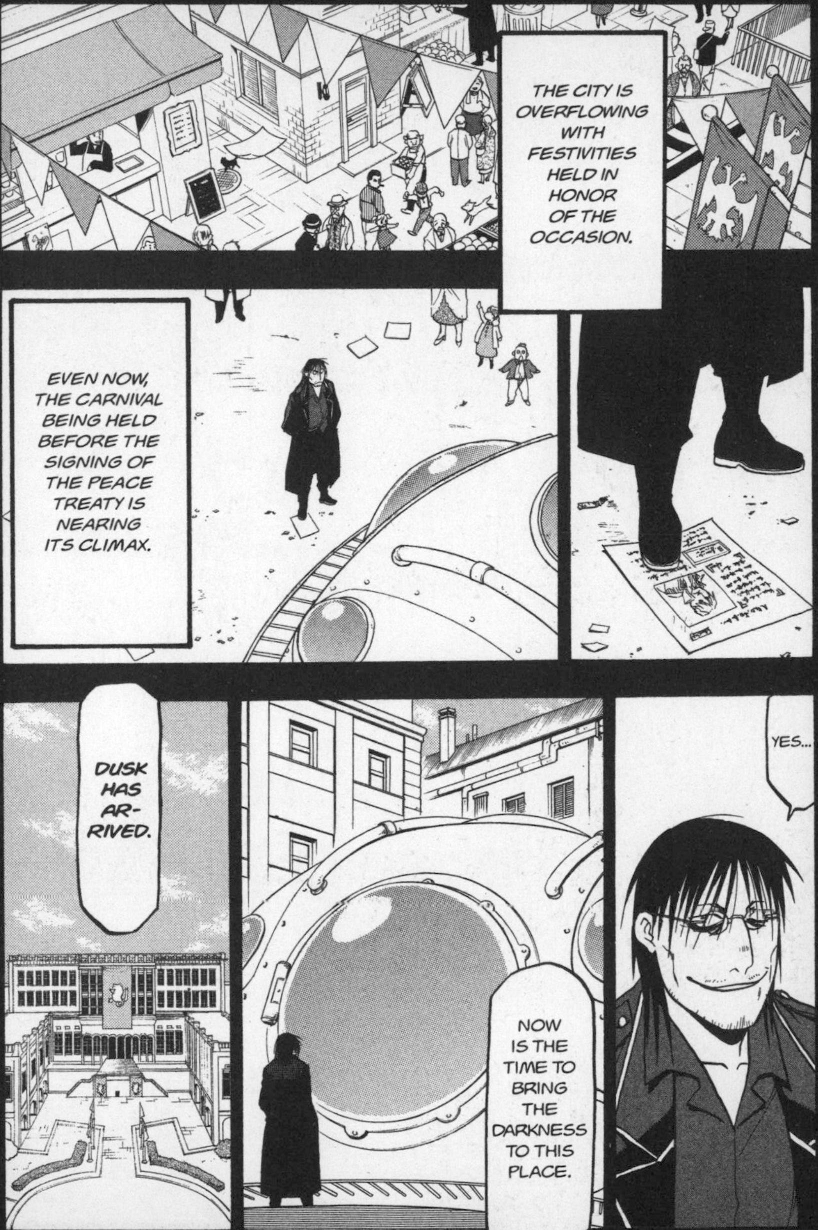
THE CITY IS OVERFLOWING WITH FESTIVITIES HELD IN HONOR OF THE OCCASION.
EVEN NOW, THE CARNIVAL BEING HELD BEFORE THE SIGNING OF THE PEACE TREATY IS NEARING ITS CLIMAX.
YES...
NOW IS THE TIME TO BRING THE DARKNESS TO THIS PLACE.
DUSK HAS AR-RIVED.

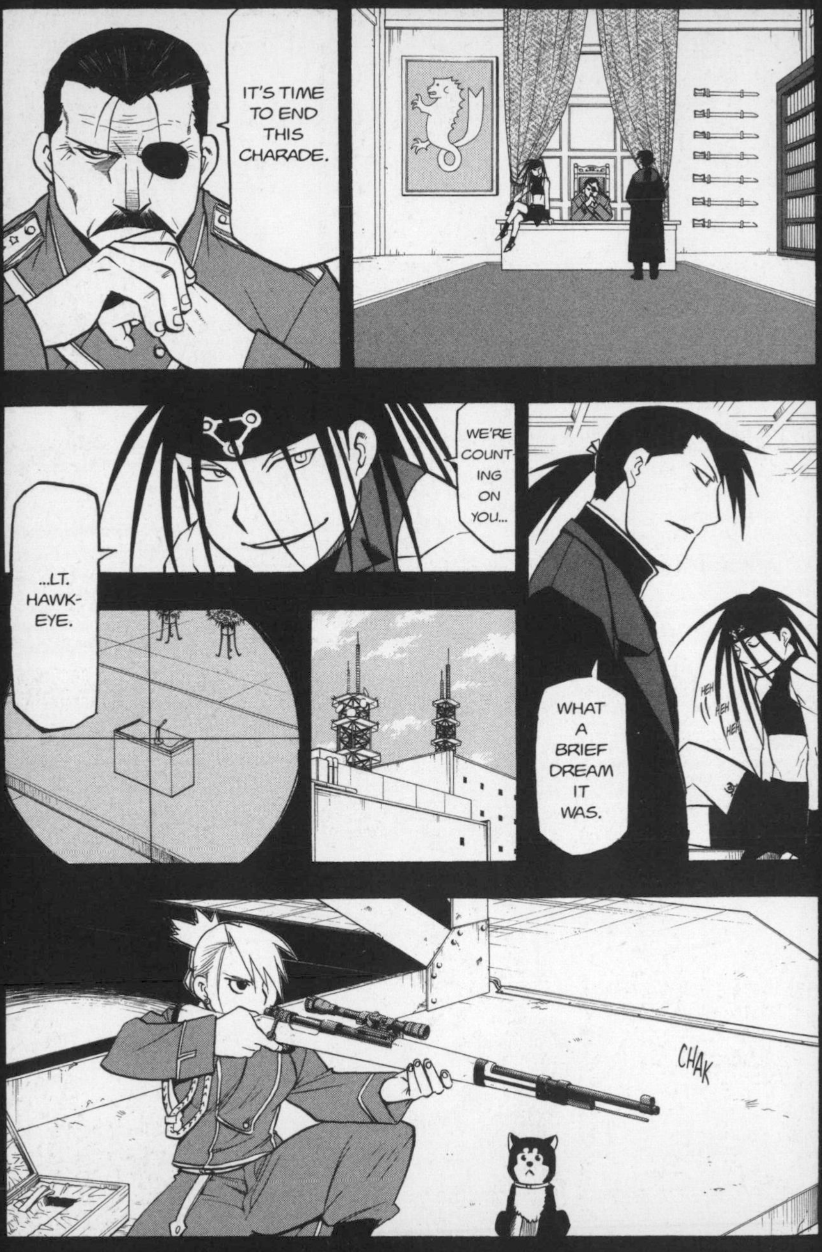
IT'S TIME TO END THIS CHARADE.
WHAT A BRIEF DREAM IT WAS.
HEH HEH HEH
WE'RE COUNTING ON YOU...
...LT. HAWKEYE.
CHAK

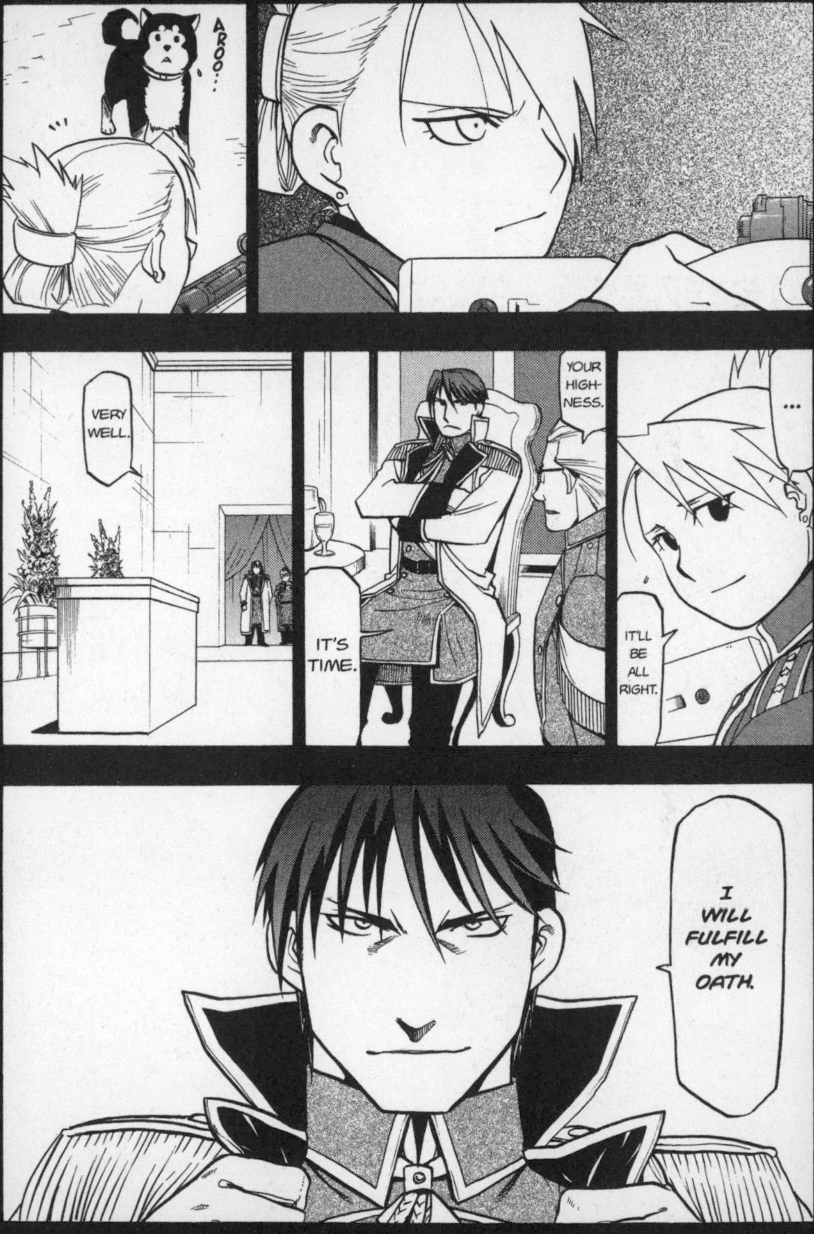
AROO...
...
IT'LL BE ALL RIGHT.
YOUR HIGHNESS.
IT'S TIME.
VERY WELL.
I WILL FULFILL MY OATH.

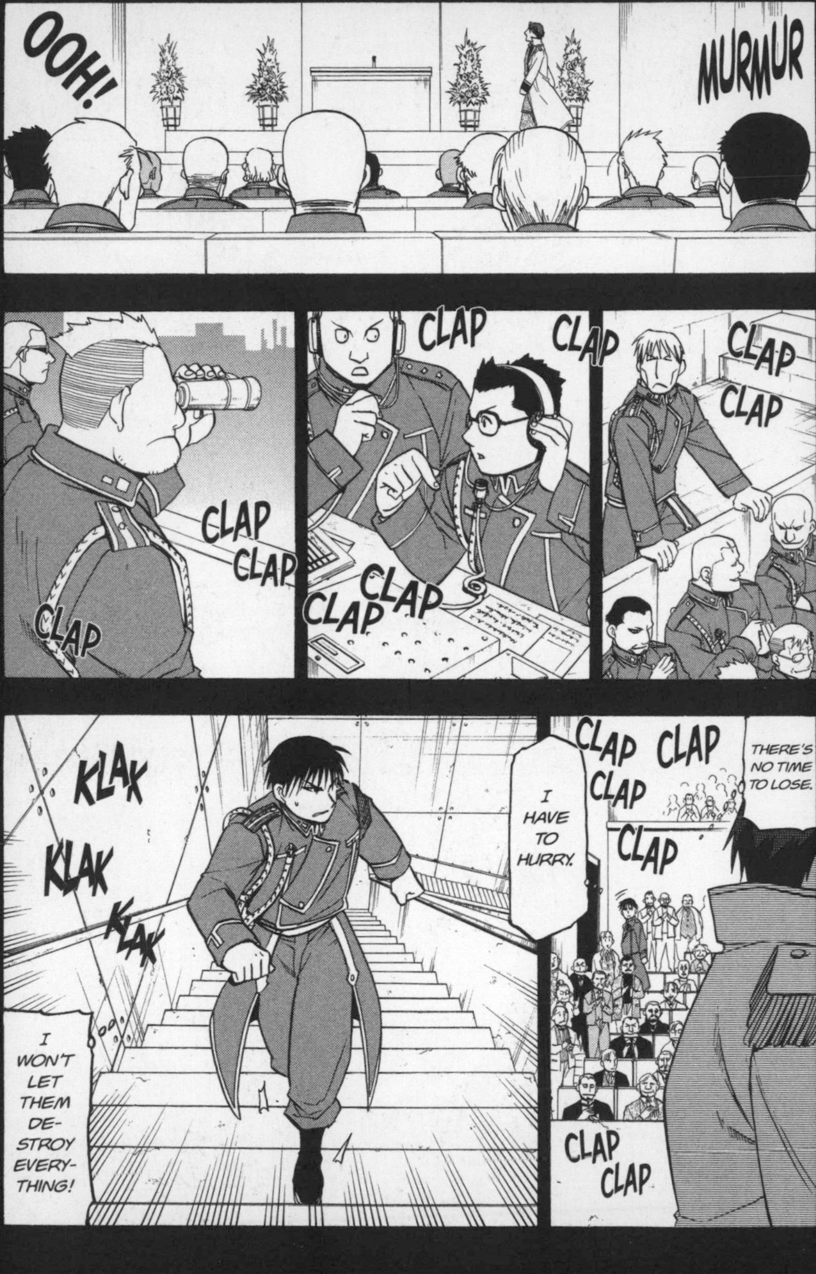
MURMUR
OOH!
CLAP
CLAP
CLAP
CLAP
CLAP
CLAP
CLAP
CLAP
CLAP
THERE'S NO TIME TO LOSE.
CLAP
CLAP
CLAP
CLAP
CLAP
CLAP
I HAVE TO HURRY.
KLAK
KLAK
KLAK
I WON'T LET THEM DE-STROY EVERY-THING!

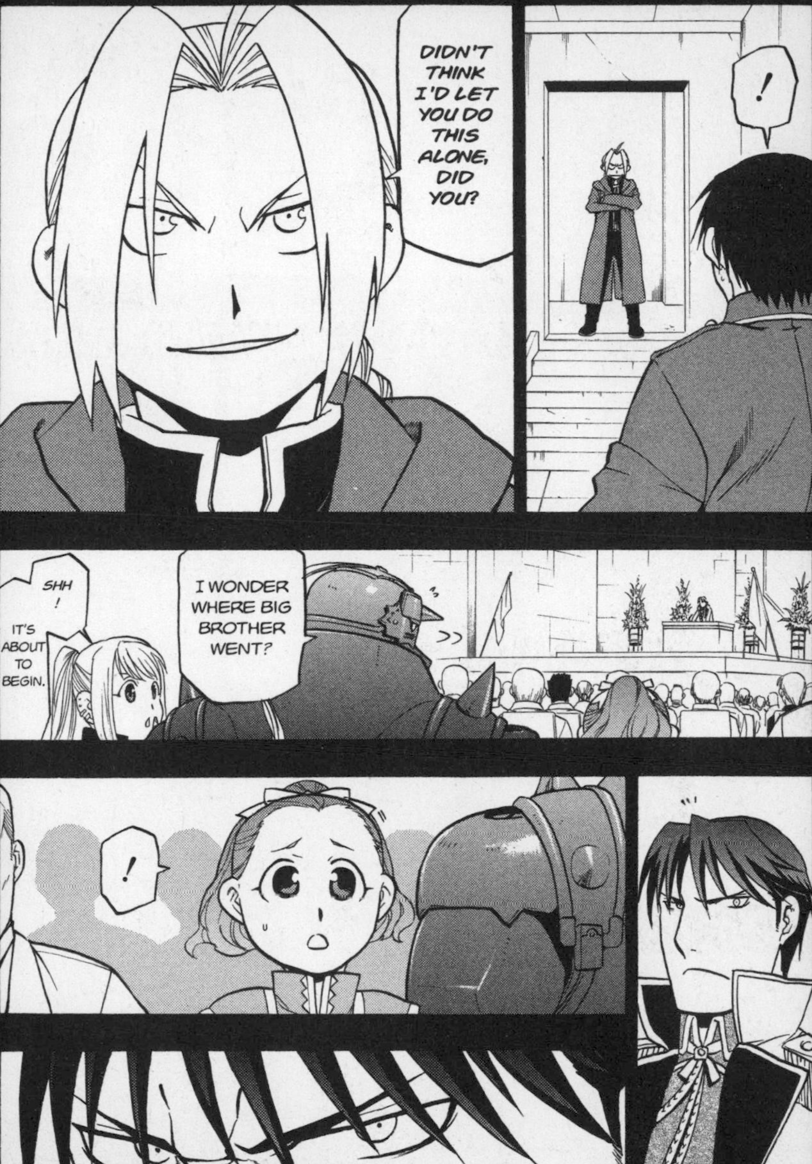
!
DIDN'T THINK I'D LET YOU DO THIS ALONE, DID YOU?
I WONDER WHERE BIG BROTHER WENT?
SHH!
IT'S ABOUT TO BEGIN.
!

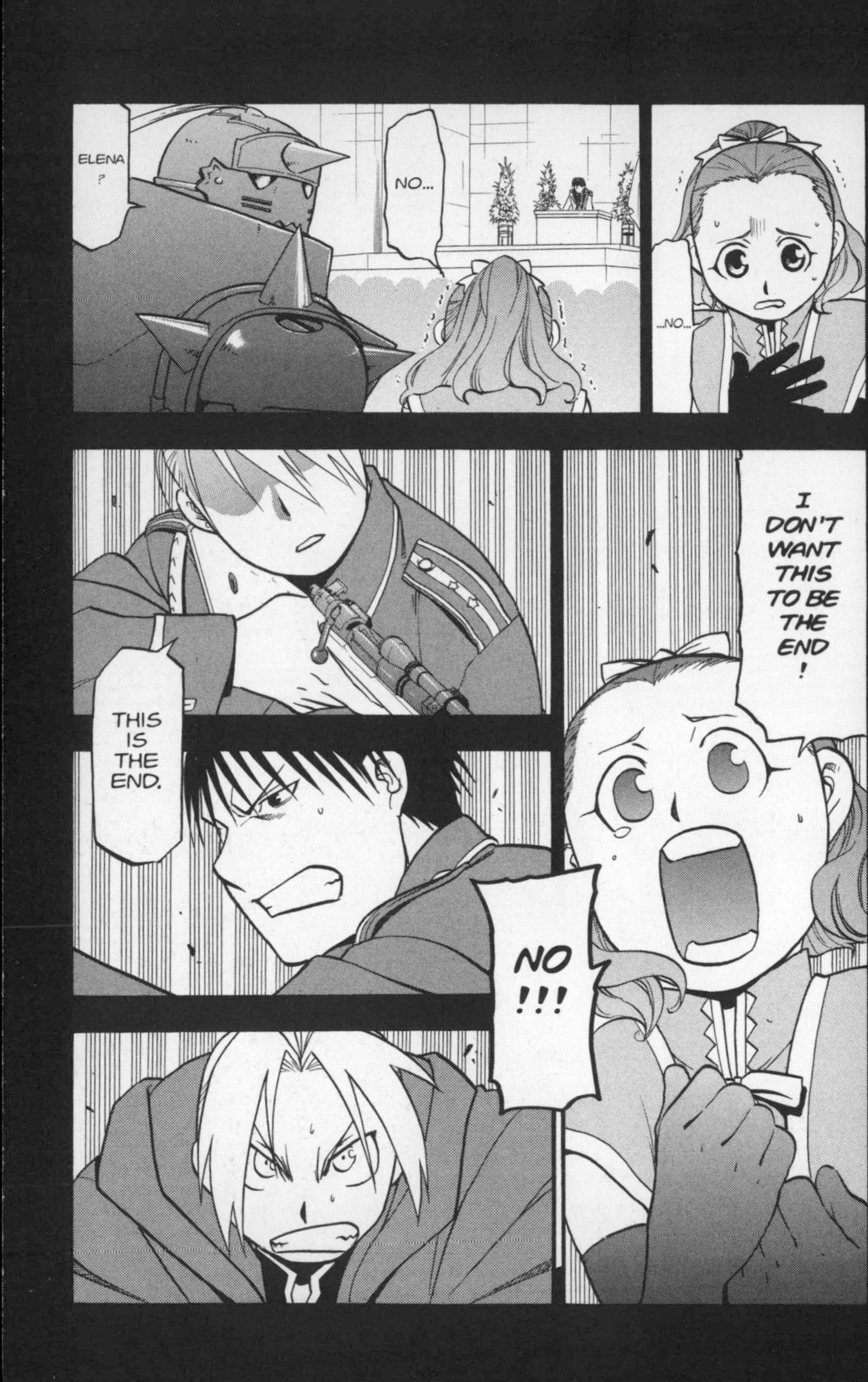
...NO...
NO...
ELENA ?
I DON'T WANT THIS TO BE THE END !
NO !!!
THIS IS THE END.

# FULLMETAL ALCHEMIST
# Daughter of the Dusk

She's come to find something to believe in.
Coming soon to the Nintendo Wii

# FULLMETAL ALCHEMIST 24

## FROM CHAPTER 97.

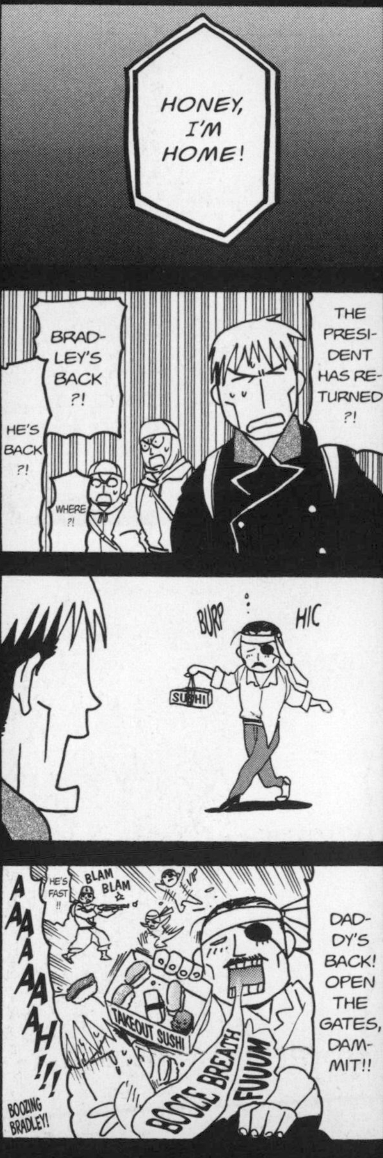
HONEY, I'M HOME!
THE PRESI-DENT HAS RE-TURNED?!
BRAD-LEY'S BACK?!
HE'S BACK?!
WHERE?!
HIC
BURP
SUSHI
DAD-DY'S BACK! OPEN THE GATES, DAM-MIT!!
VIP
BLAM BLAM
HE'S FAST!!
VIP
TAKEOUT SUSHI
FUUUM
BOOZE BREATH
AAAAAAAH!!!
BOOZING BRADLEY!

## SPECIAL THANKS to:

Jun Tohko
Masashi Mizutani
Coupon
Noriko Tsubota
Haruhi Nakamura
Kazufumi Kaneko
Kori Sakano
Manatsu Sakura
Kei Takanamazu

My Editor, Yuichi Shimomura

## AND YOU!!

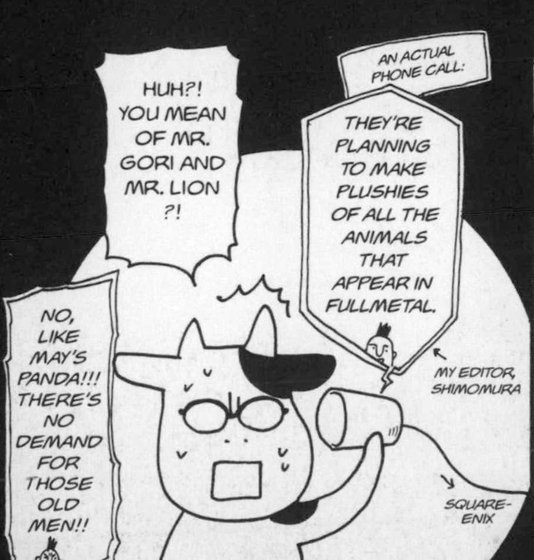
AN ACTUAL PHONE CALL:
THEY'RE PLANNING TO MAKE PLUSHIES OF ALL THE ANIMALS THAT APPEAR IN FULLMETAL.
MY EDITOR, SHIMOMURA
HUH?! YOU MEAN OF MR. GORI AND MR. LION?!
SQUARE-ENIX
NO, LIKE MAY'S PANDA!!! THERE'S NO DEMAND FOR THOSE OLD MEN!!

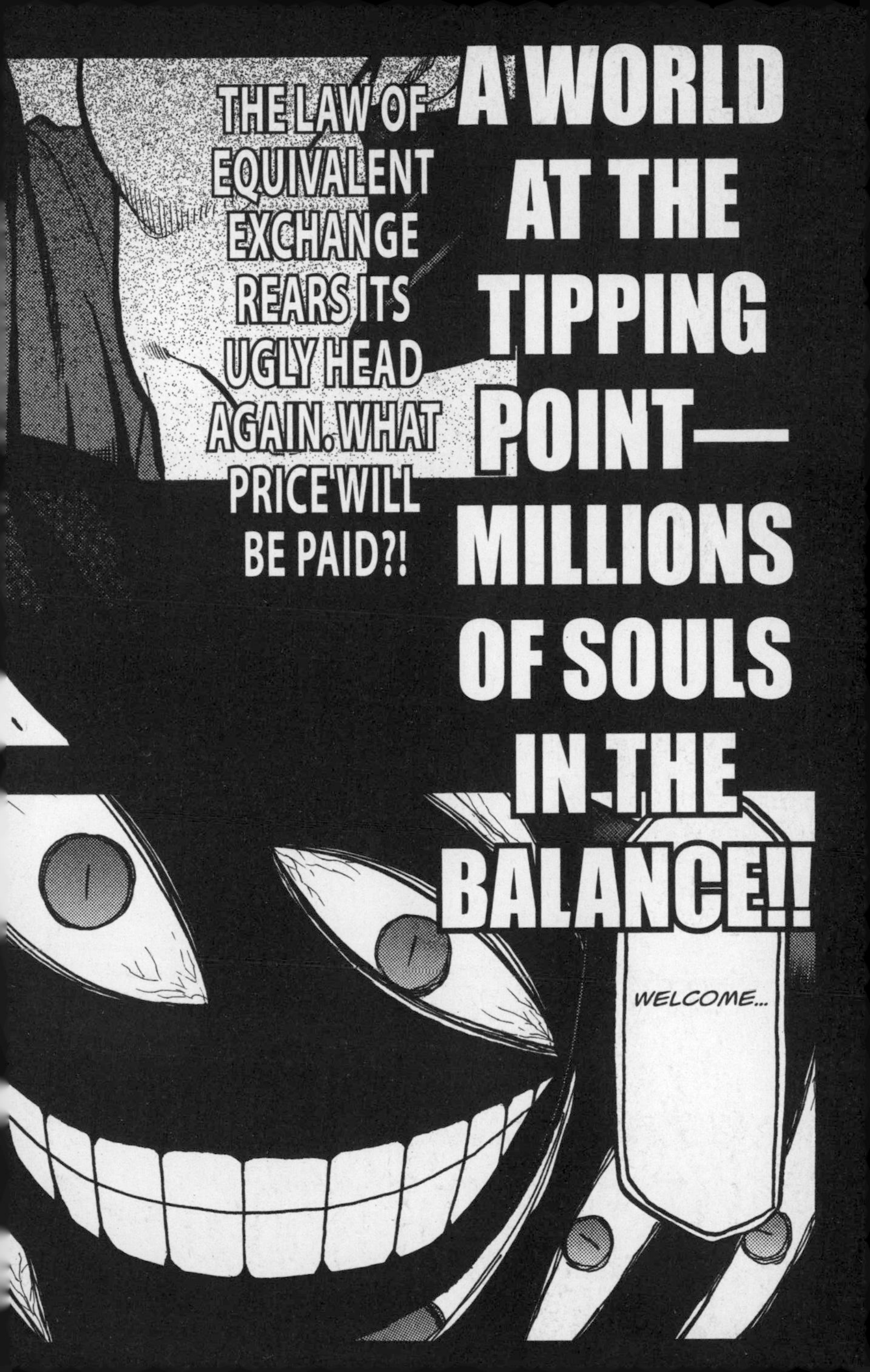
A WORLD AT THE TIPPING POINT—MILLIONS OF SOULS IN THE BALANCE!!
THE LAW OF EQUIVALENT EXCHANGE REARS ITS UGLY HEAD AGAIN. WHAT PRICE WILL BE PAID?!
WELCOME...

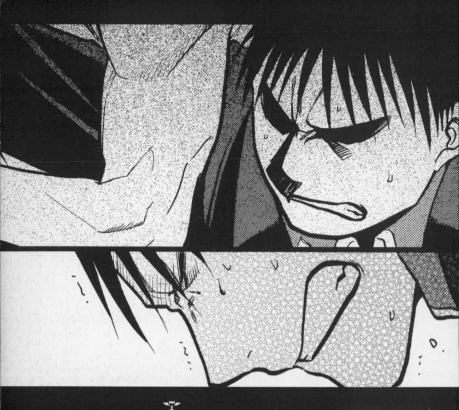

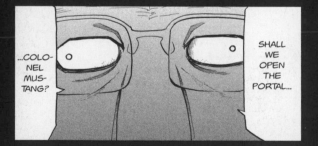

Fullmetal Alchemist
...MY SACRIFICES.
SHALL WE OPEN THE PORTAL...
...COLONEL MUSTANG?
THE EAGERLY ANTICIPATED
FULLMETAL ALCHEMIST
VOLUME 25--COMING SOON!!

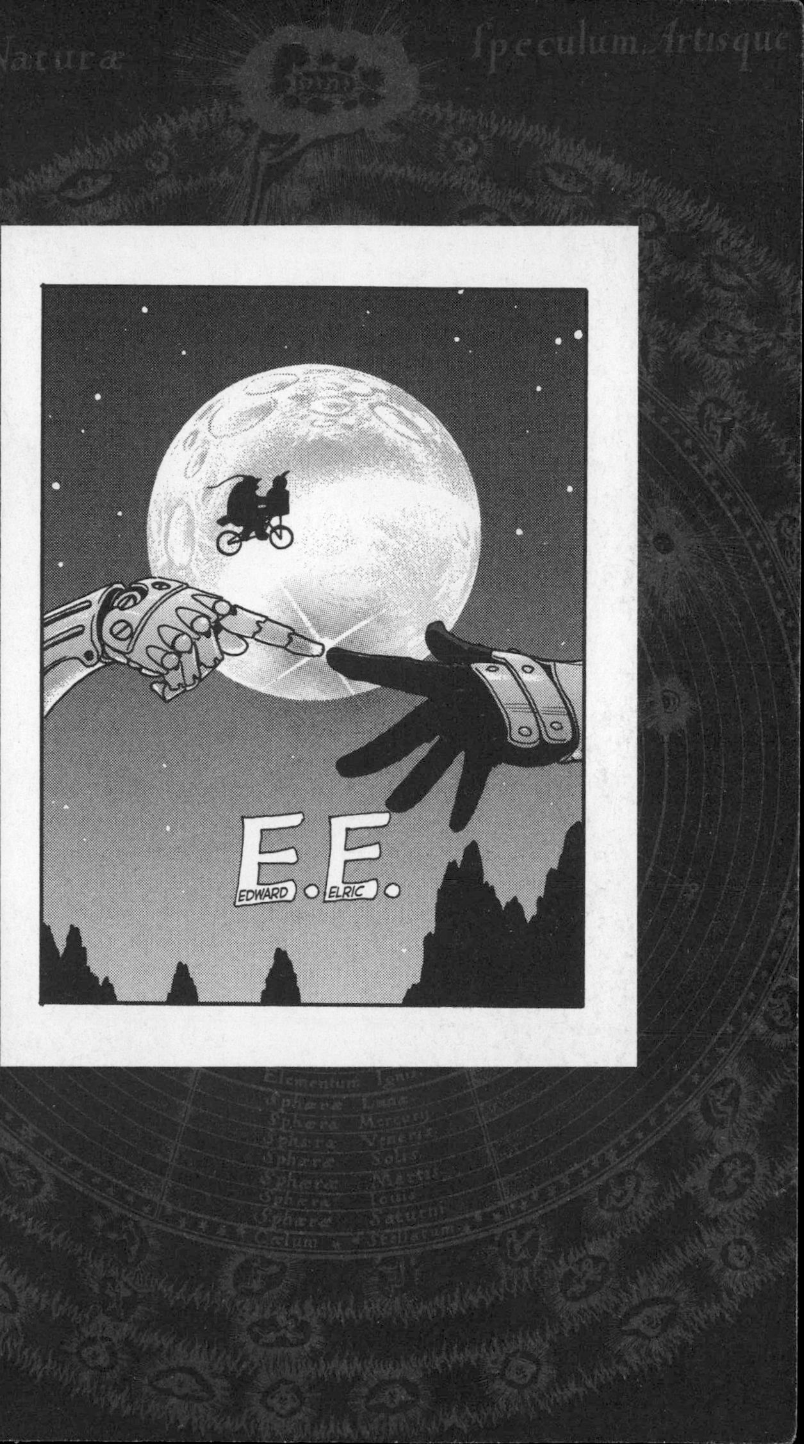
E.E.
EDWARD
ELRIC

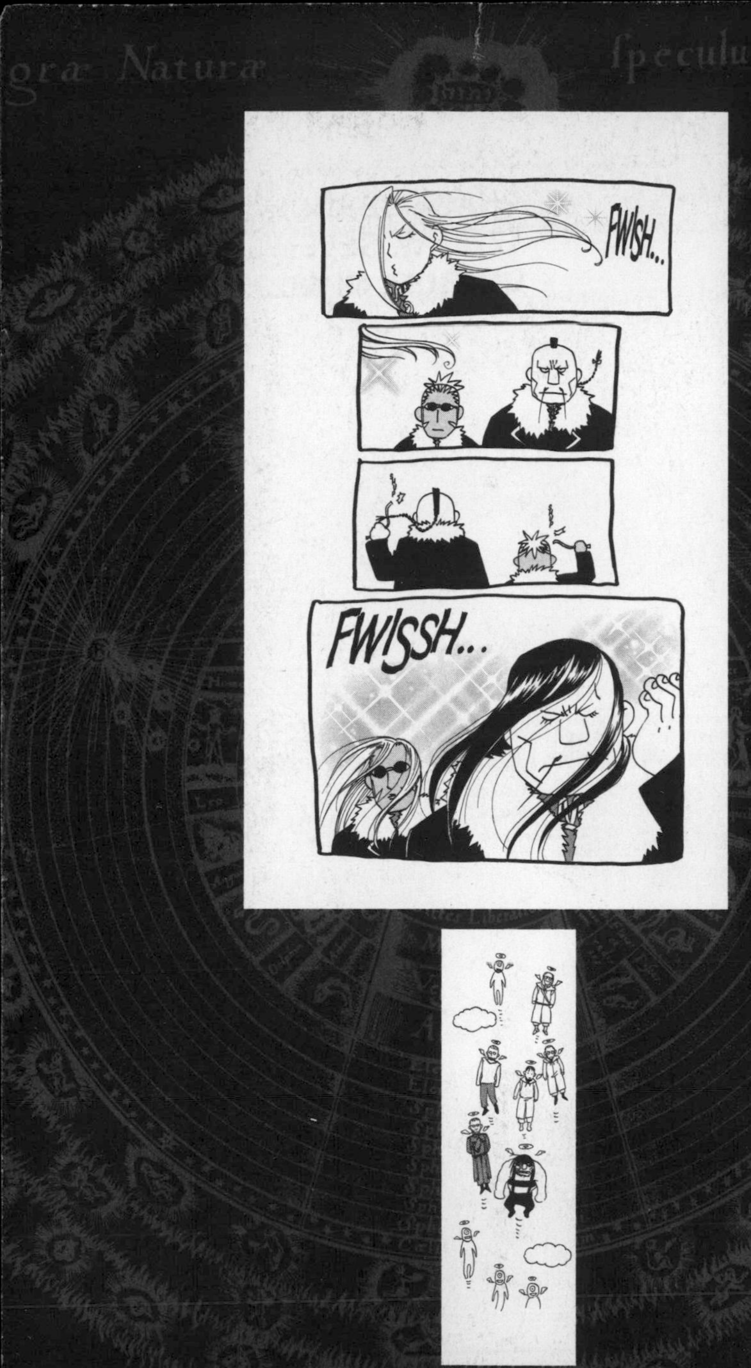
FWISH...
FWISSH...

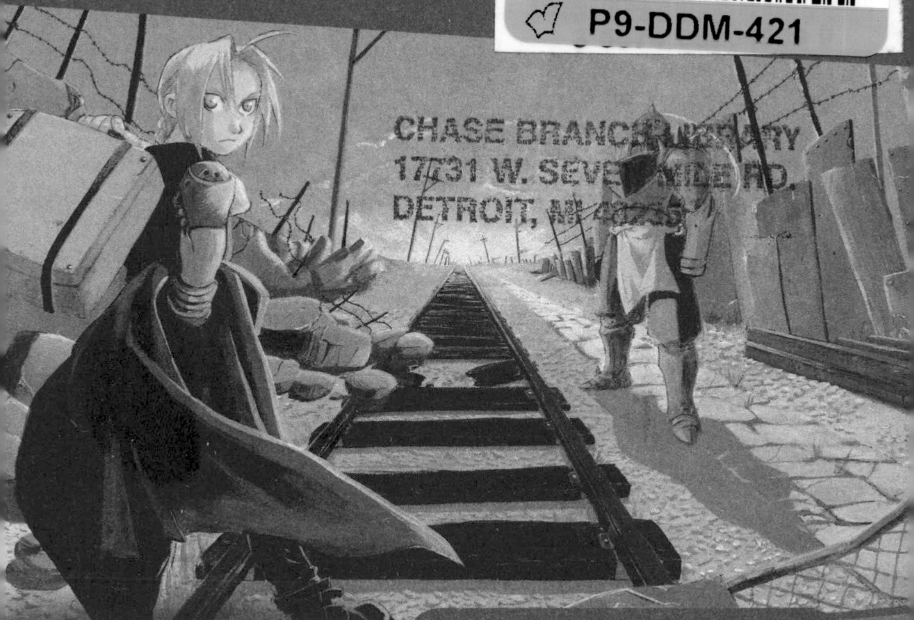

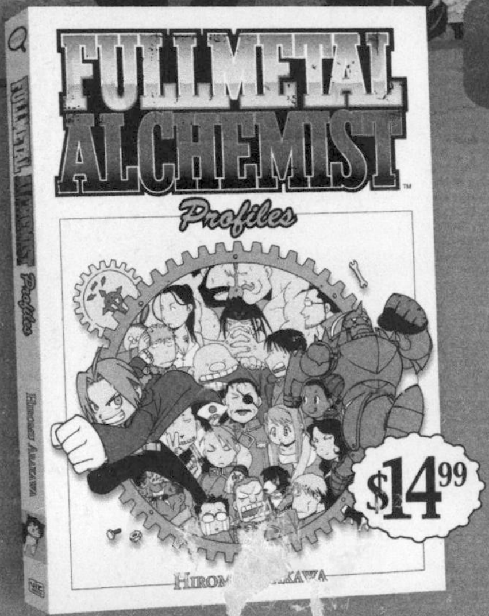
FULLMETAL ALCHEMIST
Profiles
$14.99
HIROMU ARAKAWA

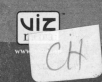